BUSINESS CYCLES

Their Nature, Cause, and Control

BY

JAMES ARTHUR ESTEY, PH.D.

PROFESSOR OF ECONOMICS
PURDUE UNIVERSITY

NEW YORK

PRENTICE-HALL, INC.

First Printing ....February, 1941
Second Printing ....July, 1941
Third Printing ....March, 1942
Fourth Printing ....February, 1946
Fifth Printing ....October, 1946
Sixth Printing .... May, 1947

To Nem and Marty

PREFACE

THE purpose of this book is to supply a brief, simple, but reasonably comprehensive introduction to the subject of business cycles, including therein some description of cyclical behavior, a survey of business cycle theories, and an analysis of proposed methods of control.

It is hoped that, by having in the compass of a single volume the threefold subject of description, causation, and control, the reader will be better able to see the full scope of cycle problems, and better served in his study of them.

The book is divided into three parts. The first part is concerned with description. It answers the question: What do cycles look like, and what happens to business in the course thereof? The second part has to do with causation. It sets forth the principal theories now current as to why cyclical fluctuations occur. It is mainly expository and indulges only in such limited criticism as will enable the reader to see how one theory may develop into or give place to another. The third part is devoted to the problem of control. It sets forth the various ways by which the extent of economic fluctuations may be reduced, and subjects these proposals to critical analysis.

Select references are given in the brief bibliographies at the end of each part, and appropriate references to specific subjects are made in the course of the chapters. No attempt has been made to develop elaborate footnotes. This book is not a work of research. The materials are familiar, and the author's debt to the literature of business cycles is evident in every chapter.

All summaries and quotations from *Business Cycles, The Problem and Its Setting,* by W. C. Mitchell, are used through the courtesy of the National Bureau of Economic Research, Incorporated.

JAMES ARTHUR ESTEY

CONTENTS

Part I

DESCRIPTION

ILLUSTRATIONS

PART I

DESCRIPTION

CHAPTER I

BUSINESS FLUCTUATIONS OF VARIOUS KINDS

IF THE statistical records of business activities, particularly as exhibited in the graphic form of charts so characteristic of our day, are examined, it is immediately seen that the course of business, like true love, is not smooth. The evidence is unmistakable, whether the chart gives a graphic record of a single business activity, like bank clearings, or railway tonnage, or iron steel production; or whether it pictures a composite record of business activity in general, like the *American Telegraph and Telephone Company's Index of General Business Conditions,* or *The Annalist* index of business activity; or whether a chart depicts the course of prices, such as the wholesale price index, or of ratios such as interest rates. Fluctuation and change rather than constancy are characteristic of our business world.

These fluctuations of business are of many kinds. Some are abrupt, isolated, discontinuous, like the great economic changes brought about in the world by the First World War. Some are continuous for long periods of time in the same direction, such as expansion of output, or in some cases contraction of output. Other changes are essentially fluctuations of a rhythmic nature, such as the changes due to the seasons, or those longer periods of ebb and flow of business activity commonly called "business cycles." Some of these fluctuations are limited to specific fields; others, such as business cycles, tend to spread over the entire field of business activity and reflect changes in what may be called "business as a whole."

Even this brief statement has disclosed the fact that business cycles are but one example of a number of fluctuations to be found in the activities of modern business. The purpose of this chapter is to examine briefly these various kinds of fluctuations so that the particular kind of fluctuation to be studied in this book—that is, business cycles—can be segregated and distinguished from the others.

Our purpose will best be served by some classification of these fluctuations. The most common classification is as follows:

1. Secular trends.
2. Seasonal fluctuations.
3. Cyclical fluctuations.
4. Miscellaneous random fluctuations.

Secular trends represent the upward or downward course of sustained development exhibited in any activity over periods that are relatively long.

Seasonal fluctuations are the variations in activity that take place within the period of a calendar year, and presumably are due to causes connected directly or indirectly with the physical season.

Cyclical fluctuations are wavelike fluctuations of business activity characterized by recurring phases of expansion and contraction in periods longer than a year.

Miscellaneous random fluctuations are irregular, uncyclical variations of activity due to the incessant interference of all sorts of causes affecting business. They are "accidental" fluctuations.

As we shall see later on, a statistical technique has been developed for separating the cyclical fluctuations from secular trend and seasonal variation in the indexes which measure the activity of business, although the elimination of random fluctuations has not yet been attained.

An alternative classification, based on the distinction between changes in economic structure and fluctuations within a given structure, is offered by Ernst Wagemann: [1] ·

1. "Isolated changes, or changes in structure."

(a) "Discontinuous changes, involving a breach in the course of development." These range from the miscellaneous minor changes, which we may call "accidental," to fundamental changes in the whole "structure" of economic organization such as were caused by the First World War.

(b) "Continuous changes," or changes that exhibit the course of development, expansion, contraction, continuous transformation. These are essentially "secular trends."

2. "Periodical fluctuations."

(a) "Fluctuations occurring in a fixed rhythm." These are seasonal fluctuations, covering all fluctuations with a regularly recurring invariable interval.

(b) "Fluctuations occurring in a free rhythm." These include "cycles" of all kinds that show a continual recurrence of expansion and contraction, but with no fixed or invariable period. As we shall see, this type includes not only the familiar "business cycle" but any variation of a proved cyclical character.[2]

Out of these classifications may be drawn the observation that there are two broad types of change in business activity. There is (1) the nonrecurring, nonperiodical change, such as is exemplified by trends, by accidental or random fluctuations, and by important structural changes; and there is (2) the periodical or rhythmic fluctuation such as is exemplified by the season on the one hand and the various cyclical fluctuations on the other.

The detailed discussion which follows is organized according to this fundamental distinction.

---

[1] E. Wagemann, *Economic Rhythm*, New York, McGraw-Hill Book Co., Inc., 1930, Chapter 3, "The Basic Forms of Economic Movement."

[2] The distinction here brought out between fixed rhythm and free rhythm is similar to that developed by Irving Fisher in *Booms and Depressions*. Fisher distinguishes "forced" cycles from "free" cycles. "Forced" cycles are all cycles forced on the business system from outside—all seasonal fluctuations, for example. "Free" cycles are not forced from outside. They arise within the business mechanism itself.

I. Nonrecurring or Nonperiodical Change

(a) **Trends.** A trend may be defined as a continued and continuous movement of the data of any activity in a recognizable direction over a period of time that is long relative to the business cycle.

Such movements are commonly thought of as upward. For example, industrial production in all developed countries has an upward trend. For this reason, secular trend is sometimes regarded as the factor of growth, arising from the effects of (a) increasing population, (b) increasing economic efficiency through education, invention, improvements in technique, and so on, and (c) the gradual growth of accumulated wealth and productive capital. But it is more exact to observe that trends may be downward as well as upward and may even reverse themselves from time to time. Thus, for several decades, the volume of railway construction in the United States has had a downward trend. There is evidence that interest rates during the nineteenth century had a marked downward trend. Some time series have no apparent trend at all, or, if one cares to use an alternative phrase, show a horizontal trend—for example, the percentage of unemployed workers in England before the First World War, or the percentage of unemployed in the United States in the period 1897 to 1926.[3]

As suggested before, it is possible for series to show reversing trends—sometimes upward and other times downward. This trend might be said to exist in the case of wholesale prices in the United States, which, over considerable periods of time, move upward, to move down again over relatively equal periods. Here, however, is raised a problem of classification and definition. Possibly such fluctuations should be called "long cycles" rather than "reversing trends"; and this question may be raised in regard to other aspects of business activity as

---

[3] P. H. Douglas and A. Director, *The Problem of Unemployment*, New York, 1931, 33.

well as prices. After all, production may not grow indefinitely; population may cease to grow and begin to decline.
Possibly even output series, were they followed long enough,
would show reversing trends. Certainly this tendency would
be true in respect to the output of many individual commodities which find their way into use, rise to some importance, and
eventually are displaced by something else. This experience
is presumably the explanation of the downward trend which
replaced what, for a long while, was an upward trend in railway construction. However, these are remote matters and can
be neglected in this study. We will continue to use the term
trend, therefore, for movements in one direction over periods
that are long—that is, long in relation to the business cycle.[4]

(b) **Irregular (or accidental) fluctuations.** It is apparent that there are many nonrecurring causes of fluctuations
that affect business as a whole. Fires, storms, floods or other
disasters, strikes, revolutions, wars, elections, legislative changes,
and judicial decisions may cause business to prosper or to decline to some degree and for some longer or shorter time.

Such causes differ from trends, cycles, and seasonal fluctuations in that they are relatively noncalculable, not easily foreseen or guarded against, and not easily removed.

Theoretically, such factors, being in the nature of random
factors, might at any given moment be expected to cancel out.
By the law of probability, this should occur provided the factors are fairly numerous and are independent of each other in
origin, and provided none preponderates over the rest. These
conditions are rarely fulfilled since the factors are likely to be

---

[4] If one will study the admirable series of measurements set up by Carl Snyder
in the chapter on "Economic Growth" in his *Business Cycles and Business Measurements* (New York, 1927), he cannot fail to be impressed by the evidences of the
persistence and stability of the growth factor in many of the important processes of
our economic life. Trends really are trends; and though they may reverse themselves, the reversal lies in an uncertain future.

In the *Encyclopaedia of the Social Sciences* trends are defined as "cumulative, irre-
versible changes," as compared with "cancellable reversible changes" represented by
cyclical fluctuations of various kinds. Vol. XIV, 631.

mutually interrelated or else dominated by one or two powerful ones. The result is the production of fluctuations in business, often considerable in amplitude, that are not explainable
by trend, cycle, or seasonal variation.

It might be said that it is largely this collection of accidental
variations which make business cycles (when considered apart
from trend and seasonal variation) differ from each other. It
is this, too, which makes prediction and forecasting of business conditions so difficult. As Pigou says, cycles are all of the
same family, but no two are twins. And one must therefore
note that, while business cycles may show a certain pattern or
type, each cycle differs from others in some aspects. Therefore, business forecasters, if they do not follow a purely mechanical procedure, take pains to note marked departures from
the typical or expected course of events and to find some acceptable explanation to account for the irregularity.

(c) **Structural changes.** At times these irregular (in the
sense of isolated, nonrecurring) changes in the economic process are of such magnitude that they are better designated as
"structural changes." Structural changes, to follow Wagemann,[5] are organic, constitutional transformations of the economic system. Thus the change in the rate of growth of the
population due to birth control is a structural change The
First World War introduced many structural changes, as, for
example, turning the United States from a debtor to a creditor
nation and Germany from a creditor to a debtor nation; and
the hindrances to trade by new territorial alignments and
tariff barriers. Again, the setting up of new central banking
systems, such as the Federal Reserve System in the United
States, can be classified as a structural change.

The growth of agriculture in the New World in the third
quarter of the nineteenth century led to a structural change
that was essentially the cause of chronic depression in England

---

[5] Wagemann, *Economic Rhythm*, 26.

and Germany in the 1880's. The unification of Germany in 1870–1871 was a structural change. The great gold discoveries in South Africa and changes in the technique of gold mining in the late 1880's and 1890's were structural changes. England's adoption of free trade in the 1840's was a structural change; so was the withdrawal of Russia from the relatively uncontrolled European economy after the Revolution; so also was the technological revolution of the last two decades; and so on.

Such important modifications in the essential elements of economic society may profoundly affect the behavior of the recurring and cyclical changes. And doubtless this helps to account for the prolonged and world-wide depression of the 1870's, following the Civil War in America and the Franco-Prussian War in Europe. And again the profound depression of recent times, so much greater and more widespread than any that the world has yet known, has its roots in structural changes.

II. Recurring or Periodical Fluctuations

(a) Seasonal fluctuations. Seasonal fluctuations are imposed upon business by the fixed rhythm of the seasons and are characterized by a recognized periodicity in time.

Some of these fluctuations are "natural" fluctuations in either demand or supply, or both, due to the physical influence of the season. Others are "artificial" or "conventional," originating doubtless in the physical or meteorological season, but now dependent on institutions, customs, regulations, and law.

The output of agricultural commodities in temperate zones, at least, is obviously affected by seasonal changes. Along with changes in the activity of agriculturists go changes in railway traffic, in bank clearings and interest rates, and in the activities and payments of many industries. Similarly, road building, house construction, lumbering, and all out-of-door occupations have marked seasonal swings.

The demand for goods and services undergoes similar natural fluctuations. Tourist travel and sports and the demand for clothes, for fuel, for automobiles, and for certain types of food are seasonal and, unless the production is adapted to storage, these factors impose seasonal variations in output on a supply which otherwise would be regular.

The conventional aspect of seasonal variation in activity is illustrated by the increases in retail trade at Christmas and Easter, by the variations in banking activity due to the customary interest and dividend periods, by the semiannual (or other periodic) receipts of taxes, and so on. These are determined by custom and convention and, while not unavoidable, have effects similar to variations due to physical and meteorological causes. Some of the apparently purely physical backgrounds of seasonal variation are often partly conventional. Thus the house-building industry has always been seasonal—busy in summer, dull in winter. But changes in building methods have made winter building much more feasible than formerly, and it seems that, if the business is still seasonal (as it is), it is more because of habit than necessity. In short, a physical season has been transformed into a relatively conventional season.

Where the data are reported as monthly aggregates, an odd seasonal variation is introduced by the conventions of the calendar. Thus February, except in Leap Year, is nearly 10 per cent shorter than January or March, and February output tends to show a proportional dip. Similarly, monthly aggregates are affected by the distribution of Sundays and holidays. The variation thus exhibited may be called a *spurious seasonal variation*. The statistical effect of this, which after all is only a slight form of deception, can be reasonably avoided by expressing activity during each month as a daily average, found by dividing the activity index by the number of actual working days.[6]

---

[6] That this does not completely solve the problem is well indicated by E. C. Bratt in his *Business Cycles and Forecasting*, Revised Edition, Chicago, 1940, 13–14.

The sum of these direct seasonal influences amounts to a formidable total, which, when taken in conjunction with various repercussions on the industry of the country as a whole, together with similar consequences from similar causes in all countries of the world, is apparently capable of producing short-time variations of industry away from the normal line of development and trend. In practice, however, this potentiality is considerably reduced, for a number of reasons.

For one thing, the actual seasonality of economic activity due to the operation of these changes in demand and supply is affected by conscious measures designed to introduce stability. Thus the production of goods subject to seasonal variations in demand may be regularized by storage or by appropriate price or advertising policies designed to stimulate off-season buying. The variations in consumption apparently imposed by seasonal production of crops are almost completely eliminated by the proper processes of storage and marketing. Many other examples could be cited.

Furthermore, the seasonal fluctuation observed in any given economic activity is subject to change from circumstances not connected with any conscious program of stabilization. Seasonal fluctuations in automobile manufacture have gradually changed as good roads and closed cars made all-year driving more common. Likewise, the marked seasonal fluctuation in the New York money market associated with the moving of the crops has been notably reduced as a consequence of the organization of the Federal Reserve System.

Finally, the economic consequences of seasons, whether climatic or conventional, affect so many industries so differently, and are themselves so scattered over all the months of the year, that the business of a country as a whole is substantially less subject to seasonal variations than any of its component parts. In the business of the world even more than in the business of any given economic area, seasonal variations tend to cancel out.

A quasi-seasonal fluctuation of some kinds of economic activities is found within periods shorter than the seasons as usually defined. These fluctuations take place within the month, the week, and the day. There may be fluctuations of a regular sort within the hour.

A German investigation described by Wagemann [7] shows these variations in retail trade. As to monthly variations, retail sales are high in the last days of the month, falling away thereafter—at first sharply, then gradually. The fall is checked briefly at midmonth and then continues until the end-of-the-month activity begins. This variation is attributed to rhythm in the buying habits of the salaried classes.

Retail business is heavy during the week-end, light in midweek. This variation arises apparently from the buying habits of the wage earners, and the rhythm varies with different classes. Even the day shows its rhythm, with a slight liveliness in the late morning hours and a maximum activity toward the end of the day—a rhythm obviously imposed by employment conditions and by the personal habits of the consumer.

Similarly, there is a marked weekly variation in the sales of gasoline, with heavy bulges at week-ends; and a daily variation in the output of electricity, with a normal bulge in the late hours of the day.[8] Perhaps such changes may be regarded as negligible in a study of industrial fluctuations, but they are significant enough to modify the business habits of many concerns. As a result, electric power companies and street railway and bus companies have to think in terms of peak loads as normal incidents of the day.

It is conceivable, of course, that even the hour is affected by quasi-seasonal changes similar to those described as concerning the month, the week, or the day. Thus refreshment stores catering to students in a university community may well be affected by the conditions imposed upon student life during certain parts of the day by the customary arrangement of

---

[7] E. Wagemann, *Economic Rhythm*, 60–61.

[8] See the charts in W. I. King, *The Causes of Economic Fluctuation*, New York, 1938, 11.

lectures. The dismissal of classes at ten minutes before the hour might well cause a measurable peak of business at the end of each hour and in the early minutes of the following hour, so that the hourly business would show a marked fluctuation, with relatively heavy sales in the early minutes and late minutes of each hour and reduced activity in between. After the normal end of the university day, say 4 P.M., this hourly seasonality would disappear, and no measurable congestion at any given part of an hour would occur.

(b) **Cyclical fluctuations.** It is possible by various statistical devices, which will be explained in detail in Chapter II, to eliminate from a time series both the trend and the seasonal variation. When this is done, most measures of business activity show another well-marked series of fluctuations, which differ from trends in being alternating ebbs and flows rather than continuous movement in one direction, and from seasonal fluctuations in occurring within longer, and at the same time less regular, periods of time.

These fluctuations are characterized by alternating waves of expansion and contraction. They are not periodic—that is to say, they do not have a fixed rhythm—but they are cyclical in that the phases of contraction and expansion recur frequently and in fairly similar patterns. These patterns are most marked in those countries which are built up on "business" rather than agriculture, and have been particularly notable in England and the United States for well over one hundred years.

These fluctuations are properly called "cyclical fluctuations," or "cycles." They may be distinguished from periodical fluctuations by the nature of their rhythm. "It seems desirable to use cycle as the inclusive term for all recurrences that lend themselves to measurement, and period or periodicity for those with a definite time interval, recognizing, however, that there is no fixed line between the two." [9] That is to say, cycles have

---

[9] Definition adopted at a Conference on Cycles in 1922 and quoted in W. C. Mitchell, *Business Cycles, The Problem and Its Setting,* 1927, National Bureau of Economic Research, Inc., New York, 377.

a free rhythm, and periods have a fixed rhythm.   Cycles have irregular timing but a recognizable pattern; periods—for example, seasons—have a (practically) fixed timing as well as a
recognizable pattern.

The tendency to cyclical variation is seen in many aspects of
business activity. The production of steel, the sale of automobiles, the movement of freight, building construction,
wages, interest rates, profits, the level of wholesale prices, imports and exports, stock exchange prices, new issues of securities, the volume of savings, bank clearings, employment, and
even marriage and birth rates exhibit cyclical variations.

These recurrent fluctuations in individual time series may be
called, to follow Mitchell, "specific cycles."

The most characteristic aspect of these cyclical fluctuations,
however, is their tendency toward simultaneous appearance in
all the important aspects of business. The successive phases
that mark a cycle tend to spread more or less promptly over a
large part of the economic processes of a country. In addition, these relatively synchronous fluctuations in so many
aspects of industry appear also in various countries at much
the same time. Indeed, these international similarities have
tended to become more and more marked. Especially is this
true since 1870, as more and more countries find themselves
enmeshed in the typical developments of modern capitalism
and, therefore, exposed to the conditions which, under capitalism, as we shall see, tend to bring about cyclical fluctuations.

In short, the great number of specific cycles which appear
in our economic processes are clearly interrelated. And this
"congeries of interrelated phenomena," to use Mitchell's
phrase, may be defined as a *business cycle*. That is to say,
business cycles are fluctuations in general business activity that
appear through the interrelated fluctuations of innumerable
specific cycles.

(1) *Minor and major cycles*. While both specific cycles and
business cycles, properly speaking, include all fluctuations that

follow the general pattern of alternating expansion and contraction of activity, further examination of the history of these
episodes discloses a considerable difference in the amplitude of
their fluctuations, so much so that it may be appropriate to
make a distinction between minor cycles and major cycles.

Major cycles may be defined as the fluctuation of business
activity occurring between successive "crises." They may also
be called "intercrisis" cycles. In 1860, Clement Juglar, French
economist, showed that trade fluctuations were cyclical in nature and that periods of prosperity, crisis, and liquidation followed each other always in the same order. He called his
book Des Crises Commerciales, and thereafter economists began to speak of commercial crises and of commercial cycles and
to locate these cycles by the recurring appearance of "crises."
Thus Cassel, the well-known Swedish economist, in his Theory
of Social Economy, set up the years 1873, 1882, 1890, 1900, and
1907 as locating-points for cycles in Germany, on the ground
that each of these years was a year of recognized crisis. Similarly, Mitchell, in his Business Cycles and Unemployment, begins his section on the nature of business cycles as follows:
"Fifteen times within the past hundred and ten years American business has passed through a 'crisis.' The list of crisis
years (1812, 1818, 1825, 1837, 1847, 1857, 1873, 1884, 1890, 1893,
1903, 1907, 1910, 1913, 1920) shows that the periods between
successive crises have varied considerably in length."

Therefore, we may agree that intercrisis cycles are to
be distinguished from cycles in general. So distinguished,
they are called "major cycles," "commercial cycles," or Juglar
cycles, in recognition of Juglar's pioneer work in establishing
the cyclical nature of business fluctuations; but always they
refer to variations of business between recognizable crises.

However, further study of the history of business fluctuations
discloses that activity has frequently turned downward following a period of expansion without being accompanied by
the major disturbances in the money market associated with

crisis. What has occurred is a "recession" rather than a crisis. There has been a turn downward, but no abrupt break. If one counts the cycles between recessions, what we may call *interrecession cycles,* one will find that they are shorter and more numerous than intercrisis cycles. The intercrisis cycle may include two or even three (as between 1920–1930) alternations of prosperity and depression. The average duration of intercrisis cycles in the United States in the period 1790 to 1925 is practically twice as great as that of interrecession cycles. Where the longer cycles average 8⁶⁄₇ years, the shorter average not quite 4.[10]

These shorter cycles, or interrecession cycles, may be called *minor cycles,.* In late years the evidence is that they average close to 40 months.

Joseph Kitchin makes this distinction between major and minor cycles, after a careful measurement of certain indexes during the years 1890–1922 in both Great Britain and the United States.[11] The indexes examined were bank clearings, wholesale prices, and interest rates. By calculating the average interval between successive maxima and again between successive minima, he finds a strong tendency toward a minor cycle averaging 3⅓ years, or 40 months. This finding, moreover, is confirmed by an investigation of W. S. Crum, who, using a periodogram analysis on data of interest rates on commercial paper, finds an average period of 40 months also.[12]

Kitchin proceeds to state that major cycles are merely aggregates, usually of two, less commonly of three, minor cycles, and that the limits of these major cycles are marked by a high maximum of the indexes, and sometimes a panic. The average of these major cycles is eight years, and the most usual interval seven or ten years. These major cycles are the intercrisis or Juglar cycles described above.

---

10 Mitchell, *Business Cycles,* 388.
11 *Review of Economic Statistics,* January, 1923.
12 *Ibid.*

It would be accurate to say, therefore, that business cycles may be classified into two broad divisions (the boundaries of which cannot, of course, be precise): (1) major or intercrisis cycles, and (2) minor or interrecession cycles.

Of these two, the intercrisis cycle is economically the more important, and, as far as the public is concerned, the one in which it is interested. Minor oscillations are not dramatic; they may scarcely be recognized as they go by. Sometimes they can be recognized only by scrutiny of statistical indexes; sometimes even some statistical indexes do not show them, as, for example, the depression of 1927. But the major cycles are dramatic and have serious results. The social consequences of cycles, their effects on employment, on prices, and on the distribution of income between the various classes of society are impressive only when the cyclical fluctuation is well marked. From the point of view of the public, minor cycles might well be regarded not as cyclical fluctuations in the true sense but rather, to use the apt phrase of A. B. Adams, as periods of "oscillating equilibrium."

On the other hand, from the standpoint of scientific classification and for the purposes of systematic analysis of the essential patterns of cyclical behavior, the interrecession cycle offers, perhaps, the greater interest. Minor and major cycles do not differ in their fundamental behavior. The characteristic pattern of the cycle is found in both. In both occurs the normal sequence of prosperity, recession, depression, revival. Even the great depressions, such as 1873–1878, 1893–1897, and 1929–1933, while affected by abnormal and specific influences, display the underlying and essential features common to all cyclical fluctuations. It is for this reason that Mitchell in his classic studies uses the term *business cycle* for *all* cyclical fluctuations, whether minor or major, whether intercrisis or interrecession, reserving the words *commercial cycles,* when needed, for intercrisis cycles as such. As this usage is probably most effective for scientific analysis, it is the one adopted here.

Major and minor cycles, therefore, are subdivisions of the broad category of business cycles, which themselves may be taken to cover all *recurring* fluctuations of general business activity that take the form of alternating expansions and contractions.

(2) *Long waves.* There is some evidence that economic activity is subject to rhythmical fluctuations of a duration longer than the business cycle as described above. Various economists, by careful analysis of the available statistical material, claim to have demonstrated the existence of what are commonly called "long waves," occurring in a fifty- or sixty-year cycle.

The starting point of these investigations is the well-established fact of wavelike fluctuations in the level of wholesale prices. Index numbers of wholesale prices, no matter how calculated, all show long waves of the price level, with the trend of prices changing direction five times in the 140-year period 1790 to 1930. The exact turning points vary with the index chosen, but the general picture is clear. Both in England and in the United States, where available data make it possible to construct an index number of prices covering the whole period involved, six periods of alternately rising and declining prices are disclosed.

The timing of these periods is as follows:

Rise	1790–1815
Fall	1815–1849
Rise:	
United States	1849–1865
Great Britain	1849–1873
Fall:	
United States	1865–1896
Great Britain	1873–1896
Rise	1896–1920
Fall	1920–

The symmetry of behavior in the price levels of two countries, broken only by the effect of the Civil War and the green-

back standard in the United States, which hastened the peak
of prices that ended the period of price rise, is a convincing
proof of the existence of long waves in wholesale prices.
What is disclosed is a price cycle with a wave length of some
50 years. And one might assume that, in the absence of interference by governments intent on controlling the value of
money, there would have been a downward trend of prices,
following 1920, until about the year 1945, thus finishing the
downward phase begun in 1920, and rounding out, to the satisfaction of the statistician, the third great cycle of prices.

Furthermore, these long cycles of prices, which are generally
attributed to variations in the rate of increase in world gold
supply relative to the volume of production and trade, seem to
be associated with (and may be the cause of) similar long
cycles of economic activity, in such wise that the general trend
of economic activity is higher in periods of rising prices. The
annals of business indicate a change in the ratio of prosperity
to depression in periods of rising and falling prices, respectively.
In periods of rising prices, prosperity tends to be long and
depression short; in periods of falling prices, prosperity tends
to be short and depression long. In his study of business annals, Thorp gives the evidence for the United States as follows: [13]

Ratio of months of prosperity to months of depression in
periods of rising prices:

1790–1815	2.6
1849–1865	2.9
1896–1920	3.1

Ratio of months of prosperity to months of depression in
periods of falling prices:

1815–1849	.8
1865–1896	.9

One might properly deduce from this evidence that the general pace of activity in the periods of rising prices would be

---

[13] See Mitchell, *Business Cycles*, 411.

greater than in the periods of falling prices. This expectation finds some confirmation in the evidence of the variation of economic activity offered by different investigators who claim to have discovered the existence of long waves, particularly in the studies of the Dutch economists Van Gelderen and de Wolff [14] and the Russian economist Kondratieff.[15] Of these, the studies of Kondratieff, being the most accessible, may serve to show the nature of the conclusions.

Kondratieff Cycles

Kondratieff collected and examined a great variety of time series extending over long periods. He found that long waves similar to those already recognized in British wholesale prices were to be observed also in interest yields on French and English government bonds and in French and English wages. Then he examined various series showing physical quantities or aggregate values. He put these through a refined statistical process. The original data were computed on a per-capita basis, mathematical trend lines were calculated, and the deviations from the trend were computed and smoothed by nine-year moving averages (to remove cycles). The resultant index, when plotted, showed a wavelike deviation about the trend in the production of coal, pig iron, and lead in England, the consumption of coal in France, French imports and exports, English exports, and some others. The timing points of the various waves thus discovered tended to coincide in a broad sort of way, and to produce waves with more or less established timing, and of international scope. The data, which covered the period 1780–1920, seemed to establish $2\frac{1}{2}$ long cycles, each full cycle being in the vicinity of 50 years. Where there was no trend, as in the price series, the cycles took the form of a wavelike movement above and below the

---

[14] *Der Lebendige Marxismus;* 1924, 13–43.
[15] "Long Waves in Economic Life," *Review of Economic Statistics,* November, 1935.

average. Where there was a trend, the cycles showed not so much a rise or fall as an acceleration or retardation of the rate of growth. The periods of these long cycles are as follows:

1st cycle	Incline: 1780–1790 to 1810–1817
	Decline: 1810–1817 to 1844–1851
2nd cycle	Incline: 1844–1851 to 1870–1875
	Decline: 1870–1875 to 1890–1896
3rd cycle	Incline: 1890–1896 to 1914–1920
	Decline: 1914–1920 to ?

On the face of it, this seems to indicate an ebb and flow in the pace of activity that is not accidental but due to causes in some way embedded in our industrial economy. But the evidence cannot be regarded as more than suggestive. The data cover but two and one-half cycles, certainly not enough either to establish a probability of further cycles or to predict that the period 1920–1945, say, will be one in which the rate of progression will fall below the average. Furthermore, not all the series examined by Kondratieff showed unmistakable signs of these long cycles. There were no such waves in French cotton production or in American wool or sugar production. Therefore, one cannot regard these "Kondratieff cycles" as being established as the ordinary business cycle is established.

However, one may accept provisionally the possibility that the fundamental changes which go on in economic activity include three kinds of cycles: the short or minor cycle, of some 40 months' duration; the major or Juglar cycle, made up of two or three minor cycles; and the Kondratieff cycle, made up of perhaps six Juglar cycles.[16] Furthermore, the possibility of such long waves or cycles gives rise to the suspicion that, if we knew more, what are commonly called "trends" might turn out to be merely segments of very long cycles. In the period for which we have knowledge, they are trends. For periods longer than this, they may be cycles. Even the longest trend

---

[16] Cf. J. Schumpeter, "The Analysis of Economic Change," *Review of Economic Statistics*, May, 1935.

may in time reverse itself. Even the long and relatively uninterrupted progress which seems to mark the "magnificent
episode" of the nineteenth century may be but the rising phase
of a very long cycle, the downward slope of which perhaps the
twentieth century will eventually disclose. In short, cycles
may well be the rule of all activity.

Conclusion

It seems clear from the evidence of statistics and business
history that the economic activities of a country are subject to
a great variety of fluctuations, and that some of these are so
well marked as to lend themselves to identification and systematic classification. Seasonal variation, business cycles, commercial or intercrisis cycles, possibly long waves, and secular
trends are recognizable forms of business fluctuation. Along
with these occur a multitude of uncertain, unclassifiable, unpredictable changes, which may be called "accidental factors"; together with those more formidable but also nonrecurrent transformations of the whole economic scene called "structural
change."

The business cycle, to the study of which this volume is devoted, is, then, one out of a number of fluctuations to which business is subject. It is tempting to assume that it is the most
important. Its effects upon social welfare, and perhaps on the
very continuance of modern capitalism, are profound. It is
the most dramatic of fluctuations, and the one which has cap-
tured public attention and claimed the most prolonged and
intense scrutiny on the part of economists.

What is proposed in this book is to examine in detail the
characteristic behavior of business during the course of cycles;
to set forth the explanations advanced by economists to account for them; and to analyze the various means by which
these cyclical fluctuations might be reduced in the interests of
the economic welfare of the people as a whole.

CHAPTER II

TIME SERIES AND THEIR ANALYSIS

THE statistical materials from which our knowledge of business cycles is derived take the form of "time series." "A time series is a number of quantitative measurements arranged in chronological sequence." [1]

The following is a time series showing the *per capita* income in the United States for the years 1932 to 1938.

TABLE I

Year	Per Capita Income
1932	$320
1933	336
1934	395
1935	433
1936	494
1937	540
1938	472

Time series in their original form may be values such as prices or wages; or physical quantities such as pig iron output or railway tonnage; or ratios such as interest rates or reserve percentages; and so on. To be most useful for study, the units of such time series should be available at frequent intervals—weekly or monthly. Annual data, while useful in the absence of others, do not admit of fine measurements of such relatively short-period fluctuations as business cycles.

---

[1] *Encyclopaedia of the Social Sciences,* Vol. XIV, 629.

Simple Index Numbers or Relatives

As time series in their original form are not well adapted to interpretation, it is usual to refine the raw series by various statistical processes. One convenient device is to reduce the actual data as given to a series of percentages of some convenient base.

Thus each·item of the per capita income series can be expressed as a percentage of the year 1932 (or any convenient year). The result is given in Table II.

TABLE II

Year	Relatives (1932 = 100)
1932	100
1933	105
1934	123
1935	135
1936	154
1937	170
1938	148

These percentages of a given base are sometimes called "simple index numbers." One would speak of the index for 1934 as 123. But it is considered more correct to call these numbers a series of "relatives." Such relatives enable comparison to be made of the changes in time series expressed in various units, such as pounds, tons, yards, bushels, and so forth. They are particularly useful in enabling various time series with similar fluctuations to be brought together and merged into a single series of index numbers. Such index numbers are called "composite index numbers."

Composite Index Numbers

A composite index number is designed to show the relative change in a whole group of related time series which all pertain to the same kind of activity.

The following example shows an index of pig iron production, an index of automobile production, and a composite index of production, found by averaging the two.

TABLE III

1935–1939 AVERAGE = 100

Year	Pig Iron Output	Automobile Output	Composite Index
1933	48	50	49
1934	57	71	64
1935	76	102	89
1936	110	116	113
1937	132	125	128.5
1938	68	65	66.5
1939	114	93	103.5

This composite index is thus an average of the two series in each year. It may be taken to be an index of production in general, in so far as pig iron and automobile output can be taken as representative samples. Were a larger number of series taken into account so as to cover a wide area of output, the composite index number so calculated might properly be called an "index of industrial production." Thus a composite index number enables one to get some idea of a magnitude which cannot be known by any direct observation—that is, the total volume of productive activity.

Weighted Index Numbers

As the different kinds of output in the total productive activity of the country clearly are not all of equal importance, a more accurate "index" of the general state of activity—that is to say, a better representative picture—is obtained by the device of weighted index numbers. Weighted index numbers are calculated by estimating the relative importance of each series in production (say, by the relative volume produced or consumed in some given year) and, on the basis of this, assigning weights to the relatives included in the average. Thus if pig iron and automobile production were estimated to be of the importance of 5 and 2 respectively, then, in taking the average, pig iron relatives would be multiplied by 5 and automobile relatives by 2. For example:

Year	Pig Iron Output	Automobile Output	Composite Index
1933	48×5	50×2	$\dfrac{(48 \times 5) + (50 \times 2)}{7} = 48.6.$

The result is a series in which pig iron changes exert more influence than automobile changes, and pull the index more in the direction indicated by the pig iron series.

Most of the familiar time series which are currently published are weighted in this fashion. Thus the price index of the Bureau of Labor Statistics is an aggregate of many prices, each weighted by the consumption of the article in question in a basic year, and the total reduced to percentages of the data for the year 1926. Again, the index of industrial production of the Federal Reserve Board is a weighted average of numerous relatives, all expressed as percentages of the average of their respective series for the years 1936–1939 inclusive.

Such refined index numbers (and, of course, any time series) may be graphically represented by curves drawn upon a chart, a procedure which facilitates the understanding and interpretation of what might otherwise seem abstract.

Obtaining Comparable Scales of Variation

In putting together composite index numbers, one often finds great differences in the variations of the individual time series. Thus, though all series have the same general pattern and commonly show much the same timing in the occurrence of expansion and contraction, they do not show the same "amplitude" of change. Some swing very widely; others have but small variation. Thus the production of capital goods varies much more widely through business cycles than the production of consumers' goods. Again, bank clearings have greater variations than interest rates. Yet these different amplitudes are all expressions of the same general cyclical fluctuation.

If, now, a composite index is made by averaging the series as they stand, the picture is distorted by the different scales of fluctuation. It would be as if a series expressed in pounds were averaged with a series expressed in tons. Somehow they should be brought to a similar scale.

The means of doing this is to reduce each series to percentages of its own characteristic "deviation" as expressed in one of the familiar measures of deviation known to statistics.

Measures of deviation give a picture of the degree to which the individual items of a series deviate from the average of the series. They are essentially measures of consistency of behavior. If, in general, the items differ but little from the average of the series, the deviation is low and the behavior consistent. If they differ much from the average of the series, the deviation is high and the behavior erratic. Thus a ball player whose batting average was .300 and who can be expected to bat close to .300 on any given day is a very consistent batter, and the measure of his deviation is low. But a batter with the same average of .300 who might have a perfect score one day and no hits the next is an inconsistent hitter, and the measure of his deviation would be high. (Incidentally, the club would be willing to pay more for the former than for the latter.)

The best-known measures of deviation are the *average deviation* and the *standard deviation*.

To find the average deviation of a series, one first finds the arithmetic average of the series, then calculates the deviation of each item of the series from this average, and finally finds the arithmetic average of these deviations. In equation form:

$$\text{Arithmetic deviation} = \frac{\text{sum of deviations of items from average}}{\text{number of items}}.$$

To find the standard deviation, one again calculates the arithmetic average of the series and the deviations of each item from the series. But the deviations are then squared, the squares averaged, and the square root of the average taken. In equation form: .

$$\text{Standard deviation} = \sqrt{\frac{\text{sum of squares of deviations}}{\text{number of items}}}.$$

Both measures of deviation imply that any given item has a tendency to vary by this much (up or down) from the average of the series.

Let us see now how these measures can be used to improve comparisons between one time series and another.

Suppose two series of varying amplitude are as follows:

TABLE IV

Year	Consumers' Goods	Producers' Goods
1	90	70
2	100	120
3	110	140
4	110	100
5	90	70

Chart 1 shows these disproportionate fluctuations.

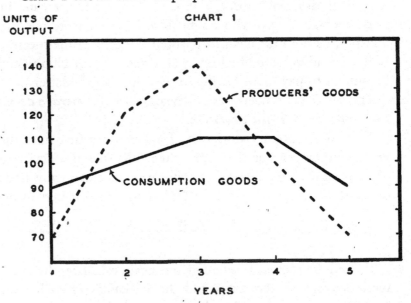

UNITS OF OUTPUT

CHART 1

PRODUCERS' GOODS

CONSUMPTION GOODS

YEARS

The average deviation is now calculated as follows:

TABLE V

Year	Con-sump-tion Goods	Deviations of Consumption Series from Average	Pro-ducers' Goods	Deviations of Production Series from Average
I	90	− 10	70	− 30
2	100	0	120	20
3	110	10	140	40
4	110	10	100	0
5	90	− 10	70	− 30
	5⟌500	Ignoring Signs	5⟌500	Ignoring Signs
average . .	100	Av. Dev. $= \dfrac{40}{5} = 8$	100	Av. Dev. $= \dfrac{120}{5} = 24$

Now divide the actual deviation of each item in the respective series by the average deviation of the series. The result is a series expressed in units of average deviation.

TABLE VI

Year	Consumption Goods	Production Goods
I .	$\dfrac{-10}{8} = -1.25$	$\dfrac{-30}{24} = -1.25$
2	$\dfrac{0}{8} = 0$	$\dfrac{20}{24} = .83$
3	$\dfrac{10}{8} = 1.25$	$\dfrac{40}{24} = 1.66$
4	$\dfrac{10}{8} = 1.25$	$\dfrac{0}{24} = 0$
5	$\dfrac{-10}{8} = -1.25$	$\dfrac{-30}{24} = -1.25$

Thus, for example, in year 3, consumption goods output is 1¼ units of deviation above the average, and production goods 1⅔ units of deviation above the average.

Chart 2, with the scale in units of average deviation, shows the result.

Thus the variations have been reduced to a comparable scale. The generally greater variations of the production goods series are now reduced to the relatively smaller variations of each item from its own typical variation. Zero on the scale means that at that point the item did not vary at all from the average of the series; 1 on the scale means that the variation of the item from the series was equal to the average variation of the series; and so on.

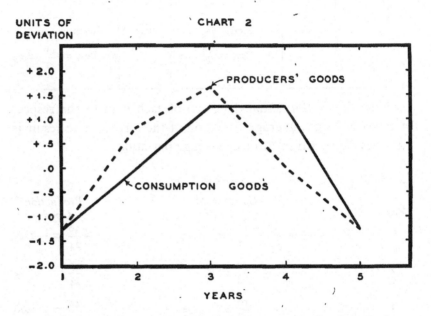

UNITS OF
DEVIATION

CHART 2

PRODUCERS' GOODS

CONSUMPTION GOODS

YEARS

Similar results can be had by calculating standard deviations. The reader will find various charts in which the scale is in units of either average or standard deviation—for example, the charts used in the monthly survey of business in the *Review of Economic Statistics* or the *American Telephone and Telegraph Company's Index of General Business*. Whenever either device is used, the purpose is to secure greater comparability of various time series, and particularly to be able to average them together into some significant composite index number.

Deflation, or Correcting for Price Changes

Many of the available time series useful for business cycle study are expressed in values and represent money volume. As such, they are a product of two variables, activity and price. They are volume of activity multiplied by a price factor.

As such, they do not adequately disclose the variation in activity which is the essence of boom or depression. Thus, for example, an index of department-store sales which is expressed in dollar volume is not an unambiguous index. A rise of this index *may* mean that more goods are being sold, but it may also mean merely that prices are rising. It does not inform us definitely that activity has increased.

Hence it is desirable to eliminate the effect of price change and leave only the "real" change which values tend to obscure. This is done by a process of "deflation," which consists of dividing the items of a series by corresponding items of an index of price.

For example, Table VII is an index of *per capita* income in the United States from 1926 to 1932, a period during which an expansion was followed by a drastic reduction.

TABLE VII

Year	Per Capita Income in the United States
1926	$643
1927	624
1928	648
1929	668
1930	555
1931	434
1932	320

The national income is designed to serve as a measure of the goods and services annually produced, and the drastic reduction here displayed from 1929 to 1932 seems to indicate the

great severity of the depression. But, during this period, the
price level was also falling, so that the reduction in the volume
of goods and services is not fairly represented, but in fact is
exaggerated, by data expressed in values. Hence if changes
in "real" income are to be shown, the data must be deflated by
being divided by an index of the price level._ This process is
shown by Table VIII.

TABLE VIII

Year	Per Capita Income	Price Index	Real Income $\left(\dfrac{income}{price}\right)$
1926	$643	100	$643
1927	624	95	658
1928	648	97	658
1929 . .	668	95	703
1930 .	555	86	645
1931	434	73	595
1932	320	65	492

The last column displays the deflated figures. This column
is income in "constant dollars," in this case 1926 dollars. It is
what income would have been on the assumption that prices
had been constant throughout the period. It is an index of
"real" as compared with "money" income and, because of this,
is a better representative of the changing flow of goods and
services that constitutes the national income, particularly in
periods of rapidly falling prices such as 1929–1932. Thus,
whereas money incomes of 1932 were only 48 per cent of those
of 1929, real incomes were 70 per cent of those of 1929.

Any time series expressed in money values can be satisfac-
torily deflated in this way, provided an appropriate "deflator,"
or index of prices, is used.

Thus wages should be divided by an index of cost of living
to get "real" wages. Department-store sales should be deflated by an index of retail prices or preferably (if available)
of department-store prices themselves. Both bank clearings
and national income, reflecting as they do the whole activity

of the economy, should be divided by an index of general prices, including rents, wages, security prices, and other important values, as well as the customary wholesale prices. Whatever deflator is used, the result is an index which, so far as the process is correct, represents activity, not values.

Correcting for Trend and Seasonal Fluctuation

Most time series in their original form are not properly adapted to disclose business cycle fluctuations, for the data is the expression of a complex of variations—not only cycles, but trends, seasonal variations, and accidental fluctuations of various kinds. All of these fluctuations are registered in the varying behavior of time series, and some procedure must be used to separate these several fluctuations if a measure of cyclical change alone is to be obtained.

Unless this separate measurement is made, not only is the study of cycles made more difficult, but serious confusion and deception will lie in wait for the unwary user of statistical data. If the trend of production, for example, is upward, every year tends to be a "record" performance. But breaking all records is no infallible index of prosperity, for unless the "record" is enough to include the normal year-to-year growth, it is not a sign of prosperity; it may even be a sign of depression. Hardy and Cox [2] noted that, in the summer of 1925, car loadings were running above a million a week, a figure rarely reached except in the abnormally prosperous year 1923. Yet business was not abnormally active in the summer of 1925. There is an upward trend in railway traffic of about 4 per cent per year, so that a record of 1,000,000 cars a week in 1925 is comparable to 800,000 in 1920, and indicates only normal traffic.

Seasonal variations make the same kind of trouble. If, for example, the output of pig iron in March is ordinarily 10 per

---

[2] Hardy and Cox, *Forecasting Business Conditions*, New York, 1927, 28.

cent above the average for the year, then the observer must be-
ware of assuming that an actual increase of 10 per cent in a
given March is a sign of prosperity. It is not a sign of prosperity, but only of the regularly recurring seasonal bulge.
Only an increase of more than 10 per cent would indicate
above-normal business in that month; and an increase of only
5 per cent would have to be interpreted as a sign of depression.
At the end of depressions, when everyone is eagerly looking
for signs of revival, the ordinary normal improvement of certain months may be mistaken for evidence of a genuine recovery, and people congratulate themselves on a March that was
8 per cent above the average for the year, when they should
have been mourning because it was 2 per cent below the
normal.

Although it is not feasible to segregate all the various fluctuations compounded in a time series, fortunately statistical
technique has developed effective devices for calculating and
removing trends and seasonal variations. The methods used
in these calculations will be found set forth in any textbook on
statistics. It is enough to indicate here in nontechnical language what the procedure means and the kind of corrections
it makes.

The Elimination of Trend

To measure the trend is to find out what is the amount by
which the data tend to increase from year to year or from
month to month. It is fairly evident by glancing at a charted
time series whether there is a trend, and whether it is upward
or downward; and some idea of the amount of the trend can
be obtained from a line drawn through the data, in such wise
that the area above and below the line is substantially equal.
This can be illustrated by Table IX and Chart 3.

Let us put these figures on a chart, together with what seems
to be the trend. It is evident from this chart that the trend is
upward, despite the downward move in 1937 and again in

1940. The dotted line may be taken as fairly representative of this trend, showing at each successive year the amount which might be "expected" at that time.

TABLE IX

Year	Sales in Thousands of Dollars
1936	85
1937 ....' ..	70
1938	90
1939	130
1940	125

The amounts indicated on the trend line may be called "the ordinates of the trend" and the increase from year to year the "increments of trend."

CHART 3

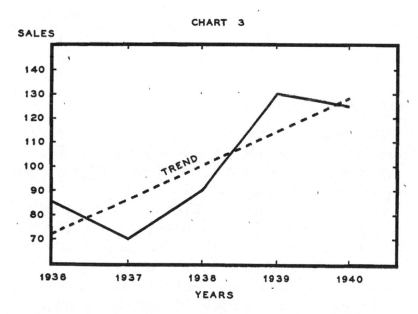

If we may assume that the trend figure for 1936 is 72 (thousands), then, with an increase of 14 (thousand) each year, the ordinates of the trend are as given in Table X.

TABLE X

Year		Ordinates of the Trend
1936	. . . .	72
1937	.	86
1938		100
1939	. . . . .	114
1940	.. . .	128

The degree to which the actual sales differ from the expected sales may be taken as the measure of cyclical fluctuation. Hence cyclical fluctuation can be disclosed (and the trend "removed") by expressing the actual sales in each year as a percentage of the trend figure for that year, as is shown in Table XI.

TABLE XI

Year		Original Data	Trend	Original Data as Percentages of Trend
1936	....	85	72	118
1937	.. .	70	86	81
1938	... . ..	90	100	90
1939	. . ..	130	114	114
1940	..	125	128	98

The figures in the last column may, therefore, be properly considered to be an index of cyclical fluctuations. Thus, in 1936, business was 18 per cent above "normal," but, in 1940, 2 per cent below "normal."

The result is as shown in Chart 4. The trend then is an expected amount of increase from period to period, and cyclical fluctuations are revealed as variations above or below this expected amount. In other words, they are variations from "normal" as expressed by the successive positions of the line of trend. Thus, in our illustration, the increment of trend is $14,000 a year—that is, each year is expected to be $14,000 better than the year before—since this increase is "normal" for the period involved.

The time series has now been "corrected" for trend. There is no trend in this curve. It is merely a fluctuation around a level of 100 per cent, which itself represents that changing normal level which the trend is supposed to be.[3]

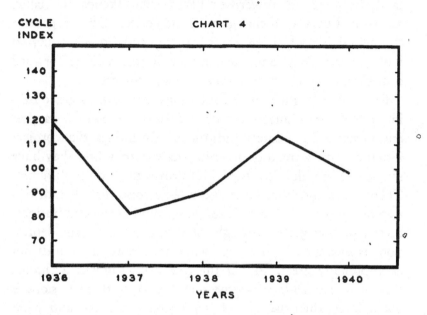

CYCLE
INDEX

CHART 4

YEARS

Some Problems of Interpretation

Trends thus discovered must be interpreted with care and a fair mixture of scepticism. The trend must be established for a definite given period, and this period must be chosen with discretion. The conditions at the two extremities of the curve must be reasonably alike. More particularly, the same phase of the cycle should occur at each end. If the period begins with prosperity or depression, it should end with prosperity or depression. Furthermore, there should be no fundamental disturbances in the conditions involved during the period. If

---

[3] Trend figures obtained by inspection, as illustrated above, are not likely to be satisfactory to statisticians who have devised very exact mathematical techniques by which trend can be more scientifically established. These techniques are explained in every textbook on statistics. However the trend is established, the method of correcting for trend is the same as illustrated above.

the conditions are subject to abrupt change, the trend cannot be considered as established.

Even when these two conditions are fulfilled, the trend is accurate only for the period it covers. It cannot with any certainty be projected forward or backward. Trends are liable, as Mitchell puts it, to change without notice. They represent the period for which they are drawn, and no other period with surety. They cannot reliably be projected either forward or backward with any certainty of being correct.

Failure to recognize these limitations may lead to grave misinterpretations of current events and, in some cases, to dangerous mistakes in business judgment. Businesses that project into the future a trend of booming activity may find they have seriously overbuilt when the trend proves to be quite different. There is evidence that some automobile concerns fell into this trap in the 1920's. Again, if the long trend of general business up to 1930 is projected through the next eight years, the depression, as measured by the area below the "normal," stands out as imposingly great. But if the trend has suffered a change (and it is reasonable to assume that it has), so that the slope is not so steep, then the area of depression is smaller, and what seemed to be the greatest depression of all time turns out to be, at least in part, a matter of changing trend.

If statistical methods cannot be said to "establish" trends with precision, still less can they, by "eliminating" trends, "establish" business cycles. A trend may be removed statistically, but it cannot really be removed. Were the trend actually removed, the behavior of the business cycle would certainly be different from what it now is. Trends make cycles what they are; cycles make trends what they are. If the trends are to be considered the resultants of progress, they can be removed only if progress is removed. But progress being removed would change cycles too. At least some explanations of the cycle indicate that progress, invention, and change are

important determinants of cycles as we know them. On the
other hand, if cycles are a cause of progress, and some hold
that it is the periodic expansion due to cycles that makes us go
on the upward path, then trends are the result of cycles and
cannot be eliminated in order to show cycles except by eliminating the cycle, or the very thing which is to be shown.

Therefore, while it may be convenient to regard cycles as
variations from the line of trend, to be measured by the degree
of this variation, one must recognize that the task of separating
two such interdependent components as cycles and trends is
really insuperable. It is one of those cases where $2 + 2 = 5$.

The Elimination of Seasonal Variation

A seasonal variation is the tendency for an index in any
month of the year to vary from the average for the year. Thus,
in the building industry, construction for January, because of
adverse weather conditions, will be only 70 per cent of the
average monthly construction during the year. On the other
hand, construction in April, when seasonal conditions are very
favorable, will rise to 135 per cent of the monthly average.

It is possible, by appropriate statistical technique, to establish
an index of seasonal variation. Such an index will show by
how much the behavior of any given month may be expected
to diverge from the average behavior of the whole year. Based
as it is on past records, it cannot infallibly imply that a given
month *will* behave as expected, but only that, in general, the
month in question *has* so behaved and may be expected to continue doing so.

Table XII is an index of seasonal variation of pig iron production. This table expresses the typical or average seasonal
behavior for each month as a percentage of the average behavior for the year. It assumes that the seasonal influence of
any actual month is reasonably allowed for by the level of this
index.

Seasonal indexes, like indexes of the trend, are bound to be empirical. They reflect what has occurred in the period in which the index has been calculated. They may or may not continue to reflect the facts. If the index is primarily due to the compulsions of the physical season, it may continue to be representative. However, conscious effort to avoid the objectionable results of seasonal fluctuations may change the behavior of industry. If the seasonal fluctuation has been due to custom or habit, this either may be broken down by planning or may break down of its own accord through the changing

TABLE XII

January	102	July	98
February	93	August	101
March	104	September	98
April	101	October	103
May	101	November	102
June	97	December	100

caprice of the consumer. There is no certainty, therefore, that a seasonal index based on the past 20 years will continue to be reliable. Automobile production has gradually become less seasonal, as closed cars and good roads have made year-round driving commonplace. In addition, on this has been imposed a conscious attempt to stabilize still more in the interest of good industrial relations, as when the Auto Show was pushed back into the late fall. Hence, the seasonal index for auto. production is substantially different from what it was 10 years ago.

Furthermore, a seasonal index, no matter how carefully calculated and adjusted to satisfy changing seasonal conditions, either physical or conventional, measures the typical, not the specific, monthly variation. The specific or actual variation may differ from the typical or average variation, and, when this happens, the cyclical measure is bound to be distorted. If the specific variation is less than average, the cycle index will understate the cyclical level. If the specific variation is more than the average, the cycle index will overstate the cyclical level. Thus one expects a certain bulge in jewelry business in June because of college and high school graduation. If the bulge is greater than expected, it is attributed to the cycle and is supposed to indicate a general rise in business. But it may merely mean a larger than average set of graduates or a more generous than average set of friends.

Adjusting for Seasonal Variation

A time series can be adjusted for seasonal variation by dividing the output (or value) for each month by the corresponding seasonal index. This process is shown in Table XIII.

TABLE XIII

Month	Output (Thousands of Tons)	Seasonal Index (%)	Adjusted Output
January	85	102	$\dfrac{85 \times 100}{102} = 83.3$
February	70	93	$\dfrac{70 \times 100}{93} = 75.3$
March	90	104	$\dfrac{90 \times 100}{104} = 86.5$
April	130	101	$\dfrac{130 \times 100}{101} = 128.7$

The seasonal index for January being 102 per cent of normal, the unadjusted figure overstates the normal output. The adjusted figure, which is found by dividing 85 by 102 per cent ($= 83.3$), shows the output which would be expected were seasonal variation absent. Similarly, as February output is expected to be 93 per cent of normal, the unadjusted figure understates the normal output, which is shown by the adjusted figure of 75.3.

The adjusted figures of output are, therefore:

		Thousands of Tons
January		83.3
February	. . . . . .	75.3
March	. . . .	86.5
April	128.7

Adjusting for Both Trend and Seasonal Variation

When both seasonal variation and trend have to be removed, the process is similar. What is sought is a figure that will express the actual data as percentages of the "expected." In this case, the "expected" is the trend modified by the seasonal variation.

Table XIV shows the actual performance over a period of months, as compared with what might be called the "expected," or normal, performance during the same period.

TABLE XIV

Month	I Actual Sales (Thousands of Dollars)	II Seasonal Index (%)	III Ordinates of Trend (Thou- sands of Dollars)	IV Expected, or Normal, Performance
January ..	85	102	72	$72 \times 102/100 = 73.5$
February .	70	93	86	$86 \times 93/100 = 80$
March	90	104	100	$100 \times 104/100 = 104$
April . . .	130	101	114	$114 \times 101/100 = 115$

In Table XIV, Column III is a supposed trend, beginning with 72 (thousand) in January and increasing by 14 (thousand) each month. Column IV is clearly an index of "expected" sales. Thus in January the trend indicates sales of $72,000. But as January is a better-than-average month, as indicated by seasonal index of 102, the full expectation for January is 102 per cent of the trend (102% of 72 = 73.4). Similar calculations give the expectation for other months.

The final correction must, therefore, be to express the actual performance as a percentage of the expected. When this is done, one has a picture of deviations away from normal, which may be taken to be a picture of whatever fluctuations are left after trend and seasonal variations have been "removed." Table XV shows this completed process.

TABLE XV

Month	Actual Sales	Expected Sales	Corrected Index = Actual as Percentage of Expected
January	85	73.4	116
February	70	80	87.5
March	90	104	86.5
April	130	115	112

To sum up: if the ordinates of the trend are calculated and a seasonal index discovered, then the process of correcting a time series for trend and seasonal fluctuation is represented by the following equation:

$$\text{Corrected index for each date} = \frac{\text{Actual datum}}{\text{Trend} \times \text{seasonal index}} \times 100.$$

That is to say, the actual performance is reduced to a percentage of expected or normal performance, and the result is a picture of cyclical fluctuations undistorted by the effects of either trend or seasonal variation.

Random Fluctuations Not Eliminated

While the elimination of trends and seasonal fluctuation is necessary for the statistical measurement of the business cycle, it must not be assumed that the statistical residue after these eliminations represents the business cycle and nothing else. It does not. It represents the business cycle modified by the effect of accidental, random, or irregular fluctuations.

These random fluctuations cannot be segregated in the present state of statistical knowledge. They do not occur in recognizable periods like the seasons and they are not subject to the persistent continuing movement of trends. It is possible that their distribution may be subject to the law of probability, that their number is so considerable, their nature so varied, and their effects so differing that they might be thought of as canceling each other out. But the evidence that this is true is lacking, and, in respect to major factors such as wars or great inventions, canceling out is, *prima facie,* improbable. We will presumably have to accept the difficulty as insurmountable for the present and to be satisfied with having eliminated the effects of trends and seasons.

It is the interposition of these irregular and accidental causes which helps to make cycles as we know them differ from each other in shape. And it is these uncertain factors which make the art of forecasting so difficult. Cycles seem to be the combined result of various generating causes and certain typical business responses. Both the generating causes and the responses, but particularly the generating causes, are affected by these unpredictable, accidental influences that we call random fluctuations. Some day the pattern of wars, strikes, droughts, epidemics, and inventions may be better known. When it is sufficiently well known, "accidental" fluctuations will no longer exist, and business forecasting will be a science rather than the intelligent guesswork it perforce now is.

CHAPTER III

THE RECORDS OF BUSINESS CYCLES

When Cycles Began

It has been pointed out 'that, although business cycles are not periods, they are properly described by the term *cycles* and are, therefore, capable of being measured. Such measurement must be obtained from the records of cyclical fluctuations wherever they may be found, reaching back as far as possible and into all countries of the world.

The records of business fluctuations, at least in the recognizable pattern of recurrent ebb and flow of activity, do not in all probability extend back of the Napoleonic Wars. It is true that all economic life in the past, as far as records go, has been subject to many vicissitudes and changes, but the kind of fluctuation to which the term *business cycle* applies seems essentially to be a characteristic of relatively recent industrial history, more particularly of that modern industrialism which has developed since about the time of the Napoleonic Wars.

The economic records of the past show good times and bad times. They show many crises. But these variations of economic activity do not take on the recurring rhythm of cycles. They do not arise from characteristics inherent in, and forces developed by, the world of business.

In his minute study of English business from 1558 to 1720, Dr. William R. Scott of St. Andrews has discovered 30 crises during this period of time. Characteristically, they are due, principally, to the following causes: famines, plagues, wars, civil disorders, irregularities of government finance, high-handed acts of government, early speculation (such as the South Sea Bubble of 1720). Most of these alleged "causes" play little part in modern cycles. The older crises, moreover, were apt to be of long duration. One fifth of them lasted three years or more. Modern crises tend to be short. Whole cycles are ended in three or four years. In earlier times, crises did not necessarily follow periods of prosperity; 12 of the 30 came in periods of depression. Modern crises tend to follow periods of prosperity, for the reason that prosperity induces stresses and strains that bring it to an end. Again, whereas modern crises are brought about by factors inherent in the nature of our business process, the older crises were seemingly precipitated by nonbusiness factors and could, therefore, occur at any time. They tended to be isolated, unpredicted disturbances and produced an irregularity of sequence such as is not characteristic of the fluctuations of modern business activity. Essentially they were "occurrences of the unforeseen."

One may conclude that business cycles are a phenomenon of a highly developed business civilization, and that the earlier English crises "were not business crises of the modern type and that the intervals between these crises were not occupied by business cycles." [1]

Some time in the late eighteenth century, in all probability, crises brought on by nonbusiness factors begin to give way to crises that are part of a regularly recurring cycle, and are brought about by the various circumstances in the cycle itself. Just when this occurred is a matter of doubt and speculation. For example, Tugan-Baranowski (*Les Crises Industrielles en Angleterre*) holds that what we would call "business cycles" began with the English crises of 1825. He regards the crises that marked the close of the Napoleonic Wars, 1811, 1815, and 1818, as nonperiodical, attributable to the war, and properly

---

[1] W. C. Mitchell, *Business Cycles, The Problem and Its Setting*, 80, and section one of Chapter II.

to be grouped with the "nonbusiness" crises of the eighteenth century. On the other hand, Bouniatian (*Geschichte der Handelskrisen in England 1640–1840*) calls the crisis of 1793 the first of England's great industrial crises followed by a general business depression. One might argue that the sensational panics following the collapse of John Law's Mississippi Company in France and the South Sea Bubble in England (1720) were to some extent forerunners of the modern crisis, possibly marking in some way the transition from the old nonbusiness crisis to the modern business cycle. While these speculative excesses did not arise out of the production and distribution of commodities and had no inherent connection with the general business system, they did on the other hand spread beyond the circle of speculation and had notable effects on business activity, raising commodity prices and stimulating industrial production and building activity.

Cycles Arrive with Modern Industrialism

Probably the arrival of business cycles cannot be precisely dated, but it is certain that their first definite and undeniable appearance occurs in England at the beginning of that modern period ushered in by the end of the Napoleonic wars. This occurrence is highly characteristic, for it was England which, by that time, was beginning to display the essential characteristics of modern industrialism and what Mitchell calls "a fully developed business economy." It is in this business economy where "a large proportion of the people begin to rely on making and spending money in a large proportion of their activities" that recurrent alternations of prosperity and depression slowly begin to appear.

In a society where the economic life is centered in the family; where production is for the family, not for the market; and where the guide to activity is immediate need, not prices or the stimulus of profit, business economy is lacking. It is a subsistence economy, and subsistence economies do not ap-

pear to generate cycles.   In such an economy, there is no reason
that would encourage people, nor any force that would compel them, to vary their activities from year to year; no reason
why economic activity should be very active for a few years
and then very dull for a few years.   In such a society there
would be variations of output, but they would not arise from
the business activity of the people.   They would be the result
of agricultural vicissitudes—would arise from good or bad
crops and other vagaries of nature.

Simple agricultural communities, living off the soil, with
little surplus, would be of this sort.   In all countries, the agricultural community, so far as it is engaged in simple farming,
is not particularly exposed to business cycles.   More exactly,
the activities of agricultural communities do not fall into the
pattern of the business cycle, although of course they may be,
and in fact are, affected by the variations in activity in "business" as such.

But when a large part of the population makes a living by
making money, producing goods for wide markets, using
credit and a widespread credit and banking system and or-
ganizing their enterprises on a relatively large scale with many
employees, then business cycles seem to become a necessary
part of their economy.

In this sense, business cycles are a function of what has
come to be called "modern capitalism."   It is characteristic
that cycles appeared first in the countries having the most
highly developed capitalistic system; and, conversely, that the
least capitalistic countries today are affected to the least
extent by such cycles; and that, even in the countries where
business cycles make their most noted appearance (as, for example, the United States), the occupations and industries least
affected by the characteristic processes of modern capitalism
seem at the same time to be least exposed to the fluctuations
of the business cycle—such occupations, for example, as agriculture, retail trade, personal service, and the handicrafts.

Thus it was that England experienced business cycles before the United States. In the United States, the early periods of prosperity and depression were derived largely from agrarian conditions, and cycles, as we know them, had to await the great and characteristic growth of industrialism that followed the Civil War. Carl Snyder holds that

. . . it was not until the development of steam power, the wide use of coal and iron, and the extraordinary burst of mechanical invention which followed, that modern industry, and therefore modern trade, could arise. It was from these that the business "cycle" was born.

Up to the 1840's, the United States had only "rudimentary experience" with business cycles. The panic of 1837 was essentially a financial and banking episode. Railway construction, canal traffic, tonnage of merchant marine, and coal and iron production were affected little. Prior to the 1840's, such waves of prosperity and depression as appeared were largely years of plenty or dearth in the yield of farms. Even the panic of 1857 was largely a financial and banking convulsion rather than the beginning of a serious industrial depression. The advent of the unmistakable business cycle, in the modern sense, appears to Snyder to date about the late 1860's.[2]

Germany's cycles emerged with the unification of the Reich and the industrialization of its economic structure following the Franco-Prussian War. It is illuminating that France, which has remained to such a large degree the home of small-scale business and industry, as well as the least capitalistic types of agriculture, has been less affected by business cycles than her contemporaries, the United States, Great Britain, and Germany. In the countries which are least developed in this type of capitalistic, money-making, business economy—China, India, Brazil, South Africa, Russia (at least before the Revolution)—the fluctuations are produced, as of old in England,

---

[2] Carl Snyder, *Business Cycles and Business Measurements*, 1927, Chapter 1.

more by "nonbusiness" than by business causes. Droughts, floods, epidemics, and civil disorder are more likely to be the disturbing causes. When fluctuations of the more modern type occur in these countries, they are found in those areas which have been most exposed to the money-making organization—as, for example, the coast cities of China.

The Records of Business Cycles

From this survey we may conclude that the data for the study of business cycles must be obtained from the records of business in modern industrialized countries since the early nineteenth century. It will be convenient to classify these records, following Mitchell's usage,[3] into two general divisions which, however, must not be taken to be mutually exclusive. These two divisions are *business annals* and *business statistics*. Business annals are qualitative records exhibiting the state of business as recorded by businessmen, financial reporters, and other trained observers. They state that business was good or bad, active or sluggish, rising or falling, and so forth. Business statistics, on the other hand, are quantitative records showing the state of business in the behavior of certain statistical indexes, which purport to register the behavior of business in general. They state that business has risen 10 per cent, or fallen 15 per cent; or that business is 5 per cent above normal or 20 per cent below; and so on.

But this is only a definition of our two measures. To penetrate their significance, they must be examined in some detail.

Business Annals

To repeat, business annals are the pictures of business conditions taken by the business reporter. They are to be found in financial papers like the *Economist* of London, in annual reviews, from consular reports, and from similar sources. As

---

[3] Mitchell, *Business Cycles*, Chapters III and IV.

classified by Thorp in his important study,[4] they give contemporary opinion on: (1) industrial, commercial, and labor conditions as reflected in output, trade, and employment; (2) loan, security, and foreign exchange markets as shown in interest rates, stock prices, and exchange rates; (3) agricultural output and prices; and (4) noneconomic conditions such as politics, wars, floods, and so on.

To some extent, as can be seen from the above list, this evidence is statistical and objective. Perhaps to a greater extent, especially in the early years, the evidence is nonstatistical, subjective, and personal. Even where the data happen to be statistical, they come down to us as seen by the eyes of the financial editor, and the statistics themselves appear in crude form not corrected for the disturbances caused by seasonal fluctuation or secular trends. Hence annals cannot be relied on to give a completely objective picture. There is conflict and confusion of interpretation as observers take different standpoints. There is also the distortion caused by the personal equation, so that, for example, after a depression any rise may seem to be prosperity, or after prosperity any fall a depression.

This handicap is inevitable and is particularly notable in those more remote years when, because of the absence of reliable statistics, the annals are our only source of cyclical information. But it can be said that, as years go by, the reliability of the annals is greater. Sources of information are more numerous and more reliable. One can check one source against another. The various parts of the economic world tend to lose their sectionalism, and violent differences of opinion tend gradually to be eliminated. Business reporting becomes a profession, with special periodicals and more and more competent aid from public agencies, especially consular reports. These developments remove some of the limitations of the annals, and help to make them almost as reliable and

----

[4] W. L. Thorp, *Business Annals*, 1926.

perhaps more usable than the more "scientific" statistics.

Of course, the principal advantage of the annals is that they cover periods reaching back before adequate statistics are available. In no country in Europe can cycles be traced back to the beginning (Napoleonic Wars) through statistics alone. For the same reason, the spread of cycles to the newer countries cannot be traced by statistics. In England and the United States, the annals cover at least twice as many cycles as are covered by any save the scantiest statistical data. In England and the United States, annals are available from 1790; in France, from 1840; in Germany, from 1853; in Austria, from 1867; and in Italy, Netherlands, Sweden, Russia, Canada, Australia, South Africa, Argentina, Brazil, British India, Japan, and China, from 1890.

What the Annals Reveal

While business annals cannot give quantitative evidence or make quantitative statements in respect to the behavior of business cycles, they do establish beyond question a generalized pattern of fluctuation. Even the simplest inspection of business history shows those notable setbacks to industrial advance that are known as crises. These stand out as dramatically as wars, elections, coronations, or any of the events to which history is commonly devoted.

The annals collected by Thorp and his associates reveal, as one would expect, these familiar timing points, but they reveal also a great deal more. Out of the vast amount of detail which this study of commercial histories and consular documents brings to light emerges a continuously repeating pattern in the long history of industrial and business change. Again and again activity leads to relapse; again and again depression leads to a revival, and a renewal of active trade. What is found is a frequently recurring sequence in which the familiar crises that have found their way into history are only one of the more dramatic aspects.

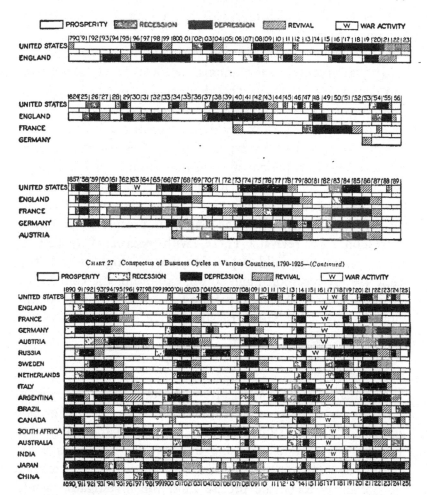

Conspectus of Business Cycles in Various Countries, 1790-1925

Taken from Willard Thorp and W. C. Mitchell, *Business Annals* (National Bureau of Economic Research, 1926), pp. 94–95.
Reproduced with permission of the National Bureau of Economic Research, Inc.

This picture of continuous oscillation is not always clear-cut. Not all business is dull or active at the same time, and sometimes conditions are so mixed that no analysis can reveal what is going on. But these cases are not common; ordinarily there emerges a "prevailing tone," and it is this prevailing tone, or average, which marks the current phase of business at any given time.

The recurring phases through which business activity seems to pass, as visioned in the annals, are, broadly, two: advance and decline, or prosperity and depression. But the transition from prosperity to depression is ordinarily so well marked, sometimes, as noted above, by definite crisis conditions, that it is useful to regard it as a separate phase. When this is done, the corresponding period of transition from depression to renewed prosperity seems equally deserving of recognition. If this is granted, then the most convenient summary of the recurring cycle exhibited in the annals is prosperity, recession, depression, and revival. These, with occasional qualifying adjectives, such as mild depression, boom (high prosperity), panic (severe recession), and so on, exhibiting the continually changing degree of intensity found at various times, are the captions chosen by Thorp to summarize his findings of the state of business.[5]

Business Statistics

It seems to be true that, although statistical data exist in what appear to be enormous quantities, they are still grossly inadequate for the study of business cycles, particularly over long periods of time. Arising as they do, largely as a by-product of some governmental or business activity, these data are not likely to be the precise kind the investigator would take if he had the choice. They are rarely available for the particular processes or periods wanted. If they are available for one period, they will be missing at another, so that comparative study of numerous cycles is made difficult. The farther back the study is carried, the more glaring the gaps, so much so that most of our knowledge of cycles before 1870

---

[5] Table 32, "A Conspectus of Business Fluctuations in Various Countries," in Mitchell's *Business Cycles*, 425–437, exhibits the phases in detail for all available countries from 1790 to 1925.

must come from an intelligent use of business annals. Statisticians are beggars who cannot be choosers. They take what they can get, not what they want.

Since 1870 in the United States and probably 1855 in Great Britain, statistical indexes are, however, so much more complete that they offer a reasonably valid method of examining the fluctuations of general business. But it must be realized that no statistical indexes of any sort can give a direct picture of the "congeries of many fluctuations" to which is given the name *business cycles*. All that any time series can do is to reveal the cyclical movement of a particular process. True, a statistician can put together various indexes into an "index of general business," and in so doing he may assume that he is presenting a picture of business cycles; but, as a matter of fact, this is not the case. There is no way of picturing the business cycle directly, except perhaps by setting out faithfully on a single chart all the available indexes representing specific activities of business. Unfortunately, a faithful picture of this sort is little more than a hodgepodge of varying curves, proving, if it proves anything, that faithful pictures are of doubtful value.[6]

However, these difficulties do not prevent the statistician from proceeding with the work of analyzing business cycles. He takes the data he can get, refines them into usable shapes, and avoids the confusing complications of the statistical picture by selective devices designed to give a fair representation of the "general drift" of many fluctuations. These methods may be classified into three general divisions: (1) Some simple index may be picked out which may be regarded as representative of all fluctuations. (2) A composite index may be constructed representing a wide section of production as such. (3) A more elaborate composite index may be constructed

---

[6] For example, see the charts in Mitchell's *Business Cycles*, 310–311, where twelve or fifteen components, respectively, of two of Snyder's indexes are plotted on single charts.

covering not only production but trade, distribution to consumer, financial transactions, and any other important aspect
of economic activity as a whole.[7]

1. **Simple representative indexes.**   There are some processes so central to the economic system that they are affected
by any broad changes in general activity. For this reason,
they serve as useful gauges of the extent of this activity, and
the record of their variations might be regarded as a reasonably
satisfactory picture of the changes in activity as a whole.   Such
indexes are: (a) the output of pig iron or steel ingots, (b)
bank clearings or bank debits, (c) railroad transportation, and
(d) electric power production.

The activities represented by these indexes are all central
in the economic system; the indexes are simple and easy to
comprehend; and, with the exception of the index of power
production, they are available, or can be made available, for
long periods of years.

(a) Iron and steel.   Iron and steel are so fundamental to all
types of output that the variations in the production thereof
have always been regarded as an important measure of business activity and for many years, when available statistics were
none too numerous, served as a handy clue to the fluctuations
of business.   Iron production has been recorded since 1903 and
estimated since 1884; production of steel ingots has been recorded from 1917; and the unfilled orders of the United States
Steel Corporation are available since 1901.   It is a merit of
these indexes that they reflect particularly the changing demand for buildings, railway construction and equipment, industrial machinery, and similar heavy capital, the variations of
which are so characteristic of business cycles.   In so doing, they
doubtless tend to give an exaggerated picture of the fluctuations of industry in general, but experience shows that they
indicate at least the timing and direction of general fluctua-

---

[7] For a discussion of these various indexes, see Chapter XVIII in E. C. Bratt, *Business Cycles and Forecasting*, Revised Edition, 1940.

tions as accurately as any equally available index. For the period 1899 to 1919, for example, the correlation between the pig iron index and an index of manufactures was +.97, indicating extremely close correspondence.[8]

(b) Bank clearings or bank debits. Bank clearings or bank debits serve to reflect business as a whole as it passes through the central machinery of bank payments and should reflect with reasonable accuracy the direction and amplitude of general change. Probably 90 per cent of payments are made by bank check. Bank clearings have a long history as a statistical measure, but, of late years, bank debits have been looked on with more favor. The total number of clearinghouses has generally increased, and with them the total number of checks passing through clearinghouses. For this reason, it is more satisfactory to use a measure of check payments which is complete in itself. This is supplied by bank debits, or debits to individual accounts, which, in respect to reporting banks, is an evidence of *all* checks debited against accounts, and not merely, as in case of bank clearings, that (changing) part of checks which happens to have gone through a clearinghouse.

To be the best index, bank debits must, of course, be deflated (that is, corrected for price changes) if they are to reflect increase and decrease of activity. As the total bank debits are unduly influenced by financial transactions arising out of the money market and the stock exchanges, and hence tend to show variations out of proportion to changes in business activity, it is best to use an index that excludes New York City —that is, "bank debits ex New York." With these corrections, bank debits may be made a reasonably satisfactory single index of variations of business activity.[9]

---

[8] Hardy and Cox, *Forecasting Business Conditions*, 163.

[9] Carl Snyder (*Business Cycles and Business Measurements,* Chapter VI) found that a clearings index ex New York, multiplied by a factor to raise it to the level of a general bank debits index and corrected for prices, corresponded so reasonably well with a volume of trade index that he regarded it as an adequate indicator of business cycles in the period 1875–1922.

(c) Railway transportation. The volume of business done by railroads has always been regarded as a most useful guide to general activity, both because of the extent of the available data and because of the tendency of the statistics of freight movements to reflect the expansion and contraction of almost every kind of business. Furthermore, unlike bank data, they are not affected by purely financial variations not directly evidencing business activity. Although other indices are available, such as idle cars or revenue tonnage expressed in ton-miles, the most commonly used index of transportation activity is carloadings. Available transportation indexes are, at best, a defective clue to general activity. They overemphasize heavy as compared with light traffic. Particularly, they suffer from the limitation that railroad transportation is a changing and declining proportion of total transportation. The carriage of commodities by trucks and airplanes and the transmission of power by electricity have given railroad transportation a downward trend, the degree of which is difficult to estimate. There is evidence, too, that the percentage of transport carried on by railroads changes during the phases of the business cycle, rising in prosperity, falling in depression. For these reasons, railroad transportation indexes are likely to be less satisfactory indexes of general business activity as time goes on.

(d) Electric power production. Like iron and steel, electric power is coming to be an ubiquitous commodity used by industry in general. Were its use sufficiently common and widespread, it would seem to give a very accurate indication of the changes in volume of industrial output. It suffers, however, from being a somewhat unrepresentative sample. Clearly, as it stands, it would overemphasize the mechanized industries. And, although its scope is continually increasing, the trend of this increase is uncertain and subject to sudden and spasmodic upward changes. For the period for which this index is available (monthly since 1919), it is, however, a fairly useful general index. Carl Snyder considers that it is

a good barometer, "showing a very smooth cyclical movement synchronizing well with the volume of trade, except for a lag through 1919 and part of 1920." [10]

2. Composite indexes of business activity, more particularly production. The indexes examined above are all relatively simple indexes assumed, because of their strategic position, to give a fair picture of the fluctuations of business in general. They are the sensitive gauges that, it is hoped, might conveniently register business change. But as gauges of this sort are clearly imperfect, the question arises whether general business activity itself might not be measured, and its changes or, more exactly, the average of the changes of its various parts be ascertained directly rather than through the movement of some more or less sensitive gauge.

A completely adequate measure of general business would be found in a weighted index of all branches of economic activity. In the present state of our statistical data, such a comprehensive index is not available. But it is possible to get data from, and calculate indexes of activity in, the major branches of production in the United States, particularly mining and manufacturing industry. Such indexes are actually available and are found in two alternative forms: indexes of employment and indexes of production, both of which might be thought of as measuring the variations of business activity in the fields covered.

(a) Indexes of employment. An index of employment and an index of production should, on the face of it, tend to coincide in both direction and amplitude of change; and they would so coincide but for variations in the average output per worker. Because of these variations an index of employment is not quite the same as an index of production.

An index of employment measures the changes in the total number of persons employed in a given field. When the num-

---

[10] Snyder, *Business Cycles and Business Measurements,* 169.

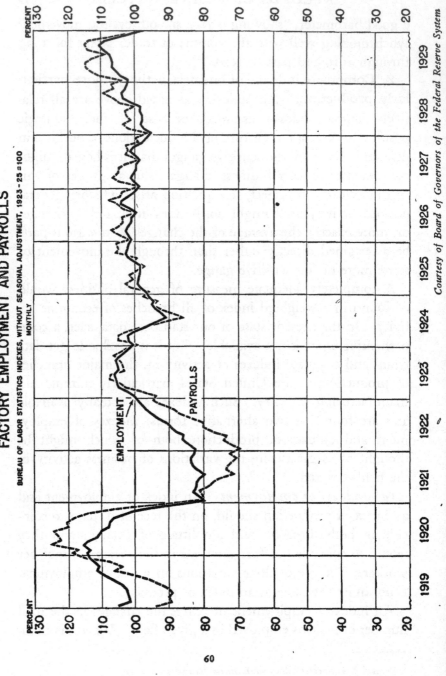

FACTORY EMPLOYMENT AND PAYROLLS

BUREAU OF LABOR STATISTICS INDEXES, WITHOUT SEASONAL ADJUSTMENT, 1923-25 = 100
MONTHLY

Courtesy of Board of Governors of the Federal Reserve System

60

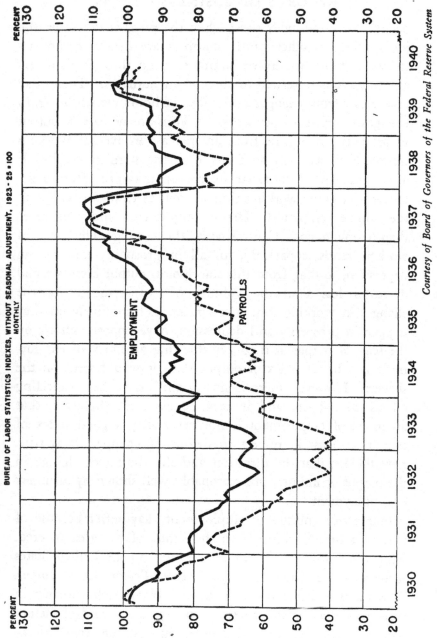

FACTORY EMPLOYMENT AND PAYROLLS

BUREAU OF LABOR STATISTICS INDEXES, WITHOUT SEASONAL ADJUSTMENT, 1923 - 25 = 100
MONTHLY

EMPLOYMENT

PAYROLLS

Courtesy of Board of Governors of the Federal Reserve System

61

ber increases, the index rises; when the number decreases, the index falls. In other words, numbers are measured, not activity. But the activity or output may go through considerable variations unrelated to changes in numbers. These may arise either from changes in number of hours worked or from changes in efficiency per worker. Thus an increase of output in prosperity may arise from an increase in average working time as well as from an increase in the number employed; and a decrease of output in depression may arise from a decrease in average working time as well as from a decrease in the number employed. Hence, output rises and falls more than employment. Contrariwise, the average efficiency of workers tends, apparently, to fall in prosperity and rise in depression, so that, from this standpoint, output increases and decreases less than the volume of employment. As the changes in working time and efficiency, respectively, as they happen in prosperity and depression, have opposite effects on the scale of output, it is conceivable that an index of employment is a better index of output than it would seem on the surface. However, there is no certainty that these canceling effects do happen, and it may be assumed, therefore, that an index of employment is not necessarily a good index of output, at least in respect to degree of change. It is true, nevertheless, that the direction and the timing of change in the output of industry are reasonably well shown by an index of employment.

In practice, indexes of employment may suffer because of a further defect arising from the limits of the area covered. Thus the best-known index of this kind in the United States is the *Bureau of Labor Statistics Index of Factory Employment*. This index is based on data derived from establishments in some 90 industries and covers probably 50 per cent of factory wage earners. Yet even this index suffers from two defects. In the first place, it covers only factory employment and hence can be representative of industry as a whole, only provided factory employment can be regarded as a fair sample of general industry. But factory employment cannot be regarded as a representative sample. There is no reason to suppose that occupations outside of factory employment have the same employment changes. Some of these, such as trade, particularly retail trade, probably have fewer fluctuations. Others, such as the rapidly growing and dynamic service industries, may have more fluctuations.

In the second place, even in respect to factory employment, the index may be a faulty fraction because of the difficulty of adjusting it to continual changes going on in the field of manufacture. Old concerns are disappearing; new concerns appearing. In practice, it is difficult to bring the list of reporting establishments sufficiently up to date to enable it to be continuously a fair sample of industry. At present the index is weighted in favor of the existing list and so may tend to understate not only the long-time volume of employment but also the degree of fluctuation of employment, for the newer industries may possibly, because of their newness, be both the most rapidly expanding and the most fluctuating.

(b) *Indexes of production.* Probably the best index of changing economic activity would be an all-inclusive index of production containing the production of both goods and services. Such indexes as are available, however, are more likely to measure production of goods than of services and, in respect to the production of goods, standardized rather than nonstandardized commodities and durable rather than nondurable goods. A good example of indexes of this limited sort is the *Federal Reserve Board Index of Industrial Production,* available since 1919, which is based on a wide sample from representative industries in both manufacturing and mining and may be regarded as a reasonably effective indicator of the position of business as a whole. Nevertheless, it must be conceded that, by not covering services and by overemphasizing heavily the durable-goods industries (themselves subject

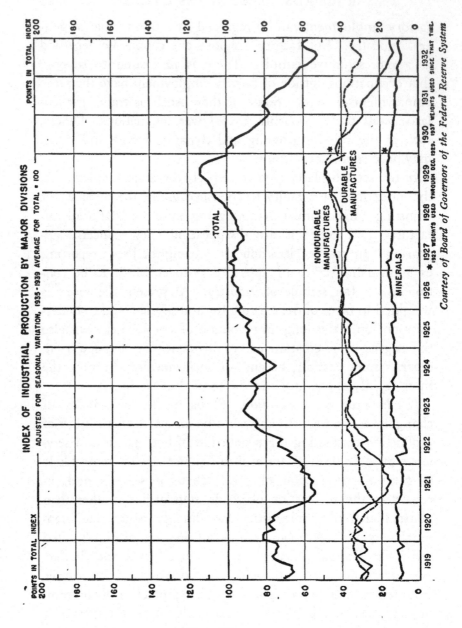

INDEX OF INDUSTRIAL PRODUCTION BY MAJOR DIVISIONS

ADJUSTED FOR SEASONAL VARIATION, 1935-1939 AVERAGE FOR TOTAL = 100

Courtesy of Board of Governors of the Federal Reserve System

64

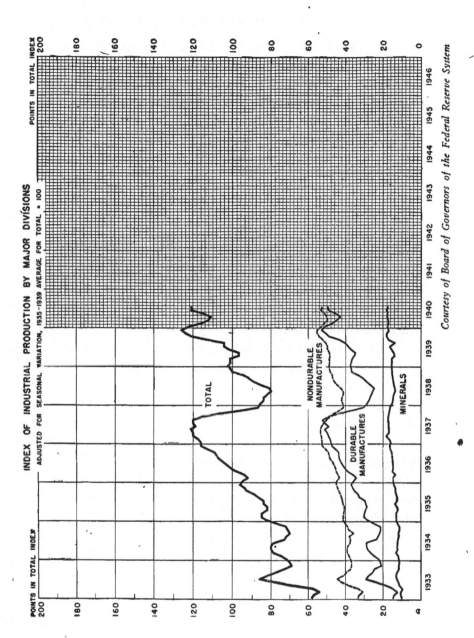

INDEX OF INDUSTRIAL PRODUCTION BY MAJOR DIVISIONS

ADJUSTED FOR SEASONAL VARIATION, 1935-1939 AVERAGE FOR TOTAL = 100

POINTS IN TOTAL INDEX

POINTS IN TOTAL INDEX

TOTAL

NONDURABLE MANUFACTURES

DURABLE MANUFACTURES

MINERALS

Courtesy of Board of Governors of the Federal Reserve System

55

to larger-than-average fluctuations), it will tend to fluctuate more violently than does total production. Hence, while it may be very sensitive to business change and may accurately reflect the timing of such change, the index will give an impression of industrial instability that is exaggerated and must be corrected by judicious interpretation.

Historically, indexes of production (and, even more, indexes of employment) suffer from inadequate data. As Mitchell points out, when compilers go back before the war they are forced to resort to one of two undesirable shifts:

Either they must change the composition of their indexes from time to time, accepting less satisfactory and smaller samples as they work backward, or they must use materials which do not show the physical volume of trade.[11]

Thus Carl Snyder, in making his "clearings index of business," fell back on the latter alternative, using a deflated "pecuniary" index as a reasonable physical-volume index for years when other data were too scanty to be effective.

3. **Indexes of general business conditions.** The indexes above described have been one of two kinds: either they were simple representative indexes capable of standing for the whole, such as bank debits, steel production, and so on; or they were indexes of "production"—meaning essentially manufacturing production—designed to show the change in the physical volume of output.

However, there are indexes which attempt to go beyond these simpler types and purport to give some kind of picture of what might be called "the general condition of business." Since business cycles are "congeries of fluctuations in many business processes," it would seem possible and desirable to include in an index thereof more than the monetary volume of trade, the physical volume of production, or any other in-

---

[11] Mitchell, *Business Cycles,* 319.

dex of a single type of change.   Therefore, such an index will include physical production, dollar volume, interest rates, price indexes, the volume of employment, and so on.   For example, at one time the *American Telephone and Telegraph Company's Index of General Business* included such diverse data as Bradstreet's price index, the production of pig iron in tons, and bank clearings outside of New York.

It is obvious that the resultant index is not an unambiguous index like those already examined.

It corresponds to no sum in dollars, to no inventory of goods, to nothing we can count.   By nature it is not an aggregate amount but a synthesis of relatives.[12]

The series which are thus synthesized are, strictly speaking, incommensurable.   They cannot be combined except as a statistical expression.   Indeed, it is not easy to say just what an index of this sort is supposed to represent.   As a problem of statistics, no special difficulty is involved.   It is easy enough to combine indexes of various processes into a single index, and to give what seem to be appropriate weights to the several parts.   However, no statistical ingenuity can hide the fact that indexes of general business conditions are the least definite and the most artificial of all indexes of the cycle.   The index of the American Telegraph and Telephone Company looks like a simple picture of economic fluctuations, and to the observer seems to show clearly just how high and how low business stands in the various cyclical phases.   In actual fact, the index is the result of a highly complex and sophisticated process, at each stage of which the judgment of the statistician has entered in.   In making it, secular trends and seasonal variations were eliminated from each component index; the remaining fluctuations were expressed as multiples of their standard deviations; the several series thus refined were weighted and a weighted average computed.   These means were multiplied

12 Mitchell, *Business Cycles*, 320.

by 10 (the approximate weighted average of the standard deviations of the constituent series), and the result was charted to make the index.

Such an index must inevitably be faulty, inexact, and only relatively reliable. Indeed, it is something like the composite photographs that are occasionally set forth as the picture of a type. Such pictures may possibly gain in comprehensiveness, but there is no question that they lose in distinctness and outline. Although a composite photograph of college presidents may be a sort of college president, it is no actual college president and may give a very poor idea of what any particular college president is really like. The same is true of composite pictures of business.

Furthermore, as of indexes of production, so, *a fortiori,* is it true of general indexes of activity, that the farther back they attempt to go, the less reliable they become. The sample used has to be changed from period to period, and the two ends of the series may be radically different. Because of this, the particular merit statistical indexes have over the business annals—namely, that they permit quantitative statements—largely disappears. They do little more than measure the direction and the timing of change. They cannot accurately measure intensity or amplitude of fluctuation. Indeed, in the United States for any period earlier than the Civil War, the annals are the more useful record.

An Example of a Complex Index

The kind of difficulty involved in these historical series is well illustrated by the *Index of General Business Activity* constructed by Col. Ayres for the Cleveland Trust Company, purporting to show quantitatively the fluctuations of general business about a "normal" from 1790.

From 1919 to date, there are adequate monthly figures—namely, the *Federal Reserve Board Index of Industrial Production.* From 1901 to 1919, there is an equivalent index

(*Thomas' Index of Manufacturing Production*), but with annual figures only. These are relatively simple, representative indexes of general activity. From 1855 to 1901, no single index was available, and a composite index had to be constructed from 10 series—namely, pig iron consumption, railroad freight ton miles, cotton consumption, canal freight, coal production, railroad construction, blast furnace activity, rail production, locomotive production, and ship construction. (Note the heavy weight given to various indexes of transportation.) Finally, from 1790 to 1855, still another composite index had to be constructed from another set of 10 indexes, as follows: commodity prices, imports, imports retained for consumption, government receipts, ship construction, government expenditures, coal production, exports, iron exports, and tons of registered shipping. Both the composite indexes were made to overlap the period following, and devices were used to correct the index where deviation of the original from the overlapped index was noted. Since these indexes were constructed as annual indexes only, monthly data from available single indexes were used to fill in the months. For this purpose, the following indexes were used: from 1877 to 1919, *American Telephone and Telegraph Company's Index of General Business* and data for blast furnace activity; from 1861 to 1877, bank clearings and stock prices; from 1815 to 1861, security and commodity prices; from 1790 to 1815, commodity prices.

The result of all this elaborate calculation is the apparently smooth curve of American business activity since 1790. Although the statistical method is ingenious and reliable, it remains unfortunately true that such an index gives us very little effective measure in any but the second half of the chart. It adds little to the evidence available through the annals; it certainly does not put us in a position, for example, to compare the magnitude of depressions in the early and later periods, respectively. The area of black above and below the line of trend (normal) is deceptively exact in appearance; it would be a rash man, indeed, who would venture to say, from inspection of this chart, how serious the depression of 1837 and the early 1840's was as compared with the depression of the 1930's.

The Validity of the Picture

The preceding discussion has shown that the complex of economic fluctuations to which is given the name of business cycles can, with some degree of fairness, be portrayed by a variety of indexes, but accurately measured by none. The indexes that are simple and definite are not comprehensive enough to be regarded as a satisfactory representation of business cycles. On the other hand, those that are more comprehensive have to be built up by such ingenious and artificial devices that they cannot definitely be said to represent anything save a statistical fiction. Any collection of statistical indexes, either those examined in this chapter or any suitable alternatives, will be found to have the same faults. Each one represents a somewhat different aspect of the economic process, and none can claim to be representative of the cycle as a whole. If the indexes reach into the past, they will be found to have changed their character as time went on. In addition, one must recall always that the methods of eliminating trends and seasonal fluctuation are rough at best.

However, there is this to be said. Although none of the indexes gives the whole picture; and although they differ in details, yet when a group of well-known indexes for a period are compared with one another, they will be found to agree in the broad outlines of the picture presented. Furthermore, if evidence from statistical indexes is compared with that to be found in the business annals for the same period, these also will be found to agree with sufficient fidelity to justify a confidence in their conclusions that could not be had from each standing alone.

These comparisons are made in Mitchell's classic treatment, a brief summary of which is here presented.[13]

Five Indexes Compared

To test the comparability of various statistical indexes of business cycles, Mitchell compared the five indexes of business conditions in the United States which covered by months the longest period of time.   These five indexes were as follows:

Index of the Pecuniary Volume of Transactions
   (a) *Frickey's Index of Outside Clearings 1875–1914*
Indexes of the Physical Volume of Trade
   (a) *Snyder's Clearing Index of Business 1875–1924*
   (b) *Person's Index of Trade 1903–1923*
Indexes of General Business Conditions
   (a) *American Telephone and Telegraph Company's Index of General Business 1877–1925*
   (b) *Snyder's Index of Deposit Activity 1875–1924*

The examination of these five representative indexes reveals a number of interesting similarities and some variations in detail.

(a) In their rise and fall, all the indexes show a "saw-tooth" contour. They are not smooth curves but jerky advances and declines. The indexes change direction every two or three months (sometimes more often) possibly because "the cyclical movements themselves keep producing and overcoming small checks." These reversals are most frequent at the top and bottom of the curves, indicating "that business has a ceiling and a floor, both somewhat elastic or irregular."

(b) All the indexes show resemblance in respect to the amplitude of their month-to-month changes. The distributions of these changes show a marked symmetry and are highly con-

---

[13] Mitchell, *Business Cycles*, Chapter III, Section VI, 3, for a comparison of five general indexes; Chapter IV, Section II, 2, for a comparison of business annals and business indexes.

centrated in an area from $+5$ to -5 change in points. In all cases the distribution is slightly skewed to the left or negative side, indicating that the most violent changes are declines. In all the indexes but one (Snyder's deposit index), the number of month-to-month declines is smaller than the number of advances, but the average decline is greater, signifying that contraction is the briefer but more violent process. However, most of the changes are small in magnitude, less than one half exceeding two "points" on the scale used.

(c) In respect to identifying individual cycles, all the indexes showed major cycles such as those culminating in 1882, 1893, 1907, 1917, and 1920. Minor fluctuations do not show such unanimity: twice the top of one curve remains below the base line of another index; twice the bottom is above the others' base line. However, "one who studies all five curves with care can draw up a list of business cycles which anyone else can identify with confidence in every curve."

(d) Time sequences, such as the timing of crest or trough, do not show the same degree of uniformity. On no occasion did all the indexes reach the crest or trough of a given wave in the same month, although, on four occasions, three out of the four series then available agreed. This fact probably means that turns take place in periods rather than at points of time, and during these periods the various processes measured by the different indexes have time to culminate in either upswing or decline. The time taken for *all* the indexes to reach trough or peak varied from 1 or 2 months to as long as 16 or 17 months, the average at crests being 8 months, and at troughs 6.1. *Snyder's Index of Deposit Activity*, probably from being heavily influenced by speculative transactions, reached the crest first 12 times out of 13, and the trough 8 times out of 13.

(e) Since the five indexes never reach crests or troughs at the same time and since neither the order nor the lag of the time sequences is constant, the duration of periods of rise and fall as shown in the respective indexes varies considerably. On the other hand, the average length of rise and fall is relatively uniform. Four of the indexes (excluding Snyder's deposit index) show an average rise of about 2 years (23–25 months) and an average fall of a little over 1½ years (18, 18, 19, and 21 months, respectively). That is to say, the "mode" in cycles is two unequal segments: 2 years of gradually increasing activity, 1½ years of less gradually shrinking activity.

(f) The duration of cycles as a whole shows a relatively uniform average for all the indexes, although the duration of particular cycles differs from index to index. More particularly, the four series that cover the whole period of some 45 years all show the average duration of the cycle to be 42 or 43 months.

(g) The least uniformity among the indexes is found in respect to amplitude of fluctuation as measured in percentage deviations from the line of trend. Neither the deepest depression nor the greatest prosperity is the same in each index. The greatest prosperity by the clearings index was in 1881; by the American Telephone and Telegraph index, in 1907; and by Persons' index, in 1917. The deepest depression was 1878 and 1896 in the clearings index, but 1921 in the indexes of trade and general business conditions. Mitchell suggests that these differences should not be regarded as discrepancies in the indexes, but rather as indications that the processes to which the several indexes relate really attained their highest or lowest levels in different cycles.

The conclusions of this comparison undoubtedly help to establish confidence in the validity of the methods used and the usefulness of the evidence obtained. When we consider that the data came from five different sources covering nearly half a century and including twelve cycles, or, as Mitchell puts it, when we consider that the indexes "were made by different hands, with different methods from different data, to show different things," the substantial similarity in their results and in the picture they give of business fluctuations must give us confidence in their validity as business cycle indexes.

Annals and Business Indexes Compared

Mitchell's second comparison has to do with the business annals and the business indexes over comparable periods of time.

Before, say, 1870 in the United States and 1855 in Great Britain, statistical data were so scanty and so unreliable that only one picture of business is available—namely, business annals. Thereafter, there are two pictures, and it is for this later period that a comparison is made. By reducing the annals to successive periods of prosperity, recession, depression, and revival, and comparing these with the variation in a general business index above and below "normal," the reliability of each in terms of the other can be put to test. This was done for the period 1875–1925 in the United States, and the period 1855–1914 in Great Britain.[14] For the United States, the annals are compared with two statistical indexes, the *American Telephone and Telegraph Company's Index of General Business* and *Snyder's Clearings Index of Business*. On the whole, the agreement is notable. The 13 recessions shown in the annals are all marked by a decline in the indexes; and the decline is proportional to the severity of the recession as noted by the observers. The same is true of the revivals and other phases.

When the annals report revivals the curves ascend; when the annals report prosperity the curves fluctuate on levels decidedly higher than in the preceding or following depressions; when the annals report depressions the curves are relatively low.[15]

The chief difference is, as one would expect, that the annals "show but vaguely and irregularly the degrees of prosperity and depression."

---

[14] See the charts in Mitchell, *Business Cycles*, 368–369, 372–373.
[15] Mitchell, *Business Cycles*, 370.

In the English case, the annals are compared with *Thomas'*
Quarterly Index of British Cycles. Here the similarity is not
quite so marked. The annals report no recession in 1860–1861
when the index falls (due to being heavily weighted with cotton). In 1874–1875, the annals report depression when the
curve, though declining, is above the base line. In 1881, 1897–
1898, and 1910–1911, the annals show prosperity when the index lies below the base line, possibly because reporters tend to
regard any recovery after depression as prosperity and any
slackening as depression; but these are exceptions. On the
whole, the correspondence of annals and index is close.

The curve usually rises when the annals report revival, stands
high when the annals report prosperity, sinks when the annals report recession, and runs on a low level when the annals report depression.[16]

These results help to confirm the validity both of the annals
and of the statistical indexes. They make it possible to have
confidence that the statistical picture of business fluctuations
available in modern times is a reasonably true one and, what is
more, that the period when statistics are too scanty to be relied
upon can adequately be represented by the longer and wider
record which the annals fortunately can give.

---

[16] *Ibid.,* 371.

CHAPTER IV

MEASUREMENT AND DESCRIPTION OF CYCLES

THE annals collected by Thorp and his colleagues give us the record of the largest number of cycles over the longest period of time. When it is considered that cycles can be said to emerge only with a certain type of economic organization which, even in the Western World, has been dominant for perhaps but 150 years, it may be safe to hold with Mitchell that the total number of past business cycles "may well be less than a thousand." Of this total of less than a thousand, the annals isolate and measure 166, which, although not a large number, is a fairly large sample drawn, especially in later years, from a considerable number of countries in all parts of the world. As such, it furnishes an imposing exhibition of cyclical behavior which can yield many interesting clues to the characteristic pattern of this kind of fluctuation. These clues, together with the evidence afforded by the business indexes during the period since 1870, are the basis of the general picture of business cycle behavior set forth in this chapter.

1. The Phases of the Cycle

As noted in the previous chapter, the evidence of the annals seems to justify the division of the business cycle into four recurring phases: prosperity, recession, depression, and revival. But this apparently simple and now familiar classification was not arrived at without much careful analysis of the problem of naming and delimiting the successive cyclical phases. This question deserves some detailed examination at this point.

The idea that business activities may be subject to alternating periods of expansion and contraction seems to have arisen from the study of those dramatic economic episodes known as crises. These periods of tension, strain, and often panic had been known and marked for years. For many years, economists have included a section on commercial crises in their textbooks. Critics of orthodox society regarded them as proof of the inadequacy of the economic system. Jevons developed a sun-spot theory to account for their apparent periodicity, in the nineteenth century.

But it came to be seen that crises are not isolated phenomena. They are a part—a dramatic one—of a cyclical movement and continuous ebb and flow in the activity of the national economy. For this reason, one might properly consider the crisis to be a phase of a cycle, and the cycle to be a three-phase fluctuation made up of prosperity, crisis, and depression.

The term *crisis,* however, is not quite free from ambiguity. Even today, two distinct meanings are attached to the term: the one regards crisis as part of a cycle and defines it as the turning point at which prosperity passes into depression; the other retains its more popular meaning and defines it as an organic disturbance of economic life bringing loss and often complete ruin to enterprise. That is to say, a crisis, by the one definition, is a turning point in general, but by the other only such a turning point as is accompanied by severe disturbance. (Indeed, one might add a third term—a "panic"—which might be defined as a crisis of unusual severity.)

The definition of crisis as a transition from prosperity to depression is clearly more appropriate to the study of cycles; but it has been so long associated in popular (and even professional) usage with the idea of financial strain that it causes confusion. Many transitions in cycles cannot be described as involving financial strain of such degree as to make the strain, rather than the turning point, characteristic. Hence it would seem desirable to give up the term *crisis* as descriptive of a phase and adopt, with Mitchell, the noncommittal and more scientific term *recession*. The term *crisis*, along with the term *panic*, may then be reserved for their more recognizable and popular meanings, as descriptive of intense strain.

Some writers (for example, W. M. Persons in his work for the Harvard Research Committee) subdivide the period of recession into two parts: financial strain, marked by monetary stringency and stock market depression; and industrial crisis, marked by fall in price level, distress selling, and the beginning of industrial decline. Probably this division serves no useful purpose, since even broad subdivisions are often hard to define exactly or, in fact, to recognize.

Complicating the Picture

The recognition of a turning period at the height of prosperity would seem to call for the recognition of a similar period at the end of a depression, for, doubtless, the behavior of business in the transition from depression to recovery has some particular characteristics not displayed in either of the adjacent periods. Thus we get the sequence of four phases: prosperity, recession, depression, and recovery or revival.

- It is sometimes useful for scientific analysis to avoid with great care any words or phrases which, by long popular usage, have certain established meanings. Thus depression has almost come to mean, popularly, not any contraction, but only a severe one, just as prosperity is not any expansion, but only a generous or considerable one. However, cycles are not all severe in respect to contraction or generous in respect to expansion. Hence, following Mitchell's lead in his treatment of business cycles in the *Encyclopaedia of the Social Sciences*, we may become quite noncommittal by eliminating the somewhat overcolored terms *prosperity* and *depression* and substituting the purely quantitative terms *expansion* and *contraction*.

The cycle phases then become: expansion, recession, contraction, revival.

However, there are cycles in which it would appear that during the so-called phase of contraction there is no actual shrinkage in many economic activities. What really occurs is a slowing of the rate of increase or growth.[1] Contraction in this case becomes a relative, not an absolute, term. Possibly, therefore (particularly if the stabilizing efforts of society are reasonably successful), it may become more appropriate to speak not of expansion and contraction but of acceleration and retardation. What we would have would be a gradual and continuous expansion, modified only by the inevitable effects of a not completely controlled economic society as expressed in an increase (acceleration) or decrease (retardation) of the rate of growth.

It is to be noted, however, that, whatever may be the most suitable terms to apply to the several phases of the cycle, it is really more easy to give them names than to know precisely where each succeeding phase emerges into the next. The boundaries of these successive periods cannot be exactly defined. It is clear, of course, that both recession and revival, as becomes turning points, are relatively short periods. In his *Business Annals,* Thorp notes that in business cycles in 17 countries from 1890 to 1925 the phases of recession and revival accounted, between them, for 23.9 per cent of the time —that is, something less than one quarter of the average cycle.[2] (In the same period, prosperity, or expansion, took 39.3 per cent and depression, or contraction, 36.8 per cent of the time.) But whether these transition periods have been correctly measured is not easy to know. Not all the indexes of activity or other economic process change direction at the same time. Some of them lead others, perhaps by several months; and no one index is so representative of the cycle as

---

[1] J. M. Clark, *Strategic Factors in Business Cycles,* New York, 1934, notes that in the average cycle pattern bank loans rise strongly during the upswing of general business and remain approximately stable during the downswing (p. 103).

[2] W. C. Mitchell, *Business Cycles,* 408.

to be taken by itself alone. Thus, when revival is going on, prices are rising, interest rates are rising, production is rising, and so on. How much rise in how many indexes must there be before revival has passed into expansion? Clearly, expansion is here when all these indexes have markedly changed for the better, but the degree of change must be a matter of judgment. Mitchell notes that "when it is necessary to define revivals and recessions as the periods within which all of the statistical series in a large collection turn up or turn down, these two phases become relatively long."[8] This statement seems to throw the measurement of transition periods into some little uncertainty, and with it the timing of all the phases.

Another Classification of Phases

In his book *Forecasting Business Cycles,*[4] Warren M. Persons has made a classification of the phases of a cycle that differs in some respects from that used by Mitchell. His phases are prosperity, recession, trough, and recovery. Prosperity is the interval of supernormal business, during which the index is above the line of the trend and has not yet turned downward. Recession is the interval of persistent decline from the turning point of prosperity to the trough or bottom of the fall. The trough is a relatively short period when the index is on a "dead" subnormal level, neither declining nor rising persistently. Recovery is the interval between the trough and prosperity. It is the period when persistent advances take place up to the level of normal business.

Compared with Mitchell's description of expansion, recession, contraction, and revival, Persons' terms have a less neutral connotation. Furthermore, they appear to have the logical disadvantage (1) of having two phases in the incline, but only one in the decline, and (2) of having a phase to mark the turning (often rapid) of recession into recovery, but none to

---

[8] *Ibid.*, 420, Note 5.
[4] W. M. Persons, *Forecasting Business Cycles*, New York, 1931, 197–198.

mark the turning (sometimes delayed) of prosperity into recession. In addition, there are cycles which cannot be described in these four phases, as where the peak is reached at a level below normal ("submerged peak"). Thus some indexes show the rise of 1896 as a submerged peak, and most indexes place the down turn of 1937 (which followed several years of expansion) at a level below the line of normal. In such periods, the cycle would apparently be a three-phase cycle only—that is, recession, trough, recovery. It would be more desirable to define the phases so that they would be applicable to cycles in general, without exception. Mitchell's phases have this merit.

Some relatively simple descriptions of cyclical fluctuations seem to reduce the phases to prosperity and depression, prosperity being measured by the area above an assumed line of trend and depression by the corresponding area below. This is a popular dichotomy which may serve the particular theories of its authors, but it suffers from the anomaly of being compelled to include in prosperity a period when business is actually declining, and in depression a period when business is advancing. In retrospect, such areas of prosperity and depression may give a sufficiently illuminating picture of good and bad times, but, as a means of describing a cycle actually in process and of throwing light on the sequence of events, they are obviously less effective than the four-phase description of either Mitchell or Persons.

2. The Length of Business Cycles

There was a time in the latter part of the nineteenth century when observers were much impressed with the apparent "periodicity" of cycles. The crises which were taken to mark the transitions from cycle to cycle appeared with such startling regularity as to lead students to believe that the cycle must have a normal and almost invariable time interval. The great English crises of 1815, 1825, 1836, 1847, 1857, and 1866 were the background of this not unnatural conclusion. The evidence that we have today does not bear out this oversimplified picture. There is no normal, relatively unvarying duration of cycles. We have to be content with an average and the distribution of the various time intervals about the average, as in other statistical observations.

There are various ways in which the average length of cycles can be measured. The oldest, as already noted, is from crisis to crisis. A common statistical device is to measure the intervals between the crests and the troughs of the index when plotted on a chart, assuming that the crest or trough can be precisely identified.[5] When averaged, these intervals indicate the typical duration of a cycle. On the assumption of some periodicity in the data over a reasonably long period of time, a mathematical approach to the problem is available through periodogram analysis and the calculation of a sine curve.[6] When this is done, a period is established which is, essentially, the typical time interval underlying the many actual variations. When the annals are used, intervals are usually established by the distance between successive recessions. But it must be noted that these recessions cannot be as exactly dated as would be wished. The data for the annals come by years, not months, and for this reason the duration of successive cycles has to be reckoned to the nearest whole year.

Let us now turn to the measurements.[7]

Intercrisis Cycles and Interrecession Cycles

The length of a cycle depends upon the points of measurement. If cycles are measured from crisis to crisis, they are longer and less numerous than if measured from recession to

---

[5] Cf. A. C. Pigou, *Industrial Fluctuations*, London, 1927, Chapter II, Section 15.

[6] Cf. W. I. King, *The Causes of Economic Fluctuations*, New York, 1938, Chapter 11, 236–244.

[7] See Mitchell, *Business Cycles*, Chapter IV, Section IV, where the duration of cycles as exhibited in the annals is fully analyzed and from which the material of this chapter is largely drawn.

recession. That is to say, intercrisis cycles are longer and less numerous than interrecession cycles.

For the period 1796–1920 in the United States and the period 1793–1920 in Great Britain (the only countries for which annals for such long periods are available), we find the following results:

1. Intercrisis cycles:
   United States, 14 cycles, range 2 years to 16 years, average 8⁶⁄₇ years.

   Great Britain, 16 cycles, range 4 years to 13 years, average about 8 years.

2. Interrecession cycles:
   United States, 32 cycles, average duration about 4 years, most common period 3 years.

   England, 22 cycles, average duration 5¾ years, most common period 4 years.

It appears from these figures that: (1) England and the United States have had much the same experience in respect to crises, both countries having nearly the same number of intercrisis cycles; (2) recessions, on the other hand, have been decidedly more frequent in the United States, interrecession cycles being more numerous and of shorter duration than in England; (3) interrecession cycles in the United States are about one half as long and twice as numerous as intercrisis cycles, so that on the average it takes two interrecession cycles to make one intercrisis cycle.

Furthermore, it is particularly worthy of note that the most common length of the interrecession cycle in the United States is three years and the average four, since this bears out the evidence offered by the available statistical indexes. The average length of the cycle, as shown by the five statistical indexes supposed best to measure the activity of general business in the United States, turns out to be in every case, as has been pointed out elsewhere, either 42 or 43 months. The same evidence is given by *Person's Index of Industrial Produc-*

tion and Trade for the period 1878–1932, which shows an average cycle of 42.8 months. It will be remembered that Joseph Kitchin, after an analysis of bank clearings, interest rates, and wholesale prices in both Great Britain and the United States for the period 1890–1922, established the length of what he calls "minor cycles" (equivalent to our own usage of business cycles) of 40 months or 3⅓ years. W. I. King fitted a sine curve to the *Axe-Houghton Annalist Index of Business Activity* and disclosed a wave length of substantially 40 months, although in certain years the business graph departed rather widely from the sine curve.[8] Finally, to end this collection of testimony, there are Mitchell's measurements for cycles in the later period in the United States, in which he finds that 13 cycles, 1885–1927, average 39.3 months, and 19 cycles, 1855–1927, average 46.1 months.[9]

One may be fairly safe in holding, therefore, that the typical or average cycle in the United States as measured from recession to recession is likely to be more than three but less than four years long.

Although useful for fixing types, averages do not tell us all we want to know. They give no idea of the variation in the length of individual cycles. They give no clue to sequences, or whether cycles are getting shorter or longer, or whether long and short cycles occur in any recognizable order; and they cannot be taken as any more than the vaguest clue to the future. That is to say, there is no particular reason to suppose that any future cycle will be, say, 42 months long, or even that the average cycle will continue to be 42 months long. The forces that make cycles what they are, both outside forces and inside responses, are subject to continual variation, and these variations may at any time radically change the average length of the cycle. What evidence we have establishes average length only for the period from which it is drawn.

In any event, averages are not significant without some

---

[8] King, *The Causes of Economic Fluctuations,* 237–238.
[9] *Encyclopaedia of the Social Sciences,* article on Business Cycles.

knowledge of the distribution of the individual items. This must now be examined.[10]

Distribution of Cycle Length

The 32 cycles which have occurred in the United States in the period 1796–1923 show the following frequency distribution:

Length in Years	Number of Cycles
1	1
2	4
3	10
4	5
5	6
6	4
7	1
8	0
9	1

The notable feature of this distribution is its heavy concentration, with a pronounced mode, at three years. This may be compared with two other distributions, one showing 39 cycles in England, France, Germany, and Austria in 1866–1920, the other showing 134 cycles in all countries except the United States at various dates to 1920–1925. They are as follows:

England, France, Germany, and Austria, 1866–1920, 39 cycles:

Length in Years	Number of Cycles
1	0
2	4
3	7
4	6
5	4
6	5
7	2
8	6
9	1
10	2
11	2

---

[10] Mitchell, *Business Cycles*, 391–407.

Here there is no pronounced mode and no marked decline in numbers up to cycles eight years in length.

All countries except the United States, various dates to 1920–1925, 134 cycles:

Length in Years	Number of Cycles
1	2
2	13
3	20
4	20
5	17
6	18
7	16
8	12
9	6
10	6
11	3
12	1

Here again there is no pronounced mode, no heavy concentration of cycles in any given time length. The distribution does not show a marked peak as do United States cycles, but rather a rounded top.

When the whole array of 166 cycles is put together, the rounded top is much modified by the inclusion of American cycles, and the distribution shows once more a modal tendency and takes a more regular form, of the sort common in studies of social phenomena.

All countries, various dates to 1920–1925, 166 cycles:

Length in Years	Number of Cycles
1	3
2	17
3	30
4	25
5	23
6	22
7	17
8	12
9	7

Length in Years	Number of Cycles
10	6
11 .	3
12	1

Mitchell fits a logarithmic curve to this frequency distribution and finds that the fit is on the whole rather close.

From this we infer that, like other biological and social phenomena whose distributions are well described by some form of the normal curve, the durations of business cycles may be regarded as the net resultants of a multitude of factors which are largely independent of each other.[11]

It is doubtful if this pleasing semblance of regularity can be taken to indicate that cycles, like other social phenomena, are subject to the compulsion of underlying law.   One hundred and sixty-six observations are not many; further, they are not homogeneous, being drawn at various dates from various countries with different economic characteristics, aspects which cast some doubt upon the validity of gathering them together into a single array.

Periodicity Not Proved

The variation in the duration of individual cycles from the average as shown above—a variation which is as notable in the case of the longer, intercrisis cycles as in that of the shorter, interrecession cycles—is fatal to the hypothesis of periodicity. There is no "period" for a cycle such as was once thought to exist.   The apparent periodicity of the crises in the nineteenth century, such as their appearance in England in 1815, 1825, 1836, 1847, 1857, and 1866, breaks down when one examines the facts of the case.   Furthermore, the annals do not disclose any regularity in the sequences of cycles of different length. It is impossible to predict at any time the length of the next

---

[11] Mitchell, *Business Cycles*, 419, Chart 25.   See also 420, note 4.

cycle. This length cannot be deduced from the average, the modal length, the duration of the immediately preceding cycle, or any group of preceding cycles.

Joseph Kitchin found evidence that in addition to "minor" cycles, averaging 40 months, there are major cycles, aggregates of two or three short or minor cycles. Such major cycles are marked by high maxima of indices, sometimes by panic. They average eight years and usually occur at seven- or ten-year intervals.[12] The annals do not give any support to this hypothesis. The evidence does not indicate that two or three minor cycles make a major cycle. If this were the case, the frequency distributions shown above would show two modes: a primary mode at, say, three and one-half years, and secondary modes at seven and ten years. These secondary modes are not disclosed in the annals; and, as the number of samples increase, such secondary modes as may be discovered in smaller groupings tend to disappear.

It is a popular opinion, based probably on such evidence as that of Kitchin, that depressions come every three and one-third years and that every third depression is a major one. Current popular journalism in the 1930's prophesied a major depression in 1940. There was one in 1920, another in 1930; hence one can be expected in 1940. The evidence of the annals does not substantiate these naive expectations.

If any semblance of regularity in this array of cycles exists, it is not in their sequence but merely, as already pointed out, in their tendency to group themselves in the positively skewed curve of the sort often found in biological and social phenomena. Again it should be noted that, while this may indicate some underlying symmetry of behavior, it cannot be explained by any rational process, and it gives absolutely no ground for prediction. Thus, if one examines the pattern of distribution of United States cycles for 1796–1923, one finds

---

[12] *Review of Economic Statistics*, January, 1923.

no cycle of eight years. However, this fact does not justify the statement that we may soon expect a cycle of eight years to complete the symmetry of the curve.

Secular Changes in Length

The annals give some evidence that the average duration of business cycles tends to undergo secular change from one period to another. The extent of this change and, indeed, whether there is any perceptible change depend upon some more or less arbitrary method of determining the several periods; for, clearly, the records could be divided into any number of periods, and in any number of ways. An interesting experiment of this kind was made by F. C. Mills, who examined minutely the annals of 17 countries for evidence of secular trend.[13] As a result of his inspection, he classified his materials into periods determined by the stage of industrialization reached in each of the countries involved. Having made this arrangement of periods and recognizing the somewhat arbitrary nature of a division based on so elusive a concept as degree of industrialization, Mills presents the following results:

> Early stages of industrialization—average duration of cycles, 5.86 years.
> Stage of rapid economic transition—average duration of cycles, 4.09 years.
> Stage of relative economic stability—average duration of cycles, 6.39 years.

Mills suggests, therefore, a general tendency for cycles to be relatively long during early stages of a country's development, shorter during rapid transition, and longer again when relative stability arrives. This tendency might account for the fact that American cycles are shorter on the average than English, since the United States was, at least up to the First World

---

[13] See Mitchell, *Business Cycles,* 412–416.

War, still in a rather prolonged stage of transition and, on the other hand, Great Britain had reached relative stability. It might indicate, too, that the United States may expect to move into a period when cycles will be of somewhat longer duration. Of course, this evidence is far from conclusive, particularly since the dates assigned to the stages of industrialization are quite arbitrary and subject to wide divergences of opinion.

3. The Length of the Phases

We have now to examine the length of the various phases of the cycle, as commonly described, and such changes in length as seem to occur with any regularity. In so doing, one must realize that, while annals, our principal source of evidence, give fair pictures of length of cycles as a whole, they leave the length of the several phases subject to a much greater margin of doubt. If the cycle were divided into two phases only—advance and decline—dating and measurement would be relatively easy. The introduction of two more phases, both difficult to establish exactly, makes precision unattainable. The length of periods of recession at the crest and of revival at the trough of cycles is subject to possibly wide differences of opinion, an ambiguity which, of course, makes the measurement of the other two more important phases equally uncertain.

With these qualifications, we will follow Mitchell's examination of what the annals and the indexes seem to show.

It will be recalled that the five indexes of American cycles which Mitchell examined for the period 1878–1923 show the average duration of interrecession cycles to be 42 months, or three and one-half years. The ascending phase of these cycles, from trough to crest, averaged about 23 months (22.75), and the descending phase, from crest to trough, averaged about 20 months (19.82). A similar story for the period 1878–1932 is told by *Person's Index of Industrial Production and Trade*, which indicates the average length of the phase of incline (recovery and prosperity combined) to be 27 months, of decline (recession and trough) to be 16 months. The difference in the ratio of expansion to contraction is doubtless to be explained by varying opinions in respect to the precise duration of periods of recession and recovery.

This indication of the greater length of prosperous and depressed periods seems to be borne out by the evidence of the annals covering various countries and periods of time.

The following table shows the distribution of months between the various phases during business cycles in 17 countries, 1890–1925.[14]

	Per Cent
Months of prosperity	39.3
Months of depression	36.8
Months of recession and revival	23.9

If we allow for the difficulty of separating the phases, which, after all, is an arbitrary proceeding, it would appear that the transitions take approximately one quarter of the time, and that the rest of the time is divided between prosperity and depression in the ratio of 1.07 to 1.

On the basis of this varying evidence, perhaps one might be justified in making the rather broad statement that, since 1870, the typical cycle in the United States is about three and one-half years long, of which expansion takes about two years, and contraction about a year and a half.

Changes in Relative Length of Phases

Between individual countries, the ratio of years of prosperity to years of depression shows wide variation, even for approximately the same periods of time, indicating to some degree how much business conditions are affected by the relative degree of political or economic stability. Even countries with settled political structure and mature economic development

---

[14] Mitchell, *Business Cycles,* Table 28, 408.

show varying degrees of relationship between the phases. Thus, in England, the prosperity-depression ratio—that is, the ratio of years of prosperity to years of depression—for various periods is as follows:

1790–1925	1.11
1890–1913	1.24
1890–1920	1.71

For similar periods, the United States shows the following ratios:

1790–1925	1.50
1890–1913	1.57
1890–1923	1.79

The most important example of variation in the ratio of prosperity and depression is shown when the long period 1790–1920 is broken down into subperiods of rising and falling price levels. When this is done, a striking variation in the prosperity-depression ratio is exhibited. The following tables drawn from Thorp's *Annals*.[15] show this variation.

England	Years of Prosperity Per Year of Depression
1790–1815 Prices rising	1.0
1815–1849 Prices falling	.9
1849–1873 Prices rising	3.3
1873–1896 Prices falling	.4
1896–1920 Prices rising	2.7
United States	
1790–1815	2.5
1815–1849	.8
1849–1865	2.9
1865–1896	.9
1896–1920	3.1

Similar evidence is given by Spiethoff, who has examined the periods 1822–1843, 1844–1873, 1874–1894, and 1895–1913. In the first and third periods, both periods of falling prices,

---

[15] Mitchell, *Business Cycles*, Table 30, 411.

depression is more common than prosperity. In the second and fourth periods, both periods of rising prices, prosperity is more common than depression. In detail, the distribution is as follows: [16]

Period	Years of Expansion (Aufschwung)	Years of Contraction (Stockung)
1822–1842 (England) . . .	9	12
1843–1873 (Germany)	21	10
1874–1894 (Germany)	6	15
1895–1913 (Germany)	15	4

The evidence that close connection exists between the movements of the general price level and the behavior of cycle phases seems unmistakable. When prices are falling, prosperity has been relatively short, and depression relatively long. When prices are rising, prosperity has been relatively long, and depression relatively short. The rationale of this relation seems to be found in the long-time variations in the rate of increase of the supply of gold, which furnishes the impulse for rising or falling price levels. A relatively high rate of increase in the volume of money (based on gold) furnishes the means of carrying production somewhat farther in prosperity and restoring its level somewhat earlier in depression than would otherwise be possible. In the opposite case, a relatively low rate of increase in the volume of money checks the expansion of production in prosperity somewhat sooner and retards its recovery in depression somewhat longer.

Therefore, the shape of business cycles is to some extent a function of the secular trends of prices and hence of the long-time variations in gold production.

Depression Makes Cycles Long

One further point in regard to relative duration of phases should be noted. When cycles are unusually long, it is the

---

[16] See *Handwörterbuch der Staatswissenschaften,* Fourth Edition, article on Krisen, 60.

depression rather than the prosperity which is long. Thus Thorp's *Annals* show that, of 166 cycles with an average length of 5.2 years, 17 lasted 9 years or more. For the whole group of 166 cycles, the ratio of years of prosperity to years of depression averaged 1.14. In the 17 long cycles, the ratio was 0.79; in 11 out of 17, the phase of depression was longer than the phase of prosperity. For the 17 cycles listed, the average depression was 55 months, and the average prosperity was 44 months—that is, depression averaged nearly a year longer than prosperity. The longest period of prosperity was 72 months; of depression, 72, 76, and 100 months, respectively. In the only cycle in the American *Annals* lasting 9 years or more (1873–1882), depression lasted 57 months, prosperity 42.[17]

Similar conclusions are reached by Bratt in his *Business Cycles and Forecasting*[18] from analysis of the evidence furnished in *Person's Index of Industrial Production and Trade in the United States, 1878–1932*. He finds that the length of cycles that include major depressions is distinctly greater than of those that include minor depressions and that the difference in length is primarily in the length of the depression:

> The cycles including major depressions (i.e., depressions in which the index has fallen more than 15% below normal) have had an average length of 46 months compared to an average length of 35 months for cycles including minor depressions. This is solely the result of the fact that major depressions average longer than minor depressions.

Since the annals are qualitative rather than quantitative, they throw no light on the amplitude of the respective phases, but some evidence in this respect can be obtained from statistical indexes.

Mitchell's survey of the five major indexes of general business in the United States in the period 1878 to 1923 gives us

---

17 Mitchell, *Business Cycles*, 411–412.
18 E. C. Bratt, *Business Cycles and Forecasting*, 1937, Business Publications, Inc., Chicago, 170–172.

some measure both of the average intensity of the phases and of the variations in this intensity. Measuring the intensity of prosperity and depression by the percentage deviation of the index from the line of their respective trends, and averaging these deviations, Mitchell gets the following results:

(1) The average amplitude of rise and fall does not differ greatly. The arithmetic means of 111 observations give 12.6 points from normal in troughs and 13.0 points from normal in crests. The medians are 13.5 for troughs and 12 for crests. These varying results seem to imply that the amplitude, in general, does not differ greatly in these two principal phases.

(2) The variation of individual instances from the average is not strikingly different, as is shown by the following table: [19]

	Average Rise or Fall	Standard Deviation	Coefficient of Variation
Trough	12.6	7.88	63%
Crest	13.0	7.55	58%

The indication from this table, covering 111 observations (56 troughs, 55 crests), shows depressions to be slightly more variable in intensity than prosperity, but clearly this variability is not very important.

One may conclude from this evidence that the phases of prosperity and depression do not differ greatly either in their average intensity or in the consistency of their intensity, if one takes a long period with major and minor cycles.

In his *Business Cycles and Forecasting,*[20] after some justifiably skeptical remarks on the problem of comparing the intensity of depressions from one time to another, Bratt commits himself to some guarded conclusions in regard to the variation of depressions in amplitude. Taking fluctuations in 1919–1932, as shown in *Snyder's Total Volume of Trade Index,* and showing deviations of the index from normal at crest and·

---

[19] Mitchell, *Business Cycles,* Table 21, 351.
[20] Pp. 172–174, 1937 edition.

trough, he finds that, whereas the successive prosperities run
10, 6, 8, and 10 above normal, the successive depressions run
11, 3, and 46 below normal. This exhibition of the greater
variability of depression, although obviously based on very
scanty data, does, Bratt thinks, harmonize with theoretical considerations which indicate that upper limits are much more
inflexible than lower limits in cyclical fluctuations. However,
it is to be noted that Mitchell, covering a longer period, does
not bear him out in this.

4. International Cyclical Relations

One of the most interesting contributions made by the annals is the light they throw on international relations among
business cycles.

It is plain from the annals that business cycles are to be
found in every country of the world, apparently in proportion
to the particular degree of industrialization. However, the
relation between the cycles in various countries, in respect to
their magnitude and the timing of their phases, and so on, is
complicated and changing. Let us see what the annals have
to say about it.[21]

It seems that the great financial crises are international,
rather than national, in scope. The crises of 1815, 1825, and
1837 were common to England and the United States; of 1847,
common to England, the United States, and France; of 1857, to
these three plus Germany; and of 1873, to these four plus
Austria. All five countries showed recessions in 1882-1884.
In 1890, 17 countries were included in the annals. Ten had
recessions in 1890-1891, 15 in 1900-1901, 15 in 1907-1908, 12
in 1912-1913, 11 in 1918, and 14 in 1920. The annals of business show that, by the end of 1930, practically all countries
with statistical records had entered the great depression. It
is true that the intensity of such crises were not equally severe.

---

21 See Mitchell, *Business Cycles*, Chapter IV, Section V, 2.

In 1873, the United States, Germany, and Austria suffered more than England and France; 1890 was more severe in England than in the United States or Germany; 1900 was most severe in Germany; 1907 in the United States. All countries seemed to find 1920 severe, but 1929 was most severe in New York, as 1931 was most severe in London. For all that, however, financial and economic crises in any major country tend to produce crises in other countries as well.

Furthermore, other phases of the cycle—booms, depressions, and revivals—tend to be international in scope. The depressions of the 1870's, of 1920, and of 1929–1932, the boom of 1906–1907, and the revival of the middle 1890's are found in various countries. The five countries whose records reach back to the 1860's—namely, England, France, Germany, Austria, and the United States—show more years in which the business cycles were passing through the same phases than years in which they were passing through opposite phases. English cycles, probably owing to the peculiar international position of the country, are most nearly correlated with cycles of other countries, particularly with French and German cycles. However, English and American cycles tend to show considerable agreement, particularly in the later period.

When any two of these countries are compared for earlier and later periods, it appears that, as time goes on, the degree of similarity between their cycles tends to increase. There is always some difference in the behavior of different countries; indeed, this is to be expected both from the occurrence of purely domestic events and from the different stages of development at which the several countries stand at any one time. But as time goes on, local differences seem to count for less. Industrialization of newer countries goes on apace, and out of this appears a silent and almost unperceived tendency to uniformity which has come to impress the cyclical pattern, even in respect to timing, more and more on all countries alike.

The greatest source of divergence has been the influence of

agriculture, the experience of which must, according to its importance, impose some degree of variation on the economic processes of the several countries. Mitchell suggests that the history of business in such a country as the United States is a single story, diversified by agricultural episodes; and that the world, too, is showing the same general picture. The greatest. divergence from the pattern is found precisely in those coun-.tries where industry is backward and agriculture is still the dominant activity of the people. The greatest similarity is' found in those countries where agriculture has given way in importance before a highly developed industry, finance, and trade. Therefore, one would expect that, as agriculture lost its relative dominance, the influence of cycles and their relative uniformity would grow. This growth will be fortified by the increasing urge to turn agriculture from a way of life into a "business," organized and run under business motives, consciously trying to reduce the disturbing influence of purely natural forces.

Cycles Tend to Be International in Scope

When "business" is dominant, and international relations reasonably free, powerful influences tend to make each phase of a cycle, as it appears in one important area, appear also in others. Any generating force in a major country, such as an invention or a substantial increase in agricultural crops, will tend to increase the demand for raw and semifinished materials from other countries. The increase in prices which usually accompanies this expansion, and which is made possible by an increase in bank credit or other monetary means, will stimulate imports from abroad. Prosperity will encourage the sale of foreign securities and the export of capital. Easy money conditions may cause a flow of gold abroad, easing conditions there also; and so on. Considering the international nature of the market for all kinds of goods, and particularly the international nature of the money market, with the leveling effect it must have on interest rates and prices, it is to be expected that business expansions and contractions, wherever they originate, would spread to all parts of the industrialized world.

No better example of the intimate relations between all countries of the world can be given than the experience of the great depression that began in 1929.

The great crash in the New York stock market from which the slump is commonly dated shocked the financial system of the whole world. Almost immediately in every important country, liquidation first of securities and then of commodities set in. The fall of prices of 1930 was a world-wide fall, differing from country to country according to the types of goods heavily involved.

In 1931, a new impulse to depression began with the collapse of the Credit-Anstalt of Austria in May. This collapse brought a wave of fear lest the whole banking structure of Central Europe, none too strong after the First World War, should prove unliquid; and with this fear began a great liquidation of holdings in Germany. Germany had been closely associated with Austria and was weakened by the long struggle over reparations. The result was a run on German banks that brought the whole financial structure low. The Hoover moratorium belatedly seemed to have saved the situation.

The freezing of credits in Germany turned those who wished to have liquid funds to Great Britain, which, for particular reasons, had also begun to lose the confidence abroad she had so long enjoyed. The summer of 1931 saw a great and continued drain on the gold of Great Britain, which eventually, in September, forced the country off the gold standard. The repercussions of this unprecedented action were enormous. Most of the stock markets of Europe were promptly closed, and many of the countries of Europe and the greater part of the British Empire were compelled to abandon the gold standard.

The United States, reasonably free from the complications to which Europe is exposed, was not able to avoid this unprecedented unheaval. Investors unable to cash in in Europe turned to the United States. Securities, especially bonds, were sacrificed in great quantities, causing further stock exchange losses, great export of gold, and much internal hoarding. The industrial slump continued worse than ever.

These financial breakdowns, together with the collapse of prices and the cessation of foreign lending by the great creditor nations of the world, England, France, and the United States, brought almost insuperable troubles to all debtor countries. Most of these countries were producers of agricultural products and raw materials, the prices of which had been subject to the most grievous fall. Unable to finance their normal imports by the sale of exports at such disastrous prices and equally unable to borrow further funds or to pay even the interest on former loans, these countries brought additional damage to the economic structure of the world by defaulting on loans, dumping goods at ruinous prices, and setting up restrictions of every kind on imports and on the ordinary freedom of exchange. The wave of retaliation which this induced in every country of the world brought world trade to the lowest ebb and added one more difficulty to the internal economy of every nation.

One may conclude, therefore, that both economic reasoning and the evidence of the annals of business in various countries indicate that business cycles tend to be international in extent and that, as more countries are drawn into the scope of industrialization, this tendency increases rather than decreases in intensity.

Whether or not these tendencies will be checked by the growing nationalism of our day is another matter. We are in a period of international restrictions. The international gold standard has broken down; trade is subject to numerous and burdensome restrictions. Isolation is the order of the day, and regional autarchy seems to be the ambition of powerful national groups. If nations isolate themselves sufficiently from the world, their fluctuations may no longer tend to march with fluctuations in other nations. With the aid of powerful bureaucratic control as in Russia or Germany, they may even reduce business cycles to negligible proportions. It may well be that business cycles themselves are on the way out and that they will come to be regarded as one phase of what Keynes has called "the magnificent episode of the nineteenth century." As to this, only time can tell. Meanwhile, we can but note with Mitchell that "the quiet business forces working toward uniformity of fortunes must be powerful indeed to impress a common pattern upon the course of business cycles in many countries. And the increasing conformity to an international pattern which the annals reveal in recent years shows that the international influences are gaining in relative importance." [22]

---

[22] Mitchell, *Business Cycles*, 450.

CHAPTER V

THE GENERAL PATTERN OF A BUSINESS CYCLE

WE HAVE seen that cycles, as they are disclosed in the annals of business, develop in a series of phases which, for convenience, have been called "expansion," "recession," "contraction," and "revival." It will now be desirable to sketch a picture of what characteristically happens during these successive phases. In this picture, only broad outlines and tendencies can be presented. A typical cycle is described, not any actual cycle. The details of cycles differ; no one cycle is the same as another. The order of events as well as the events themselves is ever changing. Yet there is sufficient that is uniform, characteristic, and significant to develop a pattern. As Pigou puts it, cycles may not be twins but they are all of the same family. Like families, they have characteristics which are capable of description.

It will be convenient to think of the economic system as being temporarily in equilibrium, in such wise that the entrepreneurs who make the decisions in respect to the use of resources have no motive, taken in the aggregate, to either contract or expand their activities. This situation is not to be found in real life, but it is a convenient assumption and starting place from which to describe the wavelike fluctuation of a business cycle.

This equilibrium is subject to disturbance at all times, and the possible disturbing factors are almost innumerable. Some of these apparently disturbing factors do not, however, have any significant effect. They are merely shifts of resources from one place or occupation to another, as, for example, the continual changes in demand which are proceeding at all times in the economic system. The effect of these changes may be considerable on individual industries but inconsequential on the total of industrial effort. There is an expansion of A's output, a contraction of B's. The net effect on total activity is nil.

Starters and Responses

However, other disturbing factors seem capable of affecting, broadly, the whole economic process. They are not of the nature of increases of A at the expense of B. They stimulate the whole system; they move the entrepreneurs in general to expand their activities, put more resources to work. These stimulants to general activity have been called "originating forces" or, more colloquially, "starters." They are sometimes thought of as originating *outside the economic system*, rather than being generated within; as such, they may be called "exogenous forces." They are best exemplified by changes in agricultural crops, wars, inventions and discoveries, large additions to gold supply when gold is used as money, and substantial changes in consumers' wants. These are real starters in the sense of being powerful enough to engender a general increase of economic activity on the part of entrepreneurs; and they are exogenous in that they do not originate in the ordinary working of the economic system but come in, as it were, from outside, as nonrecurrent isolated and episodic forces.

Now these originating forces set up a series of business responses, the nature of which is dependent on the general complex of industrial and financial conditions. These responses find their expression not only in changes in the volume of productive activity, but also in the volume of bank credit and its rate of circulation, in changes in the rate of interest and profits and wages, in rising and falling prices, and in changes in the ordering and installation of capital equipment. Furthermore these responses seem to be cumulative in their nature. The impulse from the starter is taken up and amplified by the financial and industrial system, so that changes once begun proceed at a progressively increasing pace and cover wider and wider areas of financial and industrial life.

As little evidence exists that originating forces come at periodic intervals or arrange themselves in any recognizable pattern of appearance, one may conclude with J. M. Clark [1] that it is the cumulative responses rather than the starters that give the characteristic wavelike and rhythmic effect of cycles. That is to say, the originating causes (or starters) produce the effect they do because they operate upon and through a particular business system that tends to behave in certain ways. This conclusion is indicated by the fact that business cycles tend to reproduce the same characteristic pattern, irrespective of the nature of the starter or originating impulse, and even though these impulses from outside continually change. As the fundamental financial and industrial relations in our modern economic world do not change much from year to year or to any great degree even from country to country (provided they fall within the scope of modern capitalism), one may expect that various initiating causes would produce, at different times and places, much the same series of economic reactions, and cause the appearance and reappearance of much the same events. In all probability, this tendency produces the roughly similar appearance of cycles over considerable periods of time and over widely separated regions and areas, while allowing for the variation in the behavior of individual cycles such as we would expect from the varying character of the originating causes.

As these business responses are responsible for the shape of cyclical changes, they may be regarded properly as essential causes of cycles. As they are produced by the operation of the

---

[1] J. M. Clark, *Strategic Factors in Business Cycles*, 17.

system and within the system itself, they may be called "endogenous forces."

Thus the equilibrium with which we started may be disturbed by two rather different forces: on the one hand, originating causes, or exogenous forces, such as war, invention, agricultural changes, and gold discoveries; and on the other

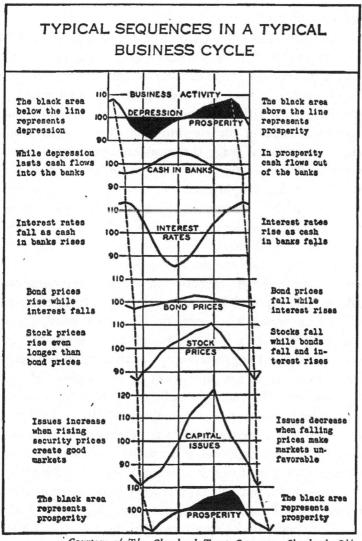

Courtesy of The Cleveland Trust Company, Cleveland, Ohio

hand, business responses, or endogenous forces, shaped by the reaction of the whole business structure to the originating force, and being themselves active causes of further and continuing change.

Let us now examine the operation of these business responses through the several phases of the cycle.

Expansion Begins

Under the stimulus of whatever originating cause may have come into play and in the expectation of rising profits, entrepreneurs increase the scope of their activities, put more people to work in their plants, and order more raw materials. The demand for materials puts people to work in other plants, as does the demand for consumption goods when workers spend the additional wage disbursements made by the entrepreneurs. If the position from which expansion started was one of incomplete employment of resources (as might be the case even on the assumption of equilibrium unless there is perfect competition), the increased demand for goods is satisfied by rapid increase in supply; and the expansion is marked by increase in production but not in prices.

As a considerable increase in wage disbursements is made to men engaged in producing materials or equipment, and as their wages are spent, on the other hand, for consumption goods, there is apt to be a lag in the production of such goods behind aggregate wage payments, and, when this occurs, there is a rise in prices. The records of cycles show that expansions are normally marked by an increase in the price level, an increase which appears to be delayed during the early stages of expansion but is stepped up sharply in the later stages. This early delay is usually attributed to the fact that plants are not at the time being used to capacity, so that an increase in output can take place without a proportionate increase in total costs. But as time goes on, output becomes less elastic; bottle necks appear with rising costs, deliveries are more difficult, and plants may have to be expanded. With these things, prices rise.

This rise of prices is accompanied by, and, in fact, dependent upon, an increase in the volume of monetary means of payment, an increase largely effected by an expansion in bank deposits, a marked feature of prosperity. It would be quite impossible for an increase of output to be sold at an increase of average prices without this increase of money. An increase in the velocity of circulation, were it sufficiently great, would accomplish the result. However, the evidence seems to indicate that, while velocity of circulation increases in periods of boom, its increase is only enough to account for the increase of output. The increase of prices must be accounted for by an increase in the volume of money.

The rise of the general price level is more marked when the productive activity includes much building of substantial plants, factories, steel mills, or other expensive and durable equipment. The payrolls of these building operations add greatly to the volume of spending while no substantially equivalent addition is being made to the output of consumption goods; and this goes on until the processes of construction are completed, and the addition to output for which the construction was designed made available. As we shall see in more detail later, this period of construction, usually called the "period of gestation," is considered by some economists to have a predominant part in making the cyclical process.[2]

Disturbances in Price Relations

The rise in prices which is characteristic of the expansion phase is, however, by no means uniform. Wholesale prices rise more than retail prices. Indexes of the cost of living which reflect retail prices rise but modestly. Of the whole-

---

[2] See Chapter X.

sale prices, it would seem that the greater the distance from the consumer, the greater and the quicker the rise in price. Thus raw materials rise higher than semifinished goods, and the semifinished goods rise higher than goods ready for the consumer. Prices of farm products tend usually to have the swings of raw materials in general; but they are more erratic and uncertain, owing to the vagaries of nature which at any time may make for unexpectedly higher or lower prices. These variations in the behavior of different prices are an example of a tendency toward price dispersion which seems to be characteristic of periods of changing general price levels. They disturb to some extent the symmetry of the price system, distort price relations, change price spreads between one level and another, and bring about at the same time some more or, less considerable changes in the distribution of the national income. .

Expansion is marked not only by changes in the relative prices of goods, but also by changes in the various elements of the cost structure. Some elements of cost change quickly; others, slowly. We have seen that raw material prices commonly move up quickly. On the other hand, wages (that is, wage rates) have, in the past, tended to lag, possibly because of the relatively conventional aspects of wages, determined as they commonly are in relation to the cost of living. It may arise, too, from the existence of a reserve of labor, the employment of which delays the rise of wage rates. But there it is. Wages and, even more, salaries do not rise so quickly as prices at wholesale. Interest, particularly long-period interest, is slow to rise, and in respect to existing debts is fixed. Similarly rentals, insurance changes, and taxes, especially property taxes, lag behind in expansion.

This typical distortion of the cost structure brings about a tendency in every expansion period to increase the margin of profit. Because various elements of cost lag behind the general rise in the price level, the margin between receipts and expenditures is widened. Supplementary or overhead costs particularly, and even prime or operating costs in respect to salaries and wages, are slow to move; hence the increased receipts are not eaten up in increased expense, and hence profits are enlarged. Here, again, there are variations in behavior. Those concerns that enjoy the earliest increase in demand, whose overhead charges are relatively large, and whose operating costs consist more in wages than in materials reap the largest profits; those with opposite characteristics reap the least.

The Boom

This increase of profit and the prospect of its continuance commonly cause a rapid rise in stock market values. All securities, including bonds, rise under the influence of improving confidence. The outstanding change is in stocks, which, reflecting the capitalized values of prospective earnings, register in an exaggerated form the rising profits of enterprise.

The general improvement in the condition of entrepreneurs, arising primarily from the slow rise of costs, is, presumably, the principal source of the cumulative expansion which is observable in periods of prosperity. Stimulated by the prospects of profit, further investment is made by entrepreneurs. This development is dependent on the expansion in the nation's monetary circulation, especially its bank credit; an expansion which the evidence shows takes place. The improved prospects of business and the high values of securities on the stock exchanges make the banking authorities willing to expand credit facilities. The same circumstances tend to speed up the velocity of circulation of all credit available. This further investment, facilitated by bank credit, is likely to consist not so much in increase of working capital as in additions to fixed capital, plant, machinery, and equipment. This capital expenditure is particularly potent in adding to the expansion, making for substantial increases in wage disbursements, and, especially, during the period of gestation, tending to add still further to the demand for consumers' goods and the strengthening of the price level.

Part of the background of this expansion is to be found in the spirit of confidence and optimism which the increase of output, prices, and profits seems to engender. The records of every cycle bear witness to the importance of the wave of optimistic sentiment which sweeps the business and financial community in periods of expansion. The most dramatic exhibition of this is found in the real estate and stock market booms characteristic of these periods. The general run of businessmen, even the conservative fraternity of bankers, share the sentiment of the time, seem to be caught up in its sweep, and become moved to liberality in credit extension. An aspect of this optimistic sentiment is seen in the tendency by retailers, wholesalers, and manufacturers alike to add to inventories. Presumably, the moving cause of this behavior is the rise of prices, the continuation of which being assumed makes buying for the future a profitable venture. Of course, so far as this stocking up of commodities takes place, it will increase the activity of producers at a pace out of proportion to even the increasing pace of consumption.

Looking back now over this process of expansion, one can see how, beginning with what perhaps was a relatively small stimulus, activity grows in cumulative fashion until the whole economic system is brought to a relatively high pitch of production. The originating cause sets off a series of productive activities, each one leading to still more, engendering a rise of prices and, with this, a rise of profits, and cumulating in an increase in permanent investment and capital building with construction of buildings and machinery, and back of them, possibly, buildings and machinery for the making of other buildings and machinery until the whole pace of economic activity has reached a very high level.

One might suppose that this process of expansion would proceed until full employment of resources is reached; and furthermore, since the production of goods by each producer is the source of demand for the goods of other producers, that this high level of production might be maintained indefinitely. Unfortunately, this is not what happens. Instead, the rate of activity begins to be slowed down, and sooner or later, by gradual change or abrupt transition, the phase of expansion ends and turns into the phase of recession. The turn of the cycle has come.

The End of Expansion

The circumstances surrounding the phase of recession indicate that the cumulative forces making for expansion are progressively weakening, or, if one prefers to put it in another way, are being overcome by a series of limiting forces brought into play by the expansion itself.

1. The first of these is the gradual rise of costs relative to prices. The lag of costs which is largely responsible for the growth of profits in the stage of expansion now at last disappears; and the bulge of profit begins to be cut down. The tremendous pressure of the productive demands in the market for materials and labor and money capital begins to make itself felt in rising prices, wages, and interest rates, rates which have been held back by available reserves but now feel the influence of scarcity. Cost of production rises as the best equipment, workers, and management are gradually all in use and as resort must be had to substandard equipment, inferior workmen, and less effective management. The average efficiency of workers and management alike tends to fall. There may be a good deal of overtime work, which is both costly and inefficient. Labor scarcity in the face of high demand encourages trade union restrictionism; discharge becomes more difficult; and industrial disputes probably are more numerous. If a new plant is built, there is a sudden rise of overhead cost,

all the greater because of rising costs in the construction and equipment industries where production has reached the dimensions of a boom.

All these factors conspire to raise unit costs and make the price level less profitable to entrepreneurs than they had expected.

2. The problem of rising unit costs, which fundamentally springs from the ultimate scarcity of efficient means of production, might be met were it feasible to continue to raise selling prices. But this possibility seems to meet with two formidable obstacles: one of these is the limit imposed by the diminishing elasticity of bank credit; the other is the apparently increased difficulty of raising prices without encountering the resistance of consumers.

(a) Bank credit expansion is an indispensable prerequisite for the continuance of rising prices. The selling of an increased volume at an increased average price level must, as we have seen, be accompanied by equivalent increases in the volume or in the velocity (or both) of bank credit—particularly the volume, since velocity seems, from the evidence, to expand *pro rata* but no more than *pro rata* with the volume of output. In countries on a gold standard, the volume of bank credit that bankers are willing or able to supply has more or less definite limits. As loans and the volume of deposit liabilities grow, there is an increasing pressure on reserves, a pressure which is the greater because the public demand for circulating medium when wages are high and retail trade active tends to withdraw cash from the banks. The situation would be relieved if gold were to flow in from mines or from abroad, but there is no evidence that this tends to occur. More likely, the very opposite will happen. High price levels make gold mining relatively unprofitable and discourage marginal output; and they tend, if anything, to encourage imports and discourage exports, creating an unfavorable balance of trade and a tendency to gold outflow.

The pressure on reserves, brought about by expanding deposits and internal and external drains, is bound in time to make banks raise their rates of interest, scrutinize more carefully projects brought to them, and even put pressure on less desirable borrowers to repay loans. This increase of interest rates and the beginning of credit "rationing" are likely to put a sharp check on further rise of prices. By so doing, they check, also, and probably more abruptly, the rise in stock market values and thus, by putting limits on the value of collateral, may add still more to the restriction of credit.

(b) This check to rising prices from the action of the banks is apparently reinforced by the accumulating difficulties of marketing. Of course, some prices, such as freight rates and public utility prices, are regulated and not easily increased. Others are fixed by long contracts. Still others have been built up by advertising and, if changed, may stir up consumer resentment. Possibly the standards of living are conventional and not easily raised in times of expansion, so that increased incomes are more readily saved than spent on consumption. Much of the expansion is in the field of durable goods such as houses and automobiles, the demand for which may not easily be increased once the initial expansion has taken place. After all, one house is usually enough. In due time, the great increase in productive equipment characteristic of this boom must reach the stage of active output of consumers' goods, the flow of which is bound to be a depressing influence on the general level of prices. The evidence of these difficulties may appear in a piling up of inventories, indicating production outrunning current consumption, or in a great increase of advertising and high-pressure salesmanship. For a while, this effect may be overcome by installment selling, but this involves the credit mechanism and the banking system, and will have the same limits imposed upon it as upon other forms of borrowing.

These strains appear in the economic structure as expansion proceeds. They are not great at first, but they grow; and although they may be overcome for a while, particularly if favorable impulses from outside emerge from time to time, they will reappear again and again. As they do, they are bound to weaken the optimistic expectations of entrepreneurs. If unfavorable events occur—crop failures, disasters at home or abroad, and legislative changes of magnitude—they may be all that is needed to throw the whole business machinery into reverse and will be blamed for the recession which now begins. Fundamentally, the trouble lies in the strains in the economic structure which seem the inevitable accompaniment of a period of expansion—strains which perhaps can be tentatively described as the result of the inability to maintain adequate balance between all the various parts of the economic process. If, on the average in the last 50 years, the phase of expansion rarely passes two years in length, it is because it takes this period of time for the strains to accumulate and reach the breaking point.

The Recession

The recession proper, as we have defined it, covers a relatively short space of time. It marks the turning period during which the forces that make for contraction finally win over the forces of expansion. Its outward signs are liquidation in the stock market, strain in the banking system and some liquidation of bank loans, and the beginning of the decline of prices. Production may continue for a while, as goods in process are carried through to completion and some manufacture goes on for stock; but there is a sharp reduction in orders for equipment and in construction contracts, and many projects are abandoned. Indeed, there is evidence that the earliest sign of recession, and the efficient cause of the weakening of the whole industrial structure, is the fall of production and orders in the capital-producing trades.

The fall in the stock market is the dramatic signal of recession's advent. The sensitive pulse of the state of industrial and financial sentiment is influenced by the various discouraging aspects of the economic situation. Doubtless the fall is due largely to the realization that profits cannot be maintained and the reflection thereof in the minds of the speculative fraternity skilled at discounting the future. Part of the slump may be due to sales by insiders anxious to get out early; part, too, to the pressure of banks on the volume of brokers' loans. The funds loaned in the stock market on call tend to be drawn in when business pressure on funds has grown severe. The rise in call loan rates discourages some speculators and causes a sale of securities to liquidate loans.

The fall in stock market values not merely forecasts the fall in prices and profits but helps to bring it about. Borrowers on stock market security find their collateral shrinking and may have to pay off some of their loans. When they do, they may find it convenient to liquidate holdings of commodities, weakening their price. The weaker market in securities causes corporations which had considered expansion by sale of new issues to hold these new issues off the market, thereby reducing what would have been orders for equipment or buildings. The weakening of the basis of credit which all this implies tightens the money market and makes banks unwilling to expand or even to maintain the volume of loans.

This cumulative wave of liquidation which thus sets in in the stock market, the money market, and the commodity market is the prelude to the more or less prolonged phase of declining activity—to the business contraction—which presently sets in. Whether the beginning of this period will be reached by an orderly, though none the less trying, transition, or whether it will be accompanied by the explosive financial excitement of a crisis or panic, depends partly on the nature of the previous boom, partly on the incidents and accidents of the time as they affect the state of mind of the people, and partly on the good sense and effective organization of the banking community. Some recessions have passed without much sense of financial strain. Thanks to the Federal Reserve System, even the great stock market panic of 1929 was passed through without the accompanying run on the banks which would have been expected in former cycles.

The Collapse of Confidence

When a crisis, and more particularly a panic, does occur, it seems to be associated with a collapse of confidence which causes sudden demands for liquidity which, by the nature of things, feed on their own impossibility of satisfaction. This crisis of nerves may itself be occasioned by some spectacular and unexpected failure. A firm, a bank, or a corporation announces its inability to meet its debts. This announcement weakens other firms and banks at a time when ominous signs of distress are appearing in the economic structure; moreover, it sets off a wave of fright which culminates in a general run on financial institutions—everyone for himself and the devil take the hindmost. If the banks attempt to meet this situation with an attitude of studied liberality, preparing to advance funds to all who have good name or security and meeting promptly the early demands for cash, the situation may be saved even then. Otherwise, little can halt the panic; and banks may be compelled to issue a general refusal to meet their obligations, commonly concealed behind specious measures such as meeting no cheques except those going through clearinghouses or allowing only limited withdrawals. Such was the experience of the United States in 1873, in 1893, and in 1907. The dramatic closing of the banks in February and March 1933 was of the same sort, save that it came at the end of the depression, not at the beginning as one usually would expect.

Whether the end of the period of expansion is a mild recession, a crisis, or even a panic, a more or less prolonged period of industrial contraction and stagnation follows, during which prices continue to fall and a curtailment of productive activity and a decrease in the volume of employment occur.

This phase of contraction must now be described.

Contraction Begins

The characteristic of the period of contraction into which recession merges is the general decrease in economic activity. There is a notable fall in the production of goods and services and in employment. This fall is general throughout the whole field of activity, but it is by no means uniform. Some fields, such as retail trade, are relatively little affected. Others, such as agriculture, show irrational variations due to the weather and the relatively noncommercial nature of the occupation. In manufacture, mining, construction, and transport, the reduction is substantial, especially in the field of capital goods, buildings, machinery, and equipment. As in the expansion, the production of goods near the consumer shows the least variation; that of goods remote from the consumer, the most variation. Communities devoted to the latter type of production have very great unemployment and suffer most from the depression.

Despite the reduction in output of goods and services, the contraction is marked by a fall in the average price level. In the earlier stages, this fall may be caused by the liquidation of inventories piled up during expansion. As the contraction proceeds, it seems to be the consequence of a great reduction in the volume of money in actual use. The general reduction in activity and the deteriorated prospects of all business result in a substantial fall in the volume of bank deposits. Loans are paid off, as much as they can be. New loans do not take their place. Neither banks nor business seem willing to continue the normal scale of borrowing. This fact reduces greatly the total credit money available. What is available, as well as what currency is outstanding, suffers a substantial reduction in use as expressed in indexes of velocity of circulation. Fear of the future moves many to save for emergencies; the inadequate prospects of profit cause business deposits to be idle; the very fall in the price level which this engenders makes postponement of purchases profitable.

Irving Fisher estimates that, in the great depression, deposits subject to check fell from 22 billions in 1929 to 15 billions in 1933, while velocity of circulation fell from perhaps 30 per annum in 1929 to 20 per annum in 1933.[3] These figures represent a very great fall in the total monetary purchasing power actually in use.

This fall in purchasing power is the fundamental background of the fall in prices which, despite the general reduction of output, characterizes the depression.

Distortions in the Price Structure

In contraction, as in expansion, the rate of change in prices is quite unequal. Some goods fall but little; others suffer a veritable collapse. Highly manufactured goods fall less than raw materials or semifinished goods. Agricultural products fall farther than manufactured goods. Wholesale prices fall more than retail prices. Some prices are held up by custom or by regulation; some appear to be subject to private control. All these are relatively inflexible. Other prices have great flexibility. These unequal changes in the price level distort the price structure, change the distribution of income, and may serve to prolong the depression.

Along with this distortion in the price structure appears a distortion in cost-price relations. There is no equal and harmonious fall in costs along with prices. Some costs fall; others are rigid or fall but slowly. Wages and salaries tend to lag behind the price level. Public opinion, custom, trade-union regulation, and resistances of one kind and another conspire to

---

[3] Irving Fisher, *100% Money*, New York, 1935, 5–6.

bring about this result. Various expenses lumped as over-head continue for a while without reduction. Interest rates, rents, insurance, and taxes are slow to move downward. For existing debts, interest is fixed and can be changed only by the difficult process of negotiation or the disgraceful resort of bankruptcy. Because of these relative changes in prices and costs, the margin of profit tends to disappear and be replaced by loss. All of this is very disheartening to business and in-duces a mood of pessimism which exaggerates the potential losses and, as long as it continues, contributes to inactivity and stagnation.

Thus the circle of cumulative trouble is completed. The weakening of expectations from which the recession started brings about price fall, output reduction, and further fall in prices with fall in profits; and so under the discouragement of falling profits, which now replace what had been at first only a fear thereof, comes another wave of reduction of output with further unemployment, further reduction of purchasing, further fall in bank credit and velocity of circulation, and more deflation of prices. It is this cumulation of forces which makes the contraction so dangerous and in great depressions so severe.

Indeed, there seems nothing in the situation which could ever bring the contraction to an end save the complete dis-ruption of the economic activities of the nation. Expansion has obvious limits, set by the physical resources of the nation, which may soon reach their practicable maximum of output. Contraction, on the other hand, has no lower limit short of zero. Long before this lower limit had been reached, how-ever, either governmental intervention or else revolution would have put an end to the disaster. In past cycles at least, other limits to contraction have operated to induce recovery without the necessity of such drastic interferences. Just as in expansion various forces which tend to bring the expansion to an end are eventually set in motion, so in contraction limiting forces arise to bring the contraction to an end.

Revival Sets in

The most important of these forces, perhaps, are those that are working towards restoring the normal price relations and price-cost relations so badly distorted by the deflation. Prices at last cease dropping, doubtless partly due to the gradual exhaustion of inventories and the accumulated stores of the period of expansion. Even the most extensive stocks are gradually sold out; and, with the slowing up of production, supplies ultimately reach scarcity levels. This stage is reached faster in those fields like mining where output can be controlled; slower in agriculture, where nature and rampant individualism interfere with restriction. However, even here limitation of supply eventually does emerge.

In the meantime, the durable goods on which consumers have been coasting along are wearing out. Purchases can be delayed but become more and more urgent as time goes on. Clothes, furnishings, automobiles, and ultimately houses are wanted, and they furnish a backlog for future business activity. In industry, reserves for depreciation and obsolescence have been withheld from use under the stress of bad times and the excuse of little wear, but replacements cannot be indefinitely postponed. Even idle factories and equipment deteriorate and get out of date. So much is this so, that sudden bulges of demand may find industry scarcely equipped to take care of them. The mere presence of these potential needs weakens the forces of depression and stagnation. As time passes, these needs become more insistent, likely to overcome greater and greater resistance and be responsive more readily to any favorable events.

While this is going on, the cost-price relation tends to become more favorable. The lagging costs which pinch profits so badly at last begin to fall. The resistance of custom or law or organized groups seems gradually to weaken. Under the growing pressure of funds piled up in financial markets de-

prived of the ordinary commercial outlets, interest rates sink
to low levels. Not only short-time rates but also long-time
rates fall, with the accompanying rise in the value of first-class
bonds. Long-time interest fixed by contract is brought down
here and there by agreement, oftentimes by recapitalization
or other financial reconstruction. Rents, insurance, and taxes
become adjusted to the lower levels of output and prices.
Wages under the harsh influence of unemployment eventually
are compelled to come down, sometimes breaking rapidly to
levels equivalent to the level of prices. With these direct reductions in labor cost, favorable changes in efficiency appear.
The elimination of less effective labor and, possibly, the greater
zeal of workmen anxious to hold their jobs tend to increase
the output per man and, along with the fall in wage rates,
make for substantial reductions in labor cost. Indeed, it may
be said that just as in expansion the general level of efficiency
falls, so in depression it gradually rises. Not only the less
efficient workers but also the less efficient plants and the less
efficient managements are dropped, thus lowering the average
cost of production. Under the influence of all these changes,
the margin of loss is reduced; in some quarters, under increase
of demand and strengthening of prices, it may be replaced by
profit. As this goes on, any quickening of business may readily start a substantial wave of recovery. It is true that recovery
may be delayed, despite these relatively favorable influences.
Outside events of an unfavorable nature may come in to retard revival, or even to start off another and secondary depression, as happened to the world in general by the financial
collapse of the central European countries in the summer of
1931. The longer the revival is postponed, the more the favorable forces which we have described grow in power; and it
would seem that in due time, perhaps with the aid of some
"originating cause" from outside, they are bound to break
through the weakening forces of depression and begin the
phase of recovery.

The Forces of Recovery Get Under Way

The first signs of this change of phase, apart from the restoration of price and cost relations characteristic of and essential to the end of the trough of depression, seem usually to be found in the level of stock exchange prices and in the activities of the construction and equipment industries.

Stock exchange activity has a tendency at all times to lead production, and the conditions preliminary to revival are all favorable to this tendency. The imminent recovery of profits is certain to be reflected in the price of securities as long as the exchanges fulfill their function of discounting the future. Moreover, the low level of interest is favorable to an increase of brokers' loans and encouraging to a growth of bullish sentiment.

This increase of stock market prices is accompanied by, and favors, an expansion of construction and other capital projects. Not only does this rise of security prices give fair warning of a coming revival and so hasten building in preparation therefor, but the improvement in prices is favorable to new issues and makes the financing of long-time projects easier. Furthermore, the difficulty of making profits during depression tends to encourage invention and improvement. It is a common observation that, at this stage in the course of the cycle, inventions are most likely to be made or, having previously been made, to be put into active operation. For various reasons, therefore, capital expansion is likely to proceed, and it has been the experience of many recoveries in the past that the capital-producing industries lead the others out of the depression.

If this expansion proceeds on any substantial scale, the payrolls and other incomes paid out will serve as the starter for still other projects, and, by the kind of cumulative process we have already examined, industrial activity gets rapidly under way, and the phase of recovery tends to move on into the phase of expansion; the cycle is ready to repeat itself once more.

Are Starters Needed for Complete Recovery?

It is a debatable question whether recovery to anything more than relatively modest heights can come about in the absence of some one or other of the originating causes, which, as we have seen, are commonly responsible for the beginning of a period of expansion after equilibrium has been attained. Some writers hold that the recovery from depression is so stimulating to confidence, the necessary production to make up for the low output of depression so substantial, and the conditions imposed by lagging costs on the upward path so favorable to profit levels, that recovery will move into expansion without any outside or "exogenous" cause. In this view, cycles once started are continuous and self-generating, each phase producing the conditions necessary to the appearance of its successor, and so on in an endless chain of causation.[4]

However, there is some ground for believing that this self-generating process could not go on indefinitely. Frictions of one kind and another are likely gradually to bring the cyclical tendencies to a halt in the absence of sporadic originating causes whose function in this respect is to keep the cycle going. Possibly, too, entrepreneurs would be able to foretell the behavior of a self-generating cycle to such a degree as to enable them to make stabilizing plans that would effectually iron out cyclical fluctuations. However, there is a good deal of doubt whether any purely self-generated expansion has ever existed. It is probably true that every recovery can be found to be associated with favorable events of the "originating" kind. In the United States, a long tradition has caused business in slump to look for favorable agricultural conditions to bring about revival; and a good deal of the disappointing

---

[4] See also W. C. Mitchell's account of the phases in the article "Business Cycles" in the *Encyclopaedia of the Social Sciences.*

difficulties in the recent prolonged depression is attributed to the fact that agriculture, once the helper, is now in a state of having also to be helped.

It is possible, too, that various other factors may delay recovery and make more than usually important the possibility of a starter emerging to give the desired impetus. Thus, at the present time, the slowing growth of population may deprive industry of one of its most reliable aids to recovery, for population growth is claimed to be the principal source of the continued demand for houses, construction, and equipment. Again, there is some evidence, which will be discussed more in detail later,[5] that wages are becoming more rigid. There is a greater unwillingness to lower wage rates, an unwillingness which is rationalized as a need for maintaining the purchasing power necessary for industrial prosperity. Whether justified or not, this rigidity of wage rates may make it harder to bring costs into relation with prices after recession. There has been also a growing reluctance to scale down capitalizations. Bondholders are not willing to reduce their claims. Furthermore, evidence exists of an increasing rigidity of some prices, apparently under the control of monopolistic groups or under the sway of imperfect competition—a rigidity which is particularly important in that it seems to affect the field of capital goods production, the low demand for which is the cause of some of the deepest areas of depression. One may add to this the fact that an apparently growing fraction of consumption consists of very durable goods, such as automobiles, electric equipment, and so on, the service of which can be extended over relatively elastic periods of time, thus making for still further potential postponement of replacement demands.

This formidable mass of complications, all of which tend to retard recovery, may make it more difficult to hold that recovery is self-generated out of depression. They indicate that

---

[5] See Chap. XXIII.

originating forces, such as invention, new industries or commodities, favorable crops, great discoveries of gold, or even war, may, after all, be required. Doubtless they furnish much of the background for the prolonged effort of the New Deal to supply the impetus by all sorts of government intervention.[6]

The Nature of Cyclical Disturbance

This series of cumulative responses which we have now traced through the successive phases of the cycle shows plainly enough that cyclical behavior does not conform strictly to the "normal" reaction of the economic system to disturbances of equilibrium. "Normally," the economic system is a self-regulating, self-correcting mechanism. Disturbances to equilibrium set in motion forces which act promptly to restore the equilibrium. In economic phenomena, as in natural phenomena, changes brought about by any force act to neutralize that force. A rise in prices due to change in demand increases the profits of producers and leads them to produce the additional supply necessary to restore the former price level. A fall in wages in one quarter causes a movement of workers to other quarters, thus checking the fall. It is these quasi-automatic reactions to disturbances that limit their effects and help to keep the economic system in equilibrium. In short, the equilibrium, on these assumptions, is stable.

Business cycle behavior violates the conditions of stable equilibrium. What the business cycle discloses is a fundamental instability in the economic system. If it is moved from equilibrium, the forces set in motion are not forces tending to restore equilibrium; rather, they are forces causing the system to move farther away from equilibrium than before. This progressive departure from equilibrium continues until the resultant strain sets up limits which even the cumulative forces

---

[6] See also P. H. Douglas, *Controlling Depressions*, New York, 1935, Chap. IV, "Does a Depression Cure Itself?"

of expansion or contraction, powerful though they are, cannot overcome.

Doubtless, if one wishes to strain a point, even this process might be embraced in the concept of "normal" behavior. The very process of expansion up to recession and of contraction down to recovery shows that even the most powerful disturbances set up forces which in due time bring them to an end. In this sense, what is a business cycle if not an example of the self-correcting mechanism by which disturbances are got rid of? It is true that the delay is often considerable and the disturbance seems to be a long while correcting itself, but perhaps this is only a matter of degree. Despite their familiar pattern of expansion and contraction, minor cyclical fluctuations pass off without any more disturbance than is commonly found from the multitudinous noncyclical changes to which the economic system is exposed. While major cycles are more spectacular, it is hard to draw the precise line where what is going on should be described in terms of cumulative departure from equilibrium or, contrariwise, as self-correcting reactions to disturbance.

It must be admitted, however, that a cycle, if it is an example of self-correcting responses to disturbance, is, from the point of view of efficiency, a very clumsy one. If, for example, a substantial increase of gold occurs in a country, the proper reaction is a new equilibrium on 'a higher level of money incomes and prices, just as, in the opposite case of a loss of gold, the proper reaction is to a lower level of money incomes and prices. The fact that the former can be brought about only by the troublesome and exciting process of a boom, and the latter only by the quite painful experience of a depression, is disheartening, especially since the "correction" in each case is so violent that it sets up an equally violent counterdisturbance, to be corrected in its turn by another overpowerful correction, and so on in a possibly endless series of fluctuations. It is unfortunate to be always delaying correction so long that equilibrium is never restored, for the social strain involved and the individual hardships and losses caused by this labored process of adjustment are among the most serious of our economic difficulties. For this reason, one is justified in regarding business cycles as an example of cumulative disturbance rather than of eventual correction.

CHAPTER VI

GREAT DEPRESSIONS

SOME depressions seem to stand out from all others. They may be called "great depressions." They appear like landmarks in the industrial history of a nation. In the United States, it would probably be conceded that the depression following the crisis of 1837, the prolonged depression of the 1870's, the double depression of the 1890's, and the great depression of the 1930's loom tragically above the most serious of the other recorded fluctuations in economic activity.

True, there can be no absolute agreement on the list of these great depressions. Some would doubtless include the depression of the 1840's or that of the 1880's. The difficulty lies in the problem of measuring severity. Long and short depressions are easily picked out. The annals are competent to show these; and we have seen that longer-than-average cycles, where they have appeared, take their length from the abnormal length of depression. But length of depression is not synonymous with severity. It is the *depth* as well as the length that makes depression severe, and depth or intensity is not easy to measure. Such indexes as we have covering the cyclical history of the United States are relatively unreliable in respect to the earlier period; and even if they were more reliable, they do not include homogeneous materials from one period to another. Hence it is practically impossible to compare the relative intensity of such depressions as that of 1837 and that of 1873; or indeed to know with any certitude what severity really meant in those earlier years.

After the Civil War, indexes become fairly comparable, and it is possible to compare intensity as well as length. One way of doing this graphically is to measure the distance from the top of peaks to the bottom of troughs. Another is to measure the fall of the index below the line of normal. Thus Bratt, in his discussion of depressions, determines major depressions as those in which the index falls by 15 per cent or more below the line of normal. Furthermore, these measures of intensity correspond with measures of length. The longer depressions tend to coincide with the more severe.[1]

Probably, however, the evidence of history and the consensus of opinion, rather than precise measurements, would have to be our clue to the great depressions. If we assume they can be agreed on, it is tempting to ask what causes these occasional great depressions. Are they fortuitous, the result of chance factors conspiring to produce an abnormal conjuncture of unfavorable events? Or on the contrary, do they follow some pattern, some sequence or order traceable in the history of fluctuations? The present chapter is devoted to this problem.

Are There Trends in Depressions?

Some writers hold that depressions disclose the simplest type of pattern, the trend. One group, like the optimists of the 1920's, believe the trend to be one of diminishing intensity; others, particularly Marxian socialists, believe the trend to be one of increasing intensity. The former, basing their convictions on the increasing control by central bank authorities and on the stabilizing measures of sensible businessmen, were inclined to believe that great depressions, at least, were a thing of the past. The latter, on the other hand, thinking in terms

---

[1] E. C. Bratt, *Business Cycles and Forecasting*, 170–172.

of the allegedly increasing exploitation of the working masses and the difficulties of reconciling vast expansion of fixed capital with the low purchasing power of the people, insisted fanatically that depressions were becoming more intense—each major slump worse than the last, and the worst still to come. The optimists seemed to be borné out by the relative stability of the 1920 decade; the pessimists, by the rude interruption of the 1929 crash.

Such evidence as we have, however, indicates that neither of these conflicting views is right. Statistical material for the period before the Civil War is too scanty to give any positive picture. The quantitative measurements available thereafter reveal no trend. Mitchell, after analyzing five important indexes in the years 1878 to 1923, fails to find any certain evidence that the severity of depressions is progressively changing. Snyder's clearings index of business and (less clearly) Frickey's index, of clearings suggest, if anything, a growing mildness; but the other three indexes, which perhaps measure more accurately the activity of production, disclose no observable trend.[2]

Similar conclusions are reached by A. R. Eckler in a recent study of the severity of depressions.[3] Using a statistical measure based on various activity indexes and measuring the severity of depression by the percentage decrease from the highest year after which decline began to the year marking the bottom, Eckler ranks the major depressions in the following descending order of magnitude:

1929–1932
1873–1878
1920–1921
1892–1894
1882–1885
1907–1908

[2] W. C. Mitchell, *Business Cycles, The Problem and Its Setting*, 1927, 343–349.
[3] A. R. Eckler, "A Measure of the Severity of Depressions, 1873–1932," *Review of Economic Statistics*, May 15, 1933.

These results do not indicate any persistent trend in intensity, either up or down. It is true that the depression of 1929–1932 is the most severe of all those occurring within the period for which adequate statistics are available, but there is no evidence that depressions arrange themselves in an ascending order of severity culminating in this great catastrophe. On the contrary, one has to go back to 1873 to find the depression that ranks next in severity.

Primary and Secondary Postwar Depressions

The progressively severe depressions that followed the First World War, which gave plausibility to the theory of the increasing intensity of depressions, are held by some economists to be an example of a pattern of postwar depression which can be found repeated in each of the periods following the major wars in which the United States has been involved. This theory of primary and secondary postwar depressions is advanced by Col. Leonard P. Ayres, economist of the Cleveland Trust Co.[4]

There is some evidence that great or major wars are followed by two distinct depressions: a sharp, but relatively short, depression as war ends, which may be called the *primary postwar depression;* and, after a period of recovery and expansion, a long and severe depression, which may be called the *secondary postwar depression.* Thus, at the end of the Napoleonic Wars, there was a primary depression in 1820, and a secondary beginning in 1825; after the Civil War, a primary depression in 1865, and the great secondary depression beginning in 1873; after the First World War, a primary depression in 1921, and the great depression of the 1930's.

The varying patterns of the two postwar depressions find their origins, it is held, in the great rise of prices which war engenders and the somewhat different consequences of this

---

[4] L. P. Ayres, *The Economics of Recovery,* Chapter 2.

price rise upon the two principal economic classes: those engaged in agriculture and other extractive occupations, and those engaged in manufacture, industry, and trade. When war comes, with rising prices, the extractive industries enjoy the greatest prosperity; their prices are the highest of all prices. Land values rise rapidly; there is a great increase of land under cultivation, much of it obtained by an equally great increase in the issue of mortgages. The industrial population is not having such a good time, however, for while business is brisk, cost of living is now rising rapidly and industrial disputes are common.

When the war ends, there comes a short and sharp depression, marked primarily by a collapse of the farming boom and the prices of foodstuffs and raw materials. This collapse is the primary postwar depression, which, however, is soon ended and is followed by a period of rapid expansion in which industry and the urban population enjoy great prosperity.

During this period of prosperity, when food is cheap (for farmers continue to be depressed) and real wages are high, there is a great surge of urban industry, accompanied by a boom in construction and in real estate values and by the development of a great wave of speculation in securities. In due time, this prosperity destroys itself, as the boom runs to excess and the farm population continues to suffer from low purchasing power. The result is the secondary depression, deeper than the first and wider also, since it now affects all sections. The rural community plunges back into the trough; the urban population, depressed in its turn, makes deflation and contraction general. Profits, wages, and prices have to be adjusted, and during this process the formidable volume of debt presses very hard.

There seems to be, therefore, a normal sequence of events: (1) commodity price inflation, (2) farm prosperity and farmland speculation, (3) price deflation and a short primary postwar depression, (4) a period of city prosperity and widespread speculation, and (5) secondary price deflation and a long secondary postwar depression. This sequence of events takes about 15 years to run its course. Three of these sequences appear in the history of the United States: (1) from the peak of prices of 1815 to the recovery of 1829, (2) from the peak of prices of 1864 to the recovery of 1878, and (3) from the peak of prices of 1920 to the recovery which apparently began in 1933.

The Relation of Depressions to Long Waves of Prices and Production

The possible connection of major depressions with the great wars which have afflicted this country and the world in general opens up further possibilities. Ayres has called attention to the sharp rise of prices during war, but closer examination of these war periods shows that the price rise is not merely an incident of wartime, but, in fact, the culmination, dramatic and rapid it is true, of a long period of price rise going back far before the war. The price peak of 1815 ended a rise of prices which began in 1793; that of 1864, one that began about 1841; and that of 1920, one that began in 1896. What is disclosed here are simply the peaks of the long waves of prices, the nature of which has already been discussed in Chapter I.

These long waves of prices, as we have seen, appear to be associated with the long waves of activity called "Kondratieff cycles." It is at the culmination of these long waves that wars have appeared, and it is when the long wave turns down that the dramatic collapse which Ayres calls "the secondary postwar depression" makes its appearance. Wars themselves and the depressions that follow them may be only part of the great pattern which the Kondratieff cycle describes.

Kondratieff has pointed out how many things that seem for-

tuitous can be explained in relation to long waves of activity.[5]
Long waves affect the ratio of prosperity to depression in the
shorter business cycle. In the long recession, agriculture suffers the most and has the deepest depressions. Inventions are
encouraged in these great recessions and, through their exploitation lay the foundation for the next long upswing. Gold
production tends to increase at the bottom of the downward
phase, particularly as the long upswing proceeds. The upswing is marked by the enlargement of colonial areas as great
economic empires seek markets. At the end of the upward
phase, wars tend to break out.

Thus neither invention, nor gold production, nor the exploitation of colonies, nor wars are haphazard. All are related
in some causal way to long waves of economic activity.

Hansen [6] develops this theme at length and offers the hypothesis not only that wars are bred on the upswing of long
cycles, but that revolutions are bred on the downswing. The
Napoleonic Wars at the end of the first upswing; the Crimean
War, the wars of Prussia with Austria and France, the wars
of France and Italy with Austria, the American Civil War
on the second upswing; and the First World War at the end
of the third upswing illustrate one phase. Similarly, the revolutions in Europe in 1820, 1830, and 1848 in the first downswing; the growth of revolutionary Marxism in the second;
and the revolutions in Germany, Italy, and Spain in the third,
downswing illustrate the contrary tendency during the long
downswing.[7]

It is not difficult to advance reasons for this sequence of
events. Upswings are times of advancing output, search for
markets, growth of profits, and foreign investment. The pace

---

[5] N. D. Kondratieff, "Long Waves in Economic Life," *Review of Economic Statistics,* November, 1935, 105–115.

[6] A. H. Hansen, *Economic Stabilization in an Unbalanced World,* New York, 1932,
Chapter 6.

[7] See also A. L. Macfie, "The Outbreak of War and the Trade Cycle, *Economic
History,* February, 1938.

of competition, both at home and abroad, is sharpened. The growing wealth of nations makes them able to increase armaments competitively; their growing rivalry tends to make them willing to use them. In the end, war breaks out.

War brings a long period of good times to an end. Prices rise to abrupt heights, and at the end of the war comes collapse, with many repercussions. Gold production already has declined, bringing falling prices. The general disruptions set up by the war, the disturbance of monetary systems, and the dislocation of price-cost relations are a more or less prolonged influence towards depression. For years, activity will move at a slower rate.

Such a situation breeds distress. Those classes that are most harshly affected by the situation look for violent means of restoration. Governments become chronically unpopular; measures for restoring good times are not effective. These are the conditions that make for political unrest; and only the soundest and best established governments are able to avoid internal disturbance. Some governments are overthrown, more or less peacefully. Revolutionary movements continue until the wave has ebbed its farthest. Thereupon, with the rise of prices once more and the increase of the pace of economic activity, the wave of discontent begins to wane, and the danger of revolution seems to pass.

If wars then tend to come at the end of a rising price wave and social disturbances at the end of a falling price wave, possibly the major depressions may come at the turning points in general of the great waves of prices, rather than merely at the end of rising phases. The great depressions of 1825, 1873, and 1930 are located at the top, it is true; but the depressions which followed the panics of 1837 and 1893 were equally great and certainly would have to be listed among the major depressions in American industrial history. These depressions came at the bottom of a wave of falling prices. It is tempting to rationalize these appearances and suggest that, if wars cause trouble by the dislocations they set up, revolutions or revolutionary sentiment may cause just as much trouble. Against either of these influences, the general vitality of business tends to wear itself down, and, when this occurs, the more prolonged slumps make their appearance.

Coincidence of Various Waves of Activity

The possible appearance of major depressions at the turning point of "long waves" or "Kondratieff cycles" leads to another conjecture—namely, that major disturbances may be due to the coincidence of similar phases of the various cycles which can be traced in economic activities. The amplitude of fluctuation of a given wave can clearly be intensified if it happens to occur along with a similar fluctuation of another wave. Thus there is some evidence that in prewar years the greatest danger of a crisis in the United States came in the autumn, for it was then that the seasonal drain on monetary centers took place. Because of this, in years when the rising phase of the business cycle reached its top, it more easily passed over into recession in the months of seasonal strain than at any other time.

Now there are many wavelike fluctuations of industry, not only seasonal variations but minor, Juglar, and Kondratieff cycles. Because of their different wave lengths, these fluctuations have now opposite, now reinforcing effects. Thus the rising phase of the Kondratieff cycle tends to subdue the normal depressions incident to business cycles, creating a preponderance of prosperity; whereas the falling phase of the long cycle increases the force of cyclical depressions and makes for a longer and deeper slump.

It is conceivable, therefore, that major depressions can be traced to this kind of synchronism. Joseph Schumpeter, who holds that the evidence of modern cycles indicates the coexistence of minor cycles (40 months), major or Juglar cycles (8–10 years), and Kondratieff cycles (50 or 60 years), has pointed out that the year 1930 saw each of these cycles in its downward phase. The short cycle that began in 1927 was on the normal downswing, the Juglar cycle was repeating the slump of 1920, and the long wave was now well on the downward phase that had begun around 1920.[8]

While, however, the coincidence of various waves of activity might serve, at more or less calculable intervals, to bring about a greater than normal depression, the evidence that we have of great depressions seems to indicate the presence of other factors not explicable by any cyclical fluctuation. We have broadly referred to these as "structural changes." Such structural changes may come about as the result of some great political disturbance, principally wars, and will therefore be periodic to whatever extent wars are periodic; or they will, come about through great technological changes, so great in extent and so sweeping in their consequences as to upset the normal adjustments of the economy.

Thus, in a broad way, one might offer the hypothesis that great depressions occur when a normal business cycle recession coincides with the downward phase of the Kondratieff cycle and is further complicated by the effect of structural changes brought about by either war or great technological changes, or both.

The great depression of the 1930's might be offered as an example of this conjuncture.[9] The normal business cycle recession was due by 1930. At the same time, the downward phase of a long price cycle which began in 1920 was setting in unmistakably by 1925 (to continue possibly to 1945?). Finally, there were structural changes produced by war and technology. The First World War had brought in its train deflation of prices, the collapse of national currencies, maladjustments in the distribution of gold, shifts in world trade of great

---

[8] J. Schumpeter, "The Present World Depression," *American Economic Review*, March, 1931, Supplement, 179–180. See also his *Business Cycles*, 161–174.

[9] See League of Nations, *Course and Phases of the World Economic Depression*, 1931, Chapter VI, Section A, "The Character of the Depression."

magnitude accompanied by the imposition of many trade restrictions, profound changes in the relations of creditor and debtor nations, and, to crown all, revolutions in three great nations. As for technology, it was a period of great advance, so great as to lead some observers to speak of a "new industrial revolution"; new products, new methods of production and management, and a great extension of machine technology and power production were introduced within such a short space of time that the adjustments in consumption and the transfers of capital and labor necessary to avoid disorder and disruption were difficult.

The listing of this complex set of factors contributing to a great depression raises the suspicion that probably the pattern of great depressions in the general picture of economic fluctuation will elude analysis. Cyclical fluctuations may be measured; even wars, if not their consequences, may possibly be found to conform to a pattern; but there seems to be no clue to the appearance of great technological change such as has apparently been at work during the last few decades. That is to say, structural changes are, after all, nonrecurrent, nonperiodic changes. They cannot be anticipated, nor can their effects be calculated in advance. When they come, they come as isolated episodes, not as phases of a recurrent pattern. Because they do come in this manner, the great depressions to which they probably contribute so much must be, to some extent, isolated episodes also. They are fortuitous, the result of factors that are essentially factors of chance, conspiring to produce an abnormal conjuncture of unfavorable events. There is good evidence, as we shall now see, that the great depression of the 1930's was an example of this kind of conjuncture.

The Great Depression

It is not the purpose of this section to account fully for the depression as such or for its exceptional severity. Here it is sufficient to point out how many concurrent influences were at work in this period, all of them influences which would seem likely to have added something to the difficulties of the time.

(1) In the first place, there was the familiar business cycle recession. The period of the 1920's had been marked by prolonged prosperity, at least in industry. This prosperity had been particularly notable in the field of construction and capital production, and it had gone on with only minor interruptions for nearly 10 years. That is to say, it had proceeded through three minor cycles, interrupted only by two relatively unimportant recessions. During this period, there had been the usual expansion of credit, on a larger than usual scale, with the resultant increase of profits, although this profit increase had come despite any increase in the price level and must have arisen, therefore, from rapid changes in costs. The downturn was inevitable when the cumulative strains that seem to bring about the end of periods of prosperity finally had their way.

(2) In the second place, the dislocations in world economy and in the economy of many individual countries brought about by the First World War were still causing trouble. True, the world had begun to resume to some degree its normal progress, but the return to normal conditions was far from complete, and disruption of economic relations was still serious.

The productive system of Europe had been seriously affected by war conditions. The great destruction of wealth and loss of man power had set Europe back in relation to the rest of the world. This setback was accentuated by the political settlements after the war. The large number of small states into which the Treaty of Versailles had divided the prewar empires broke up the economic unity of Europe and created areas of uneconomic size and inadequate resources, whose weakness their rulers tried to offset by various methods of protection, tariffs, trade restrictions, and similar devices. Abroad, there

had been a great expansion of the hitherto nonindustrial areas
of the world, first under the pressure of the war demands, and
later because of the ambition to capture markets lost by Europe.
Thus Japan, India, Malaysia, Australia, and Canada entered
the industrial field. These shifts of power remained a disturbing factor preventing readjustment.

In Europe also, among the belligerent countries, established
monetary systems many decades old were completely disrupted
by the events of the war and postwar periods. All without
exception abandoned the gold standard during wartime, and
all experienced various degrees of inflation. Inflation, followed in the postwar period by deflation and devaluation,
brought great hardship to the business communities and caused
sweeping and undeserved redistributions of the national in--
come. When, after much painful effort, the gold standard
was re-established in this country or that, the different valuations in gold bestowed upon their monetary units created inequalities in export and import relations that did much to
prolong the confusion and difficulty that afflicted business.
Thus England made its monetary unit so high in value in the
restoration of 1925 as to penalize exports; while France seems
to have undergone the opposite experience, undervaluing its
currency by the valuations of 1926, and stimulating exports.

As a result of these various situations, the movements of
gold throughout the world became quite abnormal. Gold
tended to pile up in some countries and be withdrawn from
others. At the end of the decade, two countries, France and
the United States, had come to have between them the major
share of the world's gold. This unusual distribution of the
gold supply tended to cause falling prices in other countries
and engender a chronic depression.

The losses of the war and the movements of gold, together
with shifts in the course of world trade, had introduced a new
situation in the relation of capital-investing countries to the
world economy. Germany, known before the war as one

of the three great creditor nations annually investing large
sums abroad, lost this status, and, as a result of compulsory
liquidation of capital holdings abroad and of the loss of territory and markets following the war, became a debtor nation
on a large scale. On the other hand, the United States, formerly a debtor nation, found it possible during the war to buy
up foreign-held capital investments within the country, and
furthermore to invest such large sums abroad in Canada, South
America, Europe, and the Orient as to rival Great Britain as
a creditor nation.

These great capital shifts were of unprecedented magnitude,
introducing into the world economy an equally unprecedented
situation in regard to the movements of imports and exports
which tend to follow the monetary investments. Added to
all these shifting currents were the formidable movements
caused by the reparations imposed upon Germany and the
correlated payments made by European countries on war debts
owed to the United States—a source of disturbance troublesome not only by the magnitude of the capital shifts involved
but by the train of uncertainty which it always carried with it.

Indeed, uncertainty and unrest marked the whole period.
Europe, torn by the war, hovered precariously between democracy and dictatorships. Even the most stable countries were
afflicted with widespread political unrest. Others, such as
Russia and Italy, had already gone the way of revolution.
Still others, such as the numerous states of Eastern Europe,
were ready to change at any time. These conditions were not
favorable to orderly economic recovery.

All these factors, hangovers of the war, conspired to weaken
the economic resistance of the civilized world, made it difficult to bring about restoration of good times, and set up a
condition when any setback might develop into a major catastrophe.

(3) In the third place, the long wave of prices which had
reached the culmination of its upward phase at the end of

the First World War now seemed to have set in definitely downward. The high levels of gold output reached before the war were beginning to recede. The high point of gold production was reached in 1915 with an output of $470,000,000. The output, after shrinking during the war, rose in the postwar period, but even in 1928 was only $408,000,000. The situation of the world gold-mining industry caused a committee of the League of Nations to anticipate even smaller outputs than this, reaching as low as $370,000,000 in 1940. Meanwhile, the increase of trade during the postwar decade and the steady pressure for gold to fulfill the reserve requirements of those countries that had been moved to restore the gold standard served to raise the value of gold and lower the price level. By 1925, the world's price level, which had seemed to have been stabilized at about 50 per cent higher than prewar, was definitely, though slowly, beginning to decline.

The experience of the past and the obvious deductions from economic reasoning indicate that this secular trend of prices downward would add to the virulence of whatever depression might finally be precipitated.

(4) In the fourth place, stimulated partly by the necessities of war production, the pace of technological change seems definitely to have undergone a considerable increase. In the United States, this development had found its expression in the burst of inventions which flowered in the period, especially automobiles and all kind of electrical equipment, and also in the rapid spread of scientific management, which in many ways was even more revolutionary. These same tendencies, often referred to as "rationalization," were working in Europe also—notably in Germany, where they had led to rapid changes in the productive equipment of the country.

These technological changes necessitate much shifting of resources, both capital and labor, and sometimes, when change comes fast enough, outrun the power of absorption which industry in general normally enjoys. The figures of

unemployment during the prosperous decade of the 1920's in
the United States, although admittedly faulty and unreliable,
seem to indicate a growing difficulty of finding re-employment
for workers displaced by technological change.

Of all the fields where technological change occurred, agriculture was perhaps the most striking example. Here mechanization and improvements making additional cultivation
possible in all kinds of soils and climates, aided by the great
demand for agricultural staples caused by the war, had substantially increased the area under cultivation and added
greatly to the annual agricultural output. The normal reduction in demand materializing at the end of the war would,
in any case, have brought about some considerable fall in agricultural prices, and one which, considering the slow response
of the agricultural community, was bound to be serious and
relatively lasting. The continued effects of mechanization and
improvement, amounting to an agricultural revolution, kept
pressing on the price level still further, with the result that,
although some recovery took place from the serious deflation
of 1920–1921, agriculture continued to be a relatively depressed
economic area throughout the entire decade.

This prolonged depression in agriculture, perhaps more than
any other single factor, greatly weakened the general economic
structure, not only in agricultural countries, but in all parts
of the world. When the slump of 1929 came, with a renewed
fall in prices, the great and added distresses of the agricultural
world promptly acted to extend the depression in every quarter. In the past, periods of depression have been brief when
agriculture has been prosperous; and in the United States,
good crops and high purchasing power of the farmers have
always been looked for as the force pulling the country out
of slump. When agriculture becomes involved in a crisis of
its own, then depressions seem likely to be of long duration
and exceptional severity. In the great depression of the 1930's,
farmers, instead of being an aid to recovery, had themselves

by all sorts of government expedients, to be lifted out of their own slump.

(5) In the fifth place, factors of an entirely different sort— possibly fortuitous, possibly the result of a long and persistent trend—entered into the picture. These various developments tended apparently to make the economic system more rigid, more inflexible, and less able to make the necessary adaptations imposed by continuous and often sweeping change.

It is a commonplace of economic observation that the economic mechanism must be sufficiently flexible to enable capital and labor and management continually to flow from places and uses where they are less valuable to places and uses where they are more valuable. Were industry static, methods of production and demand for goods unchanging, this process would be unnecessary; but the incessant changes of methods of production brought about by technology, and the equally incessant changes in demand brought about partly by technology and partly by the caprice of the consumer, demand flexibility in our economic system as a prerequisite to unimpeded operation. This flexibility can be had only by the willingness of capital and labor to move, by reasonable willingness to undergo reductions of interest and wages in occupations where, for the moment, demand is low, and by reasonable flexibility of individual prices. Where wages or prices or production are not flexible, there it is not easy to bring about that constant shifting of resources which is necessary not only for full employment and best utilization, but, at times, even for the effective continuation of productive operation in general.

From the evidence of the 1920's, it seems that flexibility was by no means perfect and may, indeed, have been gradually decreasing. This situation may have been the mere culmination to notable proportions of a trend already going on for some time, or it may have sprung up in the conditions surrounding the economic system following the great disturbances of the war. Whatever the source, there the growing inflexibility seemed to be.

In the field of wages, labor unions, backed by social insurance and to some extent by a growing public opinion which interpreted variations in purchasing power as responsible for economic instability, were moving toward establishing wage payments as fixed charges on industry. In production, monopolies and semimonopolies, anxious to avoid the instability of competitive bidding, were thinking in terms of "administered prices." In one field and another, where conditions of production seemed to be out of control and low prices a continued aggravation to the producer, governments had entered in to fix prices by intricate regulation. The period was one of "valorization" and various other control mechanisms. Coffee, rubber, sugar, and other raw materials came within their scope. Toward the end of the decade, the great agricultural staples were brought under regulation, headed by the spectacular efforts of the Federal Farm Board approved by the American government in 1929.

Whatever the merit of these mechanisms in themselves, there seems little doubt that they introduced another rigid element into the operation of national economies. This growing inflexibility of economic structures all over the world at a time when, because of the war and the impact of technological change, adjustments were unusually important, was bound to intensify any depression that might occur.

That these rigidities and controls were increased, not diminished, when depression finally broke is, of course, well known. Every effort was made to uphold wages, prevent prices from falling, peg the prices of bonds, and control the levels of exchange rates. The world as a whole gave itself up to a veritable orgy of tariffs and other restrictions on trade, which added a final touch to the sum of controls to which the world was subject.

Such was the combination of circumstances which surrounded the coming of the great depression. Business cycle recession, structural changes consequent upon the First World War, a change downward in the long cycle of prices, technological changes of magnitude, especially in the field of agriculture, and what seems to be a growing inflexibility in respect to wages and prices and output in various areas; some chance or other had brought together these formidable factors to bear upon the economic systems of the world. It seems probable that, in their various interrelations, they were responsible for the severity of the depression.

Whether this pattern of events was to be expected or could be deduced from the experiences of other periods, especially those that followed great wars, is very doubtful indeed. Perhaps it will turn out to be unique, an isolated episode, explicable but nonrecurrent, in the varied history of the vicissitudes of business. If it has more than this significance, it can be only because it may represent a marked and definite stage, a turning point in the trend, of capitalistic society. To this possibility we must now briefly turn our attention.

The Possibility of Chronic Depression

It is conceivable that the depression which has hung over this country now for a decade is not merely the result of the various forces which have been analyzed above. The difficulty which we have experienced in achieving more than a temporary recovery may indicate the presence of something more fundamental than anything we have yet examined. It is possible that powerful influences are now at work, making against complete recovery and for a more or less prolonged economic stagnation. Some have held that capitalism has reached a turning point and that the driving forces which made it such a powerful engine of economic well-being have lost their vigor—hence the great depression, the difficulty of recovery, and the continued unemployment despite all our efforts. In short, progress, so characteristic of the nineteenth century, may have been interrupted, and the long upward trend checked at last.

The problem has been admirably presented by Alvin H. Hansen in his 1938 Presidential address to the American Economic Association, and we may well follow his analysis.[10]

The great economic expansion of the last century was based on the triple foundation of: (1) technical innovations and the rise of new industries based thereon, (2) the opening up of new territory or new resources in old territory, (3) the growth of population. These three sources were the prime causes of that great and continuous increase of capital formation and investment that gave the period its vigor. Through them was made possible not only a continued rise in the level of real income, but also a fairly full employment of the productive resources, human and other, of the country. Apparently, only through great capital investments has reasonably full employment been reached.

These foundations of our economic structure are beginning to be affected, possibly seriously, by the events of our modern age. The opening up of new territory has practically come to an end. By the end of the nineteenth century, the American frontier had been closed. Today the world's frontier is closed. There are admittedly no more important areas open for exploitation and settlement. True, there is room for industrialization in Russia, India, China, and the Orient. But the monopoly of the Soviets in Russia and of Great Britain in India and the general turmoil in other parts of the Orient do not offer very promising fields for investment.

Population growth has definitely slowed down. It is almost at a standstill in some parts of Western Europe. In the United States, population is rapidly approaching its maximum level. In the 1920's, the population increased by 16,000,000; in the 1930's, it is likely to increase by but 8,000,000; in the

---

[10] A. H. Hansen, "Economic Progress and Declining Population Growth," *American Economic Review*, March, 1939, 1–15.

1940's, at estimated rates, only 5,000,000 to 6,000,000. This decline of population growth is most drastic and affects greatly the rate at which capital investment is likely to be made.

Hence, two of the props of our material progress have been largely taken away, leaving us to depend more than ever before upon the future of technology and invention. Technology and invention will have to be responsible for perhaps twice as much capital investment as when population and new territory played their part; and those who look on the dark side of this picture find little hope that this can be achieved. If it is not—if new inventions equivalent to the railroad, the automobile, and the electrical industry do not appear in sufficient magnitude—then it would seem that our economy may experience a prolonged stagnation, and the great depression extend itself indefinitely.

If now, along with the slowing up of population and the final closing of the frontier in all parts of the world, conditions put an end also to the vitality of invention, then indeed the long trend of progress may have reached a turning point. If this fact were true, then the great depression would have turned out to be not merely a secondary postwar depression or a major depression accompanying the turn of the Kondratieff cycle, or any other of the possible pattern types which we have examined. It would have been one of the major turning points of history and the beginning of the end of the capitalistic system.

Suggested Readings on Part I

J. M. Clark, *Strategic Factors in Business Cycles,* 1934, National Bureau of Economic Research, New York, especially Part II. Typical cycle patterns. A readable study based on researches of the National Bureau of Economic Research.

W. C. Mitchell, *Business Cycles, The Problem and Its Setting,* 1927, National Bureau of Economic Research, New York. One of the most important works on business cycles in modern times.

and the most valuable source for a factual description of cyclical behavior. Chapters III and IV give an admirable and detailed account of the problem of measuring and describing the cycle.

W. M. Persons, *Forecasting Business Cycles,* 1931, John Wiley & Sons, New York. This book contains the most useful and learned historical and statistical analysis of cycles in the United States since 1870.

J. A. Schumpeter, *Business Cycles,* 1939, McGraw-Hill Book Co., New York. Chapters VI and VII of this great work contain a detailed study of long waves of activity from 1787 to 1913. Chapters XIV and XV carry this study from 1919 up to 1938.

Carl Snyder, *Business Cycles and Business Measurements,* 1927, The Macmillan Co., New York. Excellent statistical studies of growth and cyclical fluctuation by a well-known statistician and economist.

W. L. Thorp, *Business Annals,* 1926, National Bureau of Economic Research, New York. Here are the detailed accounts of business behavior that give the background for much of our knowledge of cycles since the early nineteenth century.

E. Wagemann, *Economic Rhythm,* 1930, McGraw-Hill Book Co., New York. Brief and useful studies based on German researches in measurement and description before 1929.

PART II

THEORIES OF THE CYCLE

INTRODUCTION

OUR survey of business cycle behavior, as set forth in the first part of the book, should have revealed how many processes are involved in the ebb and flow of activity which constitute cycles. Originating forces impinging on the operations of business, responses of business conditioned by the framework of our economic institutions, variations in confidence and despair, increase and decrease of money in use, correlative rise and fall of the price level, changes in the distribution of income among the economic classes, changes in the ways in which, under the impact of prosperity or depression, people spend or invest their income—all these multitudinous factors are at work in determining business cycle behavior.

Of these and other factors at work, which are the essential causes of cyclical fluctuation? The answer to this question is the task of cycle theory; and to the exposition of the various answers which may be given, this part of the book is devoted.

Because of the complexity of the forces involved, the possible explanations are somewhat numerous. By the concentration of emphasis on one factor, several apparently satisfactory, but to some degree conflicting, explanations can be evolved. We will develop at length the most important of these explanations in the chapters that follow.

To facilitate this task, the explanations have been arranged under the following classification:

Real causes
Psychological causes
Monetary causes
Causes associated with variations in saving and spending.

Real causes are changes in actual economic conditions capable of setting up cycle fluctuations. They are subdivided into "Innovation" (Chapter VII), "The Principle of Acceleration" (Chapter VIII), and "Agriculture and the Business Cycle" (Chapter IX).

Psychological causes arise from changes in men's attitude of mind toward actual economic conditions. They are discussed in Chapter X.

Monetary causes originate in variations in the total money supply. They may work through changes in effective demand, as taken up in Chapter XI, "Monetary Theory of the Cycle"; or they may work through changes in the rates of interest and their effect on the output of producers' goods, as shown in Chapter XII, "Monetary Overinvestment and the Structure of Production."

Causes associated with variations in saving and spending are treated in Chapters XIII, XIV, and XV. The first of these is devoted to "Underconsumption Theories," which find the cause of cycles in excessive saving and its correlative underconsumption. Chapter XIV takes up the relations of saving and investment. Chapter XV gives an account of the theories of J. M. Keynes, who corrects and extends the simpler underconsumption theories and brings them into their proper relation with the operation of monetary factors and the price levels.

This part of the book ends with a brief appraisal of the current status of business cycle theory (Chapter XVI).

CHAPTER VII

REAL CAUSES: INNOVATION

A REAL CAUSE of business fluctuation is a change in actual industrial conditions, such as a new method of production, or a change in consumers' desire for goods. These "real" causes change the valid expectations of businessmen and, granted they are on sufficient scale, may be effective agents of expansion and contraction.

Such real causes are listed by Pigou [1] as follows: (1) variations in the yield of agriculture; (2) technical inventions or improvements in methods of production; (3) discovery and exploitations of new national resources; (4) industrial disputes; (5) "net changes in taste"; and (6) changed desire for goods involving more than mere transfer of demand from one commodity to another.

Robertson [2] classifies real causes of change as follows: (1) changes in real costs, such as, for example, technological changes; (2) changes in real demand, such as the large increase in derived demand for plant sometimes occasioned by a smaller increase in demand for consumers' goods; and (3) changes in real demand prices—that is, changes in the amount of goods a given group would be willing to offer for the goods of another group, such as would be brought about, for example, by substantial changes in agricultural output. Clearly, Pigou's

---

[1] A. C. Pigou, *Industrial Fluctuations*, Part I, Chap. IV, § 5.
[2] D. H. Robertson, *Banking Policy and the Price Level*, Revised Edition, London, 1932, Chap. II.

list of causes could be rearranged under Robertson's economic categories.

What we have now to examine is how these various real factors may set up alternating periods of expansion and contraction. To this end, detailed consideration will be given to: (1) technological innovation; (2) the variations in derived demand, commonly called the "principle of acceleration"; and (3) agricultural changes. The present chapter will be devoted to technological innovation.

1. SCHUMPETER'S THEORY OF INNOVATION

The possibility that technological change, the most characteristic aspect of a competitive capitalistic society, may be the efficient cause of cyclical fluctuation has found its most renowned expression in the works of Joseph Schumpeter. His theories, which may be found in his earlier work, *The Theory of Economic Development* (1934), and in his recent monumental treatise, *Business Cycles* (1939), may be taken as representative of all those that run in terms of invention, innovation, and technological change.[3]

In a static state, with no changes in methods of production and a stable money supply, business cycles would not and could not exist. External disturbances, such as changes in harvests, would require appropriate adjustments, but these would not be cumulative and equilibrium would be quickly restored. Even continuous changes, such as increase or decrease of population or of capital, would not cause progressive disequilibrium, for these, too, would be absorbed in the succession of small adjustments by which the equilibrating process works.

Our economy is not static; it is dynamic. Its dynamic qual-

---

[3] For a brief statement of his theory, see "The Explanation of the Business Cycle,"· *Economica*, December, 1927. A summary of his ideas is found in H. S. Ellis, *German Monetary Theory*, Cambridge, 1937, Chap. XVIII. In *Business Cycles*, New York, 1939, see Chaps. III and IV.

ity resides in the operations of the entrepreneur, whose typical function is not mere management, or the receipt of windfall profits or losses, or the assumption of risk, but the creation of the new: new ways of doing things, new commodities and services, new markets. It is his innovations, his technological or marketing novelties, that are the dynamic factor in economic life. They set in motion forces which prevail over the adapting process characteristic of equilibrium, and in so doing they create cumulative increases in activity such as characterize booms.

These innovations [4] involve not merely a new and lower cost curve, but also a new arrangement of the factors of production. They involve the setting up of new "production functions." They combine the factors of production in a new way. Furthermore, they improve the expectations of the entrepreneur and lead him, in order to take advantage of the situation, to demand extensive new productive equipment.

How Innovations Disturb Equilibrium

If we may suppose that the economic system is in a state of equilibrium, with all factors of production fully employed and entrepreneurs making zero profits (the equivalent of a static state), then the effect of innovations is to disturb the equilibrium, cause entrepreneurs to expand their activities, and particularly to set up a cumulative demand for productive equipment which has far-reaching effects.

Technological innovations carry with them an enlarged demand for capital. Investment must be carried on extensively—to some extent in additional working capital, but mostly in the relatively permanent forms, such as new equipment, new construction, and so forth. Mere increase in invest-

---

[4] Innovations are to be distinguished from inventions. Invention is the discovery of scientific novelties. Innovation is carrying these inventions into actual performance, or, in common terms, "exploiting" them. Invention is probably much less fluctuating than innovation. It is innovation that is subject to cycles, not invention.

ment by a few innovators, even though they are of considerable importance, would hardly be sufficient to account for the actual increase which occurs during a "boom." Indeed, it might be expected that the increase in investment by innovators would be at the expense of investment by their less gifted rivals, leaving the aggregate investment unchanged; or if this were not the case, that innovation would be so equally distributed over time that it would be merely a factor of growth, which, as has been said, is not to be taken as straining the adaptive process of the economic system.

In reality, technological change is likely to increase aggregate investment greatly. Innovations are not spread out in time; they come in waves. Once an innovation is effected, it attracts imitators—first a few, then more, then crowds of them. The innovation is copied, imitated by some, and forced by competition on others. This factor of imitation makes what otherwise would have been the daring innovations of those who have the imagination or the courage to pioneer, into a wave of progress and improvement that gains momentum continuously. Hence the innovation is not at the expense of others; on the contrary, it draws others along with it, enlarging greatly the aggregate volume of investment.

This expansion, however, can only take place if bank credit is allowed to increase. In a static economy, funds are fixed. What innovators and their followers get hold of must be relinquished by someone else. In a dynamic society, the banks are ready to increase the total supply of credit and to put it into the hands of those whose prospects from innovations promise ability to pay interest. When the innovators obtain their credit, they are in a position to draw productive resources away from those not so fortunate, not by getting away their funds, but by outbidding them in price. Thus a rise of prices begins and continues until enough means of production have been wrung from others to satisfy the demands of the innovators at the new level of prices.

Why the Boom Ends

Innovation can continue to support the upward swing no longer than any of the other possible forces which make for supernormal expansion. The forces which it sets in motion carry with them the seeds of their own decay. In due time, the innovation will substantially increase the output of consumers' goods, and, when these goods emerge upon the scene, the period of expansion will be checked. This expansion depends upon the length of time taken to build and install productive equipment—that is to say, upon the length of the "period of gestation." During this period of time, the efforts of society will be diverted temporarily from the production of consumers' goods, in order that the means for producing goods in the future can be enlarged. When the period of gestation is over, the output of consumers' goods will be enlarged once more, and, because of the innovation, to a level above that which ruled before. The work is done; the consequences of an innovation are here; the expansion is checked; and the boom comes to an end.

Indeed, the boom must come to an end, for the ending of the boom is not merely a cessation of supernormal activity. It involves more than this. It involves the necessity of adapting economic society to the new levels of costs and prices and the new methods of production installed by the innovators. This adaptation is a painful process that overstrains the adaptive process of economic society. The powers of absorption that can take care of a multitude of small disturbances cannot cope quickly with the effects of innovation, for innovations have the most painful consequences for many firms. The innovator is a powerful competitor who, once his output is ready, forces rough changes on his less gifted rivals. He compels them to reconstruct and modernize their plants. He may cause them to lose their markets, go through the painful process of restriction, and even suffer economic death. These acts are not quickly done, and, while they are being done, the disequilibrium which is engendered causes—indeed, takes the form of—a depression.

Were further innovations proceeding, the disequilibrium arising from the earlier ones might be overweighed by the further expansion of activities set up, but this is not likely to happen. Indeed, entrepreneurial activity on any supernormal level must eventually slacken, for two reasons. (1) In the first place, even though the fall in prices consequent to an increase of output has been taken into account in the plans of the innovators, still as output increases and pressure on the factors of production becomes intense, many costs must rise, and a position will be reached where costs and prices once more are equal, profits are eliminated, and further impulse to expansion is removed. (2) In the second place, the upset in normal relations consequent to the innovation, especially after the new or additional products begin to come on the market, introduces such confusion and fluctuation in values that planning becomes more difficult and failure more of a risk. This outcome tends to discourage additional innovation until such time as things settle down and thus removes the only force which might overcome, even if temporarily, the onset of depression.

Once entrepreneurs cease to expand, the forces of disequilibrium are bound to have their way. If entrepreneurs, even of the innovating type, moved by the increasing risks of the time, reduce their activities and pay off their bank loans (what Schumpeter calls "auto-deflation"), the effects on total purchasing power are serious and the depression takes on considerable virulence.

Progress Is Fluctuation

Thus the process of innovation brings about a change in economic activity that takes the form of the familiar pattern of expansion and contraction characteristic of cycles. We expand while innovations are being put into effect; we contract while society is adapting itself to the changes these innovations demand. Progress is not a smooth line; it expresses itself in a cyclical process. There is no conflict between progress and fluctuation. Progress *is* fluctuation. Doubtless in a different society, it might take a different form. Progress might be steady rather than in spurts. But in the particular institutional setting of capitalism, with private property and private initiative (even the collective initiative of great corporations), or more particularly in a special kind of private initiative characterized by the spirit of progress, innovation seems certain to move in a cyclical form. Innovation engenders booms, and booms are followed by depression. Indeed, booms are the cause of depression, and depression will continue until the readjustments required by innovation are reasonably carried through, as they are bound to be. Right relations between costs and prices are restored; the weaklings are weeded out; and business is adjusted to the new economic data. This painful process of adaptation eventually brings a new equilibrium in which the economic system is once more at rest, but with a greater product, new production functions, new price relations, lower prices, and, of course, zero profits. So the stage is set for a new wave of innovations, and, when this wave occurs, another boom is on the way.

Innovations, indeed, are bound to enter into the picture at this very stage, partly because innovation is a continuous impulse in our dynamic society interrupted only by those periods of adaptation which we call "depressions," and partly because depression itself brings about a further impulse to innovation. Not only do the hardships of depression cause more active search for the means of reducing costs, but the reduction of interest rates characteristic of depression makes inventions exploitable which would otherwise have had to lie dormant.

Thus it is that innovation revives and a new cycle of expansion and contraction enters the scene.

Complicating Factors

The simple expansion-contraction process described above is, however, commonly complicated by other factors. The business expansion carries along with it much speculative activity based on optimistic assumptions regarding the continuance of current rates of change. People act as if rising output and the rising prices made possible by bank credit expansion are to continue indefinitely. A "secondary expansion" is set up which becomes so conspicuous as to be taken for the real cause and hides the less obvious but fundamental motive force of innovation. All the usual errors of optimism take place with its accompaniment of great borrowing not justified by productive advantage. One need not repeat the familiar picture.

On the downward swing, the crumbling of the structure, particularly in its state of unjustified enlargement, induces a liquidation and a readjustment more formidable than that needed merely to produce the new equilibrium appropriate to the innovation. In this "secondary contraction," pessimism and the various elements of the vicious spiral of deflation do much damage. This period is what Schumpeter calls "abnormal liquidation."

Because of these secondary factors, what would otherwise be a process of expansion and contraction (or, if one likes, prosperity and recession) has added to it a period of depression and revival, thus making the four phases characteristic of cycles as commonly experienced.

To repeat, then, booms and depressions turn out to be, on examination, the way in which a progressive society adapts itself to technological change. It seems a strange kind of adaptation and a halting sort of progress: two steps ahead, one step back. In Schumpeter's mind, this is the price we have to pay for progress. Possibly there is no avoiding the price. It is conceivable that careful banking policy could make the process

more smooth. Without credit expansion, the plans of innovators and the expansion they engender could not be carried
through.   Unfortunately, while this might eliminate the boom
and with it the subsequent depression, it might eliminate the
progress too.   We do not want to forego the boon of progress.
Furthermore, it may well be beyond the art of banks to devise
just that precise combination of aid and restraint that would
give us progress without the price we now pay for it and make
innovation continuous rather than a succession of spurts.

2. CASSEL'S OVERINVESTMENT THEORY

Among the theorists who find in the forces of progress the
moving cause of cycle is the great Swedish economist, Gustav
Cassel.   Like Schumpeter, he traces the successive periods of
expansion to the dynamic forces of change in our capitalistic
society; but whereas Schumpeter traces the crises which always
follow expansion to the dislocation of price relations caused by
the ending of the period of gestation when the results of innovation are ready for the market, Cassel attributes the end of
expansion to excessive investment outrunning ·the available
supplies of capital.

Let us examine his theory in detail.[5]

According to Cassel, cycles, or, to use his own term, *conjunctures* are essentially the result of the forces of progress.   These
forces include not only technical progress as such (although
this is the chief force) but also the opening up of new countries and the growth of population (which must be included in
progress in the economic sense).   Such progress in itself is
bound to be uneven rather than regular, and from this arises
the stimulus to those bursts of activity that constitute recognizable periods of prosperity.   Every innovation or discovery is a
new opportunity to use fixed capital profitably on a large
scale.   At all times, many such opportunities are just awaiting

---

[5] G. Cassel, *Theory of Social Economy*, New York, 1923, Book IV, especially Chap.
XIX.

the profitable exploitation possible when progress has lowered their cost relatively to the existing rate of interest. When this arises, an extraordinary extension in the production of fixed capital occurs, constituting a new "high conjuncture."

One might suppose that this "high conjuncture," when the immediate impulse that caused it has disappeared, would pass gradually into a period of more moderate activity, but actually this is not the case. Commonly expansion ends abruptly, often in a catastrophe which we call "a crisis" and to the accompaniment of great losses, many bankruptcies, and destruction of confidence in general. Something must have gone wrong with the calculations of the entrepreneurs to create such a situation.

The Supply of Savings Overestimated

What, now, is the mistake which they made? It is not overproduction, which means they had overestimated the demands of the consumer. There is no evidence that this is the case; indeed, quite the opposite. The services of fixed capital have to be used to the utmost, even in the last part of a period of expansion, to meet the demand of consumption. So great is the demand that the materials used in the production of fixed capital, such, for example, as iron and steel, become unmistakably scarce and command high prices right up to the crisis and even beyond. No—what is overestimated is *not* the demands of consumers or the need of the community for the services of fixed capital, but rather the supply of capital, or, going back of this, the amount of savings available for taking over the supply of fixed real capital which is being produced. What is overestimated is the community's capacity to save. If there is overproduction, it is overproduction relative to the volume of saving, not relative to the volume of consumption.

The great volume of fixed capital which is produced in "high conjuncture" is clearly dependent on the willingness of the community to allow resources to be devoted to this kind of production for the future, a willingness expressed in the supply of savings and measured at any time by the prevailing rates of interest. The rate of interest is of crucial importance, for it is the only means the entrepreneurs have of judging the condition of the capital market. The rates of interest at the beginning of a period of high conjuncture are relatively low, since the opportunities which give the expansion its start offer more than usual prospects of return. Hence enterprises may be planned, and planned in large volume, which can be profitable only if interest rates continue on or near their existing level. As many of these enterprises, such as houses, industrial buildings, railroads, and so on, may not be completed for some time and so delay their full demand on the savings of the community, wrong estimates of the state of savings may easily be made. It must be realized that, although the process of producing fixed capital may be financed by the relatively expansible means of bank credit, where loans for pay rolls and purchase of materials are customary transactions, this cannot be done so easily when the fixed capital is ready for sale and has to be paid for by those who have ordered installation. This kind of payment is not commonly financed by bank loans; rather, it calls for the issue of securities which can be sold only in the market for the effective savings of the community.

The Crisis Due to Undersaving

The process of expansion sharply limits the growth of savings, more particularly by the relative rise of wages over profits which distinguishes the later months of a boom. Of all the classes of society, profit-makers tend to save the most; wage earners, the least. At the beginning of a period of expansion, when profits are still high, saving and the formation of capital are at their highest. But the scarcity of labor characteristic of prosperity raises wages gradually at the expense of profit (which may be pinched also by the rise in the prices of scarce materials), and, as this happens, the level of savings becomes relatively inadequate. The greatest savers find their incomes pinched; the wage earners who now belatedly gain increase their consumption. Even though the volume of savings does not fall, it may cease to rise and may become inadequate for the increasing needs of the business world.

The first expression of this appears in the rising rate of interest, which, in itself, is a source of trouble, since it brings about a falling price for instruments of production, the income of which now has to be capitalized at a higher rate. Producers of such instruments may, therefore, be disappointed in their sales price. The real extent of the difficulty tends to emerge only when a large volume of such instruments, including construction, is now completed. It is this event which causes the peak of demand for capital to carry out the necessary payments, and it is this necessity which makes the greatest stringency in the capital market. The evidence of capital shortage now becomes unmistakable. Producers of capital goods may have great difficulty in selling them. They may have difficulty even in financing their current costs of production, and thus will emerge a general inability to complete undertakings that are already begun—so much so, that some will be abandoned at great loss.

To some extent, these difficulties had been hidden by the ability of the banking system to expand its currency. But when the emergence of serious trouble, the fall in the price of capital goods, and the abandonment of enterprises begin to react on the willingness of the banks to advance funds, then the veil is finally torn away, the real scarcity of capital becomes painfully apparent, and the prosperity comes to its all-too-familiar end.

Thus the essential cause of crisis is to be found in the capital market. We save too little; we spend too much. Where the underconsumptionists find the collapse in too much saving, Cassel finds it in too little. We set a pace in the production of fixed capital that we cannot maintain, not because of over-production of goods, but because of undersupply of savings. Monetary theorists, as we shall see, find the origin of this excessive pace in the illusions set up by the elastic currency of our banking system. Cassel finds it in the forces of progress inherent in our way of life. The monetary theorist would remove fluctuations from our economic order by proper arrangements of the supply of money. Cassel, like Schumpeter, sees no way of reducing our cyclical instability save by curbing the factors of progress to which we owe the welfare of our modern world. If progress and change come to an end in a relatively static society, then economic conjunctures will tend to disappear. As long as we have progress, we will have cycles too. Even a socialist community, as long as it hoped to progress, would have cycles, for they are not, as such, inherent in a particular form of economic society.[6]

Spiethoff's Theory

Cassel's theory has been taken as representative of what Haberler calls the nonmonetary overinvestment theories. Some might have preferred Arthur Spiethoff, whose influence in cyclical theory, especially in Germany, has been great. Like Cassel, he puts much stress on the great output of fixed capital as the source of expansion and on the overproduction of this real capital as the real cause of crises. He tends to be remembered largely for his theory that the crisis arises from disproportionality in the supply of goods, whereby, while producers' goods are plentiful, labor-power and the means of subsistence for workers become relatively scarce. This scarcity is disguised in a monetary economy as a shortage of loan capital and leads sometimes to the hope that an increase of bank credit will relieve the situation. The real trouble, which no increase of credit can remove, is a shortage of certain complementary

---

[6] G. Cassel, *Theory of Social Economy*, 624.

goods without which the great supply of fixed capital becomes unworkable. Thus overproduction and underproduction exist side by side. As the result is to bring about a great fall in the demand for fixed capital and a corresponding reduction in employment and incomes, overproduction spreads from its original field and becomes general throughout the whole economy.[7]

---

[7] See Spiethoff's article "Krisen" in *Handwörterbuch des Staatswissenschaften*, 4th Ed., Jena, 1925, Vol. VI, 70–86. There is an admirable summary of Spiethoff's analysis in G. von Haberler's *Prosperity and Depression*, Geneva, 1937, 70–75.

CHAPTER VIII

REAL CAUSES: THE PRINCIPLE OF ACCELERATION

IT IS a matter of common observation that the production of producers' goods fluctuates more violently than the production of consumers' goods. This difference may be accounted for in a number of possible ways, as will be seen later. One of the most interesting of these explanations is often called "the principle of intensified fluctuations of derived demand" or, more simply, "the principle of acceleration."

This principle briefly states that changes in the demand for the output or current services of durable goods tend to cause much greater changes in the demand for the durable goods themselves. Following Haberler,[1] we may distinguish three cases of this principle: (1) durable producers' goods, (2) durable consumption goods, and (3) commodity stocks.

1. Durable Producers' Goods

Suppose 1,000 units of consumers' goods are produced in a given period with the aid of 500 units of equipment, such equipment wearing out in 10 periods—that is, being subject to a 10 per cent rate of depreciation. Then the demand for machinery under this situation, assuming no change in methods and no increase of the demand for goods, is entirely for

---

[1] G. von Haberler, *Prosperity and Depression*, 83.

replacement and consists of 10 per cent of the equipment units per period—that is, 50 units. If, now, a 10 per cent increase of demand for the products takes place, then, again assuming no change in methods of production, an increase in equipment of 10 per cent, or 50 units, will be necessary. Hence to the *replacement* demand of 50 units is added a *new* demand of 50 more, a total of 100 units. The result is that an increase of 10 per cent in demand for the product causes the demand for the equipment to increase 100 per cent.

Furthermore, the degree of this magnification of derived demand is directly dependent on the durability of the equipment. If, in the above illustration, the equipment lasted, on the average, 20 periods, then only 25 would need to be replaced each period, and in equilibrium this constitutes the normal demand. However, a 10 per cent increase of demand for products in this case will add a demand for 50 new units of equipment, increasing the demand from 25 to 75. Thus a 10 per cent increase in commodity demand causes a 200 per cent increase in equipment demand.

On the other hand, if the equipment lasted only five periods, making the normal replacement demand 100, then an addition to the commodity demand of 10 per cent would raise the equipment demand from 100 to 150, a 50 per cent increase. Finally, if the equipment lasted only one period and had to be replaced each time an output was produced (such as coal), then the normal replacement demand in our illustration would be 500. A 10 per cent increase of commodity demand would raise the equipment from 500 to 550, a 10 per cent increase, and precisely equivalent.

The table on page 171 shows this in simple form.

Derived demand decreases sooner than expected. The downward fluctuation of derived demand has a particular interest, for it begins while the demand for the products is still increasing, provided only that the *rate* of increase is beginning to fall.

Commodity Demand	Equipment Replacement Demand	New Equipment Demand	Total Equipment Demand
	(1) Equipment lasts 10 periods		
1,000	50	0	50
1,100	50	50	100 = Increase 100%
	(2) Equipment lasts 20 periods		
1,000	25	0	25
1,100	25	50	75 = Increase 200%
	(3) Equipment Lasts 5 periods		
1,000	100	0	100
1,100	100	50	150 = Increase 50%
	(4) Equipment lasts 1 period		
1,000	500	0	500
1,100	500	50	550 = Increase 10%

Thus, in our original illustration, we have seen that an increase of 10 per cent in commodity demand increases derived demand by 100 per cent. Let us now see what happens if demand increases more slowly and finally ceases to increase, although it does not fall. The following table shows what occurs:

	Commodity Demand	Equipment Replacement Demand	New Equipment Demand	Total Equipment Demand
Normal	1,000	50	0	50
10% increase	1,100	50	50	100
5% increase	1,150	50	25	75
No increase	1,150	50	0	50
Decrease	750	0	0	0

Thus, as soon as the rate of increase slackens, the absolute demand for equipment begins to fall; and, when demand has ceased to grow, the demand for equipment has returned to its original position. This statement has to be modified slightly from consideration of the fact that the replacement demand of 10 per cent of equipment will (in due time) rise to 57 (equipment now in use is 575 units). However, this increase will take place only when the present new machines begin to need replacing—that is to say, 10 periods after the increase of equipment begins to take place. Such an increase, small in any case, and particularly small if spread out over the period, may be neglected as having no importance in cyclical expansions and contractions.

Now, if demand for the commodity begins actually to fall, as is the case in recessions, and furthermore to fall below its ordinary level (1,000 units in our illustrations), at the best we cannot expect the demand in the equipment industry to be higher than 50 (as there are no new units wanted); but it may be that the general feeling of overcapacity in the business will cause business buyers to refrain from replacements (especially if they can more advantageously use the replacement reserves for wages or, even more probably, for dividends) and to reduce the demand before the normal level of 50. If they made no replacements whatever, the demand for equipment would disappear and become zero.

Thus it is possible that the demand for equipment will rise from its normal rate of 50 to a boom rate of 100, falling to 75 when demand is still increasing, and going down even to zero if demand falls much below its ordinary level. Such a situation might come about in the production of locomotives, which in a good year will rise to astonishingly high figures, but in a bad year sink almost to nothing—a range of output quite disproportionate to the change in demand for transportation.

2. Durable Consumers' Goods

Houses, automobiles, furniture, and all other articles which have a relatively long life (relative to the flow of services which they render) exhibit this principle in the field of consumers' goods. A stock of houses, rendering a given amount of service, involves some regular replacement demand, in such wise that in normal conditions, even if no new demand is arising, a regular amount of house building is going on. If demand for house space arises, the same magnification of demand for houses will take place. If the depreciation rate of houses is 5 per cent per annum (houses lasting 20 years), then an increase of 10 per cent in demand for accommodation will increase house building by 200 per cent. (For every 1,000 houses, 50 will be being replaced, and to this must be added 100 more, raising the total to 150 for every 1,000 now in use.)

The case of automobiles is similar. Suppose that cars last on the average five years, so that 20 per cent of existing cars are replaced, on the average, each year. Then an increase of 10 per cent in demand for automobiles will raise the demand for cars 50 per cent.

In this case, as in the case of durable producers' goods, the total demand for cars (replacements plus new orders) will begin to shrink when the demand for automobile service is still on the rise. In similar fashion, the demand for cars will soon fall to replacement levels, and if shrinkage in demand for the service of cars continues, causing users thereof to postpone replacements, demand for cars will fall to very low levels indeed.

3. Commodity Stocks

The same magnifying effects will appear wherever dealers or producers hold stocks in some relatively fixed proportion to sales or production; then any increase in demand for the goods themselves will tend to be magnified when passed on to the producers of such goods.   In addition to the goods ordered to satisfy the consumer, a further order will be made to raise the stocks to their appropriate level.   Thus, if a merchant sold 100,000 units in a month and kept on hand permanent stock equal to one-half month's sales (50,000), then an increase of 10 per cent in the demand of consumers will cause him to order 10,000 more for sale and 5,000 more for stock, a total increase of 15,000.   Thus an increase of 10 per cent in demand increases orders by 15 per cent.   How much this magnification may be depends on the ratio of stocks to sales—the larger the ratio, the greater the magnification.

On the downturn, as demand shrinks, dealers will meet the situation by sales from stock, thus reducing orders more than proportionately.   Indeed, they may cease orders completely until the stock reaches whatever low figure is conventionally regarded as the irreducible minimum.

This process, which is dictated by the business necessity of keeping some stock on hand, is intensified by the normal reaction of dealers to price change.   In periods of rising demand, with prices rising, dealers, for speculative reasons, increase the ratio of stock to sales; similarly, in periods of falling prices, they reduce it.   Stocks are like reservoirs.   They gradually fill up in good times; they gradually empty in bad times.   Hence a variation in demand has magnified effects as the reservoir is gradually filled and emptied.

Secular changes, on the other hand, reducing the ratio of stock to sales, will at the same time reduce the importance of these derived fluctuations.   Thus, during the 1920's, there seemed to be a growth of "hand-to-mouth" buying, originating from various causes, such as ease of delivery via improved transport, standardization of stocks, conscious efforts by dealers' associations to reduce inventories, and so on.   All this reduces derived fluctuations.

One may fairly conclude that the demand for all durable goods, whether producers' goods, durable consumers' goods,

or stock in the hands of dealers, is subject to intensified fluctuations whenever final consumer demand changes.

The Effect of Changes in Replacement Demand

This process of intensified derived demand, which, as we
have seen, is directly proportional to the durability of the
goods concerned, will be further exaggerated provided replacement demand is speeded up in expansion and slowed
down in contraction. If, in the case of producers' goods, the
demand for the output thereof is sufficiently encouraging, replacements may be speeded up, obsolescence scrutinized more
closely, and the opportunity taken to improve the productive
setup. Should this happen, derived demand will be still further stimulated. On the downturn, if the fall in demand is
sufficiently discouraging, replacements may be delayed, the
margin of obsolescence pushed out, and the management in
general be moved to get along and make things do. Under
these circumstances, derived demand will have the maximum
variability.

Similar considerations apply to houses, automobiles, and
other durable consumers' goods. We have already seen that
speculative reasons may cause dealers to increase and decrease
the ratio of stocks to sales in times of rising and falling demand, respectively.

It is to be noted that the opposite of this *might* take place.
In times of rising demand, producers may intensify the use of
existing machinery, draw into service semiobsolete equipment,
and work long hours. In times of falling demand, some producers, at any rate, may find the period convenient for mod-
ernizing their equipment, since prices may be low and, furthermore, the competition for trade puts a premium on methods for reducing cost.

To the extent that this policy is followed, the acceleration
of derived demand is made less intense, and the forces arising
out of durability of equipment are to that degree neutralized.

Moreover, there is evidence that this result may actually occur. If, for any reason, business is experiencing overcapacity, then clearly until such capacity is "used" (that is, used to some normal level, determined by the custom of the industry), acceleration will be delayed. This outcome is, of course, a normal condition as business emerges from depression, and leads to the conclusion that the forces of "acceleration" do not necessarily get under way in the phase of revival. This aspect may explain, also, why after a prolonged boom, such as occurred in the 1920's, recoveries are more than usually difficult. The equipment trades cannot experience much more than replacement demand until capacity is reached. Of course, both in the matter of durable consumers' goods, such as houses, and in durable producers' equipment, such as factory buildings and machinery, revival, wherever it takes place, is likely to encourage optimistic views of future needs and bring about some speculative replacement and additions even though "capacity" has not been reached. If capacity includes a good deal of obsolescent equipment, what looks like addition in less optimistic times may now be regarded as replacement.

All things considered, one may fairly conclude that, whatever changes may take place in replacement policy, they are likely to have the net effect of intensifying replacements in expansion and retarding them in contraction, and that this outcome will tend to increase the intensity of fluctuations of derived demand.

Cumulative Effects

It will be noted that the processes just described may be cumulative. An increase in the demand for automobiles results in a greater increase in the demand for cars from dealers. This increase, in its turn, tends to be translated into a somewhat greater demand for cars from manufacturers, since to the transmitted consumer demand dealers will add their own demand, not only to keep their stocks up to the normal ratio but to take care of possible future increases in sales at

higher prices. Provided capacity is not seriously in "excess,"
the demand for cars from manufacturers will cause them to
add new demand to replacement demand for equipment; and
the producers of equipment will go through the same inten-
sification in their own demand. So the process goes on. The
result is to translate small changes in demand by consumers
for the service of durable consumption goods into large changes
of demand for ultimate equipment and materials. Then the
fluctuations tend to increase in intensity as they reach stages
of production farther away from the consumer, the "highest"
stages showing the most marked fluctuations.

The Statistical Evidence

It is apparent from the various possibilities surrounding the
operation of the principle of acceleration that the actual results thereof in practice may be greatly varied—so much so
that attempts to establish the principle by statistical or other
process of verification are not likely to be attended by success.
Changes in the average age of equipment, changes in the inventory habits of dealers, conscious attempts to stabilize production by increasing plants in recessions, inventions which
hasten obsolescence—any or all of these currently operating
tendencies will obscure any simple relation in actual practice
between changes in consumer demand and changes in the
demand for equipment.

Such evidence as is available cannot be considered conclusive.[2] Clark presents confirmatory evidence in respect to automobile production, 1917–1932. He finds also a significant correlation between increase of rolling stock and *rate* of increase
in traffic demand in the United States. Kuznets finds the
amplitude of cyclical change in the demand for capital equipment in railroads falls far short of that indicated by the net

[2] See J. M. Clark, *Strategic Factors in Business Cycles*, New York, 1934, 38, and
Economics of Overhead Costs, Chicago, 1923, 394–396. S. Kuznets, "Relation between Capital Goods and Finished Products in the Business Cycle" in *Essays in Honor
of W. C. Mitchell*, New York, 1935. J. Tinbergen, "Statistical Evidence on the
Acceleration Principle," *Economica*, May, 1938.

change in the demand for their services. Tinbergen, on the other hand, finds this relation to be high in Germany, but low in France and the United Kingdom. The same author finds no significant correlation in either cotton spinning or shipping, or between changes in production indexes of investment goods and the rate of increase in indexes of consumer demand (although the latter were agreed to be inadequate). This conclusion in regard to general indexes is borne out by Kuznets.

Moreover, even were significant statistical correlation established, it would not prove that the explanation lies in the principle of acceleration and the technological factors involved therein. Thus, even if one established beyond question that durable producers' goods had similar but greater fluctuations than those displayed in consumers' goods, the reason for this would still have to be sought. The reason could be found in a number of possible factors, such as stimulus of profits in rising price periods, tendency of bank loans to be made to producers in periods of credit expansion, tendency to excessive saving and cumulative investment, cyclical fluctuations in inventions, and rigidity of prices of durable goods causing excessive rise and fall of production in the face of changing demand. Thus Tinbergen found that such correlation as existed between output of durable goods and variations of demand could be better explained as a reaction to profits than by the principle of acceleration.

This principle, one must conclude, remains therefore an interesting but unproved hypothesis.[3]

---

[3] The acceleration principle is not commonly regarded as the fundamental factor making for cyclical change. It establishes one reason for the excessive fluctuations of capital goods production, but it does not in itself offer any reason why the advance it initiates comes to an end or how the decline is in time replaced by a period of good times. It merely offers an explanation why expansions and contractions, when they are brought about, are so considerable. It does not account for the origin of these variations. An exception to this general conception of the acceleration principle is offered by R. F. Harrod, English economist, who holds that this principle, which he calls the "Relation," occupies the "pride of place" in the forces which make the cycle. His rather ingenious theories are set forth in his book *The Trade Cycle*, London, 1936, especially in Chapter II.

CHAPTER IX

REAL CAUSES: AGRICULTURE AND THE BUSINESS CYCLE

THAT the national welfare depends upon agricultural prosperity is a common opinion in this country. Businessmen have taken it for granted that changes in the volume of the principal crops are an important factor in business prosperity or depression. They accept good crops as a sign of good business and poor crops as a potent cause of depression. Always they have looked to agriculture to lift them out of slumps, and they are ready to attribute the prolonged depression of the 1930's to the inability of agriculture to stage a recovery of its own. They tend to regard good crops as a spontaneous source of new demand that fills the pockets of the farmer with money, and, at least in the past, they have commonly adjusted their plans to the state of the harvest and the general prospects of the rural districts.

This belief in the importance of the crops has been shared by economists, at least to the extent that they include agricultural changes among the contributing causes of cyclical variation in industry. A few not only accept agricultural factors as important, but also regard them the chief generating cause of cycles. Among them are those who trace cycles to meteorological causes (such as are associated with sunspots) operating through the medium of crop variations.

Therefore, we may ask: Are these opinions well-founded? Are changes in agricultural output capable of bringing about important changes in total activity of business? Are these changes of output independent and autonomous changes, not brought about by changes in business itself? Are they outside forces, "exogenous factors," which, through their effects on the demand for industrial output, may claim to be "real" causes of business fluctuations?

Is Agricultural Change a Cause or an Effect?

First of all, we must know how the line of causation runs. Even if agricultural and business prosperity go together, we cannot deduce that the former is the cause of the latter. It would seem just as probable that business changes would bring about changes in agriculture. Unless we can establish that agriculture is a cause and not just an effect, we can draw no useful conclusions.

However, it seems that both the nature of agricultural changes and the observed behavior of agriculturists point to agriculture as the causal force.

The output of the principal crops, which is what lies in the mind of those interested in the agricultural factors in the cycle, seems to follow a pattern imposed largely by variations in weather and climatic conditions. The important changes in agricultural output arise from changes in yield per acre rather than from changes in acreage planted. Furthermore, although changes in yield per acre could be due to more or less inten- sive cultivation of the soil, they appear to be caused principally by changes in climatic conditions, such as wind, sunlight, rain- fall, and storms. In short, the cause of variation is to be found in the vagaries of nature rather than in the deliberate action of men. Hence, if any relation is established between changes in agricultural and industrial output, the cause will run from agriculture to industry rather than the reverse. Changes in business output *might* induce similar changes in agriculture, but in fact they do not appear to do so, since the observed changes in agricultural output seem due largely to other causes than human volition.

The probability that agriculture is the causal factor is forti-fied by the observed behavior of agriculturists in the face of external change. Obviously, changes in business activity, in-cluding as they do substantial changes in the demand for the output of agriculture, should induce similar changes in agri-cultural activity. But for economic as well as physical rea-sons, the adjustments of agriculture to those changes are not easy. Indeed, it is apt to be so delayed that, for periods as short as the business cycle, it cannot be counted on as an im-portant factor in the situation.

Decisions to change agricultural output must anticipate by many months the actual marketing of the product. This fact makes forecasting difficult and tends to discourage change unless the conditions of demand seem to be reasonably endur-ing. Change often involves (especially where one crop is to be substituted for another) the whole farm organization plan, and this often is greatly limited by the nature of the region, the soil, and the arrangement of the crop rotation. The cost of this transformation is bound to increase the slowness of decision characteristic of agricultural producers. When de-mand falls, production is not reduced so quickly as would be supposed, partly because farmers feel that prices are beyond their individual control and that any reduction of output merely reduces income; even if prices are low, they may still cover direct charges and out-of-pocket expenses, thus making it worth continuing output. Moreover, farming is not merely a source of income but a way of living.

For these reasons, it can be assumed that variations in agri-cultural output are effective causes rather than consequences of accompanying changes in industrial production. They are not only "real" causes, but they are independent causes, not induced by changes in business activity. We can now pro-ceed to investigate how these causes work out and how im-portant they are.

The Consequences of Changes in Agricultural Output

Changes in agricultural output affect business in two distinct ways. One is through changes in the *volume* of crops, particularly in bringing about changes in all the activities directly or indirectly connected with the outturn of the crops. The other is through changes in the *value* of the crops, which bring about changes in the relative purchasing power of the agricultural and nonagricultural population, and thereby various repercussions on business.

Effects of Increase in Volume of Output

The most obvious effect on total business activity comes from larger volumes of crops that must be harvested, transported, marketed, and processed. The harvesting then needs more men; railroads are more active hauling goods; more materials must be put through the various processes; more materials enter storage for carry-over; and a greater flow passes through the wholesale and retail channels. If the increase in output is considerable, farmers may have to add to their equipment. Railroads, elevators, and mills may also have to add to their facilities; and so a new circle of activities that will affect business over wide areas is brought into play.

The increased output of agricultural goods will cause a fall in agricultural prices, the extent thereof depending upon the elasticity of demand for these goods. If, as is commonly held, the demand is inelastic (has an elasticity less than unity), the fall may be considerable. In any case, there will be a fall; if the price level is rising, the fall will be relative to the prices of industrial output. This influence is most favorable on all business using agricultural raw materials because it increases the margin between their own prices and costs. Furthermore, the fall in foodstuff prices reduces the cost of living of workers, disposing them toward acceptance of at least the ruling level of money wages. This fact may be a general encouragement to all manufacturers, as the pressure of activity induced by the volume of crops hardens the price level of nonagricultural output.

It should be noted, too, that these encouraging effects do not have to await the actual realization of good harvests. The machinery of forecasting the state of the crops has become so effective that industrialists may proceed with confidence well before the crops are harvested. Prices are affected in the speculative market for futures before the actual movements of the visible supply. Indeed, it has been noted that the interval between agricultural causes and industrial effects has apparently diminished. Whereas in the 1870's abundant harvests took two years to work out their full effect on the iron industry, and whereas in the 1890's one year was·required, in recent years the effects tend to be simultaneous.[1]

This speeding up of consequences may be furthered by the psychological attitudes of business, which cause entrepreneurs to think of big crops as advantageous and move them to produce more in anticipation of the increased demand they suppose will arise.

There may be still another reason for this anticipatory action. Some economists, notably Pigou and Robertson, hold that the effort-demand for agricultural output is decidedly elastic. They mean that a greater output of agriculture not only stimulates consumption (because of lower prices), but also increases the willingness of industry to expand its output by work, and thereby increase the "real" demand for agricultural products that consists of the output of other products. Robertson argues that, wherever there is less than full employment, the marginal disutility of work is so low and so slow to increase, and the marginal utility of food is so high and so slow to decrease, that workers in general are disposed to favor increase of output (and real purchasing power) and to be ready to aid entrepreneurs in bringing this about.[2]

---

[1] H. S. Jevons, quoted in Pigou, *Industrial Fluctuations*, 39.
[2] D. H. Robertson, *A Study of Industrial Fluctuations*, London, 1915, 133.

It is possible, of course, that the occurrence of a large crop may coincide with a condition of full effective utilization of resources. Nature is capricious and cannot be relied on to stage her agricultural generosity in periods of low industrial output when the stimulus would clearly do the most good. If this untoward expansion takes place, the result may be disastrous rather than stimulating. The demands for capital and labor to carry on the harvesting, transporting, storing, and processing of the crop may strain existing facilities, raise the rate of interest, and, at a time when industry is very sensitive to the slightest increase of cost, supply the one element needed to start a depression. This situation seems to have arisen in the year 1907, when an exceptionally good crop coincided with the culmination of an extended period of expansion.

It seems fair to conclude that an increased volume of agricultural output is definitely stimulating to industry, save when it comes at peaks of expansion when further stimulus is useless and likely to be dangerous.

Effects of Changes in the Value of Agricultural Output

Whatever consequences changes in the aggregate value of output may have on business are brought about through the shifts of purchasing power between the agricultural and the nonagricultural community. While it may be said that a greater volume of agricultural output definitely makes for expansion, the consequences of the shifts in purchasing power following a change in the value of output are neither simple nor certain.

It would seem that shifts of purchasing power would have no special consequence. If the farmers gain in aggregate income from a large crop, as would be the case if demand for their products were elastic, the rest of the people lose proportionately. If the farmers lose, as when demand for their products is inelastic, other people gain proportionately. In the rare case where elasticity of demand is unity, no shifts of purchasing power take place. In a broad way, therefore, and particularly in a closed economic system with no import-export relations, there would appear to be no important consequences to be expected from shifts in purchasing power.

Let us examine this in detail.

Is It Important Who Gets the Money?

On the most probable assumption—namely, that the demand for agricultural products is inelastic—one may expect the following income changes from an increase in crops: The total amount spent on farm products will be smaller. Of this smaller amount, a larger fraction will go to the transporting and distributing agencies, leaving a still smaller amount for the farmers. The railroads will carry a larger volume, with no probable changes in rates per unit of traffic. It is well known that the middlemen, the elevators, the warehouses, the wholesalers, and so on, not only increase the volume of turnover with larger crops, but, owing to relatively inflexible charges, make a larger margin of profit per unit dealt in. Thus the farmers will have less to spend, the railroads and distributive organizations more, and the general consumer will be able to turn the purchasing power released from agricultural uses into the channels of industrial buying.

Thus the aggregate of purchasing power expressed in money is redistributed in various ways, and the redistribution will benefit some industries at the expense of others. Industries catering to farmers will flag; those catering to others will enjoy a boom. Whether this redistribution will tend to generate a cyclical expansion is another matter. If the spending habits of the different groups involved were similar, it would seem that shifts of purchasing power would have no consequences. On the other hand, if habits differed, some effects might be expected. Thus, if the nonfarm population put money into circulation at a faster rate than the farm population, then the shifts involved in our assumptions would tend to stimulate activity as a whole. Or again, if the effect were to shift income from groups that spent to groups that saved and invested, the resulting expansion of investment might, via the period of gestation, set in motion the broad forces of cyclical expansion. However, as little or nothing is known about the comparative economic habits of these various beneficiaries or victims of shifting purchasing power, these possible sources of expansion may be ruled out, and the general proposition reasserted that, in a closed economic system, shifts of purchasing power such as are involved in changes in agricultural outputs are neutral in respect to cyclical changes.

The Effect of Exports

But in a system capable of export, such as that of the United States, other factors are brought into play. With larger crops, exports tend to rise. Furthermore, the wide area into which such exports are sent tends to limit the reduction of price consequent upon the increase of supply, so that the money receipts of the exporters are increased in the aggregate. The corresponding loss of purchasing power is imposed not upon other members of the same country, but upon the industrial or agricultural population of the rest of the world. Moreover, this increase in money receipts will, in international trade, take the form of gold. (Even in the disturbed period of the 1930's, gold flowed into this country, in part at least, in payment for an excess of exports.) This new gold increases by the customary multiple the available supplies of credit, tends to lower the rate of interest, and sets in motion an inflationary stimulus to industry as a whole. If the increase of home agricultural output happens to coincide with a shortage abroad (as, for example, in 1879 and again in 1896 in the United States), then the inflationary consequences are at their maximum, and the stimulus to industry in general is the greatest.

The Net Effect of Agricultural Change

From this analysis, one is tempted to conclude that, save when they occur at peaks of expansion, large crops are a definite stimulus to industry. The increased volume elicits greater activity in various fields, and the lower price reduces the cost of production in industries with the stimulus this implies. It is true that the shifts in purchasing power cannot be assumed to be stimulating, but at least they are not likely to be restrictive and, when they are associated with considerable exporting, may be definitely expansive.

Similar and opposite effects may be expected to follow short crops. The volume of industrial activity needed in connection with the various processes associated with agriculture falls. Costs rise in industries. Purchasing power is redistributed in opposite ways and, while not certainly restrictive, is not likely to be expansive. In case importation or great reductions in export come about, it may have deflationary results.

Thus one would expect to find periods of low crops and high prices corresponding with or preceding depression in industry, just as big crops and low prices would be expected to precede prosperity in industry. Were this borne out in actual experience, we would be justified in holding that agricultural changes are a genuine and potent influence in the formation of cyclical fluctuation. This evidence we will now examine.

The Evidence of Statistics

While the theory set forth above is plausible enough, it is not easy to find any real confirmation thereof in the statistics of agricultural and business output. The evidence is conflicting, so much so that well-known authorities on forecasting allege that "neither as cause nor as effect is the size of the crop related in any consistent recognizable way to the fluctuations of business activity.[8]

---

[8] Hardy and Cox, *Forecasting Business Conditions*, 154.

Some economists have found, for example, that agricultural production, when measured as deviations from a line of moving average or other line of trend, discloses recognizable cyclical fluctuations, with a measurable wave length, say seven or eight years.[4] Others find therein no evidence of cycles, but only year-to-year oscillations.[5] Even where cycles in agriculture are found, it cannot be certainly established that these bear any definite relation to cycles of industrial activity. Henry L. Moore, who is the most uncompromising exponent of the agricultural causation of business cycles, finds a high correlation ($r = .718$) between agricultural production and pig-iron production two years later. Timoshenko, while he finds some positive correlation between crops and pig-iron production, puts the coefficient at a much lower and less certain figure. Hardy and Cox, examining Day's index of agricultural production from 1879 to 1925, find no significant correlation between agricultural production and trade activity.

The Annals of Business

Those who turn their scrutiny to the annals of business activity rather than to statistical correlation seem to get better results. Mr. A. P. Andrew, writing in 1906, concluded an admirable study of the influence of crops on business conditions by these remarks:

While one must admit that the influence of the crops has not always been the predominant factor in business, one can readily perceive their usual and very extended significance. . . . Crises have not ensued invariably and immediately upon every crop failure, nor have eras of up-building followed with clock-like regularity after every bountiful harvest. Yet one cannot review the past forty years without observing that the beginning of every movement towards business prosperity and the turning points towards every business

---

[4] V. P. Timoshenko, *Role of Agricultural Fluctuations in the Business Cycle*, Ann Arbor, 1930, makes it seven years. H. L. Moore, *Economic Cycles*, New York, 1914, puts it at eight.

[5] W. M. Persons, *Forecasting Business Conditions*, 193.

decline (movements which have frequently antedated the actual out-break of crises by several years) were closely connected with the out-turn of the crops.[6]

That this outturn of the crops is essentially the physical, not the financial, outturn is indicated by two other confirmatory testimonies. Both of these, it will be noted, imply that it is the level of agricultural prices, not the level of agricultural income, which is the important factor in business fluctuations.

Thus L. H. Bean, Economist of the Department of Agriculture, after a study of the relation of agricultural prices and business cycles during the period 1875 to 1927, reaches the following conclusions: There were six periods of relatively low agricultural prices. Each of these was followed by a period of industrial recovery and prosperity. There were five periods of relatively high agricultural prices. Each of these, except one (1900 to 1903), was followed by a period of business depression.[7]

A similar conclusion is reached by V. P. Timoshenko in his recent study (1930), *The Role of Agricultural Fluctuations in the Business Cycle*. After examining the relation between changes in the ratio of agricultural to industrial prices and the ebb and flow of business activity, he concludes that revivals seemed "almost without exception" to depend on a low ratio and recessions "very often" on a high ratio of agricultural to industrial prices.

These uncertain conclusions from actual experience are doubtless explained by the somewhat unreal assumptions involved in the theory of agricultural influence.

Agricultural Influences Less Important Than They Seem

(1) We have argued as if agriculture were a unit and agri-

---

[6] A. P. Andrew, "The Influence of Crops on Business Conditions," *Quarterly Journal of Economics*, 1906, Volume 20, 351.

[7] L. H. Bean, "Some Short Time Interrelationships Between Agriculture and Business," in J. L. Snyder's *Business Statistics*, New York, 1929, 107–124.

cultural output one crop produced in one territory under a single set of conditions. Actually there are many crops and many conditions, and effects are likely to be greatly modified by this fact. The conditions favorable to one crop may not favor another. Wheat may boom when cotton is in slump, and the aggregate influence of crops on business may be much reduced in consequence. Furthermore, crops move into market at various times, and the changes in business activity which may be expected do not occur at once. The effects are diffused, and, being diffused, may not be very important as a "starter."

(2) Again the machinery of carry-over which has been developed has the effect of evening up the fluctuations of agricultural output. The bulges of production do not cause equivalent bulges in consumption, including consumption by industrialists; hence, prices do not fluctuate so drastically as they otherwise would. In good years, crops are held off the market, to be disposed of in times of better prices. The tendency on the part of governments to carry this evening-out process still farther, as exemplified by the "ever-normal granary" of the Roosevelt administration, may substantially reduce some of the important impacts of agricultural change.

(3) Finally, it should be noted that, whatever the actual consequences of variations in crops, their power to modify the course of business must depend upon the importance of agriculture in the economic system as a whole. As this importance falls, variations have less significance. As society grows, and with better methods of agriculture continually emerging, less and less of its resources are devoted to the production of its food supply. The fraction of its people devoted to agriculture, or at least that fraction which is devoted to the actual growing of the crops, tends to grow smaller. Its income becomes a smaller fraction of the national income. Indeed, this outcome is what would be expected in any society where average incomes are rising. Gains in income are more likely to be spent

on nonagricultural than on agricultural products. The result of this must be to diminish the effectiveness of agricultural changes as a factor in business cycles.

· On the basis of this rather uncertain factual evidence, one may perhaps agree with Pigou's cautious conclusion that "harvest variations occupy a significant place among the impulses behind industrial fluctuations, good harvests tending to promote expansions and bad harvest contractions of industrial activity." [8]

Meteorological Theories

The recognized fact that agricultural fluctuations are due primarily to natural conditions rather than to human volition raises the question of whether natural conditions themselves are not subject to recurring fluctuations capable of explaining the apparent rhythm that appears in both agricultural and industrial activities. We have seen that business fluctuations are genuine cycles—that is to say, although not necessarily periodic, at least subject to a recurrent rhythm capable of measurement. It has been tempting to speculate that the source of this rhythm lies in the behavior of natural phenomena, which imposes a meteorological or cosmic variation on the facts of . economic life.

Sunspots and the cycle. The most influential, certainly the most celebrated, of the meteorological theories is that of W. Stanley Jevons, the English economist, who in 1875 set forth the proposition that variations in the atmosphere of the sun, as evidenced in the frequency and magnitude of sunspots, determined the rhythmical fluctuations of industry. He was very much impressed with the periodicity of the great English crises of the nineteenth century—1825, 1837, 1847, 1857, and 1866—and with their average length of 10.5 years, the more so when it was currently established that sunspots had a cycle of

---

[8] *Industrial Fluctuations*, 40–41.

10.45 years. Moved by this coincidence, he worked back over the records of English trade in the eighteenth and nineteenth centuries, finding therein 16 crises in 157 years, with an average interval of 10.466 years. Jevons rejoiced to find that the apparently isolated episode of the South Sea Bubble fitted into the pattern.

Convinced that he had laid bare a genuine causal factor, Jevons set himself to find a rational explanation thereof in the sequence from sunspots to weather, from weather to changes in agriculture, and thence to equivalent changes in industrial and commercial activity. Hoping to verify his analysis, he examined Thorold Rogers' great history of agricultural prices but was compelled to admit that 10 to 11 year cycles were not discoverable therein. Apparently other factors besides solar cycles were at work. Nevertheless he kept to his belief that sunspots did explain the periodicity of cycles, and that this came about through agricultural variations. In 1867, John Mills had suggested that waves of emotional aberration might account for crises, and Jevons toyed with the idea that men might be so constituted as to produce a 10 to 11 year cycle of behavior provided even slight recurrent stimuli came via agriculture from variations in solar radiation. This nod to psychological influences did not change the essentials of his theory.[9]

Change in the accepted length of the sunspot cycle, the average of which is now put at 11 to 13 years, and change, too, in the intervals between crises cast a shadow of doubt over Jevons' meteorological theories. His son, H. S. Jevons, attempted to rescue them from decay by appropriate modification. It would appear that, among other meteorological cycles, there exists a three-and-one-half-year period in solar radiation and barometric pressure. The younger Jevons found a three-and-one-half-year period of crop yields and an apparent tendency for trade cycles to appear in seven- or ten-and-one-half-

---

[9] See the papers on commercial cycles in his *Investigations in Currency and Finance,* London, 1884.

year intervals. He thought that two or three cycles of crops were needed to bring about the observed cycles in business, but he made no attempt to demonstrate this connection.

American variations on sunspot theories. The most systematic of recent attempts to establish the relation between meteorology and business cycles is the work of the American economist, Professor Henry L. Moore.[10] Professor Moore, by harmonic analysis, claimed to have discovered an eight-year cycle of rainfall in Ohio and Illinois which he regarded as causing like variations in the yield of agricultural crops. Furthermore, he found a high coefficient of correlation between crop yields per acre and important indices of business conditions. For pig-iron production, the coefficient of correlation was .718 with a two-year lag, and, for the wholesale price level, .800 with a four-year lag. Thus the connection which Jevons was seeking seemed to be at last completed. The cycle of rainfall determined the cycle of crops, and they, in turn, determined the cycles of business activity. But sunspots were not responsible for the meteorological variations; the real cause was the transit of Venus which, at intervals of eight years, comes directly into the path of solar radiations and through its magnetic field affects the streams of electrons flowing from the sun, and hence earthly magnetism and the weather.

In all these variations of the original Jevonsian theory, agriculture is the medium through which meteorological influences are transmitted to industry. However, it appears that this is not the only possible medium. Indeed, it is conceivable that agriculture has nothing to do with the problem. Professor Ellsworth Huntington, always a bold generalizer in his field, offered the theory in 1919 that variations in health, which often seemed to be a result of business cycles, were in fact a cause thereof; and that they themselves were the resultant of variations in weather and solar radiation. The possibility that the

---

[10] See his *Economic Cycles*, New York, 1914, and *Generating Economic Cycles*, New York, 1923.

link between meteorology and business may lie in human, rather than agricultural, vitality has been explored recently in the interesting investigations of Garcia-Mata and Shaffner.[11] After elaborate statistical measurements, the authors conclude that there is a clear correlation between the major cycles of nonagricultural business activity in the United States and the solar cycles of 11 years. The evidence made it almost impossible to believe that this connection is accidental, and, as no correlation was found between the solar cycle and variations of crops, it is clear that the causal connection must be found in some other medium than agriculture.

This medium, the authors suggest, may be found in variations in human vitality brought about either by the variation of ultraviolet rays or by the variation of magnetic activity associated with the cycle of sunspots. Changes in ultraviolet radiation are capable of causing variations in health and vitality, while changes in magnetic activity conceivably may affect the mental state of people and make for the variations of optimism and pessimism which have been observed to be a factor in business cycles. The fact that sunspot cycles have been found to correlate with such evidences of growth as the number of tree rings and the receipts of rabbit pelts indicates that ultraviolet radiation may be the important factor. If these hypotheses are valid, then we have booms simply because we feel good, not because of any impelling change arising from agricultural or any other nonhuman source.

Meteorological influences unproved.   Our survey of meteorological influences has thus led us into conflicting and confusing testimony. That there are meteorological cycles capable of affecting human affairs seems plausible enough, and the correlations discovered by statistical analysis are often, like other correlations, quite impressive. But economists seem content to remain skeptical in regard to these theories, and perhaps

---

[11] C. Garcia-Mata and F. I. Shaffner, "Solar and Economic Relationships," *Quarterly Journal of Economics*, Vol. 49, November, 1934.

it will be enough to accept agricultural change as among the factors contributing to cycles, without any commitment as to the validity of meteorological causes.

Indeed, agricultural influences are probably, at best, an example of episodic initiating causes, or. starters, determining often the time of revival or recession and thus the length of particular cycles. They are in themselves not adequate to account for the actual shape of the cycle, which is more probably the result of the responses made by the business world to originating forces, responses which are determined by monetary, psychological, and institutional factors.

CHAPTER X

PSYCHOLOGICAL THEORIES [1]

THE theories which we will now examine are founded on the distinction between real causes and psychological causes of expansion or contraction of economic activity. A real cause is a change in actual economic conditions. A psychological cause is a change in men's attitude of mind toward actual economic conditions. When a real cause emerges, it can be only because economic conditions have actually changed, as, for example, an increase in the output of agriculture because of favorable weather. A psychological cause can exist even though no change in actual conditions has occurred, as when, in a boom, each businessman is prone to exaggerate the expectations of profit likely to be obtained by himself as compared with others. Ordinarily, the two causes are closely related and interconnected. A change in actual conditions (a real cause) sets up a similar change in men's attitudes, so that the consequence on activity is partly a result of a valid reaction to the real change and partly a further and added result of seeing this change in a somewhat different attitude of mind.

In a world where no real cause leading to change in activity arises (a stationary state), it would seem unlikely that psychological causes of change could exist, since circumstances would repeat themselves with such regularity that change in attitudes of mind towards economic data would scarcely tend to occur.

---

[1] See especially A. C. Pigou, *Industrial Fluctuations*, Part I, Chapters VI and VII.

Nevertheless, even here psychological causes *could* arise, as, for instance, if variations in vitality occurred such as would lead to periods of optimistic or pessimistic attitudes among the generality of persons. On the other hand, even in a world of real causes of change (a nonstationary state), psychological causes need not arise, provided persons were perfectly intelligent and capable of forming valid judgments (unbiased by changes of attitudes) in respect to the real causes which occur. People being what they are, a world of real causes is likely to be a world in which changes of attitudes do take place; consequently, judgments are rendered and actions are taken which are not valid judgments or correct actions and which would not appear if we were not prone to mistakes.

Fundamentally, therefore, psychological causes arise from mistakes or errors of judgment. We get a wrong view of the facts. We are misled. We change our view of the facts, although the facts have not changed; and when the facts do change, our frame of mind is somehow so influenced that we cannot make correct judgments as to the significance of the change.

Therefore, we may speak alternatively of psychological theories as theories based on the working of error. It is now our task to examine the sources of error in economic society and lay bare the various reasons why mistakes in judgment occur, and particularly why, instead of canceling out (mistakes in one direction canceling mistakes in another), they tend to work all in the same direction for considerable periods of time.

Errors of Forecast

The fundamental cause of error, or, to be more exact, errors of forecast, is to be found in two different but interrelated aspects of modern industrial societies. The first of these aspects is the long and roundabout processes of production imposed on us by a capitalistic economy. The second is the individualistic organization of production by which a multitude of independent entrepreneurs, bound together by no central authority, but each one specializing on his own part of the whole, try to satisfy as best they can society's demand for goods. Both of these aspects happen to be found together in the typical modern economy; but both are not equally inherent or inescapable. The first is fundamental to any society using capitalistic methods. It would be here, even if the second were not. The second, on the other hand, is not essential or inherent. In fact, there is evidence that it is disappearing.

Let us now see how these features of our economy open the way for errors of forecast, such as are capable of producing alternating periods of expansion and contraction.

Roundabout Processes of Production

Owing to the complex division of labor and the organization of production into many stages from the raw material production to the delivery of the goods into the hands of the ultimate consumer, there emerges a more or less extended period of time between the decision which a producer must make and the final results of his decision in a flow of consumable goods. The major activities of our society are undertaken in anticipation of demand. Goods are not made to order. "Expected facts are substituted for accomplished facts as the impulse to action," and, when this is so, the way is opened for errors of forecast. The result is a possibility of mistake and wrong adjustment, the realization of which is postponed too long to be of corrective value. When the belated realization has come, the evil has already been done.

Furthermore, the longer the average interval which elapses between decision and final result, the greater the possibility of mistake and the more serious the probable maladjustment. Hence one would expect to find and one does find the greatest variation in activity in those industries which are farthest removed from the ultimate consumer, the iron and steel industries, the copper mines and smelters, and the construction trades—in short, the industries producing capital goods or production goods. If it is merely a question of deciding, for example, whether, with existing plant, to produce more shoes, the range of error is small. Forecasts can be made of the probable market for shoes a month hence without much danger that, in so short a time, unexpected influences will come in to change the demand. But if a plant for making shoes, which may take many months to construct and to put in working order, is to be erected, what must be made is a forecast of the demand for shoes a year or two years hence. During this interval of time, in a dynamic society, the possibilities of disturbing factors are so great that the range of error is much enlarged.

Hence, the more dynamic the society, the more important is the operation of error as a cause of fluctuation. A dynamic society is a society in rapid change, and rapid change means more readiness to make far-reaching decisions, at the same time that it introduces more uncertainty as to the ultimate usefulness or value of the results of the decisions. Thus some of the most notorious booms and crises of the nineteenth century, first in England, then in the United States, were directly associated with, and presumably attributed to, the excessive expansion of railroad building. The enthusiasm created by the development of a new industry and, later, the successive waves of expansion of railways into new territory made errors of forecast easy; while the lapse of time between effort and fruition, with all the possibility of change involved, exposed even sensible forecasts to unusual hazards.

Other Causes of Mistakes of Forecast

The same danger of mistaken forecast which arises from the time interval that modern methods have inserted between production and consumption is imposed on us by distance. Producing for a distant market makes forecasting more difficult by imposing on the forecasters the problem of calculating the demand, exposed as it is to every conceivable change, of remote groups of purchasers. One might add that, as modern ways of living are increasing both the time and the distance intervals between the various stages of production and final consumption, the problem of forecasting may well be becoming more formidable and the danger of cumulative error more serious.

There is some ground to believe, further, that the possibility of error is enhanced by the increasing variability of consumers' choices in a highly complex industrial economy. Consumers in a wealthy society have, on the average, a relatively high standard of living; a standard which, by its very nature, is bound to include not only a great variety of goods, but many goods which are well above the level of staples. In a lower standard, staple and relatively unvarying consumption rules. In a higher standard, the importance of staple goods is much less. Probably, therefore, merely from this angle, producers cannot depend upon the certainty of consumption and find themselves exposed to greater variations than would be existent in a simpler society. Their expenditures on advertising and on all the means and maneuvers by which they try to carve out and keep a particular market seem to offer proof that this proposition is true. Curiously enough, these very efforts to standardize and stabilize individual markets may increase the uncertainty of all. The competition in advertising and marketing is keen, and the result may well be not to increase the certainty of any one producer's market but, by enlarging the consumer's area of choice and encouraging him to shift from this commodity to that, to increase the uncertainty of all. Clearly, this outcome must increase the probability of errors of forecast.

The Influence of Competition

The errors of forecast imposed upon entrepreneurs by the time-consuming processes of production are reinforced by the fact of industrial competition.

In a competitive society, the output of any industry is the work of many independent producers. They have no agreements with each other to produce any given output. No one knows what the others are doing or what the aggregate output is going to be. The total output is the unplanned result of the efforts of all these uncoördinated producers. In these circumstances, an increase of demand is likely to result in an excess of output. Each producer, as he feels the impact of demand, will move to increase his output. As he has no way of knowing what his rivals are doing, and as his natural reaction to a favorable situation is to be overhopeful, he will seek not only to obtain his due share of the expansion, but also to improve his competitive position. A few producers may expand in this way with impunity; but if all attempt to do so, they will surely exceed the level of profitable output and glut the market with goods.[2]

To put it otherwise, if the lengthy processes of production may make it possible to miscalculate total demand, the fact of competition makes it probable that each producer will miscalculate his expected share of this total.

Furthermore, just as each producer in a competitive society overestimates his probable share of sales in a period of expansion, so he will underestimate his costs. In order to produce his added output, he must be prepared from time to time to buy more materials, hire more labor, and invest more capital. He must estimate as best he can the supplies of these factors and the prices at which they are likely to be available. For some materials, he can protect himself by "forward contracts" or "futures"; for others and for all labor and capital, he must pay the current price. As each has no way of knowing what others are doing, and as each is apt to give too little weight to probable rivalry in the market, the ultimate result is likely to

---

[2] See W. H. Beveridge, *Unemployment, A Problem of Industry*, Revised Edition, London, 1930, 59–60; and C. O. Hardy, *Risk and Risk Bearing*, Revised Edition, Chicago, 1931, 83–85.

be a general and unexpected scarcity of labor, materials, and capital, and a rise in prices, wages, and interest beyond all expectation.

These errors, of course, are the result of ignorance, and it would seem that adequate information should eliminate them. If we knew the relevant facts on the state of production, the stocks of goods in store, and the movement of goods into the hands of consumers, errors of this sort, even in a competitive society, would be greatly reduced. But these and other pertinent data have been notoriously lacking in our supply of economic statistics. We have no adequate data on expansion of capacity, either indirectly in the volume of savings designed for capital investment or directly in the volume of new issues placed on the capital market. Indexes of general production we have, but indexes of inventories or stocks on the way to the consumer are glaringly defective. Even consumption is represented only by such data as the sales of department stores in certain cities or the sales of the great mail-order houses. In the face of this scanty supply of statistical barometers, each businessman does the best he can, guided by experience and particularly by the current changes in price.

The Period of Gestation

The errors of forecast which these conditions foster are admirably illustrated by the behavior of business during what is commonly called the "period of gestation."

The period of gestation is the period of time covered by any given process of production. It is the period during which goods are being born and is measured from the inception of production to the day when the product is ready for delivery. This period of gestation may be short or it may be long; but for most commodities it is an appreciable interval. For some goods, such as additional consumable goods from existing equipment, the period may be very short—a day, a week, or a month. For others, such as mills, steel plants, office buildings, and railroads, the period may be one, two, or several years. For slowly ripening resources, such as orchards, coffee and rubber plantations, forests, and so forth, years may have to elapse before they are ready to produce.

In a competitive society, this period of gestation gives rise to a very definite form of cumulative maladjustment directly traceable to errors of judgment induced by the situation itself. These errors of judgment are the entirely natural, and apparently appropriate, responses of entrepreneurs to the situation disclosed to them.

Let us suppose that the demand for goods has increased (either from without, as by an invention or an increase in crops, or from within, as by an increase in money in circulation and use), and that, therefore, the price level of consumable goods is rising. Under these conditions, entrepreneurs proceed (and rightly) to increase their output. Activity therefore increases. But during the period of gestation, despite this activity, output of consumable goods is not increased. The original increase in demand remains unsatisfied, prices remain high, and the motive to increase output still operates. What is more, to the degree that activity has already increased (and quite apart from any increase in consumption goods), more wages have been paid to workers as a whole. This increase in total wages (as well as all incomes from productive factors) tends to add to the demand for consumption goods, precisely at the time when no more consumption goods have yet been made available. As a result their price level is bound to rise.

So long, therefore, as producers judge the situation of the market by the level of prices (and this they are bound to do in a competitive market where the only practicable clue to demand is price), they will be more and more led astray. Were they monopolists, or were they organized into highly integrated associations, they might be able to realize that what is going on is not a growing (relative) scarcity of consumption goods, but only the delay in their appearance incident to the period of gestation. As it is, they have no clue to the volume of production already set in motion and, therefore, tend to follow, even if somewhat cautiously, the indicator of price; and this indicator remains set at a high level.

Thus, during the period of gestation (which, of course, is no single period, but many different periods), a powerful and continuing tendency to produce is at work, and as a result the response to any given increase in consumptive demand is a magnified increase in the output of consumption goods. When, in due time, the period of gestation comes to an end, and the volume of goods coming on the market turns into a flood, the consumption goods markets will be overloaded and prices will fall.

From this angle, a boom is due to an error of forecasting arising from the period of gestation. The magnitude of the error and, therefore, the extent of the boom clearly depend on the length of this period. If it is short, the boom does not go very far. If it is long, it may be very extensive indeed. Thus a boom involving a demand for nondurable consumption goods, what might be called a "consumption boom," must be a short boom, because the interval between demand and actual output is short. (Such, it is argued, was the post-armistice boom of 1919–1920.) Where the boom is caused by an increased demand for producers' goods (itself based on the expectations of a sustained demand for consumption goods) or for the more durable and more slowly produced consumers' goods, then the boom is likely to be relatively long. All booms come to an end; and the end of every boom comes when, the (average) period of gestation being over, producers are brought face to face with the realities and find that available output at current prices has outrun the demand.[3]

---

[3] The French economist Aftalion, who is an exponent of this aspect of the period of gestation, has compared the process to the time between kindling a fire and the moment when it begins to give heat. If one were guided purely by the thermometer

Speculative Influences

This tendency to overexpansion as a result of watching price indexes is reinforced by the activities of speculative middle-men, who, scenting an upturn of prices, add to their inventories in order to reap the advantage of the price change. When they do this, they are bound to distort still more the picture which producers of commodities have drawn of the state of demand; for they convey the impression that ultimate demand has increased by the total amount of their orders, when in fact part of the increase represents only speculative dealings and not any net increase in the demand of consumers. This speculative demand ceases just as soon as the expectations of rising prices begin to appear unfounded. When prices begin to fall, it is replaced, as far as speculative dealers are concerned, with disinvestment in inventories, and so adds a further weakness to the price structure.

There is a tendency also on the part of dealers or intermediary manufacturers, under the fear of scarcity of materials, to give more orders to manufacturers than they expect to be filled; and when this is done, a false sense of buying activity may be engendered which is given a rude shock when, later, dealers, as they must do, cancel their excess orders.

Mutual Generation of Errors

We are now in a position to answer a question which has been lurking in ambush throughout this discussion—namely: Why is it that errors of forecast all move in the same direction

---

(and not by experience), one would be led to alternate overheating and under-heating of the room. When the thermometer was low, one would put on more fuel, and because the delay in getting heat keeps the thermometer low, one would add to the fire continuously. Eventually the heat would come and the temperature rise uncomfortably. As it remained high for quite a while, no effort would be made to keep up the fire, and it would eventually go out, leaving a cold house and the necessity of starting all over again.

See also the amusing illustration in Keynes, *Treatise on Money*, Volume II, 223.

rather than move now this way, now that, as one might expect? After all, the laws of probability would seem to indicate that errors would cancel out. If a producer makes an error in one direction, another producer should make an error in another direction. If producer A overestimates the demand, why does not producer B underestimate it? The one kind of estimate would seem as likely to occur as the other; and that being so, why should we expect a cumulative kind of error which alone could lead to a boom (or a depression)?

The reaction of producers to the gestation period throws light on the answer to this riddle. Errors are in the same direction for a very good reason. All businessmen tend to make the same error because all guide their operations by the same index—namely, the index of consumer prices. This index, throughout the period of gestation, persists in telling them to add to their production.

If businessmen watched another index, such as an index of construction (were such an index available), or even if they kept their eye on the price index but watched it with that higher degree of skepticism which one would suppose the experience of previous booms would have sown in their minds, these cumulative and reinforcing errors, all in the same direction, might not occur. Businessmen being what they are, and thinking, as they always do, in terms of price, this kind of excessive reaction to what was originally a small change in demand is held by theorists of the psychological school to be unavoidable.

There is still more to this situation of generalized error. Not only does generalized error tend to arise from a common reliance upon what really is, at the moment, a faulty index, but, in addition to this, the emergence of an error in forecast in one quarter tends to cause similar errors in other quarters as well, and so on in a widening circle until whole areas of activity are being affected. In Pigou's language, what we have to deal with are "waves of optimism and pessimism" generated by the nature of human beings and the conditions of modern business life.[4]

Waves of Optimism and Pessimism

Businessmen, whether in the same or different occupations, are bound together by the invisible ties of social psychology. Optimism in one quarter of business tends to generate optimism in other quarters, particularly if the original burst of optimism is displayed by powerful business personages whose sentiments impose themselves readily on the mass of business "followers." Optimism, as Mitchell suggests, is really one of the social states of mind. One can be optimistic as an individual; in a crowd, it is vastly easier. The close contact among all businessmen that modern business life makes easy, the conventions, the luncheon clubs, and the cheer sessions, where optimism is deliberately developed—all these make common sentiment spread quickly. In good times, the wave of optimism eventually affects even that constitutionally cautious, not to say pessimistic, creature, the banker; and when this happens, the easier conditions which follow in the money market, the less forbidding aspect of banking officials which is found in financial institutions, make an even more favorable environment for the spread of optimistic attitudes of mind.

Furthermore, the actual operation of error for a while strengthens this optimistic sentiment by making it appear that everybody is right. If A overestimates the reasonable expectations which he should be entertaining, he puts more incomes in the hands of all those who work for him or supply him in any way; and this rising income increases the business of B, who, in turn, can afford to be optimistic, thus eventually increasing the income of C (and, of course, of A also), and so on in ever-widening circles.

A further cause of interrelated sentiment is the intricate

---

[4] A. C. Pigou, *Industrial Fluctuations*, Chapter VII.

debtor-creditor relation which is found throughout all business connections. Most business concerns are both borrowers and lenders. They get materials on credit; they sell them on credit to others. If, because of an excess of enthusiasm on the part of the producers from whom a concern buys its materials, it is able to get larger and longer credits, then it is more inclined to pass on the same concessions to its customers, to whom it grants in turn longer and larger credit. Thus good feeling is apt to pass on from one manufacturer to another, backwards, forwards, and laterally, each concern to some degree aiding in the good fortune of the others. By this financial interdependence, a generalized attitude of optimism, which makes for broad-scale increase of activity throughout the whole business system, is engendered.

As the psychological theorists see the matter, business is living, during expansion, in a state of great expectations, which however, being false, are obviously doomed to disappointment. Some day (the time being largely determined by the length of the gestation period for important processes of production) the truth is bound to come out. When it does, the whole airy fabric collapses. The dream is over; we wake to the unpleasant reality. The expectations of profit give way to fears of loss. Once this has occurred, the process of contraction, closing down factories, canceling orders, putting people out of work, and leaving productive resources idle or partly occupied sets in with increasing intensity.

Psychological Influences in Depression

The cumulative process of deflation and reduced activity characteristic of depression is essentially due to the same type of psychological influences that made the boom. The very magnitude of the boom, which is another way of saying the very magnitude of the optimistic error, tends to make an equally great excess of pessimism. The first check to business activity, brought about, presumably, by the disappointed expectations of some business concern, extends to all firms with which the former has business dealings. The long chain of debtor and creditor relations which made possible the "mutual generation of optimistic error" now works in the other direction. Each concern that finds its own credit-obtaining capacity reduced reduces in its turn the credit it is willing to extend to others. If, to cope with this deflationary situation, business turns to the banks, it commonly finds that already the banks, sensitive as they are to turns of business sentiment and threatened moreover in their most sensitive place—namely, their reserves—are beginning to draw in their loans or, at least, to scrutinize requests more severely. This discovery adds to the universal spirit of pessimism.

If transactions have been heavily financed by borrowing, particularly if plant construction and other equipment activities characteristic of a boom have been financed by bond issues, the trouble is greatly increased. The pressure of debt payment induces despairing attempts to keep things going; to continue production by borrowing still more; and to hold off the inevitable price collapse by various devices for keeping up prices. This attempt must be futile in the end. When the inevitable collapse comes, it is accompanied by greater fall in price, greater restriction of production, more bankruptcies, and a more prolonged period of gloomy views and pessimistic attitudes; so much is this so that the reduction of activity is as much exaggerated in the period of depression as was the increase of activity in the period of boom. The period of gestation now works the other way. Just as it took time to get products ready for consumption, so it takes time to reduce all along the line the processes by which output is made available. During this period of reduction, the flow of goods is only gradually reduced. It cannot be shut off immediately. For this reason, prices continue to fall, and fall farther than they would fall were output reduction more speedy. In due time, however, the full effect of the reduction in activity at last reaches the ultimate market, and, when that occurs, it becomes obvious that the reduction has been excessive. Demand was not so low as pessimistic views had estimated. By this time, stocks have been exhausted, and demand is actually incapable of finding satisfaction.

Thus the foundation is laid for another period of revival. Shrewd producers who have forecasted these events begin to make money. Prices begin to rise once more. Expansion is now justified. But once again the period of gestation makes quick expansion difficult and so lays once more the train of causation which, as we have seen, generates the errors of optimism characteristic of booms. Thus the cycle is completed, and a new cycle begins.

Conclusion

Psychological explanations of cycles can hardly claim to be more than elucidations of one important factor in the process of expansion and contraction. The errors of forecast which they discuss could scarcely arise independently. Fundamentally, they are faulty reactions to "real" changes. Without the "real" change, the conditions necessary for the operation of error could not be expected to emerge. For this reason, psychological causes alone seem insufficient to account either for the beginning of a revival, after a period of depression, or for the crisis at the end of a period of expansion. Doubtless the crisis is caused by the realization of the extent of an error of forecast. Some particular event precipitates the trouble, such as a shortage of capital due to inadequate savings; or (from a contrary point of view) an insufficiency of consumers' demand due to excessive savings; or the limits of bank credit; or a scarcity of labor and its accompaniment in rising costs. Similarly, some "real" cause seems necessary to explain the revival after depression, a scarcity of consumers' goods, the effects of the application of invention, an influx of money, and the fall in the costs of production. The operation of these "real" causes furnishes the background for the emergence, once again, of the psychological factors, the atmosphere of optimism, in an area of uncertainty, and so prepares the way for the errors of forecast which lie at the heart of this type of theory.

One must admit the existence of these changes of confidence, of business "tone," of the general mental atmosphere or "climate." The annals of business history confirm this at every point. While the writers whose theories we have examined in other chapters would regard these psychological manifestations as merely contributory factors in a process of expansion or contraction fundamentally produced by other causes, the psychological theorists (embracing all those who put major emphasis on errors) raise these manifestations to first place in the scheme of causation.

CHAPTER XI

MONETARY THEORY OF THE CYCLE[1]

THE monetary theory of the cycle is based on the following propositions:

(1) That the known behavior of the cycle could not occur in the absence of an elastic money supply.

(2) That the monetary supply of all countries with modern banking systems is elastic and capable of expansion and contraction.

(3) That such expansion and contraction, when they occur, lead to cumulative expansion and contraction of industry and are sufficient to account for the business cycle, even if no other causes were present.

(4) That the normal behavior of bankers is such as to cause them to bring about these contractions and expansions instead of controlling the monetary supply in the interests of stabilization.

(5) That, therefore, the business cycle is essentially the result of variations in the money supply produced by the banking systems of advanced industrial communities.

---

[1] The best-known exponent of a monetary theory of the cycle is R. G. Hawtrey, English economist, who has set forth his views in many books and articles. The following books may be consulted: *Good and Bad Trade*, 1913; *Currency and Credit*, 3rd Ed., 1928; *Trade and Credit*, 1928; *The Art of Central Banking*, 1933; *Capital and Employment*, 1937.

The student will find a systematic discussion of the relation of monetary factors to business cycles in A. C. Pigou, *Industrial Fluctuations*, Part I, Chaps. XII to XVII inclusive. See also W. C. Mitchell, *Business Cycles: The Problem and Its Setting*, Chap. II, Sec. IV, "The Monetary Mechanism," for an acute analysis of money as an active or passive force in cycles.

The Necessity of an Elastic Currency

The most striking characteristic of the business cycle is the simultaneous fluctuations in the volume of production and the general level of prices.   A period of expansion is marked by the concurrent increase of production and prices; a period of contraction, by their concurrent decrease.   Yet this behavior is contrary to reasonable expectation.   One would naturally assume that the increased volume of output would result in falling prices; the decreased volume, in rising prices.   This outcome is precisely what would happen if the total purchasing power of the community remained unchanged.

If the total purchasing power is constant, any increase in aggregate output must be accompanied by a lowering of the price level, just as any increase in the price level must be accompanied by a reduction in the aggregate level of production. In other words, with an unchanging purchasing power, either a general rise in prices or a general increase in production, but *not both,* could occur.   In fact, as both occur in the typical expansion phase of a cycle, it would seem that the total purchasing power must have increased.

This proposition can be stated in terms of the familar equation of exchange, $MV = PT$.   In this equation, PT, the product of output and price level, undergoes alternate increase and decrease during the expansion and contraction phases of the business cycle.   This change could not occur without a corresponding increase and decrease in MV, the product of the money supply and its velocity of circulation, which is the total purchasing power of the community.

Carl Snyder of the Federal Reserve Bank of New York, after a study of American statistics, finds such a close relation over a period of years between the variations of velocity (V) and the volume of trade (T) that he is moved to hold that the change in price (P) is accounted for substantially by the variations in the money supply (M).[2] Professor Pigou, on the other hand, basing his conclusions on English statistics, finds that the variations of money (M) more consistently parallel the variations of trade (T) and that the variation of prices (P) is primarily accounted for by the variations in velocity (V).[3] These opposite conclusions indicate how difficult it is to separate out the precise relations between the changes in M and V and the changes in P and T, respectively. At least it can be said that only a concurrent change in total monetary purchasing power, implying a concurrent change in both volume and velocity of money, can account for the actual increase in the monetary value of trade which is expressed in the product PT.

One may conclude that the behavior of the cycle is dependent upon the existence of an elastic currency, in the broad sense of a variable volume of purchasing power in use, and that, if this elasticity were not present, the changes in the price level so characteristic of the cycle could not occur. Were this elasticity not present, indeed, it is difficult to see how, except in the case of a reduction in costs of production due to technology, any expansion such as marks the prosperity phase of a cycle could get under way, for expansion must then be accompanied by a falling price level and be speedily brought up against sharp limits. As costs do not fall proportionately with prices, profits must contract, and whatever optimistic impulse may have started the expansion must surely fade away. It would be possible under an inelastic currency to expand production in one quarter at the expense of production in another, but the general business expansion which distinguishes the rising phase of the cycle could not occur. However, this consideration is not important since, as a matter of fact, the currency of the typical industrial community is notably elastic, in respect to both money supply and its velocity of circulation.

---

[2] C. Snyder, "New Measures in the Equation of Exchange," *American Economic Review*, Dec., 1924.
[3] A. C. Pigou, *Industrial Fluctuations*, Part I, Chap. XV.

The Elasticity of the Money Supply in Fact

The monetary systems of most advanced industrial countries during the period in which cycles have been noted consist of bank deposits and paper money based upon a foundation of gold. If the supply has cyclical variations, they must be found either in the gold supply or in the superstructure of credit money.

1. **Gold.** Variations in the monetary gold supply of a country can arise from variations in the output of mines (if there are any), from changes in the proportions of gold going into monetary and industrial uses, and from variations in the import and the export of gold, this being, in turn, dependent on variations in the balance of international payments. Let us examine briefly these different sources.

Rationally, one would suppose that all these sources of gold supply would be subject to cyclical fluctuations. For example, a sudden increase of gold by discovery would start a rise of the price level. Then, as prices rose, the operative costs of gold mining encroaching on the fixed price at which gold is sold would make marginal mines unprofitable and gradually shut off supply. The rising prices would turn gold from the mints to the industrial market, where it would be worth more. With rising home prices, imports would tend to increase relative to exports, and gold would flow abroad to meet adverse balances. Thus all the sources of supply would work together to bring expansion to an end.

With the end of expansion, a period of falling prices, in which all the conditions would be reversed, would begin. Operative costs in gold mining would fall relative to prices and encourage marginal mining. The industrial market would be less attractive to gold than the fixed price of the mint. The falling prices would encourage exports over imports and would start an inward flow of gold. All this would reverse the trend once more, and so on in an endless cycle.

However, the evidence reveals that these rational expectations are not borne out. Gold supply, at least in the United States, does not have these short-time variations; or, if they occur, they are of such small magnitude as to be of negligible importance. Significant short-time changes in the volume of gold, largely from importation, as in the period of 1915–1924, have occurred, but they have not been regular features of business cycles.

Gold mining is primarily speculative and not in any certain way connected with the level of prices. Discovery of new mines and new ways of working old ones may counteract high costs of mining, just as exhaustion of available veins may counteract otherwise low costs of mining. Capital scarcity in depression may be a restrictive factor even if costs are low, just as ease of raising capital in prosperity may be a stimulating factor even when other costs are high. In any case, the enormous size of the existing stock of gold belittles the importance of changes in the annual output. With output averaging perhaps 3 per cent of the existing stock, only continued increases or decreases of output over prolonged periods are capable of exercising important influences over the price level. Hence they will cause not cyclical variations, but, if anything, long-period fluctuations such as have been observed by Kondratieff. As such they do, of course, influence the proportions of prosperity and depression over long periods of time.

Variations in the use of gold in the arts seem to follow rational expectations; but the total amount of gold involved (ordinarily about ¼ of mined gold goes into the arts) is too small to make important effects over short periods of time. In severe depressions, where the discrepancy between the currency value and the industrial value of gold may be very substantial, large sums may be added to monetary gold by the process of diverting to the monetary use large fractions of mined gold and quantities of treasure, representing past industrial and artistic production, such as plate ornaments, temple roofs, crowns, and so forth.

This diversion was spectacularly exhibited in the great depression, when gold released from hoards during the years 1931-1935 was estimated to have been equal to some two-years' normal output from all the mines of the world. Of course, this case was exceptional, encouraged as it was by the changes in the price of gold involved in the devaluation or depreciation of the various national currencies. Ordinarily, the amount added to monetary gold from such sources is of no great magnitude.

The effects of international trade on the movements of gold must be set down as quite uncertain. The movement of gold inwards toward the end of depression and outwards toward the end of prosperity implies a localization of the cycle which cannot be counted on. Furthermore, the movements of capital, which are oftentimes imposing in volume, and which more than any other item may determine the direction of gold flow, are affected as much by the state of confidence and the interest rate as by the price level, and may cause gold to move out in depression and in in boom. So complex are the various forces involved in these international movements that no simple and reliable statement as to the flow of gold in the various phases of the cycle can be made.

One may fairly conclude that gold is not to be relied on, in any predictable way, to supply cyclical variations in the volume of money.[4]

2. Paper money. It might be thought that, since government paper money is under the control of a specific monetary authority, and not dependent, like gold, upon the relatively uncertain behavior of a multitude of mining companies, industrial users of gold and the possessors of gold stocks in other countries, it could have elasticity and that this elasticity might take the form of cyclical variations. The government could enlarge and contract the currency at will and, if it chose, make it expand and contract in conformity with the phases of the cycle.

---

[4] Mitchell, *Business Cycles*, 119–121.

In fact, however, this possibility does not seem to be what actually happens. If the nation is on a gold standard, the volume of paper money is a fraction of the gold supply, whose variations we have examined. If it is not on the gold standard, either the changes in the volume of paper money will be an emergency operation in time of urgent need, or it will be regulated so as to keep prices stable. In neither case will the supply of paper money be capable of being an active or passive cause of cyclical fluctuations.

3. **Bank credit.** The principal means of payment in modern communities is, however, neither gold nor government paper money, but bank credit, in the form of either notes or deposits subject to check. In the United States, deposits subject to check are of overwhelming importance, accounting on the average for probably 85 per cent of the total volume of monetary transactions.

Contrary to what we know about gold or government paper money, bank credit, particularly deposits subject to check, does have the kind of elasticity which facilitates cycles. It can be readily increased and diminished; and the evidence shows it to be subject to cyclical variations. When the statistical data either of bank deposits or of bank loans and discounts (either of which is a fair measure of bank credit) are corrected for trend, there is unmistakable evidence that the resultant figures have cyclical fluctuations which correlate closely with indexes of industrial activity.[5]

The total volume of available bank credit is some multiple of the reserves. It can be increased or decreased by varying the reserves legally or conventionally required to be carried or, even though the reserve ratios are kept constant, by increasing or decreasing the volume of available reserve money (gold or credit at central banks). If reserves were always required to be 100 per cent (as some reformers now advocate), the variation

---

[5] Cf. A. C. Pigou, *Industrial Fluctuations*, 1927, Part I, Chap. XIII, and W. I. King, *Causes of Economic Fluctuations*, 1938, 153–157.

of bank credit could be only the same as the variations in available reserve money. In this event, banks could, for example, increase bank credit only by importing gold from abroad, or receiving gold from circulation (if gold were legally permitted to circulate), or by acquiring, through rediscounting or borrowing, additional reserve credit from the central bank.

If fractional reserves were permitted, as is the most common procedure in bank systems, but by custom were kept substantially at a fixed percentage of deposits—say, 10 per cent—then variations in total available credit would have to be brought about by the same alternatives as with 100 per cent reserves. But any change in reserves would make possible a multiple expansion of deposits. If reserves were kept at 10 per cent, deposits would be increased tenfold for every increase in reserves. A small change in reserves makes possible a large change in deposits.

Sometimes not only are fractional reserves permitted, but also banks are left free to carry varying fractions (as long as they satisfy minimum requirements). In these circumstances, not only may the total deposit credit vary in proportion to every change in available reserves from any of the three sources (gold import, inflow of gold from circulation, and increase of reserve credit at central banks), but also it may vary in inverse proportion to every change in the actual reserve proportions that the banks in fact maintain. Thus if, in depression, because of low demand for money on the one hand, and the banks' urge for liquidity on the other, bank reserves are 20 per cent and, in the return of the demand for money and of bank confidence, are allowed to fall to 10 per cent, bank credit can be doubled with no increase whatever in the absolute volume of reserves in the possession of the banks.

If with variable fractional reserves, which in themselves permit wide variations in the total of bank credit, is coupled a willingness of the central bank to increase or decrease the amount of available reserves to the credit of the banks, then the maximum variability of bank credit is attained. This willingness is made effective by lowering or raising the rate of discount, or by purchase and sale of securities in the open market, the results of which are to increase or decrease the total of central bank credit in the possession of member banks.

Degrees of variation in bank credit. The degree of variation in the supply of bank credit and, hence, of the total supply of money in most advanced countries depends, therefore, on what combination of arrangements is in force. The 100 per cent reserves for member banks, coupled with determination on the part of the central bank to control the volume in the interest of stability, would reduce the variations of bank money to their smallest proportions. At the other extreme, variable fractional reserves for member banks, coupled with willingness of the central bank to vary the available volume of reserve money in the interests of elasticity, would give the variations of the bank money their greatest range.

The actual degree of flexibility in the volume of bank deposits would, of course, vary from country to country. An interesting contrast can be made between Great Britain and the United States.

In Great Britain, although fractional reserves are neither required nor sanctioned by law, practice has made them the normal procedure for the joint-stock banks. Moreover, in practice they have been maintained within quite narrow limits. As Keynes points out, the banks find large reserves unprofitable and smaller reserves imprudent. Still further, along with these fixed fractional reserves has come a custom of not borrowing at the central bank. The central bank, on its part, has had the custom, in the past, of avoiding open-market operations such as would increase or decrease the reserves of the joint-stock banks. In these circumstances, the variations in bank credit have come largely from the flow of gold in and out of the country and out of and into circulation. These practices tend to reduce somewhat the variations of bank credit as a whole; although even then, because of the volume of gold in circulation and the importance of Great Britain as a world trading and financial center, the fluctuations in bank credit have been substantial.

In the United States, on the other hand, especially after the advent of the Federal Reserve System, with its stress on the elasticity of the currency, circumstances seem to have made possible the maximum variability of bank deposits. The banks have fractional reserves which, in practice, have had wide variations above the minimum required by law. With the advent of the Federal Reserve System, the banks were encouraged to rediscount when in need, and the central banks were prepared to buy securities in the open market, if necessary, to find an outlet for their idle funds. The professed aim of the Federal Reserve Act of 1913 was to establish an elastic currency —that is to say, a bank currency capable of expansion and contraction. The actual arrangements of American banking seem to have satisfied this aim in the highest possible degree.

4. **Velocity of circulation.** Snyder's investigations indicate that velocity of circulation of bank deposits (the principal currency) in the United States, while showing no trend (no tendency over long periods to either increase or decrease in the average), does have marked cyclical variations, which, as noted above, are strikingly similar to the variations of trade. Keynes, after a careful examination of the English evidence, concludes that the velocity of deposits increases in good times, decreases in bad; and that this is indicated both by statistics and by rational analysis. In good times, the rise of interest rates and prices increases the sacrifice of holding cash balances and impels everybody to lend funds or buy commodities; the opposite occurs in bad times.[6]

Randolph Burgess gives similar evidence for the United States. Tracing the variation of the velocity of bank deposits in various cities from January 1919 to February 1923, he finds

---

[6] J. M. Keynes, *Treatise on Money*, Vol. II, Chap. 24.

velocity rising above average in prosperity, falling below in depression; the range of variation away from the average being as high as 68 per cent for Albany and as low as 22 per cent for Chicago.[7]   Similar indexes for 140 cities outside New York City for the period 1927–1933, based on 1919–1925 as 100, show the following yearly averages:[8]

1927	107	1931	88
1928	115	1932	78
1929	128	1933	74
1930	107		

It is held by some writers that the variations in velocity of circulation, which seem to indicate an elasticity in this field independent of the elasticity of the money supply, are, however, not really independent. As Pigou has pointed out,[9] they are induced rather than autonomous, being brought about by the effects of changing price levels and the subsequent changes in business expectations—that is, they are themselves secondary consequences of the price changes brought about by changes in the supply of money.   True, they have further effects of their own, but, being themselves produced by monetary factors, they must be regarded as of secondary importance.

Fundamentally, therefore, the elasticity which is related to the business cycle is the elasticity of the money supply which, in modern industrialized communities, is substantially equivalent to the elasticity of bank credit.

Hawtrey's Monetary Theory of the Cycle

We must now show how the potential elasticity of bank credit becomes a reality and how monetary theory relates it to the fluctuations of the business cycle.   This demonstration can best be made by following the argument of R. G. Hawtrey, who en-

---

[7] R. W. Burgess, "The Velocity of Bank Deposits," *Journal of American Statistical Association*, June, 1923, 727–740.

[8] Federal Reserve Bank of New York, *Monthly Review.*

[9] Pigou, *Industrial Fluctuations,* Part I, Chap. XV, Section 8.

joys the reputation of adhering most uncompromisingly to a purely monetary explanation of the business cycle (or trade cycle, as English economists call it).

"Variations in effective demand," says Hawtrey, "which are the real substance of the trade cycle, must be traced to changes in bank credit." Or again, "The trade cycle is a monetary phenomenon, because general demand is itself a monetary phenomenon."

First we must familiarize ourselves with some of Hawtrey's definitions:

The *consumers' income* is the total of incomes expressed in money.

The *consumers' outlay* is the total of money payments made out of income. It is the most important of all concepts, for it constitutes the effective demand of the community. (Some money receipts, such as gifts, sale of capital assets, and so forth, are not counted as income and hence not as outlay if expended.)

Cash balances are the holdings of the community in cash and bank deposits; they are the sum of the balances of consumers and traders (traders being all who carry on business for profit).

The total cash balances = the *unspent margin* = the total monetary supply of the community. This total cannot be changed save by the increase or decrease of bank credit or by the import or export of gold. Individual cash balances can change by shifts from one to another.

Velocity of circulation (income velocity) is the ratio of consumers' outlay to cash balances in a given time.

1. **The phase of expansion.** The effective demand for commodities is constituted by the total money outlay of consumers. This money outlay is determined by and, barring changes in cash balances, tends to equal the money income of the consumers, which is the total money income of the community. Outlay is less than income when balances are

being increased and greater than income when balances are being diminished. In equilibrium, consumers' outlay equals consumers' income; consumption equals production; the cash balances of consumers and traders are being neither increased nor diminished; the banks are neither increasing nor diminishing bank credit; and there is no net export or import of gold.

Hawtrey regards this situation as one of extremely delicate balance which can be disturbed by any number of causes, and, when disturbed, tends to move into a transitional period of cumulative disequilibrium. Thus an expansion can be originated by an increase of gold from abroad, an increased inclination on the part of traders to increase their stocks of goods, an increased inclination by consumers to spend and release cash, an increased willingness by banks to make loans and so put funds into the hands of the community, and so on. Of all these possibilities, the increase of spending by consumers out of their balances is the least probable. Consumers' balances are so much a matter of deep-seated habits that once established at certain proportions of income they are not likely to be changed, especially in short periods. It may fairly be agreed that increased consumers' outlay is commonly the result of increased income. The release of cash by traders and the increases of bank credit by bankers are another story. Any improvement in expectations will cause traders to increase their purchases of commodity stocks (enlarge their working capital). Any increase in their reserves or any feeling that existing reserves may safely be decreased causes bankers to seek to increase their loans and lower their rates of discount in order to do so. These lower rates of interest infallibly increase the borrowings of traders, particularly for the purpose of adding to working capital, for interest changes are the principal expense in respect to working capital, and changes therein quickly encourage or discourage investment, as the case may be.

Now in each of these instances, the consumers' outlay is likely to be increased. If consumers release cash, their outlay is in-

creased directly. If banks release cash, which is commonly
done by increasing loans to traders and so increasing traders'
expenditures, or if traders release cash on their own initiative
and so move their idle deposits more freely into circulation,
consumers' income somewhere in the economic system will be
increased; this will be an increase in the aggregate money income of the community, not merely a transfer of income from
one group to another. Doubtless, it cannot be assumed that
this increase of consumers' income must infallibly increase consumers' outlay. The increase might be added to cash balances
instead. Conventional attitudes toward cash balances being
what they are, Hawtrey assumes that the increased income will
be largely spent and so become a source of increase in effective
demand.

Cumulative consequences.   Now this increase of effective demand on the part of consumers sets up a cumulative process of
expansion in which more and more cash is released by traders
and by banks, and more and more additions are made to consumers' income and outlay. Traders, who have released cash
to add to their stocks of goods, find that the increased demand
by consumers, which is thus set in motion, has reduced their
stocks again and so frustrated their intentions of expansion.
They will be moved, therefore, to order still more from the producers and continue to do so until they succeed in getting and
holding the additional stocks they regard as appropriate.

As they do so, they must eventually use up their idle balances
and be compelled to arrange loans at banks, which the banks
(under the circumstances of increased velocity, and assuming
adequate reserves) would be quite willing to grant. This credit
increases the total money income still more ("When the banks
lend, they generate income."), and again, barring an improbable
increase in idle balances, increases also the consumers' outlay.

At some stage in this process, probably early if the start is
from equilibrium, the general level of prices rises. There
are places where output cannot readily be increased, labor

is scarce, or the plant is temporarily at capacity. There prices rise, and a general rise gradually sets in. The general rise of prices adds still further to the forces of expansion. The lag of costs caused by the relative rigidity of wages and interest increases the profits of entrepreneurs and makes them willing to borrow still further from banks. The increased monetary value of output increases the demand for credits to finance its production. It becomes less advantageous to hold balances, and an increase in the velocity of circulation of the money supply takes place, which adds still further to the expansion of effective demand and the rise of the price level.

Why the expansion ends. Now this process of enlarging the money income and outlay, with its concurrent expansion in output, goes on just as long as the banks are willing to add to income by expansion of credit. Even after industrial capacity has been reached, and further increases of credit mean nothing but inflation, the process of monetary expansion could go on if the banks were willing to abandon the gold standard and if society were willing to endure the growing friction between economic classes involved in continuous inflation. In practice, this expedient has been resorted to only in the great economic disruptions of the postwar period. Ordinarily, the gold standard is not abandoned, and, when this is the case, the inevitable though delayed shrinkage of the cash reserves of banks forces an end to the period of expansion.

With the rising monetary volume of transactions and the increased monetary income and outlay of consumers, there sets in, at first slowly, then with increasing force, a drain of cash out of banks into circulation. Consumers want more cash in hand; merchants want more cash in tills. Payrolls involve more cash withdrawals. There may be an increase of imports over exports and a flow of gold abroad. This flow of cash out of the banks at a time when their deposit liabilities have been increasing endangers their conventional reserve ratios and leads them to put brakes on borrowing, primarily by raising their

rates of discount. Unfortunately, this action comes too late.
Had they raised their rates earlier in the expansion and raised
them high enough, and had they taken warning from the increase of consumers' outlay, they might have kept the expansion
within bounds. Since they were keeping their eyes fixed on
their reserve ratios, they were bound to act too late. The deple-
tion of reserves is almost the last of the series of changes which
mark the expansion. Increased credit, increased consumers' income and outlay, rising prices, and, at last, drain of cash and
of reserves is the normal order of events. Because of this, when
banks are at last moved to act, the expansion has gone so far
that any check sets up a drastic and cumulative reaction.

2. The phase of contraction. The contraction which follows, like the preceding expansion, is a function of the change
in effective demand. The restrictionist policy of banks and the
high interest rates discourage dealers from investment in commodity stocks. As a result of reduced orders, producers are
less busy, and income paid out by them falls off. Thus begins
the first contraction of the consumers' income. Unless consumers now draw on their balances, which they may do for
a brief period but not for long, consumers' outlay and effective
demand also contract. Traders find stocks left on their
hands and contract their purchases still more. Many use
the opportunity to pay off bank credit, thus reducing the sum
total of money. All of these things put down the price
level and, with this, profits. With the prospects of falling
prices, balances are held unspent and the circuit velocity of
the money supply falls, weakening prices even more. As
the monetary volume of output falls, the volume of credit
needed to finance it is reduced, and loans are still further
reduced. In short, effective demand for goods has collapsed.

In the meantime, the forces which will halt the decline get
under way. The fall in bank credit begins to ease the position
of banks, and, as depression proceeds and the low volume of
trade and of prices reduces the need for cash, there sets in a re-

turn flow of money to the banks. First merchants and dealers and then, after they have overcome their early fear-induced tendency to hoard, the consumers, return cash to the banks. If the slump has not been international in scope, exports will have increased over imports, causing an inflow of gold. All this takes time it is true, but, once begun, the flow to banks continues increasingly, and this, with the low levels of deposit credit, substantially increases the reserve ratios and moves the banks to more liberal attitudes to borrowers. In industry, costs have been gradually falling, stocks of goods are at a low ebb, and, with the lowered rates of interest now ruling, the way is open for revival. Once more the situation is favorable to an increase of investment by dealers, and, once they start, consumers' income and outlay begin to rise once more, and the whole process of expansion is ready to be repeated.

Such, in brief, is Hawtrey's account of cyclical behavior. To his mind, this behavior is fundamentally a monetary phenomenon. He does not deny that nonmonetary causes (such as invention, discovery, increases of crops, and so on) may affect productive activity, but he holds that they can affect general productive activity as compared with the activity of particular industries, only through their monetary effects. Nonmonetary causes have no periodicity; the periodicity which appears in trade cycles is due to their monetary effects, and even these could be removed by appropriate banking policy. The actual behavior of cycles is due to cumulative variations in bank credit, produced by an elastic currency and a banking policy that keeps its eyes glued on the state of reserves. It would not exist were the money supply inelastic, or were an elastic supply subject to rational rather than conventional control.

Why Do Banks Permit Instability?

One might, therefore, ask the question: Why do not banks exercise this rational control? Merely that bank credit is capable of elasticity does not mean that it must have elasticity.

It would seem quite possible for banks to change their methods, even to the point of maintaining a fixed volume of credit facilities irrespective of the demands of trade. At the least they could adopt policies making for stability rather than fluctuation; indeed, self-interest would seem to demand it. Why do they not do so?

(1) To this bankers are apt to answer that it is their business to supply the needs of trade, not to control the volume of money. It is not for the banks to decide how much credit the business community is to have. This job belongs to the business community itself. The banks are the servants of the public. It is their business to supply bank credit, within their capacities, when it is wanted. They increase credit facilities (for worthy business, to be sure) when it is wanted, and reduce it when business wishes to pay it off. They stand ready to serve at all times, and, if there are fluctuations of business, then business is to blame, not banking.[10]

This notion of the passive (and blameless) banker is, however, not commonly held save by bankers, and not even by all bankers. Common sense would reject this passive idea of the banker's behavior. He is not passive; neither is he blameless. It is his specific policies which actively generate the cycle. He leads, rather than is led. He could have chosen other practices that would have mitigated cycles. He has not chosen them. There must be other reasons than pure passivity.

(2) The more probable situation is that the banks would like to prevent these fluctuations as much as anybody else, but are unable to do so in the face of the realities of profit-making competitive banking. It is not so much that they are averse to control as that they are not in a situation to exercise any.

Consider what happens in expansion and contraction. Banks, like other private concerns, are in business to make a profit and,

---

[10] See J. L. Currie's discussion of the "commercial loan theory" as compared with the "monetary theory" of banking. *The Supply and Control of Money in the United States,* Cambridge, 1934, Chap. IV.

if they are run rationally, to make as much as they can. They wish to maximize their profits, and they assume that this is appropriate economic behavior. To do this, they must keep their funds invested in earning assets up to the limit dictated by prudence, convention, or legal regulation. If reserves are above the minimum, then the banks are not earning so much as they should; if near or below what safety dictates, then they are earning too much and should convert earning assets into cash. In all cases, they try to keep that precise combination which will maximize earnings and safety.

If, now, in a period of expansion, due to incoming cash, or improved prospects of business, or other reasons, banks are in a position to expand loans (and some do), then it is quite impossible for other banks, even though they do not favor expansion, to resist the movement. Banks which do resist will find themselves with idle and excess reserves, as the proceeds of other banks' loans to some extent find their way into their hands. If, then, they refuse to add to their credit facilities, not only will they fail to behave as rational bankers seeking to maximize profits, but, what is worse, they will see their customers go to those who take a more liberal attitude. Therefore, willy-nilly, they join the procession even though they disapprove in general. Thus each is dominated by the pace of all; and so, like a remorseless juggernaut, the whole array moves on to the point of inevitable break.

Similar circumstances prevent any bank from stopping a decline. Those who persist in lending when others, more timid, have begun to close down on loans will find their reserves shrinking as adverse clearing balances begin to operate. Therefore, they, too, are compelled to be more stringent in their attitude, and thus one bank after another joins the general reduction.

What happens here is what happens so often in our individualistic economy. No one can afford to do what it is in the interest of all to have done. Each one holds off, knowing that, if he acts alone, he can only bring about his own downfall. As a result, all go on to engender an expansion or contraction that all deplore.

One might even go so far as to say that the bankers do not even know or notice what is going on. Once expansion is started at any place in the banking system, every bank tends to share to some extent in the additional deposits, as checks are deposited here and there in the system; and once this happens, "mere adherence to the routine of banking technique," as Keynes puts it, causes them to follow the originators of the expansion and expand their own credit facilities likewise.

(3) While this situation holds for competitive banks, it does not hold for central banks. They are not competitive; they would seem to have adequate powers of control over the money market. Why have they not acted to prevent instability?

Hawtrey would say that it is because they consistently use the wrong methods. It is not because they have no credit policy, or let credit take care of itself. They have a credit policy and systematically counteract any activities that clash with it. Unfortunately, it is the wrong one. They determine credit expansion and contraction by the state of the reserves; and this is fatal. As Hawtrey puts it,

So long as credit is regulated with reference to reserve proportions, the trade cycle is bound to occur. The flow of legal tender money into circulation and back is one of the tardiest consequences of credit expansion and contraction. If the central bank waits for the flow to affect its reserves, and sits passively looking on at an expansion or contraction gathering impetus for years before it takes any decisive action, we cannot escape from the alternations of feverish activity with depression and unemployment.[11]

Some hold that this view of central banking is mistaken and that the reason why banks have been so ineffective in controlling

[11] R. G. Hawtrey, *Monetary Reconstruction*, Longmans, Green & Co., Inc., New York, 1926, 144–145.

the creation of credit is not to be found in their excessive pre-occupation with reserves, but lies in a quite different quarter. The root of the difficulty is to be found in the "inflationist ideology" which dominates the central banking authorities. The reason why banks continue to make the mistakes they do, according to von Mises, an eminent German monetary author-ity, is "because the prevailing ideology among businessmen and politicians looks to the reduction of the interest rate as an im-portant aim of economic policy, and because they consider an inflationary expansion of credit the best means to obtain their objective." "The root cause of the phenomenon that one busi-ness cycle follows another is thus of an ideological nature." [12]

Only the central banks are thus affected. Commercial banks could never bring about a dangerous inflation on their own; only the willing aid of central banks makes this possible. Cen-tral banks, not the others, are the real inflationists, and they in-flate because the community, thinking in terms of easy money and believing that more money is more capital, wants them to inflate. Central banks are not independent. In the last anal-ysis, they are subject to political control. Politicians, reflecting public sentiment, including business sentiment, are inflationists at heart. In this view, the Federal Reserve System of the United States, devoted to the principle of an elastic currency, and a powerful agent of inflation, reflected, when it was set up, the wishes of the community rather than a scientific attitude toward banking.

As long as this situation holds, cycles are inevitable. Credit expansion is chronic, leading again and again to crises and depressions, and, after each depression, to inflation once more.

Summary

Monetary theorists hold that cycles, as compared with other variations in economic activity, are brought about by the

---

[12] G. Von Haberler, *Prosperity and Depression*, 1937, 60. See also H. S. Ellis, *German Monetary Theory*, 1937, 334–336.

elasticity of bank credit. They hold that expansion and contraction of bank credit are not only a necessary accompaniment
of similar variations in economic activity but are an efficient
cause thereof. They hold, further, that this is not a necessary
condition of banking, but that it has been brought about by the
traditional practices of bankers, under the gold standard.
These practices are dictated by the general interests of the banks
and are such as will make the best combination of profit with security. This combination is secured by maintaining the largest
possible volume of deposits justified by the state of the reserves;
and the attempt to secure it makes the state of the reserves the
key to decisions. Under these circumstances, not only are expansions checked when reserves reach levels conventionally
regarded as minima, but the slowness with which reserves are
reduced make such expansions dangerously large and certain to
lead to cumulative contractions.

The confirmed monetary theorist like Hawtrey is prepared
to argue that an intelligent bank policy designed to maintain
stability of the price level would not merely reduce but abolish
cycles. This type of theorist holds that, although all sorts of
fluctuations in business would occur, produced by the constantly
varying state of demand, costs, and so on, these would not take
a cyclical pattern. There is absolutely nothing cyclical in their
occurrence. It is only the flexibility and instability of bank
credit which seizes on these fluctuations and turns them into
rhythmic changes. Abolish the instability of bank credit (by
proper bank policy) and cycles will disappear.

Some Objections

How acceptable the monetary theory of the cycle will be
depends on what it is taken to mean. If it means that the
cycles that actually occur, and in the shape in which they occur, cannot be explained in the absence of monetary factors,
probably everybody would accept it. It is an indispensable
contributing cause, a *sine qua non* of cycles as we know them.

Whatever else happens, the compliance of the banks must be assumed.

Further, if the theory implies that the monetary factor is not merely a passive but an active factor, that monetary movements are not merely "necessary but sufficient conditions of the observed phenomena of the cycle," [13] then one must be prepared to make a fairly broad interpretation of what a monetary factor is, and also to hold nonmonetary forces incapable of causing cumulative alternations of expansion and contraction of activity. Thus, for example, is velocity of circulation a monetary factor? There is no doubt that it has important variations which spring from nonmonetary sources—that is to say, from the changing attitudes of both consumers and producers and not from the decisions of a monetary authority. These variations might cause alternations of effective demand, even in a purely cash economy, with no bank credit to give elasticity of money supply. If one chooses, with Hawtrey, to regard velocity as a monetary factor, it is undeniably easier to think of the cycle as "a purely monetary phenomenon," [14] but it might be more illuminating to regard velocity as the expression of the many nonmonetary factors, changes in real demand, changes in cost, inventions, and so on which, too, may be powerful contributors to cyclical fluctuations.

The validity of the monetary theory can be tested by the effectiveness of the controls which banks might exercise over variations in activity. Banks are in a position to remove what is claimed to be the essential cause of cycles. Experience shows that the problem is by no means easy. It is not always possible to put an early end to a boom where powerful nonmonetary influences, such as a wave of investment, are at work. Even high rates of discount and continued pressure on the market

---

[13] See Hawtrey's precise statement in "The Monetary Theory of the Trade Cycle," *Quarterly Journal of Economics,* Vol. 41, 472.

[14] Cf. discussion between Hawtrey and Pigou, *Economic Journal,* Dec., 1929, 636–643.

may not be effective.   To end a depression is even more difficult.   Dear money may end a boom; cheap money does not by any means end a depression.   Even though the monetary factor may be an active and powerful one at the end of prosperity, it is apt to be a discouragingly passive one at the end of a slump. Something else may be necessary to induce recovery, factors which are fundamentally nonmonetary in nature, even though they express themselves in monetary forms.

These considerations suggest that the monetary theory is not always "sufficient" to explain the phenomenon of the business cycle; and that other explanations will have to be given consideration.   The next chapter, however, concerns what is commonly classified as a monetary theory of the cycle; but it is not a purely monetary theory and is properly described as a monetary overinvestment theory.   It finds the ultimate cause of cycles in the instability of bank credit but traces the consequences of this, not through the variations in consumers' outlay, but through the changes in the volume of investment—that is, the purchase and production of capital goods.

CHAPTER XII

MONETARY OVERINVESTMENT
AND THE STRUCTURE OF PRODUCTION

THE most striking feature of the business cycle is the extraordinary variation in the production of capital goods—that is, buildings, machinery, and other instruments of production. No explanation of the business cycle can be regarded as adequate that does not account for the fact that the production of capital goods fluctuates so much more violently than the production of consumption goods.

An objection to the purely monetary theory of the cycle which Hawtrey so vividly develops is that, although adequate to account for the ebb and flow of production in general, it does not explain the disproportionate variation in the production of capital goods. Indeed, there is nothing in the purely monetary theory to indicate that this extraordinary variation has any particular importance.

The theory which we shall now examine seeks to remedy this defect. It is a monetary theory in that it finds the cause of disturbance in the elasticity of bank credit; but it is more than a mere monetary theory in that it tries to trace the connection between the recognized behavior of the credit system and the equally recognized distortions in the two chief classes of output. It may be referred to as a monetary overinvestment theory. Its best-known exponent is F. A. Hayek, whose statement of the theory is largely followed in this chapter.[1]

---

[1] See F. A. Hayek, *Prices and Production*, Revised Edition, London, 1935, and *Monetary Theory and the Trade Cycle*, New York, 1933. The student will find

The Structure of Production

At any given time, the resources of the community devoted to production are arranged in a number of "stages." Some of these stages are remote from the consumers and may be called the "higher" stages of production. In these stages, raw materials are being produced, equipment manufactured, buildings constructed. In short, here is being turned out our supply of capital or producers' goods. Other stages are nearer to the consumer and may be called the "lower" stages of production. There are being produced the consumers' goods which are the final object of all the previous preparation. There may be many stages of production from the nearest to the most remote. Together they constitute what Hayek calls the "structure of production."

The shape of this structure of production is, of course, not capricious. It depends very definitely on the decisions of the community in regard to the distribution of its income beween saving and spending. To the extent that the community decides to save, it indicates its desire that resources are to be put to work (that is, invested) in the "higher" stages of production devoted to the production of capital goods and the provision for the future. If it decides to spend, it indicates to that extent its desire that resources be put to work in the lower stages of production, adding to the supply of consumable goods. If the economic system is working rightly, therefore, the shape of the structure of production, particularly the number of stages between the earliest production and the final output of consumers' goods, should correspond with the spending-saving decisions of the community. Indeed (at least, in the long run), this correspondence is precisely what occurs, and what makes it occur is the operation of that extremely important factor in our economic system, the rate of interest.

---

a lucid brief statement of this theory in L. Robbins, *The Great Depression,* New York, 1934, Chap. III.

The Importance of the Rate of Interest

When people divide their income stream into the two alternative channels of spending and saving, that which is spent goes directly into the purchase of consumers' goods, but that which is saved does not go directly into the purchase of capital goods. Immediately, the flow of savings goes into the capital market and finds its way into the hands of banks, insurance companies, dealers in securities, and other financial institutions. Through them, it is put in the hands of entrepreneurs of all kinds, and finally used by the entrepreneurs to finance the production of the capital goods, for which it was designed. This process may be called "investment." The function of the rate of interest is to bring about equality between the flow of savings and the investments of the entrepreneurs, and, if it is working properly, it will tend to reach that level which will equalize the supply of and demand for this fund of savings. This level may be called the "natural rate of interest" or, alternatively, "the equilibrium rate of interest." A higher rate than this elicits more savings than can find investment; a lower rate causes more demand from entrepreneurs than current savings can satisfy. Either situation sets up such changes in the relation of the supply and demand for loan capital as will tend to restore the equilibrium position.

If, now, the rate of interest is working effectively, changes in the volume of saving, relative to spending, should be followed by equivalent changes in the volume of production of capital goods relative to the volume of production of consumption goods. If the volume of saving rises, the interest rate should fall, and more resources should be devoted to capital goods production and less to consumers' goods production. Conversely, if the volume of saving falls, the rate of interest should rise, and less resources should be devoted to capital goods production and more to consumers' goods production. That is to say, changes in the relative volume of saving and spending tend to bring about appropriate changes in the structure of production.

Moreover, there seems to be no reason why this process should not be brought about without any more than the usual friction involved in transfer of resources within the economic system. If it is possible for changes to take place in the demand for and supply of various kinds of consumers' goods without serious cumulative disturbances (and there seems to be no evidence that the necessary shifts do not proceed with reasonable smoothness), then the presumption is that shifts from consumers' goods to producers' goods, or *vice versa,* can be brought about with equal smoothness. Why should shifting of resources from one stage of the economic process to another be more difficult, or cause more repercussions, than a shift of resources from industry to industry at the same level of production? To put it in other words, why should vertical shifts be more difficult than horizontal shifts, and "vertical maladjustments" in the structure of production occur more readily than "horizontal maladjustments"?

Why Vertical Maladjustments Occur

Hayek holds that there is no reason, save one, why such discrepancies should be. That reason is the behavior of the banking system. This behavior springs from the dual nature of banking, for banks have two functions: they act as middlemen between savers and investors—that is, between the supply of and demand for capital; and they supply the principal means of payment in modern communities—bank credit. If the banking system is working properly, the middleman function should bring about continuous equilibrium between the volume of savings and the volume of investment. There should be no savings that do not find investment; no investment in excess of savings. This equilibrium would actually come about were it not for the interference of the monetary function.

If the money supply were fixed, savings would be the only fund from which investments could be made, and the mere pursuit of maximum profits would lead banks to see that all savings found their way into investment. When the money supply is elastic, investment can be increased without any increase in saving, and diminished although saving has not changed. If the market rate of interest were held below the equilibrium rate, business borrowing would be encouraged, an increase of bank credit would be brought about, and investment would rise above savings. This process would continue as long as the rate of interest remained "low." Similarly, if the market rate were raised above the equilibrium rate, investment would fall below savings and remain below as long as the market rate were kept "high."

Hayek attributes this elasticity of bank credit to the ability of the banks to raise and lower the volume of deposits relative to their cash reserves and to the nature of the competitive bank system which compels every banker to keep in step with the others. Because of this, banks are at some times increasing and at other times diminishing their deposit currency, without relation to the volume of savings which the public has put in their possession for investment. Thus, via the elasticity of bank credit, there emerges a means whereby investment can vary independently of savings, and it is this variation which, in the monetary overinvestment theory, accounts for the phenomenon of the cycle.

The Theory of Overinvestment

We will now examine this theory more closely, following Hayek's analysis of the course of events set in motion by changes in the rate of saving and investment.[2]

Hayek begins his analysis by assuming that the economic system is in equilibrium. He regards the business cycle as a disturbance of equilibrium, and the phases thereof as departures from the equilibrium position. This assumption means

---

[2] See Hayek, *Prices and Production*, Lecture III.

that there is, at the moment, no force making for disturbance or unavoidable adjustment. The rate of interest is such that savings are finding their way into equivalent investment; the structure of production is adjusted to the proportions in which the national income is divided between spending and saving; and there are no unemployed resources, save the unavoidable minimum due to incapacity or friction involved in change from one use to another. The assumption of unemployed resources is particularly important. It is justified on the ground that unemployed resources are not consistent with the assumption of equilibrium. They imply that there are appropriate reductions in wages, interest, or rent capable of eliminating unemployment of resources, which have not yet been made; that is to say, that equilibrium has not yet been reached. The assumption is important because it means that, at equilibrium, increase of output in one field of enterprise must be at the expense of output in other fields of enterprise; and particularly that any increase in the production of producers' goods *must* be at the expense of the production of consumers' goods, and *vice versa*, which is another way of saying that disturbances of equilibrium must modify the structure of production.

We will now see what happens when the relative volume of savings changes assuming (1) that bank credit is not expansible and (2) that bank credit is expansible at the will of the banks.

(1) Where bank credit is not expansible. If bank credit is not expansible, there can be no increase in the aggregate of money in use, no general rise in prices, and no possibility of increased use of purchasing power for one purpose without encroaching equivalently on the use of purchasing power for some other purpose. Let us see what happens under these circumstances when the volume of savings is substantially changed.

What happens when savings increase. Suppose now that the consumers decide to save a larger proportion of their income. This increase will lower the rate of interest and increase the profitability of all production for the future, and encourage borrowing for capital purposes. If concerns that have been borrowing at 5 per cent can now borrow at 4 per cent, they can afford to pay 25 per cent more for all their capital goods and borrow accordingly. Concerns that have been investing in instruments of 20-years' life (for the value of a capital good at 5 per cent interest is 20-years' purchase) can now invest in instruments of 25-years' life. The new rate of interest raises the value of capital goods in proportion to their length of life and encourages investment, therefore, in the more durable capital. Because of the current diminution in the demand for consumers' goods, there is a fall in their price in relation to producers' goods, the relative fall being greatest in the goods nearest the consumer. Thus the price margins between consumers' and producers' goods are reduced, corresponding to the reduction in the rate of interest and the reduction in the time preference for consumers' over producers' goods.

This change in prices discourages the use of liquid funds and readily shiftable resources in the lower stages and encourages them in the higher stages. Resources are shifted from the lower to the higher stages; replacements find their way into the higher rather than the lower stages; and production of capital is encouraged at the expense of consumers' goods. This process will clearly tend to go on until the profit margins are once more equal in all stages. The higher price of producers' goods attracts and the lower price of consumers' goods repels sufficient resources to bring about equilibrium once more. The new structure of production corresponds to the new saving habits of the community. There is a permanently lower rate of interest, a permanently lower margin between the prices at the various stages, and a permanent change in the structure of production.

What happens when savings decrease. If, instead of savings increasing, they decrease relative to consumption, then the reverse of all of these changes takes place. Interest rates rise and discourage the demand for capital funds and, with it, the demand for investment or producers' goods. Consumers' goods are in demand, however, and as a result they rise in price relative to producers' goods. Profits increase, relatively, in the lower stages of production. Consequently, mobile resources tend to be shifted from the earlier to the later stages of production, and this goes on until profits at the various stages are in equilibrium. At this point, the transition is over. The rate of interest is higher, the price margin between the stages higher, and the division of resources permanently changed to the advantage of consumers' goods, modifying the structure of production to correspond with the new division of income between spending and saving.

Thus, changes in the degree of saving, working through the interest rate, affect appropriate modifications in the structure of production. These modifications may be expressed as changes in the roundaboutness of the capitalistic process. They tend to modify the structure of production by increasing or decreasing the length of the production period or process. As saving is relatively increased, under the operation of the interest rate, the process of production tends to be lengthened; as saving is relatively decreased, again under the operation of the interest rate, the process of production tends to be shortened.

It would seem that the lengthening or shortening of the process of production is brought about both by increasing or diminishing the total resources in the higher stages relative to the lower and by increasing or decreasing the total number of stages. Even if the number of stages were not changed, a fall in the interest rate, for example, would still lengthen the process of production. The process of production really consists of a number of processes, not all of which begin or end at the same time. Some begin at earlier stages than others; some might take place at the last moment just before the consumer takes over the goods. Hence the length of the process of production is an average length, the average of the lengths of all its separate parts. The fall of interest rates increases this average by increasing resources in the longer, rather than in the shorter, processes. This increase occurs even if the number of stages does not change; but apparently the number of stages also changes. A fall in the rate of interest makes more remote, more time-consuming, more roundabout processes profitable which were not profitable before. More remote stages will, therefore, be undertaken, and not only the average length but the absolute length of the process will be increased.

Why should structural change cause disturbances? It is the essence of Hayek's argument that these disturbances and re-establishments of equilibrium are not different from other similar reactions that are continually occurring in the economic system. Every such disturbance sets up correctives which restore the equilibrium, and this particular case of changes in saving (either supply or demand) is not an exception. The change in the various price levels soon calls into action appropriate changes in the use of resources at the different stages, and these changes all move in the direction of reducing further disturbances and establishing equilibrium once more. The rise in the price of capital goods eventually makes further purchase unprofitable. The fall in the rate of interest is checked by the demand for capital. Soon the establishment of appropriate price differentials between the stages of production equalizes profits throughout the field, and any further transfers of resources or any further changes in the structure of production become unprofitable. The intelligent anticipations of producers, which enable them to act in advance of the various changes in prices, interest, and wages which events will bring about, guarantee that this process of adjustment shall be not merely inevitable, but not long delayed.

It is possible, of course, for savings to change so violently, first increasing then suddenly falling back to previous levels, that the production of capital goods is affected with excessive fluctuation. If, however, the conservativeness of most people in the division of their income between saving and spending is considered, such violent fluctuations in the volume of savings are not likely to arise, save from conditions making for extreme fluctuations in total income. In that case, the fluctuations of savings would be the effect, not the cause, of the business cycle. Even if for other autonomous causes savings fluctuated, this fluctuation could scarcely be a cyclical phenomenon. There is no apparent reason why an increase of savings of this sort should, with a certain regularity, change into a decrease, and then to an increase again, in successive waves. About all one can say is that violent changes in the volume of savings, if they occurred, would be a cause of noncyclical fluctuations. At the most, they would be a particularly complicated case of the direct process of adjustment to changes in data.[3] It seems reasonable to hold, therefore, that variations in the rate of saving involve no *cumulative* disturbances in the processes of production, and particularly no exaggerated fluctuations in the production of capital goods, such as must be explained to account for the observed phenomenon of the trade cycle. In other words, society can adjust itself without violence to the changes in the structure of production necessitated by equivalent changes in the relative levels of saving and spending, provided such changes in saving and spending arise from the voluntary decisions of the community.

(2) **Changes of savings with elastic bank credit.** The introduction of an elastic money supply brings a disturbing element into an otherwise self-adjusting economy. How this disturbance comes about must be examined.

An expansion of bank credit in use comes about when the market rate of interest trails the natural or equilibrium rate. This expansion may occur either because additions to reserves cause the banks to lower the market rate or because circumstances making for more favorable expectations among entre-

---

[3] Cf. Hayek, *Monetary Theory and the Trade Cycle*, 205-206

preneurs raise the equilibrium rate. As long as the market rate of interest is below the natural rate, it pays the entrepreneurs to borrow at banks, and so the total volume of bank credit increases. In this respect, however, the entrepreneurs respond to a fall in interest in exactly the same way, whether this fall has come about by an increase in the voluntary savings of the community or by a decision on the part of banks to expand the volume of bank credit. In the early stages, the consequences are much the same.

The recipients of the additional bank credit on these more easy terms, as in the case of an addition to savings, use them for enlarging the means of production. There is a rise in the price of producers' goods relative to consumption goods, a tendency to transfer mobile resources to the higher stages of production, and a tendency to increase the number of stages by undertaking products of a more roundabout type than could have been profitable on a higher level of interest. In short, the fall in the rate of interest brought about by the increase in available bank credit has the same consequences as when additional savings have lowered the rate—namely, a change in the structure of production. There are more plants, more durable means of production, a flow of labor and materials towards the higher stages of production, and, as a result of all these things, a growing scarcity of consumers' goods. After all, resources being limited, you cannot have expansion of everything; and if resources are to be devoted to increased volume to producers' goods, less can be devoted to the production of consumers' goods. As a further consequence, the price of consumers' goods begins to rise.

"Forced savings" and their consequences. What has happened therefore, as a result of the expansion of bank credit is that the entrepreneurs are enabled to gain command over purchasing power and, by their increased power of competition for the factors of production, to compel consumers to forego a part of what they ordinarily consume. That is to say, the real

capital needed for the increased activity in the higher stages of production has been extorted from the consumers by the rising prices which they must pay.   Thus saving has been going on just as it must always go on if investment is increased, but in this case it is not voluntary but forced saving.

There has been no real change in the sentiments of the consuming public.   They have not wished to save more, nor would they do so were it not for the compulsion of prices.   Consequently, as soon as their money incomes permit it, they revert to their habits of consumption and attempt to restore their ordinary, unchanged standards; and the increase of money income necessary to do this is soon at hand.   The increased money at the command of entrepreneurs, as it goes into use for the purchase of producers' goods, brings additional income to the holders of such goods and the owners of the factors of production needed to produce them.   Upon the receipt of this additional income, consumers proceed to expand consumption to its former (and usual) proportions.   The result of this is a decided rise in the price of consumers' goods, a rise which is the more marked because a shrinkage in the flow thereof and an increased volume of monetary demand, due to the enlarged flow of money in circulation, come at the same time.   Fundamentally, this outcome must be interpreted to mean that the consumers have never sanctioned the changes in the structure of production begun by entrepreneurs under the influence of an "artificial" rate of interest and are taking the necessary steps to restore the former arrangements; and restored they will be, for the high prices of consumers' goods make production in that field more profitable and also enable producers therein to offer higher rewards for the factors of production.   This matter is a serious one for the producers in the higher stages, who find their ventures not so profitable as they had expected.   Indeed, if they are on the margin, they find themselves incurring loss. The result is bound to be a transfer of mobile capital and labor from the higher to the lower stages, a reduction in the production of capital goods relative to consumers' goods, and an abandonment of some projects altogether.

Can the banks keep the process going? This process of reversing the changes in the structure of production that began with the increase of bank credit could be avoided by a further increase in the volume of bank credit, sufficient to prevent the enticement of mobile resources from the higher to the lower stages. This further increase, however, would have to be greater than the initial one, for the general price level and the general level of incomes have now risen; but whatever it is, it will have to be forthcoming if the abandonment of a good deal of capital production is to be avoided. For a while, banks, doubtless, will be willing to increase their loans, and the producers to make them. The rise in the price of consumers' goods may seem to offer the hope of extra profits. Entrepreneurs may be willing to pay the higher prices needed to keep the factors of production, for projects once under way cannot be abandoned easily.

Clearly, this expansion cannot go on. Under a gold standard, there are very definite limits to the expansion of credit; and, as these limits are approached, the rise of the rate of interest which the banks are bound to impose ends the continuing demand for funds for productive purposes. Even under a paper standard, the continuous rise of prices which must result from a continuance of credit expansion must, in the long run, be intolerable. It may be taken for granted, therefore, that, after a year or so of expansion (with bank rate below equilibrium rate), the banks will be compelled to call a halt.

At this point, the reversal of the changes in the structure of production is bound to begin, and somehow the structure must be restored to the arrangement appropriate to the level of voluntary savings. The difficulties involved in this restoration make for crisis and depression.

Where the trouble really lies. Thus the cause of all the

trouble is fundamentally an *overinvestment brought about by forced savings.* Voluntary savings (unless they are subject to improbably abrupt variations) bring about a change in the structure of production that is permanent. Forced savings, on the contrary, bring about a similar change in the structure of production that cannot be permanent. It is only a question of time until the changed structure becomes impossible and the former one must be restored. The real savings to support the change are not there and cannot readily be made to be there. The crisis, therefore, comes about because of a shortage of savings.

Thus Hayek's theory of the cycle brings him to conclusions diametrically opposed to the theory of those who hold that excessive saving is the cause of our distresses. There is no excessive saving. There is nothing to indicate that there can be excessive saving (that is, as a result of the voluntary decisions of the community). What really happens is that there can be excessive investment. Even excessive investment is possible only because of the illusions created by our elastic currency. Bank credit does create an illusion, an illusion which is not realized by businessmen who are in no position to know what causes the relatively low level of the market rate of interest. The interest rate looks the same to the entrepreneur whether it is caused by the voluntary savings of the people or by the enlarged credit offerings of the banks. Once bank credit is made elastic, the automatic checks to distortion of the structure of production are no longer effective or, if effective, too late to prevent cumulative depression. The bank credit is a subsidy for the producer of capital goods, but a subsidy which is certain to be withdrawn when it is needed most.

The Course of Depression

In Hayek's theory, the depression may be defined as the period during which the structure of production is being shortened to its appropriate length. This shortening process is a serious problem and cannot be done in a moment. It takes time, often a painfully long time. Like all periods of reaction, it is commonly carried too far, so that the shortening process is overdone, and a structure of production temporarily reached which is shorter and less roundabout than will be found later to be appropriate to the actual volume of voluntary saving. To overcome this exaggeration takes time also. All this explains why depressions are as long as they are.

Let us examine this painful process a little more closely. We have seen that the attempt of the consumers to restore their normal purchases, together with the stoppage in the expansion of bank credit, makes the higher stages of production unprofitable. The result of this is fairly sudden stoppage of work, at least in the higher stages of the longer processes, and a fall in the price of producers' goods. The demand for consumers' goods continuing, and the price of producers' goods of a specific sort used therein having fallen, it still pays to employ labor and nonspecific capital in the lower stages of production; and, theoretically, there should be a speedy transfer of workers and nonspecific capital from the abandoned higher stages to these lower ones. In fact, this process is slow. Shorter processes still have to be started from the beginning. Goods still have to pass through the necessary stages. In addition, it is possible only gradually, as successive stages are reached in the passage of goods to the consumer, to absorb the labor and nonspecific capital released from the longer and more roundabout processes. Moreover, this delay is increased by the uncertainty of producers in respect to appropriate methods in the shortened process where a relatively smaller amount of capital and a relatively larger amount of labor are needed.

In brief, workers and mobile resources are released from the longer processes faster than they can be absorbed in the shorter, and the consequence is a growing volume of unemployment. The forces bringing this about are intensified by the general deflation which accompanies the shrinkage of activity. The reduction in bank credit, together with the velocity of circulation induced by hoarding on the part of businessmen and consumers alike, brings about a fall in the price level. In this fall, the prices of producers' goods take an exaggerated share, and the relative rise in the prices of consumers' goods which this involves adds to the forces making for a shortening of the process of production. Under this pressure and the pressure of unemployment and low wages, less and less capitalistic methods are used, and more and more labor is employed in proportion to capital. In this way, the shortening process continues for a longer time than is really needed, and the structure of production is changed beyond the arrangement appropriate to the normal levels of spending and saving. For this reason, the length of the depression and the delay in restoring normal conditions are greater than they would otherwise have been. In other words, the attempt to restore the normal levels of consumption sets up a further disturbing factor—that is, deflation and a fall in prices—which lengthens the depression and adds to the obstacles facing recovery.

How to Cure a Depression

It follows from this analysis that the essential "cure" for a depression is to restore as quickly as possible the structure of production to the status demanded by the proportions of voluntary (not forced) saving and spending. It further follows that most of the methods used in practice to bring about this cure are ill-adapted to do so and may only make matters worse.[4]

Particularly, the evil cannot be cured by advancing money to consumers. It is not lack of consumers' purchasing power that is causing the trouble. Quite the reverse, it is the relatively high demand for consumers' goods that is at fault. To add to this demand by advancing funds to consumers makes matters worse. To increase consumer credit at the moment of the

---

[4] See L. Robbins' *The Great Depression* for a brilliant exposition of how not to cure a depression.

crisis intensifies the crisis. To increase consumer credit in depression prolongs the depression. More exactly, although such
increase may absorb resources for a time, it is an artificial stimulant which brings about a new crisis whenever it is removed.
It is no permanent cure; it merely bolsters up temporarily a
wrong and artificial structure of production.

If any credit is to be granted at all, it should be to the
producers, to encourage them to lengthen the processes of production; and this only because the effects of deflation have
caused the structure of production to shrink more than the voluntary distribution of saving and spending will eventually
justify. However, a very precise knowledge of the amount of
stimulus to be given and very careful arrangements to withdraw the credit at the precise time necessary to avoid overexpansion of producers' goods, and so another boom and crisis,
would be needed. Credits would do more harm than good
if they again caused longer processes to be started than could
be maintained in recovery without the help of continued credit
expansion. These requirements are so exacting that it would
be almost impossible for the authorities to do the job rightly.
Indeed, the logical end of Hayek's analysis is simply this:
that once an expansion gets under way, crisis and depression
are inevitable; and once depression has arrived, there is little
to do but wait patiently for the slow processes of time to bring
about revival. Once the storm has come, the storm cellar is
the only place for all of us.

For the problem of depression itself, there is only one effective solution, and that is to eliminate the elasticity of bank
credit, which is the ultimate source of the trouble. Forced
savings must disappear. The appropriate instrument for this
purpose is a fixed supply of money, subject only to such variations as will neutralize changes in the velocity of circulation
and in the coefficient of monetary transactions. This raises
questions of monetary management, which will be taken up in
Chapter XVIII.

Some Objections

Hayek's theory of the cycle is an ingenious solution of the problem posed by the disproportionate fluctuations in the production of capital goods. Based on a logical application of the theory of interest, it finds the explanation in the alternating expansions and contractions of the structure of production brought about by an elastic money supply. There are serious obstacles, however, to the acceptance of this theory. Let us examine these in order.

What are changes in the structure of production?

(1) The first difficulty arises from the ambiguity of the phrases "change in the structure of production" and "lengthening and shortening the process of production."

If these phrases mean that the number of stages is increased or diminished (and this seems to be implied in Hayek's famous illustrations in *Prices and Production*), then the theory does not appear to fit the facts. Possibly the stages may increase in number in booms (although more probably they increase gradually over a relatively long period of time), but it is difficult to believe that they are reduced in number in depressions. There seems no evidence that, in any large scale, more capitalistic methods are abandoned and replaced by less capitalistic methods. Even if, under the spur of low wages, the processes employing relatively more labor are expanded compared with those employing relatively little labor, this change is counteracted by the recognized tendency to invent and improve during depression in order to reduce cost. Capital production may decline as a whole, equipment may be idle and suffer from inadequate maintenance, and replacement may be neglected; yet this does not imply such change in technological methods as to reduce the number of stages in the process of production.

If changes in the structure of production mean changes in the average length of the process, by increasing or decreasing investment in the longer relative to the shorter processes, the theory seems to be more in harmony with the facts. Certainly, it is a more realistic description of the depression to say that investment in the longer processes suffers the greater decline and that the proportion of nonspecific resources devoted thereto falls, than to say that the number of stages has diminished. Furthermore, on this assumption, the problem of depression is lightened. It would cause less dislocation to redirect the flow of resources than first to abandon and then to reoccupy the higher stages of production.

Changes in the structure of production may mean changes in the amount of capital per head of working population.[5] This interpretation means that in expansion the total capital is. increased and in contraction decreased (disproportionately in the longer processes in both instances). While this picture may be true of expansion, it seems true only of the most severe depressions. A fall in capital per head could occur only when new capital coming forward for investment is actually less than the amount needed for replacements—that is to say, when net investment is negative. This possibility seems to have been realized in the great depression of the 1930's, but in other depressions net investment was apparently still going on. That is to say, in most depressions, capital per head was still rising and, apparently, the structure of production expanding.

In fact, what seems to happen in depressions is not so much a reduction in the number of stages or a fall in capital per head as a reduction in the capitalized values of producers' goods, a general writing down of all capital equipment. If this fall in value is what is meant by a reduction in capital per head and, therefore, by implication, a shrinkage of the *structure* of production, the whole theory is more easy to accept. Thus Hayek says: "The best equipped factory can suddenly lose its value

---

[5] "Any change in the amount of capital per head of working population is equivalent to a change in the average length of the roundabout process of production." Hayek. *Economica*, February, 1932, 42.

as a result of changes in the price structure and thus cease to be capital." [6]   If equipment can cease to be capital by losing all its value, it can be reduced as a volume of capital by losing part of its value; therefore, the revaluations and reorganization sales at reduced prices that are imposed on capital equipment in depressions constitute reduction in capital per head and hence in the length of the capitalistic process.   This way of describing the depression makes it look less forbidding. Surely it is more easy to accomplish revaluations and sales of property at values which will permit the resumption of profitable operation than to change in some physical sense the structure of production.

Forced savings not the question.

(2) A second objection concerns Hayek's theory that whereas changes in voluntary saving can be assimilated without disruption, changes in forced saving cannot.

A. H. Hansen has pointed out that this distinction is not necessarily true.[7]   Voluntary savings, if they fluctuated violently, could make for cycles.   Forced savings, if they were steady, even though steadily increasing, need not be disturbing. It is the degree of fluctuation of savings that is the trouble, not whether they happen to be voluntary or forced.   If gold reserves were steadily increasing or if bank efficiency were steadily improving, the volume of bank credit might persistently rise and be accompanied by a persistent but moderate degree of inflation, and through this bring about a gradual and permanent increase of capital.   Hansen suggests that the forced saving imposed upon society during the long period of rising prices between 1896 and 1914 was not accompanied by an excessive amount of instability.   On the contrary, it was one of the most stable periods in the last hundred years.

Perhaps, therefore, Hayek's point should be modified.   It

---

[6] Quoted by M. Hill, *Economic Journal*, December, 1933, 605, note 2.

[7] A. H. Hansen, *Full Recovery or Stagnation*, New York, 1938, 69–72.

is not that fluctuations in forced savings do any more harm than fluctuations in voluntary savings. The real point is that, as credit is organized, and with the saving habits of the people as they are, forced savings happen to be unstable, whereas voluntary savings are steady.

The assumption of full employment.

(3) There is a still further objection to Hayek's theory arising from his assumption that cycles are disturbances of an equilibrium where resources are fully employed, and the necessary consequence that expansion of production goods can be only at the expense of consumers' goods, and vice versa.

This theory is paradoxical. Not only is it belied by the evidence of fact, but it seems to mistake completely the relation of the demand for producers' goods to the demand for consumers' goods. As to the facts, far from there being at any time a complete employment of resources, what actually occurs is unemployment of both capital and labor even at the peaks of activity. One of the principal characteristics of industrial fluctuations is the simultaneous expansion and contraction in the output of *both* producers' and consumers' goods. In fact, the latter outcome is what would be expected because of the nature of the demand for producers' goods. This demand is a derived demand, dependent upon and reflecting the demand for consumers' goods. When the demand for consumers' goods rises or falls, so will the demand for the producers' goods which go to their making.

To this objection the answer might be made that the existence of unused resources and the possibility of expanding *both* producers' and consumers' goods concurrently may indeed delay, but cannot avert, the inevitable consequences of increasing bank credit.[8] The low rates of interest still encourage expansion by the producers in the higher stages of production. In this

---

[8] Indeed, Hayek makes this answer himself. See p. 258.

case, however, they do not withdraw resources from the field of consumption goods. The additional income which, via their payments to the factors of production, comes to consumers may indeed raise the price of consumers' goods, although even this can be avoided as long as output can be expanded by drawing on unemployed resources. So long as this reserve of resources holds out, expansion of both producers' goods and consumers' goods may continue. But, sooner or later all effective resources will be at work, and, if, then, credit expansion continues, there will be a flow of resources to the higher at the expense of the lower stages, and the full effects on the structure of production will set in. Indeed, even before this point has been reached, the relative advantage of low interest rates to the producers of capital goods may have already caused some "lengthening" of the process of production.

While the picture thus still retains its general Hayekian features, the outlines are not quite distinct. There is considerable room for expansion before the structure of production is much distorted. Forced savings do not have the same scope. They come into play mainly in the brief period at the end of the boom. Furthermore, it now is no longer inconceivable that recovery from depression might be hastened by appropriate aid to consumers. The encouragement this gives to the consumers' goods industries need not make it harder for the producers' goods industries. It would only if resources were hard to get. With resources available in quantity, aid to consumers is likely to be encouraging rather than discouraging to the industries making capital goods.[9]

Is the rate of interest so important?

(4) A fourth criticism is directed toward the importance

---

[9] Whether the relation of demand for consumers' goods and the demand for producers' goods in cycles is to be regarded primarily as competitive or primarily as complementary is a question that appears in various explanations of the cycle. It will be discussed again in more detail in Chapter XIV on "Saving and Investment."

that Hayek, along with other monetary theorists, ascribes to changes in the rate of interest. Evidence is growing that the rate of interest is not notably flexible; that its changes are too small or too delayed to be of consequence; and that, in actual practice, business is not much influenced thereby. Long-time changes in capital production may be caused by changes in interest rates, but the short-time variations of the cycle are more likely to be induced by changes in the prospects of profit or by spurts of invention and innovation.

To meet this criticism, Hayek has recently advanced an alternative statement of his theory in which he shows that, even if interest rates are fixed throughout the cycle, variations in the structure of production will still occur; but now it is changes in the level of profits which brings this about.[10]

An increase of demand for consumers' goods in a period of expansion (which might originate from investment by optimistic entrepreneurs) brings about, until expansion reaches a certain "critical point," a more than proportional demand for investment goods. As wage earners in the field of investment goods add to the aggregate of consumption, resources in consumers' goods production will approach full employment, and elasticity of supply begins to fail. At this point, prices of consumers' goods tend to rise, and, when they do, the relative inflexibility of wages results in a fall in real wages and a correlative rise in profits in consumers' goods industries.

Although the rise in profits would seem to encourage further demand for instruments of production, this result is counteracted by the effects of the fall in real wages. The fall in real wages makes less capitalistic methods of production more profitable. It increases the use of labor relative to machinery; it encourages entrepreneurs to substitute less durable and less expensive for more durable and more expensive machinery. Thus, although there may be some increase in de-

---

[10] F. A. Hayek, *Profits, Interest, and Investment,* 1939, Essay I.

mand for specialized machinery used in consumption goods industries, the general tendency is to reduce the demand for investment goods, particularly in the earlier stages of production. This tendency goes on as long as prices and profits rise, as they do in the consumption goods industries and in those capital-producing industries that immediately cater to them. The general result is to arrest the expansion of the more capitalistic processes, while the less capitalistic processes are expanded to their limit.

Thus the expansion of consumers' demand which accompanies a boom eventually forces a *contraction* in the demand for investment goods. This penalty on the earlier stages sooner or later forces them to reduce employment and precipitate a general collapse. If the additional incomes generated by investment had been saved, not spent, or even if labor and other resources were reasonably mobile, doubtless collapse could be avoided. But as long as additional income is spent and as long as factors are not mobile, depression is inevitable.

The depression which ensues continues until investment demand once more revives. The impulse to this revival commonly found in the fall in interest rates now comes from the fall in profits caused by the lag of wages behind prices. The rise in real wages which this implies puts a penalty on less capitalistic methods and causes a shift to labor-saving machinery and increased demand in industries in the earlier stages of production. The increase of income thus generated starts a spiral of demand which, until prices rise, reinforces the expansion of capital goods industres. In this way, the process of restoring more capitalistic methods goes on, only to be halted when the pressure of consumption demand raises prices and profits and brings up once more the critical point where demand for investment goods begins to shrink.

Thus the economic system, once moved from its equilibrium position, generates one cycle after another. Although the impetus to change is variations in profits, not interest, the essential features of fluctuation are still vertical changes in the structure of production, undue expansion of investment output, and collapse thereof because of excessive spending—that is, because of inadequate saving and "scarcity of capital."

CHAPTER XIII

UNDERCONSUMPTION THEORIES

W E NOW come to a group of theories commonly called "underconsumption theories." All of these theories, while they differ from one another in details of explanation and to some extent in degrees of plausibility, agree in this: that inability on the part of consumers to buy the products of industry at prices that will cover their costs is the fundamental cause of recurring crises and depressions. What brings industry to recurring stoppage is the inability of producers not to continue production (there is no evidence of lack of capacity or of capital) but to find an outlet, at profitable prices, for their goods.

As Haberler has pointed out in his *Prosperity and Depression,* underconsumption theories are not easily stated, largely because their scientific standard is lower than that of the theories already analyzed. Probably this ambiguity is derived from the fact that they have been developed to a considerable degree by nonprofessional economists, whose ability to grasp all the implications (and confusions) of their theories is none too great. The underconsumption approach, too, is the rational approach for the "man in the street." It sounds plausible and wins ready acceptance. For this reason, it has a practical importance, perhaps out of proportion to its scientific content. Not only is it the background of the more fantastic schemes for "sharing wealth" and of such movements as the Townsend Plan, but it furnishes the momentum behind much that is most characteristic of the New Deal. The tax on corporate surplus, the wages and hours act, the NRA, and the vast relief expenditures, in so far as they were motivated by "spending for recovery," all owe their vitality to the Administration's tendency to accept an underconsumption theory, if not of business cycles, at least of crisis and depression.

As has been noted above, the underconsumption approach is made up of a group of theories, not a single theory. In this group, some are more scientific and thoughtful than others. Some are so simple as to be called naive. They suffer from inability or unwillingness to carry the analysis far enough. We shall examine this group by proceeding from the more superficial form of the argument to the more searching.

Naive Underconsumption Theories

I. The simplest form of the underconsumption theory is that the economic system *cannot* distribute enough purchasing power to enable the output of industry to be sold at a price that will cover costs (including a reasonable profit).

The argument is based on the assumption that costs which do not represent expenditures paid out to consumers, directly or indirectly, are incurred in production (and included in price), with the result that the aggregate value of the product turns out to be higher than the purchasing power made available, and the total product cannot be sold. As it is sometimes popularly stated, "the workers in an industry cannot buy back their own product."

This popular phrase indicates the belief that wage payments are the only important payments available for purchasing power; and, indeed, even this drastic form of the underconsumption argument sometimes appears. A moment's reflection would indicate that this form of the argument cannot possibly be true. Payments are made by a producer to labor, it is true, including salaries; but he makes other payments likewise: interest on borrowed capital; rents and royalties for the use of property; payments for materials to those who produce or sell them; payments for repairs, maintenance, and replacement in respect to equipment and plant; and dividends to stockholders. All of these payments are part of the total stream of purchasing power and just as available for effective use as are wages or salaries. It is true that they may not be used as purchasing power; they may be hoarded or otherwise held out of use, but then so might wages. In any case, the theory is based on the assumption that purchasing power simply is not made available; not that, being available, it is not used.

What are the payments or items that could possibly enter into costs and price but not find their way as incomes into the hands of any individual who can use them for the purchase of goods?

Are "reserves" really reserved? Major C. H. Douglas, whose books [1] are the most well-known expression of the naive underconsumption view, would answer that, to take an example, charges for renewals, depreciation, and other reserves are precisely of this nature. They are reserves, and are therefore reserved. Since they are reserved, they are not expended, but are simply bookkeeping items which must be added to the cost of production (and price) if the industry is to keep afloat. Hence our system of accountancy forces us to send out goods at prices at which they cannot possibly be all sold, since we have simply not distributed the purchasing power wherewith to buy them. It is true these reserves are not merely for accounting purposes; they are designed to meet the eventual replacement and renewal of equipment, and, when so used, clearly constitute purchasing power in the hands of potential spenders. In the meanwhile, they are reserved; and this lag

---

[1] Douglas has many books developing his definitely unorthodox views. The reader is referred to *Credit Power and Democracy*, London, 1935, and *Social Credit*, New York, 1933. Useful summaries will be found in P. Mairet, *The Douglas Manual*, New York, 1934.

of expenditure is one factor making for the underconsumption difficulty.

Of course, while this lag may be true of any one concern, in respect to all concerns there need be no lag whatever. Concerns presumably are setting aside reserves and spending money on replacements at all intervals of time. When concern A is setting aside reserves and apparently reducing purchasing power below costs, concern B may be making expenditures for replacements out of reserves, and so increasing purchasing power above costs. With vast numbers of concerns in operation, the law of averages would imply that the aggregate money value obtained at any time from expenditures on replacements would be as much as the value set aside for reserves and added to money price. Only in the improbable event that most concerns lay aside at one and the same time would this not hold true.

There is one situation in which this concurrent setting aside of reserves and expenditures on replacements are not likely to be found. That is the period immediately following a burst of investment in fixed capital. The large depreciation reserves which this expansion will demand are likely to be continued in the slump, but, for various reasons, kept in cash and not currently invested in replacements. As long as this goes on, and provided this cash is not invested by the banks, there is a genuine instance of purchasing power not being distributed in such volume as to cover the costs of production, depreciation reserves included. But while this process exaggerates and intensifies a slump, it does not explain how the slump came about or how any period of expansion could occur.

We may conclude, therefore, that inability to generate sufficient purchasing power to support the industrial system is not a chronic defect of our society or an adequate explanation of cyclical behavior.

Income at the wrong time. The elusive underconsumptionist sometimes states the argument in another way. The whole volume of payments in respect to output is distributed *at some time or other* to consumers. But payments in respect to materials, replacements, machinery, and so forth are made 'some time before the final product emerges. These payments are received by various individuals *and spent.* They are thus no longer available for further spending. Since they were spent to consume the output of the past, they cannot be spent on the output of the present. It is this gap between the value of output now and the income distributed *now* that constitutes the deficiency of purchasing power in question.

This argument assumes that no further preparation is being made for the product of tomorrow; and, in our continuously producing economy, this assumption cannot be fairly made. On the fair assumption that production will continue, the payments made today for materials to become the goods of tomorrow will supply the purchasing power needed to cover the cost of today's goods; or put in another way, today's goods are bought by today's income, which includes the money paid to the (final) producers of today's goods plus that paid to the producers of the materials for tomorrow's goods. If the objection is made that tomorrow's goods will not be prepared for, when the income from today's goods taken alone is insufficient to buy them, it can be replied that today's goods are the result of yesterday's decisions, which, on the argument advanced, must equally have been unfavorable to further production. The argument that implies that tomorrow's goods will not be produced, virtually implies that today's goods would never have been produced either. In other words, underconsumptionists who use this argument literally prove too much; for were the argument true, production would have ceased completely long since, for no level of production could have been profitable to carry on. The mere fact that production goes on at all seems to refute the argument.

One may fairly conclude, therefore, that, in a continuously producing society, time lags of the kind described do not produce trouble, at least in the way assumed, and that, if production is reduced, it is for some other reason than the one advanced by the underconsumptionist.

However, a somewhat modified argument, which recognizes that the arguments of the preceding section are not compatible with any level of continued production, is advanced by naive underconsumptionists.

The A plus B theorem. Perhaps this argument is best shown by the celebrated A plus B theorem which Major Douglas, the leading naive underconsumptionist, uses to prove his case.

Douglas classifies all payments made by a business organization into two groups. These are:

A payments, which are all payments made to individuals, such as wages, salaries, or dividends; and

B payments, which are payments made to other organizations for machinery, raw materials, interest on bank loans, and so forth.

A payments constitute the flow of purchasing power; B payments (for reasons set forth in the preceding section) do not. Both A and B are costs and enter into price. Therefore, price equals A plus B, but purchasing power equals A. Consequently, there is a deficiency of purchasing power equal to B, and, unless this is made good, production must cease.

For a while the deficiency can be made up, by the advance of bank credit, so that a producer, for example, who expects to sell machinery, equipment, or raw materials to other concerns may borrow from a bank to pay his wage bill in advance of the sale. This practice is all right as far as it goes, but, when the buying corporation proceeds to pay for these materials and equipment (B payments), the sums received are not available for expenditure but must pay off bank loans previously contracted. Thus B payments would appear to be always on the point of extinction and disappearance from the volume of available purchasing power.

If one makes the obvious point that, even if old loans are extinguished, new ones will continually be taking their place, since, if past loans are profitable, present and future loans should be equally so, the answer of the Douglasites would appear to be that this cannot be expected under the conditions of modern banking.

This outcome is partly because interest has to be charged on loans, so that on each round the deficiency to be overcome is greater; and there are limits to the expansion of bank credit. Mostly it arises from the monopoly position of the banks, for the banks profit, like all monopolists, from scarcity. It is to their interest to keep bank credit scarce and to reap from this scarcity the highest monopoly value. For this reason, banks are normally deflationists, always interested in restricting the supply of money. Thus, while they are prepared to supply to the public the purchasing power they need, they take good care to get it back with the maximum of dispatch. Every loan must be repaid, and all money is, at all times, on a short journey which always ends up where it began, in the bank. The banks are an enormous mechanism of suction, whereby money is ceaselessly being withdrawn from circulation.

Are the banks the real villains? From this angle, therefore, underconsumptionists come round to the very old argument that finds the source of our troubles in a "monopoly" of credit and would cure our evils by making the issue of credit a public function and causing it to be increased at need. Scratch an underconsumptionist, in short, and you find an inflationist.

We end, therefore, in a criticism of the banking system and a plea for public control of the issue of credit. There are arguments for such a procedure, but the arguments are not stated by the underconsumptionist. The underconsumptionist is well-nigh compelled to argue that bank credit is continuously restricted; and if he does, once again he proves too much, for on this theory output *must* go steadily downward and result in permanent collapse—a situation which is simply not in accord with the facts.

The truth in regard to bank credit is quite different. As we have seen in other chapters, where more scientific analysis has thrown light on the actualities of banking, disequilibrium can arise from bank credit sources, but it will arise from bank credit either exceeding or falling short of the volume needed to maintain stability of production and prices. There is no evidence whatever, in either logic or experience, that it persistently falls short thereof.

It has not been demonstrated by underconsumption theorists of this particular stamp that the economic system is unable to supply enough purchasing power to enable goods to be sold at prices that will cover costs of production. They have not been able to show that money payments entering into price, even in the form of depreciation reserves, do not find their way, normally, into purchasing power; nor have they appeared to state the facts in regard to bank credit, by asserting that bank credit has what might be called a downward bias and a deflationary trend. Furthermore, the arguments by which they endeavor to establish their position would prove, not that we go through alternating periods of expansion and contraction, but that industry must sink steadily downward until the economic system has completely run down. Therefore, we may regard this form of the underconsumption theory as fallacious.[2]

---

[2] For a discussion of Major C. H. Douglas and his theories, the student is referred to the following:

A. H. Hansen, *Full Recovery or Stagnation*, New York, 1938, Chap. IV.
R. G. Hawtrey, *Capital and Employment*, New York, 1937, Chap. X.
G. D. H. Cole (Editor), *What Everybody Wants to Know About Money*, London, 1933, Chap. VIII, by H. T. N. Gaitskell.

Incomes Adequate, But Too Much Saved

II. The theories which we have examined find the source of our trouble in a fundamental flaw in our price system which makes purchasing power chronically inadequate. A more plausible form of the theory takes a quite different position. In this form, it is not argued that adequate purchasing power cannot be distributed. The real difficulty is that, after distribution, the purchasing power is not adequately "spent." It is "saving" that causes the trouble. It is saving that creates a situation where goods cannot be sold. Although those who see saving as the root of the problem call themselves "underconsumptionists," it is oversaving rather than underconsumption that characterizes their theories.

In a rather naive form of the argument, saving is regarded quite simply as refraining from consumption and no consideration is given to the process of investment by which savings are translated into demand for equipment. Thus conceived, saving is a clear and certain source of deficiency of purchasing power. Saving without investment is deflationary, reducing the total purchasing power below the aggregate current value of output and bringing about, therefore, a fall in prices, and, in consequence, losses to producers, and a reduction in the volume of business.

Clearly, it is essential not to neglect the other side of the process—that is to say, investment and the relations between saving and investment; yet the naive underconsumptionist apparently gives no consideration whatever to investment. He takes no account of the possibility of investment proceeding *pari passu* with savings, or of the relations between savings and investments which may be brought about by the intermediacy of banks. As a result, he is quite unable to account for periods of revival and prosperity. If investment is left out of the picture, the effect of savings must be not merely deflationary, but productive of continuous and unrelieved slump.

If all underconsumption theory took this simple attitude toward saving, it would hardly need to be discussed. But, although this is a popular position, it is not the position of the leading exponents of the theory, as we shall soon see. Usually underconsumptionists regard the whole process of saving and investment as a single one. Savings are designed to be invested, and it is assumed that they are. The central core of the underconsumptionist position is to be found in the effects of savings that are invested, not in the effects of savings that are not. It is held that the trouble with modern society is a persistent oversaving coupled with an increase of investment in productive capacity to a point which outruns the consuming power of the community. The sequence is oversaving, overinvestment, overproduction, and, at last, a great flow of goods unsalable at prices remunerative to the producer.

We will now examine the argument in detail, choosing for the purpose two well-known examples: (1) Foster and Catchings in the United States; (2) J. A. Hobson in England.

(a) Foster and Catchings' Theory of Oversaving

In an extreme form, those who hold this type of explanation seem to believe that savings as such, when invested in productive processes, are bound to bring about a collapse and a depression. It would not make any difference whether the volume of savings were large or small. Sooner or later, the savings would cause trouble. If they were small, the trouble would be delayed; if they were large, trouble would come quickly. But trouble there would be, in any case, as long as there were savings at all.

This type of argument is best illustrated from the writings of Foster and Catchings, who, through the Pollak Foundation, have done most to popularize it.[3] Their argument can be stated succinctly as follows.

---

[3] W. T. Foster and W. Catchings, *Profits*, Boston, 1925; also "The Dilemma of Thrift," *Atlantic Monthly* April, 1926.

Society does not spend all its income. Some part of it is bound to be saved. Some of this saving is carried out by industry itself, for not all the value product of industry is distributed in incomes; part is retained to add to productive equipment. Of that which is distributed in incomes, some part also is saved. These savings, *via* banks and security issues, find their way back to industry where they are invested; that is to say, they are used to purchase productive equipment, the means to produce more goods.

On the face of it, this volume of consumer and business saving would seem to create a deficiency of buying power in respect to goods offered for sale. It does this in the end, but not immediately. No deficiency arises immediately, for all the savings thus apparently taken out of incomes and, therefore, out of purchasing power are, by the process of investment, being paid out to wage earners (and other factors of production) engaged in the capital-producing industries. Hence the total volume of purchasing power is not affected by savings, since what is given up by one group is transferred to another. Moreover, this total volume of purchasing power is, for the while, more than adequate to buy the goods coming on the market, the volume of which has not been affected as yet by the processes of investment.

Yet this situation of adequate purchasing power is temporary and short lived. In due time, the productive equipment on which savings are being spent are ready for operation, and, after the lapse of a further period, the goods which they are capable of producing are ready for the market and added to the existing supply. When this finally happens, then purchasing power is inadequate to buy both the original and the additional flow of goods at the existing levels of prices; or, more exactly, it is inadequate to do so unless the total volume of money is increased, either by incoming gold or by the inflationary action of banks.

This simple deduction from the accepted quantity theory of

money indicates that, if output is increased faster than available purchasing power, prices must inevitably fall.

Banks unable to save the situation.   Why cannot the volume of available money be appropriately increased?   Granted that gold cannot be expected to increase in any certain volume, why should not bank credit be expanded with the expansion in the output of goods?   What are banks for if not to bring this about?

Doubtless they are there for this very purpose.   Doubtless, also, they attempt to do this very thing.   Unfortunately, even if they meet the problem for the moment, they only set the stage for further trouble at a later date.   They can postpone, but they cannot avert, the crisis.   The reason for this lies in the use of bank credit.   Bank credit is credit to producers; it is based on producers' property or producers' prospects of profit.   When it is granted, it enables producers to add to production; but it does not enable producers to add to consumption (except by adding to production).   Hence what happens is this: Credits are advanced to producers.   They proceed then to put them to productive use.   In this process, funds find their way into the hands of consumers (wage earners in the productive processes) and, to this degree, enable them to buy the goods produced with the previous savings.   When in time the additional goods from the productive processes come on the market, once more purchasing power is inadequate and the price level must fall, unless bank credit is expanded again. As there is a tendency to save a larger fraction of a larger total income, the deficiency of purchasing power which must be made up will grow at an increasing rate; and unless, therefore, bank credit is not merely expanded, but expanded at an increasing rate, prices must fall.

To suppose that banks can continue to meet this situation is to forget all the lessons of experience.   The truth is, they cannot continue to do so; sooner or later, the state of reserves calls a halt or imposes some restriction on the rate of increase.

When this time comes, the ultimate results of the process of saving can no longer be postponed. The deficiency of purchasing power, put off for a while, is finally here; and the crisis begins.

It follows that it is impossible for a society to save without causing crisis and depression. This difficulty, in short, is the "dilemma of thrift."

Saving not necessarily the cause of trouble. Two obvious criticisms of this rather extreme attitude can here be made.

(1) In the first place, the argument, when reduced to its essentials, merely states that an increase of output at a rate faster than the increase in the volume of monetary purchasing power will cause price reductions and a depression; but there are many influences that will cause this result, not merely an increase in saving. As Hansen has pointed out:[4]

> A precisely similar situation will develop in each of the following cases (among many others that might be cited), as can readily be seen without further argument: (1) increased personal efficiency of labor, (2) improved management methods, (3) new inventions and improved processes, (4) increased population and labor supply.

In short, any dynamic factor will do what Foster and Catchings attributed to the process of saving. The theory, from this angle, must really be listed among those which find the cause of cycles in the operations of progress, rather than as an underconsumption theory, such as Foster and Catchings themselves seem disposed to call it.

(2) Furthermore, it seems incredible to suppose that society cannot adapt itself to any saving whatever, no matter what its size, no matter how steady it happens to be. One still has to face the formidable arguments of Hayek that voluntary saving can be directed into investment without setting up the accumulative strains involved in prosperity and depression. It

---

[4] A. H. Hansen, *Business Cycle Theory*, Boston, 1927, 44.

is true that great variations in saving, on the one hand, or sudden substantial increases in the rate of saving, on the other, might make adequate adjustment impossible and lead to characteristic cyclical consequences. But that society cannot absorb any saving at all without dire consequences does not seem probable. Our interest rates have some flexibility after all, and, consequently, some savings could be invested, some increase of output take place, and some fall of prices be feasible (owing to falling cost of production), all without bringing about any such cumulative strain as cycles display.

This argument is, indeed, recognized even by some of those who think that cycles are caused by the processes of saving. They believe not that savings in themselves are doomed to cause trouble, but only savings in excess of what might be called the "optimum" or "equilibrium" amount. This view is well represented by the writings of the English economist J. A. Hobson, perhaps the most famous of all underconsumption theorists.[5]

(b) Hobson's Theory of Underconsumption

Hobson does not hold that insufficiency of consumption arises from any insufficiency of money income as such. He holds, on the contrary, that normally the money costs of the processes of production are currently paid out in wages, salaries, rent, interest, and profit, and are, in the aggregate, sufficient to buy the whole product of industry. Furthermore, he does not hold that saving in itself, by which he means the whole process of saving-plus-investment, need constitute a source of disturbance. True to his classical conceptions (his work is heavily buttressed with Marshall), he believes that it is quite possible to devote the energies of society to investment (saving) as well as to consumption (spending), and to make changes in the proportions in which the resources are so devoted.

---

[5] J. A. Hobson, *Economics of Unemployment*, London, 1922.

The root of his theory is not an objection to saving as such, but to undue saving—that is to say, such an investment in the means of production as to make for a supply of consumption goods greater than can be purchased (at lucrative prices). We have seen that Hayek also has found a possible source of trouble in overinvestment, but, whereas he traces this to the forced saving caused by expansion of bank credit, Hobson believes that voluntary saving can also be excessive, something which Hayek regards as unlikely, to say the least.

Indeed, this is putting Hobson's view mildly, for he believes not merely that voluntary saving can be excessive, but, very strongly (this is the central core of his thoughts), that, under modern economic conditions, voluntary saving cannot avoid being excessive. Excess is the normal condition. We suffer from a chronic evil of undue savings, and this is the root cause of our recurring tendency to periods of depression and unemployment.

The reason for this astonishing situation lies in the unequal distribution of wealth to be found in all industrial societies. The most characteristic aspect of these societies is the extraordinary concentration of wealth in the hands of the few. The great mass of the people have relatively small incomes; a small minority have large incomes and receive a disproportionate share of the total income of society. Thus in the United States in 1929,[6] 42 per cent of the families had incomes of less than $1,500 per family and, in the aggregate, received some 10 billion dollars; while 0.1 per cent of the families had incomes in excess of $7,500 per family and, in the aggregate, received some 9.8 billion dollars. Thus 0.1 per cent at the top of the income scale received nearly as much as 42 per cent at the bottom.

The effect of great inequalities of wealth. Were these disparate incomes spent to about the same degree, our sense of justice might still be outraged, but disrupting economic con-

---

[6] Leven, Moulton and Warburton, *America's Capacity to Consume*, Washington, 1934, 55.

sequences would be absent. The production of goods and services would be unduly influenced by the desires of the rich, but there would be no particular reason why periodic crisis and breakdowns should appear. But these unequal incomes are not all spent to the same degree. The actual facts show that, while the poor spend most of their incomes, the rich save more and more. The evidence shows not only that the bulk of savings comes from the higher incomes, but that the percentage saved increases with the increase of income.[7] In Hobson's view, this increase in saving with income is a natural, unavoidable result of the situation of wealthy, particularly of very wealthy, persons. Modern society has a class of persons, small in numbers, but very important in the income they receive, who are so well off that they cannot find any way of spending all their incomes. They may have the most luxurious tastes— fine houses, armies of retainers, yachts, estates, and all the elaborate paraphernalia of modern luxury—yet they are quite unable to spend the continually growing incomes they "enjoy." So we have the paradoxical situation that, while those at one end of the income scale would be glad to consume but are not able, those at the other end have the ability to consume but not the desire.

As a consequence, what cannot be spent is saved and invested. Productive facilities are added to, new capital goods come into existence, and capacity to produce is increased. This development creates an activity in business which is encouraging to the expansion of bank credit, so that prices begin to rise. Out of this situation, further expansions of saving take place. The increase of total income which is brought about by this activity and this rise in prices is, as things normally go, not evenly distributed among all the coöperant economic classes. The reason for this lies in the well-known phenomenon of wage lag. In periods of prosperity, wages invariably lag be-

[7] *Ibid.*, 95–96.

hind the rise of prices.   Real incomes of wage earners, therefore, do not increase as fast as money incomes; and the addition to incomes brought about by prosperity tends to flow in
disproportionate amounts into the hands of the non-wage-earn-
ing classes.

It is just these classes who are already unable to spend their
incomes in due proportions; and this addition to their incomes
still further increases their already powerful impulses to save
and invest.

Were the recipients of the enlarged income able to expand
their consumption pro rata, this secondary expansion of saving,
at least, might be avoided.   In Hobson's view, the arts of consumption are conservative and traditional.   They are deeply
rooted in the habits and living standards of the various income
classes.   To use Keynes' phrase, the "propensity to consume"
suffers from no little inelasticity; and this applies not only to
the upper levels of income (indeed, one might expect greater
elasticity in this region than in others) but also in the lower
levels.   Wage earners are notoriously conservative in their
habits of consumption, and such increases of income as come
to them, too, in periods of expansion (they do get *some* increase despite wage lags) may easily be added to the flow of
savings, being deposited in savings institutions or used to buy
insurance.   As a result, the volume of consumption which, by
virtue of existing inequalities of wealth, tends to be unduly
small, now becomes, relative to the increased total income, even
smaller.   Wage lag added to the normal inequality of income
is making formidable inroads on the capacity to consume.

Overproduction inevitable.   In the meanwhile, the new
factories and mines and workshops, the new equipment and
machinery, set up by the wave of saving, are all coming to the
point of output.   When they begin to get into production and
pour out the increased stream of consumers' goods which they
are capable of producing, the crisis emerges; for the consuming power of the people, reduced as it is by the drains to which

it is exposed by the rising tide of savings, cannot possibly be adequate to absorb this flow of goods at prices remunerative to the producer. When this situation is eventually reached, over-production has definitely set in, and prices begin to break; and, to avoid further loss, the productive machinery is brought to a halt, with its accompaniment of reduced national income and a great increase in the volume of unemployment.

The period of depression which now sets in is familiar enough. The attempt to avoid loss by closing down factories continues the evil unabated, for it reduces still further the consumptive power of the people. Even the activity of those businesses which produce capital goods falls away greatly, for the disappearance of profits dries up the source of those incomes from which savings and investment come. Although savings continue, they begin to lie idle in banks and find expression in an increase of hoarding rather than a continuance of their normal outlet in investment. However, while this retardation of investment is a source of unemployment in the capital-producing trades, it does in itself tend to restore in due time the right relationship between the amount of real capital and the rate of consumption. Eventually even the minimum levels of consumption put a strain on existing facilities; there is a demand for savings to flow into use, and, as they do so, a new period of "prosperity" emerges and continues until the familiar process of oversaving wrecks it once more.

Greater equality the only sure cure. The cause, therefore, of booms and depressions is to be found lying deep in the very heart of our modern industrialism—namely, in the great inequality of incomes which this structure always displays. As long as this persists, and in the absence of a revolution of consumption habits which seems totally improbable, crises and depressions will occur and we will not get rid of the greatest of all economic evils, unemployment. Furthermore, there can be no remedy for this situation, save to remove the inequality of income which is its efficient cause.

Monetary increase can do nothing to cure the evil. Increase in money must come from our banks; and banks persistently advance money not to consumers but to producers, enlarging not the ability to consume but the ability to produce. It is useless to offer abundant supplies of bank credit or investment capital to industrial concerns so long as the latter have no security that their increased output can be sold without prices falling; and they simply cannot have this security as long as the consuming public does not have the funds to purchase the additional supplies.

True, if the banks advanced money to consumers so that a larger proportion of the total monetary income could be spent on consumption goods, the evil might be, if not cured, at least reduced. But bank policy does not favor this procedure, and, although something might be done, it would be of little consequence in the face of the persistent oversavings arising from inequality of wealth. To reduce this inequality, therefore, seems to Hobson the only method capable of removing the cancer of crises and unemployment from the economic body. Hence he advocates appropriate taxation of great incomes for the purposes of enlarging the income of the masses, via the social services. He favors the growth of labor unions or any other machinery capable of raising the general level of wages and reducing the degree of wage lag as periods of increasing output and incomes. He advocates regulation of monopoly prices so as to increase the real incomes of the masses of the people, and, where necessary, such an increase of social ownership as would be dictated by inability in any other way to attack the sources of great incomes. In general, he leans toward an increasingly socialized community.

But flexibility of prices and interest rates would help. One might very well question why the expansion of output, which, according to Hobson, smashes the price level and brings about depression, is not anticipated beforehand, and why, therefore, the future fall in price is not reflected backward into the current price of output and, by being so reflected, put a gradual brake upon unwise expansion. We may further question why this anticipation of possibly falling prices, together with the force of the steadily growing volume of savings offered for investment, would not lower the interest rates, and why this lowering of the interest rate would not put a damper on savings and encourage a relative expansion of expenditure on consumption goods.

In short, why do not the changes of prices and interest set in motion by the process of saving bring about progressive and gradual adjustment, instead of the delayed and eventually catastrophic results actually experienced?

Hobson's reply to this is clear. He would grant that, if prices and interest were sufficiently flexible, such gradual adjustments might be made. But prices and interest are not sufficiently flexible. They operate, it is true, but they operate too slowly. Both prices and interest eventually fall, but only after the evil they are expected to avert has already arrived. The catastrophe of a depression is needed to bring prices and interest down. They are brought down too late, and, when they fall, they fall too far.

If prices and interest were made more flexible, these evils might be avoidable. But there seems no possibility of attaining such a flexible system that it could easily cope with the stream of savings, which, in Hobson's view, so inexorably pours into investment. Hobson, indeed, is not to be lined up with those who find the source of trouble in "rigidities." Rigidities complicate the problem, but, rigidity or no rigidity, the tendency toward oversaving will lead to crises, and there is no way of remedying this evil save to reduce it at its source in the inequalities of wealth characteristic of modern industrial societies.

American Underconsumption Theories

The particular emphasis of Hobson's theory upon the inequalities of income derives, doubtless, from his observations of contemporary England. Underconsumption theories that follow his lead in the United States do not stress this aspect so much. While the apparent inability of this country to utilize even in booms the full productive power made available by modern technology is commonly traced by exponents of this school to the great inequality in the distribution of income, cyclical underconsumption is attributed to the expansion in the output of consumers' goods without equivalent increase in the purchasing power of the masses of the people, the wage earners, the lower salaried workers, and, in some instances, the farmers. This unbalance, in turn, is traced to the rigidity of prices and wages in a period of increased production.

This increased production may arise, as in Hobson's theory, from the excessive flow of savings into investment, and thus from an increase in the supply of fixed capital; or it may arise from improvements in technology, such as appeared to be the source of expansion in the great American boom of the 1920's. In either case, unbalance is bound to arise unless either prices are reduced or wages increased in proportion to the increased output offered for sale. Unless one or the other of these things happens, then the increased output cannot be disposed of. The increase of profits which accompanies the gradually growing output does not ease the situation. Indeed, it makes it worse; for while such profits supply some upper-class consumption, they commonly seek further investment.

Now, modern developments have made prices more, rather than less, rigid as time has gone on. The growth of large-scale business, the tendency toward agreements, combinations, and monopoly, and the spread of price jurisdiction by private producers in one field after another have made for relative fixity of prices. Producers are loath to reduce their prices, even in the face of technological change, preferring rather to reduce their output when sales become no longer "profitable." Nor are wages sufficiently elastic to take up the slack. Labor unions may do something to improve the situation, but their power is limited, and they cannot prevent the emergence of great profits and the unbalance between production and consumption these profits imply and partly cause.

This statement of the underconsumption argument is common in the United States. Sometimes the emphasis is put on the increase in the profit margin and its influence in overexpansion, and sometimes on the inadequate purchasing power of the masses and its influence in bringing expansion to an end. Always there lies at the basis of their view the inflexibility of prices and wages in an economic system given to improvements in technology and the continued increase in the supply of fixed capital.

American experience, 1920 to 1930. These arguments seemed to find confirmation in the movements of output, costs, prices, wages, and profits in the United States during the years from 1920 to 1930.

Thus P. H. Douglas points out the following facts: Hourly output in manufacture probably increased not far from 30 per cent between 1922 and 1929. Hourly earnings of labor increased about 8 per cent, 1923 to 1928. Labor costs were, hence, reduced by not far from 14 per cent. On the other hand, prices fell only 2 per cent between 1922 and 1929. The result was an increase of profits in manufacture which, following Mills' figures, amount to 84 per cent between 1922 and 1929, although production was increasing only 37 per cent.[8]

The consequence of this arrangement was to stimulate enormously the capital-producing industries, with a top-heavy development in the capacity for producers' goods.

That this outcome would end in an unbalance of production and consumption appeared to Douglas to be fully confirmed by the evidence. Thus, whereas production as a whole increased 37 per cent from 1922 to 1929, his computations, as well as those of F. C. Mills, indicated an increase of 18 to 20 per cent in the purchasing power (that is, real income) of the urban

---

[8] P. H. Douglas, *Controlling Depressions*, New York, 1935, 55–58.

manual and lower-salaried groups and of less than that amount in the purchasing power of the farmers and agricultural laborers. The percentage which both wages, and wages and salaries taken together, formed of the value added by manufacture steadily fell in the period: wages from 42.6 per cent in 1923 to 36.4 per cent in 1929; wages and salaries together from 53.4 per cent in 1923 to 47.7 per cent in 1929.[9] While wages and salaries in other occupations (such as services) are not included in this estimate and may have risen in this period, there is no evidence that these incomes increased in any such degree as would be necessary to overcome the discrepancy in manufacture. On the basis of this evidence and of the fact that profits increased 83 per cent in the period, Douglas concludes that purchasing power was inadequate to take the growing supply off the market, and that this was the essential cause of the collapse of 1929.

American developments of the theory of underconsumption differ, therefore, from English in their emphasis on the relation of underconsumption to the characteristic American tradition of invention and technological change. In the traditional economy of England, where stability rather than advance colors the picture, the oversaving that comes from inequality of wealth may well seem the important factor in disequilibrium. In the United States, this disequilibrium is found in technical advance, because the very organization of society that normally accompanies large-scale production makes for inflexibility of prices and wages and prevents from operating the only means whereby the balance of production and mass consumption can be maintained and "underconsumption" avoided.

---

[9] *Ibid.*, 69–70.

CHAPTER XIV

SAVING AND INVESTMENT

THE underconsumption school, despite a certain confusion in its arguments, has rendered an important service. It has compelled economists to consider the possibility that saving in economic society might be excessive, and that the economic system might be thrown out of equilibrium by variations in the rates of spending and saving the national income.

The underconsumptionists have never had difficulty in persuading the man in the street. The notion that people have not enough money to buy the goods that are being produced is simple and direct and has an immediate appeal. But their influence in professional economic circles has been much slower in growing. The reason for this lies in a certain annoying confusion in their use of terms which has resulted in inconsistency in reasoning and considerable disagreement in the ranks. Underconsumption theory has been developed largely by heretics outside the boundaries of orthodox economic thinking. While this circumstance has given a certain vitality to their arguments that is not always found in more orthodox circles, it has been responsible for a lack of scientific precision in their theories that has hindered their acceptance by economists.

The persistence, however, with which the underconsumptionists stuck to their guns, and the growing suspicion that underneath their not-too-well-stated arguments there lay more than a grain of truth have lately brought about a considerable advance in their status; so much so that they have become not only respectable but, because of the conversion of some notable economists, distinctly formidable.

This result has been brought about partly by the more scientific discussion of the terms *saving* and *investment;* but particularly by the notable aid of J. M. Keynes, the distinguished English economist, who, in his *General Theory of Employment, Interest and Money* (1936), definitely espoused underconsumption approaches to the explanation of depression. Keynes may be said to have made underconsumption theory respectable, by clearing up its naive confusions and dressing it up in a carefully chosen scientific terminology.

The present and succeeding chapters will be devoted to this remarkable exploit. In the present chapter, some account will be given of the nature of saving and investment and the possible disturbances of economic equilibrium which may be associated with their variations. The following chapter will be largely devoted to Keynes' analysis of booms and depressions.

The Process of Saving and Investment

If we were able to take a comprehensive picture of the economic system in operation, we would see a great machine devoted to the production of all kinds of goods. Some of these would be consumers' goods; some of them would be producers' goods, the equipment for production. How much is being produced in total and how much of each of these two classes has been determined by the decisions of the entrepreneurs of the community. These decisions, in turn, have been made upon the present prospect and future expectations of the effective demand of the people.

As a result of their production, entrepreneurs are able to pay out certain sums to the factors of production. These sums are salaries, wages, interest, rents, and profits, and together they may be called "the costs of production." They also constitute the incomes of those who supply the factors of production and, taken in the aggregate, are the means of payment for whatever goods and services the people choose to buy.

This income need not all be spent—that is to say, used to purchase consumers' goods. It may, at the will of individuals, be "saved"—that is to say, withheld from the purchase of consumption goods and made to serve as an accumulation of resources for the future.

The supposed use of these savings, however, is not merely an accumulation of resources for the future. It is assumed that they will be directed through the proper channels into the hands of those entrepreneurs who desire to buy equipment, machinery, and other forms of capital goods. As commonly pictured, this direction of savings into the hands of entrepreneurs is done by the financial machine or capital market— that is, the banks and other similar institutions which receive savings via bank deposits, security payments, and so on, and see that they get into the hands of the businessmen who wish to order buildings, factories, machines, and other productive equipment.

When savings thus get into the hands of these entrepreneurs and are spent on such capital goods, they are said to be "invested." The act of using them may be called "investment," and the volume of these investment expenditures in any period may be described as "the rate of investment." Because the term *investment* is used also for the purchase of a security by an individual, some prefer to use the term *capital formation*.

Thus we may think of two streams of funds flowing back from the recipients of income to the entrepreneurs, a consumption stream and an investment stream; the former from the spendings, the latter from the savings of the community. We may think of the system in equilibrium as long as the decisions of the entrepreneurs in determining the relative output of consumers' goods and producers' goods are in conformity with the decisions of the community in dividing its income between spending and saving. If entrepreneurs decide to devote more resources to the purchase of capital goods and less to consumers' goods, what is clearly imperative is that the community be moved, at the same time, to increase the scale of its savings, and to place them in the hands of the businessmen. In this way, the reduction in output of consumers' goods will correspond to the reduction in the demand for them, and the increase in output of producers' goods will correspond to the increased resources devoted to saving. A divergence in these decisions would seem to expose the system to disequilibrium.

Conflicting Decisions of Savers and Investors

There is no reason to suppose, however, that these decisions will, in fact, be so neatly adjusted to each other. Saving, on the one hand, and investment or capital formation, on the other, are made by the decisions of two quite different groups of people, influenced by two quite different motives. Decisions to vary the rate of investment are made by entrepreneurs. New inventions, or sudden increases of demand through war, or agricultural change, or changes of business sentiments as a result of political factors may occasion their decisions. Whatever they are, they may be summed up as all the forces which may affect the expectations of profit. The decisions that determine the rate of savings are made by the public seeking to accumulate resources for future use or consumption. The motive is provision for the future in the long run and desire for liquidity in the short run.

Neither of these decisions is made with any consideration or calculation of what the other decision may happen to be. Businessmen who decide to expand resources in equipment have not usually assumed that the public is about to save on a larger scale. Nor have those who decide to reduce the scale of their business expenditures done so because they have seen beforehand that savings are about to decline. In the same way, it can safely be said that the man who puts aside $1,000 out of his income has not necessarily done so because he thinks some businessman is about to install a machine. Nor if he turns his savings into current spending is it because he thinks somewhere some entrepreneur has increased the output of consumers' goods.

To make adjustment more difficult, the rate of saving is steady, whereas the rate of investment is extraordinarily variable. Saving is essentially a steady process. It is, dominated by conventional habits of life, which change but slowly and seem not to be subject to sudden and unexpected variations. So much is this so that substantial changes in saving are likely to arise only from equally substantial changes in the level of income. Investment, on the contrary, is most fluctuating. It has no regular growth; instead it proceeds by fits and starts. Indeed, what else could it be but variable, exposed as it is to the continually shifting expectations of businessmen and likely to be suddenly disturbed by every manner of event, such as inventions, wars, changes in interest rates, and shifts in demand for this good and that?

For these reasons, there can be no certainty that the decisions to invest made by businessmen will be in harmony with those decisions to save by the public which seem necessary if the means for investment are to be forthcoming.

Savings Do Not Get into Investment Automatically

The difficulty of reaching what we may call "synchronous decisions" in respect to rates of saving by the public and rates of investment by businessmen is only one part of the problem. Another part is equally difficult.

Savings, even when they are designed to find their way into investment by businessmen, do not reach their goal by any automatic or direct process. In this, they differ from spendings, for spendings do reach their goal directly. If a person spends his income, he proceeds to buy consumable goods and thereby directly furthers their production; but this by no means is the case when he saves. Instead, his savings must go through various channels before they reach their goal. It is true, if it is a businessman or a corporation that is saving either for expansion or for replacement of equipment, then there is a direct demand for capital goods, for the entrepreneur is turning his savings back into his business. The same holds true if a person buys securities direct from a business which, in turn, will use the proceeds to install new equipment.

These are only a part of the savings of the community. The rest of them go first into the financial machine, in the form of bank deposits, payments to investment bankers for securities, premium payments to insurance companies, and so forth. It is only through the operations of the financial machine that, at the next stage, the funds thus saved reach the hands of businessmen and are used for the purchase of productive equipment and other capital goods.

Now, of course, ideally the financial machine, if it operates efficiently, should be able to get the savings into capital formation with reasonable dispatch, to bring about that harmony between the decisions of the savers and the decisions of the entrepreneurs that is desired. After all, the financial machine is the market for capital, and what is the function of a market if it is not to bring about harmony between the decisions of two groups of people, even if actuated by different motives? That is to say, any market tends to bring about equilibrium between the forces of supply and demand, and the capital market is no exception. Is it not the function of banks to equalize the supply of and demand for loanable funds destined for capital formation? Will they not, therefore, through appropriate variations in the rate of interest for the use of money, make savers aware of the demands of investing entrepreneurs and entrepreneurs aware of the intentions of savers? If they do, then an increase of saving on the part of the community would cause such a lowering of the rate of interest as to encourage an equivalent increase in investment; and an expansion by entrepreneurs would cause an increase in the rate of interest to the point where sufficient savings are attracted into the market. Thus the market rate of interest tends to become what Hayek calls the "natural" or the "equilibrium" rate.

This ideal behavior was considered to be so obviously the rational behavior of the capital market, and of both entrepreneurs and savers, that economists (and bankers as well) in the past have taken it for granted that the fund of savings finds its way into capital formation. In other words, they have practically assumed that the activities of saving and investment constitute a single, continuous process.[1] It is a self-adjusting mechanism that needs no special care and raises no special problems.

This self-adjusting mechanism being assumed, there could be no such thing as overproduction, for the income supplied to the factors of production which coöperate to produce output is both equivalent to and used for the purchase of the total output. That which is saved is not lost to circulation but returns thereto promptly and effectively through the medium of entrepreneurs' investments. Thus supply creates its own demand, and, while variations may take place in the kind of commodity produced and in the relative proportions of consumers' goods and producers' goods, the total output cannot outrun demand. This optimistic theory has long been known under the name of "Say's law," or the "theory of the markets."

How the Interest Rate Works in Practice

Unfortunately, the actual behavior of the capital market is quite different.

The reasons for this are several. One reason is that the interest rate is slow to adjust itself to changing conditions. It is conventional and "sticky," and may, therefore, remain unduly fixed at levels above or below what equilibrium de-

---

[1] As we have seen in the previous chapter (page 274), even the underconsumptionist Hobson, who was brought up on "classical" economics, made this assumption.

mands. Even classical economics would take account of this. It is one of the common "frictions" found in any market.

Another reason is found in the dual functions of banks, which not only serve as intermediaries between the suppliers and demanders of loanable funds, but also are, in modern economic systems, the purveyors of the principal form of the community's money, bank credit. These functions may not be equally well served by any given policy. We have already seen how banks may be moved to expand their elastic credit facilities in times of optimistic expectations and how this can result in inappropriate expansions of capital production.[2] This situation means that eagerness to make profit by increasing the supply of money may cause banks to keep interest rates at lower levels than would have been justified merely by their function of passing on the available stream of savings to the entrepreneurs for investment. There are other times when, because of lack of confidence, banks may withdraw, and rapidly withdraw, their supplies of bank credit and, in their desire for liquidity, raise the rates of interest above the level which the supply of available savings would justify.

Perhaps the most important reason, however, arises from the fact that the rate of interest is not really determined by the volume of savings intended for investment in relation to the demand therefor by the investing entrepreneurs. At least, these are not the only factors determining the rate. There is another factor of great importance, which can be expressed as the demand for cash, as compared with the supply of money. This demand Keynes calls "liquidity preference."

Many transactions in the money market take place between those persons who want to have cash and those who are ready to buy a highly liquid asset. The people who have cash and want to buy an asset are individuals with current accumulations, businessmen with reserves for later use, speculators of all

[2] See Chapter XII.

kinds, and the banks. Those who want cash and will sell an asset to get it are all people in need of ready money, traders reducing their inventories or other holdings, speculators who think prices are likely to fall, and, again, banks. These are the operations which are most influential in determining the short-time rate of interest. They overshadow the immediate importance of the influence exerted, on the one hand, by savings intended for long-time investment and, on the other, by the demand from entrepreneurs adding to their means of production.

It is, therefore, quite possible for the rate of interest, under these circumstances, to be either too high for business to want to borrow for investment uses or too low for the saver to be willing to lend. This outcome is particularly likely to happen considering that the banks are among the most important of those who want to acquire or get rid of money. In times of optimistic sentiment, banks are so eager to acquire earning assets that they are willing to create money for the purpose; and in times of pessimistic sentiment, they are so eager to get liquidity that they call in money wherever they can. In the one case, an unduly low rate of interest encourages investment and discourages saving; in the other, an unduly high rate of interest discourages investment and (possibly) encourages saving.

For all these reasons, it must be said that the money market does not effectively equilibrate the fund of savings and the demand therefor for purposes of capital formation. The common assumption of the past that there is an automatic connection between the funds accumulated by one set of people and the funds spent on the means of production by another set of people must be given up. There is no such automatic connection. It might happen that, at the very time the community was increasing its accumulations for the future, the businessmen were launching an expansion of capital equipment; but this would be mere chance and is quite different from saying that the one change is a spontaneous reaction to the effects of the other. In short, the interest rate, at least for short periods of time, cannot be said to be an effective mechanism for bringing into equilibrium the monetary accumulations of the people and the demands for funds for capital expansion.

The Importance of Consumers' Demand

Even if the interest rate were more effective than it is, the relation between the rate of accumulation and the rate of capital formation may still be distorted, because of the immediate effect of increased (or decreased) accumulation upon the volume of effective demand for the goods and services bought by the consumer. An increase in the rate of saving, for example, may in due time reduce the rate of interest, and this, in turn, may increase the businessman's use of funds in capital expansion; but the *immediate* effect is to reduce the total demand for goods and to disappoint to the same extent the expectations of the producers. As a result, expansion is more likely to be checked than encouraged, for a falling demand for the final output of production is hardly a favorable atmosphere for the expansion of productive equipment.

In the "orthodox" economic theories, there was no worry about the aggregate of effective demand. The demand that was apparently taken out of the system by the process of saving turned up again promptly through the investment activities of the entrepreneurs, who, as it were, restored the accumulations to circulation by putting them into the hands of workers in the capital-producing trades. Thus saving was only a transfer of activity from one kind of industry to another. But if the effect of increased accumulation is to *discourage* capital expansion, then the total activity of society is not maintained. Instead, it is actually reduced, and the effect of accumulation is to bring on what amounts to a depression.

That is to say, the effective motive creating a demand for

capital goods is the demand for the consumers' goods which they are destined to produce. The demand for capital goods is not a direct demand but a derived demand, dependent for its strength on the original demand for consumption. It is not the interest rate but the state of this original demand for consumers' goods that is the deciding factor. It may be, therefore, as Moulton points out,[3] that society faces a serious dilemma. If it sets aside larger funds for capital expansion, it diminishes the incentive for businessmen to use them. If, on the other hand, it increases its scale of expenditures, it encourages producers to expand but reduces the available monetary capital with which to expand.

To put it in another way, the process of saving has two aspects. Seen from one side, it constitutes an addition to the supply of capital funds. Seen from the other side, it is a reduction in the immediate volume of effective demand. In its former aspect, through a lower rate of interest, it makes investment more attractive. In its latter, by reducing the sales expectations of entrepreneurs, it makes investment less attractive. In the one aspect, it reduces cost; in the other, it reduces demand.

Is Business Policy Dependent on the Rate of Interest?

Thus there emerges a conflict of views. Those whose thoughts run in the older, more "orthodox" channels regard interest rate as the effective device causing entrepreneurs to make full use of the savings made available to them by the community. Those who have been influenced by the insistence on effective consumer demand regard interest as ineffective and see the real motive to the entrepreneurs' decisions in the variations of demand.

One would like to know which is, in fact, the more important as a factor in capital expansion or contraction, the rate of

---

[3] H. G. Moulton, *The Formation of Capital*, Washington, 1935, Chap. III.

interest or the effective demand for goods. Common sense seems to lean toward effective demand as the important motive; and such current evidence as we have seems to bear out this attitude.

The Harvard Graduate School of Business Administration has, since 1920, been accumulating a great collection of business cases illustrative of the problems facing business executives. Recently an analysis was made of this collection to separate out cases involving problems of expansion or contraction of output in which interest rates might have been a factor influencing decisions. There were 118 of these cases. In 91, interest rate. was not mentioned as a factor in decision. In 27, interest rate was mentioned, but in only 10 was it regarded as a factor, and in none was it held to be a controlling factor.[4]

A group of investigators at Oxford University, through questionnaire and personal interview, set out to find what actually was the attitude of businessmen toward changes in the rate of interest. They found what perhaps might have been expected, that changes in short-time interest rates, while they might affect profits, seldom affect policy. Almost all the industrialists questioned indicated that the rate of interest was relatively unimportant as compared with changing anticipations of earnings.[5]

These practical conclusions have found some support in theoretical reasoning. Eric Lundberg, in the course of a theoretical analysis of an economic system during a period of expansion, concludes that, whereas the conditions of the capital market are very important in determining investment in long-term projects such as the construction of railroads, for short-term projects the state of the consumers' demand is the dominating factor. He suggests that there may be two types of crisis, according to the dominant kind of investment. In one type of crisis, investment takes the form of capacity

---

[4] J. F. Ebersole, *American Economic Review*, March, 1938, Supplement, 74.
[5] *Oxford Economic Papers*, Oxford, Number 1, Oct., 1938.

to produce consumption goods. The impulse to output is dependent on adequate consumers' spending, and the crisis is due to an excess of saving and a deficiency of purchasing power. The other type of crisis is marked by investment in long-time projects such as railroads. This expansion is then dependent on an adequate supply of savings rather than on the current demand for consumption goods, and the crisis is due to a scarcity of capital.

According to Lundberg, there is some, although not conclusive, evidence that the expansion of 1922 to 1929 in the United States was of the former type, and that the crisis was one of inadequate purchasing power. On the other hand, the crises in Germany in 1925 and 1928 were of the latter type, as were also the great expansions in prewar United States. In these cases, capital shortage was the precipitating cause of the downturn.[6]

One may fairly conclude that, even if the rate of interest reflected better than it actually does the respective pressures of the supply of current savings and the demand for investment by entrepreneurs, it would still be ineffective in bringing about the automatic adjustment of saving to capital formation which seems to have been more or less taken for granted.

As a consequence, disequilibrium is certain to arise whenever the decisions of the entrepreneurs to increase or decrease the scale of their investments do not happen to coincide with the decisions of the community to increase or decrease the scale of their accumulations. How this disequilibrium arises can be seen readily.

Disequilibrium from an Increase of Saving

Suppose the community increases the general scale of its saving. This increase would come about ordinarily by leaving bank balances idle for longer periods of time, and amounts to

---

[6] E. Lundberg, *Studies in the Theory of Economic Expansion*, London, 1937, 254–255, and Appendix to Chap. X.

a general fall in the velocity of circulation of money. If entrepreneurs have not been moved, at the same time, to make
equivalent investments and so put equivalent money in the
hands of wage earners and other income recipients, the result
must be a fall in the effective demand for consumers' goods.
If the entrepreneurs insisted on maintaining the scale of their
output, then the result must be a fall in the general level of
prices and an increased consumption of goods. As a result,
what started out as a general increase of saving has no real
effect. The scale of consumption is unchanged. The community, instead of adding to its wealth (which would have happened had the savings found their way into productive uses),
merely maintains the scale of its consumption. The savings,
in other words, to use Robertson's useful phraseology, have not
been "applied"; instead, they have turned out to be "abortive." [7]

It is not feasible for entrepreneurs to continue their output
in the face of falling prices. The producers of consumers'
goods are now suffering losses and will be moved either to
contract their output or to reduce the level of wages and other
costs. Unfortunately, this procedure will do them no good,
for the spending power of the community is reduced by an
equal amount. Unless the effect of this is to reduce savings
or to cause the banking system to make credit so much cheaper
as to stimulate investment even in the face of falling prices
(neither of which is likely to happen), the entrepreneurs are
no better off and will continue to be no better off, no matter
what they do, so long as the community insists on its expanded
rate of saving.

Thus there are some very curious effects arising from a
tendency to save when active investment by entrepreneurs is
not proceeding. The saver thinks he is adding to his wealth,
but there is no addition to the national wealth. Each indi-

---

[7] D. H. Robertson, *Banking Policy and the Price Level*, London, Chap. V,
"The Kinds of Savings." This very acute analysis of different situations created
by savings under various hypotheses deserves investigation by the student.

vidual can save, but not all of us can save at the same time,
When losses set in, each entrepreneur thinks he can help himself by restriction of output; yet, when all do this, they are
in just as bad straits as before. In short, saving in itself has
no virtue. Thrift can produce no wealth. As Keynes puts it
in one of his more eloquent passages, "If Enterprise is afoot,
wealth accumulates whatever may happen to Thrift; and if
Enterprise is asleep, wealth decays whatever Thrift may be
doing." [8]

Thus abortive saving sets up a process of deflation which
feeds upon itself to the disruption of the whole productive
process. In the meanwhile, anything which further discourages investment or further encourages saving aggravates
the slump. If, as is common in depressions, a fear complex
seizes upon the community so that it is moved to hoard its
available means of payment, this must add to the trouble. If,
also, the practices of business and government in regard to
sinking funds and amortization quotas cause them to continue to collect these at the levels of the previous boom and to
hold them out of investment (a practice common enough, it
would appear, in business), the result may be to prolong the
slump indefinitely. The situation becomes even worse if the
government is moved by thrift campaigns to reduce public
expenditures to the lowest limits, for then the only counteracting source from which expenditure might be expected is
blocked. "Financial prudence" may then become a serious
obstacle to recovery.

The only means of putting an end to this disastrous situation is a cessation of the saving practices of the community or
such an outburst of investment by entrepreneurs as would restore effective demand for the output of industry by putting
new money into active use. Indeed, the low level of income

---

[8] *Treatise on Money*, Vol. II, Chap. 30, 149. The reader should not miss the
amusing parable of the bananas, Vol. I, Chap. 12, Section 2.

to which the depression has reduced the community may bring about these very things. Saving and "parsimony" cease to be possible. On the other hand, conditions favorable to investment gradually emerge. The need for replacements, the great ease of funds in the money market, and the lowering cost of production brought about by a general reduction of wage rates tend to encourage a revival of output, and with it some capital formation. With saving falling and the scale of investment tending to revive, the deflation ceases and equilibrium, although possibly on a low level of output, is finally restored.

Disequilibrium from Increase in Investment

Now let us see what happens when the business community is moved to increase the scale of its expenditures for capital goods—that is, increase the scale of capital formation.

This expansion must involve an available supply of funds, and implies either that the deposits of businessmen are moved faster (that is, that the velocity of circulation of money increases) or that the banking system is willing to increase the supply of credit available for business. If the community is not moved, at the same time, to increase the scale of its savings and so withdraw funds from active use, the result must be to increase the aggregate of effective demand for goods. The money drawn upon by the entrepreneurs is paid out in wages and other incomes, and is thus added to the total purchasing power of the community and, on our assumption of no increased rates of saving, to the aggregate of effective consumer demand.

The result is an increase in the prices of consumers' goods and, because of the familiar lag of costs behind prices, an increase in profits, and a great encouragement to an expansion of output. Thus the increase of activity in the field of producers' goods brings about, in its turn, an increase in activity in the field of consumers' goods. This increase is a further encouragement to investment by entrepreneurs whose derived demand for capital equipment is greatly stimulated.

Thus a spiral of expansion is started, which develops without serious interruption as long as the investments of entrepreneurs continue to be carried on. Unless, before this occurs, full employment of resources has been reached, the expansion can be brought to an end only by an increase of saving, or by the resistance of the banking system to further credit expansion, or by some cause that so changes the expectations of entrepreneurs as to make them disapprove of further investments.

Thus the effect of investment spending by entrepreneurs unaccompanied by corresponding saving by the community is essentially to bring about a boom. Just as saving without capital formation results in deflation or depression, so capital formation unaccompanied by saving results in inflation and "prosperity." One brings about a reduction in effective demand and, thereby, a reduction in the total output and income of society. The other brings about an increase in effective demand and, thereby, an expansion of the total output and income of society.

Thus we come to the conclusion that equilibrium is disturbed whenever the decisions of entrepreneurs in respect to investment and the decisions of the community in respect to saving and accumulation are not in harmony. This disequilibrium takes the form of the cumulative expansion of boom on the one hand and the cumulative contraction of slump on the other. Because the "classical" assumptions that this kind of disequilibrium is prevented from becoming serious by the operation of the interest rate have been disclosed to be unfounded, we have here an interesting possibility of accounting for business cycles through variations of saving and investment.

CHAPTER XV

THE THEORIES OF J. M. KEYNES

W E have seen in the previous chapter that the assumptions of what might be called "classical economics" in respect to the process of saving and investment are not borne out in practice. The translation of accumulations into investment and so into the incomes of the factors of production is not spontaneous. It is slow, uncertain, and unreliable. As a result, the belief of classical theory that society need not concern itself. with variations in the rate of saving and investment is quite unfounded. These variations, in the conditions of actual life, turn out to be most important indeed, for, unless they happen to coincide in a fashion that is most unlikely to occur, they may be an impelling cause of booms and slumps.

The analysis of the problems associated with these variations in saving and investment owes much to the theories of John Maynard Keynes, the eminent English economist. Keynes is the most influential representative of the revolt against the classical theories in respect to savings and investment. Although this revolt was begun in his *Treatise on Money*, 1930, it finds its complete expression in his famous *General Theory of Employment, Interest and Money*, 1936, the influence of which on current economic thinking and on practical economic policy can hardly be overestimated.

The Nature of Equilibrium

Keynes starts with the proposition that the scale of output and employment at any time is determined by the decisions of entrepreneurs. It is they who decide to produce this or that kind of output; it is they who decide whether to increase or diminish output as a whole; it is they who decide whether to expand the volume of investment and purchase of capital goods. Their decisions obviously are based, except for sentimental reasons, upon their expectations of profits, which are, as Keynes put it, "the mainspring of change in the industrial countries of the world outside Russia."

There are certain conditions under which the entrepreneurs have no motive to either expand or contract the scale of their output. These conditions constitute a state of equilibrium. They occur whenever the expected income (or proceeds) from the output of a given volume of employment is just equal to the supply price of that output, the supply price being that volume of proceeds which will just make it worth while for the entrepreneur to supply the necessary employment. Higher expectations than this are an incentive to expand output; lower expectations, an incentive to contract output.

The aggregate proceeds which may be expected consist of two parts: the amount which the community spends on consumption, and the amount which it devotes (or plans to devote) to new investment. These two taken together constitute effective demand. Hence equilibrium exists whenever effective demand is just equal to the supply price of aggregate output.

In classical economics there is only one stable equilibrium of this sort—namely, where all resources are employed. If resources are not fully employed, competition for the employment reduces the terms on which they will be available and thus encourages expansion until conditions of full employment are reached.

Keynes holds that there are many positions of equilibrium, of which equilibrium with full employment is a very special case. Thus, for example, if, in a given state of equilibrium, the community decides to save more, then, unless this is ac-

companied by an equivalent increase in the amount devoted
to investment, the effective demand falls, and the output tends
to be contracted.   If equivalent investment does not take place
(and the analysis set forth in the previous chapter indicates
that there is no certainty that it will), then the current volume
of output cannot be supported.   Entrepreneurs then reduce the
scale of their employment, and the total income of the community falls to a lower level.   When this reduction reaches
a level, where the proceeds once more cover the aggregate
supply price of the reduced output, a new equilibrium is
reached.   It is an equilibrium with less than full employment
of resources, and it is maintained as long as the tendency
to consume remains at its (relatively) low level.

Similarly, if the community turns some of its accumulations
into the purchase of consumers' goods, then, unless this is accompanied by a fall in the amount devoted to investment (and
again there is no reason to suppose this will occur), then the
aggregate effective demand is increased, the sale proceeds exceed the supply price of output, and the entrepreneurs increase the scale of their production and employment.   Thus the
total income of society is increased until it reaches the level
where the sale proceeds of the enlarged output no longer exceed
the aggregate supply price of this output.   This new equilibrium will be maintained also as long as the tendency to consume remains at its (relatively) high level.

Thus, there may be many equilibrium levels, some with high
output and some with low.   Of course, the level cannot be
higher than full employment of resources, but there is no reason
to expect that it cannot be *lower* than full employment.   Whatever the level may be, the total output of that level can be
supported only provided the consumption of the community
together with the current investment of the entrepreneurs is
sufficient to absorb that output.   Given the current rate of
consumption (what Keynes calls "the propensity to consume"),
the equilibrium level of output must depend on the amount of

current investment. This amount, in turn, depends on the inducement to invest, which thus becomes the prime mover in determining the scale of output of the community and the level of its employment.[1]

The Marginal Efficiency of Capital

This inducement to invest and, therefore, the volume of investment at any time depend on the relation of what Keynes calls *the marginal efficiency of capital* to the current rate of interest.

The marginal efficiency of capital is the ratio of the expected yield of an additional capital asset over a period of years to the supply price of such asset (that is, the price which will just induce the producers thereof to supply it). In other words, it is the expected earnings of such assets expressed as a percentage return on the supply price.

The marginal efficiency of capital at any time, therefore, depends on the state of the entrepreneurs' expectations. It is raised by invention and innovation and by the expectation of rising prices. It is lowered by the expectation of falling interest rates, expressive of the willingness of lenders to take lower returns, and by any general increase in scope of investment which threatens to reduce the yield of capital goods at the same time that their supply price is likely to be increased. It is affected by the state of the entrepreneurs' "animal spirits," for much investment is made not merely as a result of calculation but under the stimulus of irrational optimism. Always it is subject to somewhat violent fluctuations, owing to the fundamental uncertainty of the world in which we live. We have but little means of knowing what will be the value or yield of capital in the future, so•little that scientific basis on which to form any calculable probability is lacking. Consequently, we take the present as the guide to the future;

---

[1] J. M. Keynes, *General Theory of Employment, Interest and Money,* 1936, Harcourt, Brace & Company, Inc., New York, Chap. 3.

we accept existing opinion, the community judgment, and the behavior of the majority as a correct indicator of prospects; and, although this is good enough while stability reigns, it exposes us to sudden and violent changes when our expectations turn out to be unjustified.

If, now, the marginal efficiency of capital corresponds to the market rate of interest, entrepreneurs have no motive to either increase or decrease investment. But if the marginal efficiency of capital exceeds the rate of interest, and as long as it continues to do so, entrepreneurs are moved to add to investment.

What Happens When Investment Increases?

In classical economic theory (which assumes that in equilibrium all resources are fully employed), this additional investment would not at the moment increase the aggregate income or employment of the community. It could take place only at the expense of consumption, the reduction of which is insured by the higher rate of interest that entrepreneurs would obviously be ready to offer. That is to say, full employment being assured, the volume of investment has no effect on the aggregate employment of the community; nor even, for the immediate future, on its aggregate income. It merely determines how much employment is to be found and how much income produced in one section of the productive mechanism as compared with the other. The actualities of economic life indicate that full employment of resources is not the normal situation. It is not necessarily to be found in equilibrium; still less is it found in recurring periods of transition such as the phases of the business cycle. As a consequence thereof, increase of investment need not be, and in fact is not, accompanied by a coincident decrease in consumption.

What really happens when investment increases is a coincident *increase* in consumption and an increase, therefore, in the aggregate of income and employment, the amount of such increase depending upon what Keynes calls "the propensity to consume," and which he defines as "the functional relationship between a given level of income and the expenditure on consumption out of that level of income."

When investment is increased, the money incomes of the factors of production are equivalently increased; and, if the total increase of income were spent, a very rapid increase in employment would take place, each group of income recipients supplying income for the next until full employment is attained. As a matter of fact, this outcome is not what happens. It is a fundamental law, Keynes thinks, "upon which we are entitled to depend with great confidence both *a priori* from our knowledge of human nature and from the detailed facts of experience," that people increase their consumption as income increases, but not so much as the increase of income. That is to say, the "propensity to consume" is decidedly stable.

Doubtless over long periods during which habits have time enough to adapt themselves to changes in circumstances, the propensity to consume will be modified. But over short periods of time, such as the business cycle, standards of living are relatively stable and if the primary needs of a family have been covered, an increase of income may induce a greater accumulation rather than a greater consumption. Hence a man "is apt to save the difference which discovers itself between his actual income and the expense of his habitual standard; or, if he does adjust his expenditures to changes in his income, he will over short periods do so imperfectly."

As a result thereof, spending does not increase *pari passu* with investment; income of successive groups of recipients does not increase so rapidly, and the total volume of income (and employment) due to investment is smaller than it otherwise would have been. Thus the rate of investment taken with the propensity to consume determines the total income of the community. To put it in another way, there is a definite ratio, given the propensity to consume, between an increment of investment and the resultant increment of total income; a ratio which Keynes calls "the multiplier" or, more exactly, "the investment multiplier." If this multiplier is K, then an increment of investment I will bring about an increment of income KI. If, for example, investment is $100 million and the multiplier 3, then the total increment of income due to the investment is $300 million.

Let us examine the multiplier in more detail.

The Multiplier

When investment is first made, aggregate income is increased in all industries immediately affected. If the investment is house-building, then the incomes of all those engaged in building and in making or transporting materials are increased. This increase may be called the *primary* increase in income. Some of this increased income is spent on purchases of one kind or another, both by the wage earners affected and by the recipients of profits, interest, and other non-wage income. This development gives rise to further income in industries affected (largely consumption industries), and this further increase of income may be called the *secondary* increase. Obviously, beyond that there will be *tertiary* increases, and so on, which, however, we may lump together under the general title of secondary increase. Of course, as long as there are factors of production unemployed, increase of aggregate income will be accompanied by an increase of employment.

Now, clearly, the sum of these secondary incomes (in the inclusive sense indicated) depends on the propensity to consume of the community as a whole. If all the additional income were promptly spent, the secondary income would increase very fast at each turnover, and a comparatively small rate of investment would lead to a state of full employment and maximum real income. If there still persisted an unrestricted urge to spend, the result from then on, because of complete inelasticity of supply, could be only an unlimited rise of prices (that is, inflation). If, on the other hand, the propensity to consume were so inflexible that no increase in consumption is induced by the primary increase of income, then there would be no secondary income or employment whatever; and the increase of investment would have minimum effects. These varying proportions of spending and saving the increased income determine the multiplier.

If, for example, of every increment of income $\frac{2}{3}$ is spent and $\frac{1}{3}$ is saved, then the total addition to income produced by the investment of $\$1 = \$1 + \frac{2}{3} + \frac{4}{9} + \frac{8}{27} + \ldots\ldots = \$3$. The ratio of the total added income to the volume of investment is 3 to 1, and the multiplier is 3. If $\frac{1}{2}$ is spent and $\frac{1}{2}$ saved, the multiplier is 2. If $\frac{5}{6}$ is spent and $\frac{1}{6}$ saved, the multiplier is 6, and so on.

Thus the multiplier depends on the propensity to consume, which determines the fractions saved or spent out of the increment of income produced by investment. It will be noted that the multiplier is the reciprocal of the fraction saved. This fact means that the smaller the additions to savings, the larger the multiplier; and the larger the additions saved, the smaller the multiplier. Hence spendthrift communities suffer wider fluctuations of income from variations in investment than do thrifty communities. On the other hand, in the event of a slump, a smaller increment of investment would bring about recovery in a spendthrift community than in a thrifty community. If a community varied its habits (although this is unlikely in short periods) so as to make savings relatively small in booms but relatively large in slumps, it would experience great fluctuations, booming expansions being followed by periods of prolonged stagnation, stubbornly resistant to all remedial action.

In actual life, the multiplier, although always exceeding unity, is not very great. If it were, we would be subject to much greater fluctuations of income (and employment) than we actually have. Were the multiplier large, even a small increase of investment would soon produce a condition of full employment, while a decrease in investment would bring about such a fall in demand that industry would almost cease to function.   Possibly for England (at any rate, in depression), the multiplier would be no greater than 2.   For the United States, it would likely be somewhat higher.[2]

What the Multiplier Signifies

It will be seen from the examples given that, whatever the multiplier may be, the aggregate of savings must equal the original investment.   Thus, if ⅓ is saved at each turnover of income, then the total savings as the result of an investment of $1 $= \frac{1}{3} (1) + \frac{1}{3} (\frac{2}{3}) + \frac{1}{3} (\frac{4}{9}) + . = \$1$; and similarly for any fraction saved.[3]   What the multiplier fundamentally signifies, therefore, is that investment will cause income to increase to just the degree that will elicit the equivalent saving, the increase being large when the propensity to save is weak, and small when the propensity to save is strong.

In orthodox economics, investment and saving are brought to equality by the interest rate.   Entrepreneurs with hopeful expectations and a corresponding urge to investment elicit the necessary savings by offering a higher rate of interest.   In Keynes' economics, this relation, although possibly effective in the long run, is not at all to be relied on in the short.   Banks are slow to translate rising demands for capital into a higher rate of interest; and even when they do, saving, dominated by sluggish habits, does not readily respond.   What actually happens is quite different and quite unfamiliar.   Investment elicits the equivalent volume of saving, it is true, not through a rise in interest rates, however, but through a higher level of income from which, owing to the stability of the propensity to con-

---

[2] P. H. Douglas (*Controlling Depressions*, 125) puts it very close to 3.   Colin Clark (*Economic Journal*, Sept. 1938) has recently estimated the multiplier in Australia at 2.08, and, in Great Britain, 2.07 in 1929–1933, and 3.22 in 1934–1937 (the balance of payments being regarded as investment).

[3] For examples see Joan Robinson, *Introduction to the Theory of Employment*, London, 1937, 22–24.   This book is a simplified Keynes for the general reader.

sume, income receivers tend to save increasing amounts. And, furthermore, a higher rate of interest in this conjuncture would cause less, rather than more, savings, for it would depress investment, hence income, and finally savings. This situation is the reason why banks, following traditional policies of raising interest rates, can inflict such damage.

What Happens When Savings Increase?

So far we have examined how savings are brought to equality, when the initiative is taken by entrepreneurs making investment. This equality is imposed also if the process begins with variations in savings. Independent or autonomous variations in savings (in short periods) are not likely to occur, but, if they do, and investment does not happen to increase at the same time, they serve merely to reduce income. An increase in savings, being equivalent to a decrease in spending, reduces the expectations of all entrepreneurs producing consumption goods. They tend, therefore, to reduce their output and employment. This action reduces the income of the community and continues to do so until, in order to protect their customary standards of living, people reduce their savings back to the level justified by investment. An attempted increase of savings, under the circumstances, is a useless proceeding, for, there being no increase in investment, there can be no increase in saving. Any increase in savings is bound to be abortive.

Of course, if the rate of interest were effective, this outcome would be avoided; but it is not effective. It ought to be reduced to encourage investment. It is not reduced; or, if it is, is reduced too slowly. In the meanwhile, owing to the fall in consumption, the expectations of the entrepreneur in consumers' goods are worsened and his urge to investment reduced. Thus, before the fall in interest has occurred, he is experiencing losses in his output, and these will overshadow any favorable effect of the later reduction in interest. This circumstance is the reason why, even if the savings are used to purchase securities, and so raise their price and lower their yield (and the rate of interest), the action is ineffective. By this time, losses have set in, and the entrepreneur, to make good his loss, is now selling securities, with the result of canceling the purchase of the savers, counteracting the fall in yield, and rendering the rate of interest ineffective.

Investment Sets the Pace

The upshot of the argument is this. Investment and nothing else is the source of changes in output and employment. If investment is active, then either by choice or by compulsion savings will rise equally. Everyone can save or not save as he chooses, but the increase of investment will increase his tendency to choose saving.

Saving is equal to investment, because investment leads to a state of affairs in which people want to save. Investment causes incomes to be whatever is required to induce people to save at a rate equal to the rate of investment.[4]

If, on the other hand, investment is passive, then no increase in saving can be effective. Savings are reduced to the level of investment through the reduction of income imposed on the community by the restrictive actions of the entrepreneurs.

In other words, in modern society the initiative lies with the entrepreneur, not the saver. If the savers' decisions correspond with those of the entrepreneurs in their investments, then equilibrium is not disturbed. If they wish to save more or less than this volume of investment, then they will have to submit to a process designed to make them change their minds. If they try to save less, their incomes will rise until they save what the entrepreneurs have invested. If they try to save more, their incomes will fall until they again meet the decisions of the entrepreneurs. Somehow investment and saving must come

---

[4] Joan Robinson, *Introduction to the Theory of Employment,* 12.

to equality.   Apparently the *only* way in which people can be
made to increase savings when investment increases is by an
increase of income; just as the only way in which they can be
made to reduce their savings when investment decreases is by
a reduction of income.   It seems a very cumbersome process,
but it is imposed on society by the ineffectiveness of the rate
of interest.

Actual Savings and Investment Cannot Diverge

All this process may be expressed in another way.   Saving
and investment in any community *must* be equal.   If we define income as the value created by the producers of output,
and saving as the excess of income over consumption, then
saving must equal investment, for the output must be sold
either to consumers or to other entrepreneurs.   What is sold
to entrepreneurs is their current investment.   Hence current
investment is the difference between total income and consumption, which, by definition, is saving.

That is to say, consumption can be exercised only over consumers' goods.   Goods sold to entrepreneurs are not available
for consumption.   They constitute the part of income which is
saved.

Thus it is fundamentally impossible to have a divergence
of saving and investment.   They are two faces of the same
thing, just as what is sold is the same thing as what is bought.
What we have been examining is the process by which, when
the decisions of the community in respect to saving (and consuming) happen to diverge from the decisions of the entrepreneurs in regard to investment, they are brought into the
harmony which the nature of the case imposes.

The Case of Business Cycles

Although Keynes did not develop his theories as a description of business cycles, nevertheless business cycles can be described in the terms of this process.   Indeed, the cycle is a

special example, over short periods of time, and with continually reversing movements, of this process in action.

In the language of the *General Theory*, the business cycle is essentially a fluctuation in the marginal efficiency of capital, relative to the current rates of interest. It begins with something that increases the attractiveness of investment, "a new invention, or the development of a new country, or a war, or a return of business confidence as the result of many small influences tending the same way," and proceeds to that general increase in the volume of income and employment, which, as we have seen, is brought about by the operation of the multiplier.

The expansion which is thus set going is, of course, dependent on the acquiescence of the banking system, which must supply the new money that the additional investment requires. It is stimulated by the inflation of prices and profits which this new money sets in motion whenever the output of consumption goods is not elastic.

Under these encouragements, the boom may go to considerable lengths, even to the level of full employment of resources. But as time goes on, various discouraging factors come into play which put effective brakes on further expansion.

How Expansion Comes to an End

It is probable, Keynes thinks, that the "marginal propensity to consume," on the maintenance of which the inducement to invest is so greatly dependent, is subject to some decline as expansion goes on. Conventional habits of consumption cause the community to spend a diminishing proportion of an increasing income. Furthermore, expansion increases the proportion of aggregate income accruing to entrepreneurs whose tendency to consume is probably below the average for the community. Again, as employment increases, potential savings which have been spent on private and public relief are released from these uses, and in all probability not completely spent. The fall in the propensity to consume may be counter-acted for a time by the current rise in stock market values which makes people "feel" wealthy enough to spend freely, especially in the well-to-do class·which Keynes holds "may be extremely susceptible to unforeseen changes in the money-value of its wealth"; but this can only delay the inevitable decline.

The diminishing propensity to consume reduces the expecta-tions of the entrepreneurs and lowers the marginal efficiency of capital; the more so as the increase of general activity increases the pressure on the producers of equipment, raises the prices which they will have to pay for the factors of production, and raises thereby the supply price of capital goods.   It will be recalled that the marginal efficiency of capital is the ratio of the expected earnings of additional capital assets to their supply price. As expansion goes on, both factors of this ratio move unfavorably to the entrepreneurs. This outcome will lead to certain disappointment. Expectations based on a yield of (say) 6 per cent face the bitter reality of 2 per cent. With this realization, the marginal efficiency of capital may suddenly collapse.

This unfortunate result might be postponed if the rate of interest were kept sufficiently low, for the inducement to invest depends on the relation of the marginal efficiency of capital to the rate of interest. But the rate of interest actually tends to rise. This rise in interest rates is due to a change in the de-sire of people to hold wealth in the form of cash, to which Keynes gives the name "liquidity preference." Liquidity pref-erence is determined by the strength of the motives causing the public to hold cash. These motives are: (a) the *transactions* motive, or the need of cash for current personal and business exchanges; (b) the *precautionary* motive, to provide for sud-den expenses and advantageous purchases, or to meet fixed liabilities; and (c) the *speculative* motive, to take advantage of changes in the prices of goods and securities. If these motives are strong, the interest has to be high to induce people to give up cash.   If they are weak, interest can be low; and it is because interest is lower than the marginal efficiency of capital during a period of expansion that investment proceeds as it does. All the motives to liquidity preference grow stronger as expansion proceeds.   Transactions demand more money; the future may look a little uncertain; and goods and securities may appear to be valued too high.   The bankers can counteract these forces by increasing the supply of money, but their concern with their reserves makes them less and less willing to do this. Hence interest rates will rise, and this rise at a time when the marginal efficiency of capital has begun to fall will play a part in bringing about the crisis.

As a result of these unfavorable changes, the optimistic expectations of the entrepreneurs fade suddenly away.   The boom is over, swallowed up in the "sudden collapse of the marginal efficiencies of capital," and the slump sets in.

The Slump

The reduction of investment which now ensues reduces employment and income in all primary activity, which in time reduces effective demand in secondary occupations and so on.   The effect of this reduction (as in the case of increase) depends on the multiplier.   If the multiplier is large, the reduction in aggregate income will be large; if it is small, the reduction will be small.   If each group reduced its consumption with every reduction in income, the total reduction would bring activity very low.   If, on the contrary, each group reduced its consumption less than the reduction in income, falling back on accumulated savings in order to keep up its standards of living, then the total reduction would not be so great.

In any case a reduction takes place, unless active steps are taken to uphold effective demand.   This reduction may be very substantial, owing to the fears both of the community in general and of the business world.   People are then led to "hoard"; liquidity preference becomes very high.   As they try to add to their "savings," income continues to fall. In the meanwhile, confidence among businessmen will have ebbed away completely. The collapse in expectations and in the marginal efficiency of capital is so serious as to make net investment negligible. It is true that the rate of interest does, in due time, begin to fall, and possibly fall very low, as the supply of money, now no longer needed in business, becomes adequate even to the high liquidity preferences of the community. But even a low rate of interest may, for a while, be unattractive to entrepreneurs.

All this is exaggerated by the effects: (a) of the stock market slump, which reduces still further the marginal propensity to consume; and (b) of the surplus stocks of goods now making their appearance, for until they are out of the way recovery is not possible.

In due time, stocks are cleared out of the way, the sooner because carrying costs are considerable, and price sacrifice is better than further interest payments. Furthermore, in some interval of time, obsolescence and decay create a relative scarcity of capital, and with this a rise in the expected profitability of producing capital assets. When these influences have begun to set in, the marginal efficiency of capital once more increases, and, if interest rates continue favorably low, recovery proceeds, and the cycle is on the way through another swing.

What the Cycle Amounts to

Thus the cycle turns out to be a fluctuation in the marginal efficiency of capital, as entrepreneurs find their expectations rising and falling. Variations in investment are what essentially cause and constitute the cycle. They make up the major swing, and they impose a corresponding variation in the incomes and employment of the people. The rise originates in all sorts of forces and continues until the income and hence the savings of the people are brought to appropriate levels. This level might be a new and stable equilibrium were it not that the very forces bringing it about have let loose factors of disintegration which check the hopeful expectations of entrepreneurs. Upon this, there follows a collapse of investment, and, as this is not accompanied by appropriate reduction in savings, the income of the community is brought down by contraction of output, until the savings have come to their necessary equality with investment. This position, too, might be one of relatively stable equilibrium, were not forces tending to restore higher levels brought into the picture.

All these cyclical phenomena are the outcome of the decisions of the entrepreneur who, by increase and decrease of investments, imposes a multiple increase or decrease in the income and employment of the community.

But the entrepreneur of the *General Theory* is not quite the masterful agent of change that sometimes stalks through the economic picture. He may still be the agent of change, but he is no longer masterful. True, he thinks in terms of expectations; but his expectations never reach very far ahead. He really has little capacity for foresight, in general being content to hope that present conditions will continue. Because of his uncertainty in forecast, his expectations are always precarious and subject to violent change, imposing thereby great fluctuations in investment, income, and employment. He is much affected by animal spirits, both up and down, and greatly dependent on a favorable political and social atmosphere. Lacking this, he is apt to undergo a "crisis of sentiment," and is, for long periods of time, quite unable to proceed with any boldness whatsoever. He is unusually dependent on the state of consumption and continually wonders what shape the propensity to consume is about to take. For this reason, he thinks much more in terms of effective demand than of cost of production. Anything that seems likely to change effective demand apparently affects him much more and more quickly than anything that would seem likely to reduce his cost of production. He is particularly sensitive to increases of saving, for these reduce his expectations by reducing effective demand; and he is apparently quite unable to see that saving might encourage investment by reducing interest and so raising the value of capital.

Are We to Have Chronic Depression?

This timidity of the entrepreneur may be understandable enough in the conditions which have surrounded the world since the onset of the great depression, but, if it is going to be a characteristic of the modern businessman, we may be in for a rather disagreeable time. The lack of enterprise of the entrepreneur in the face of the saving habits of the modern world is so serious as to threaten us with chronic underinvestment and a persistent danger lest society be hung up for long periods in a state of underemployment, where, despite equilibrium, resources are not fully employed, and where it is only too true that there is "poverty in the midst of plenty."

Modern societies have powerful habits of saving which weaken the propensity to consume. The richer a society grows, the more savings seem to increase. Unless investment proceeds at an equivalent pace, these savings will prove abortive. The income of society will be reduced to the point where savings "will be sufficiently diminished to correspond to the weakness of the inducement to invest," and there will be equilibrium with resources not fully employed. Unfortunately, it seems highly probable that investment will not be able to proceed at the pace demanded. During the nineteenth century, "the growth of populations and invention, the opening up of new land, the state of confidence and the frequency of war over the average of (say) each decade" seem to have been sufficient to maintain the marginal efficiency of capital and the inducement to invest. But "today and presumably for the future," the marginal efficiency of capital is much lower. The very richness of the community which encourages great savings implies such an enormous accumulation of capital and such diminished opportunities for further investment that only a very rapid fall in the rate of interest will enable expansion to go on. That this fall is apt to occur is unlikely. The uncertainties of the modern world are so formidable that liquidity preference cannot be reduced rapidly. We continue to put our faith in cash, and, as long as we do so, no matter what we "save," the rate of interest will not fall adequately. Two per cent, perhaps as low as we will go, is probably too high to induce investment sufficient to take care of all society is willing to save.

In short, wealthy communities suffer from the fate of Midas. We cannot enjoy the wealth we have. We are barred from the level of employment and the standard of life which the technical conditions of production are capable of giving us.[5]

A certain pessimism which underlies Keynes' later treatment tends to turn the balance of the discussion away from variations in activity, such as are characteristic of cycles, to causes of underemployment, such as are characteristic of slumps. Primarily, the *General Theory* turns out to be a theory of depression. As such, it adds little to our knowledge of booms. The light it throws on the process of depression is searching; and his conclusions have had enormous influence, both upon the state of economic theory and upon the practical programs designed to cope with the great depression of the 1930's.

What Can Be Done?

If Keynes is right, then the means of meeting both cyclical and chronic depression are clearly indicated. The appropriate policy is encouragement of investment. This encouragement may be direct or indirect, but encouragement there must be. In a cyclical slump, the best (perhaps the only) encouragement

---

[5] This conclusion is implicit throughout a great part of the *General Theory*. But the student might refer particularly to Chap. 16, "Sundry Observations on the Nature of Capital," Chap. 23, "Notes on Mercantilism, etc.," and Chap. 24, "Concluding Notes."

to investment is an increase of consumption. Hence it would be appropriate to expand government spending (the only type likely to expand at the time) by payments to unemployed persons; conversely, it would be entirely inappropriate to lower wages. The lowering of wages does not encourage entrepreneurs by lowering their costs; it discourages them still further by reducing the aggregate of effective demand.

If private investment remains obdurate, then public investment (public works) must step in and continue either until savings are all put to work or until the spendings of the community encourage once more the habit of private investment.

For the problem of chronic underinvestment, more varied measures may be advisable: [6]

(1) The, average propensity to consume could be increased by more equal distribution of the national income. Much less inequality than we now have would still be adequate as a motive to economic activity; and the greater spending which would be brought about would help to solve the problem of investment.

(2) It may be necessary to reduce the level of interest rates below the minimum which *laissez faire* brings about. If this reduction were brought about, investment could increase, perhaps so much that even the current liquidity preference which is partly a result of fears of underemployment might be reduced. How this reduction is to be attained is a problem. As Keynes says, it means the "euthanasia of the investor"; and the banking system would hardly bring this about voluntarily. What seems to be implied is a socialization of investment.

(3) Apart from a change in the distribution of income, or forceful reduction of interest rates, there seems no method available save progressive enlargement of the field of public investment, by a liberal extension of the area of "public works." As long as private investment remains inadequate, this exten-

---

[6] Keynes, *General Theory*, Chap. 24.

sion of public activity alone seems capable of enabling the community to maintain full employment of its resources. The conditions of optimum equilibrium, where the volume of investment is equal to the excess of total income over consumption at the level of full employment, could then be fulfilled.

If the propensity to consume in modern societies continues to decline, the field of public investment would have to increase steadily, and this increase may well weaken the vitality of private investment. Increased public investment tends to spoil the climate for private entrepreneurs, and, if this occurs, the field occupied by "public works" would progressively expand. It is difficult to apply a measure of control to private capitalism without setting up a tendency to a socialistic state.

Keynes and the Underconsumptionists

It is clear that Keynes has close affinities with the underconsumption theorists. He accepts the principle of effective demand as the chief determinant of output. He would agree with Foster and Catchings that saving as such is deflationary, and the stress he puts on the importance of investment indicates that he would accept their dictum that we progress only while we are "filling up our shelves." He would not agree with Hobson that the crisis is brought on in a great flood of goods. There is no such flood of goods, for entrepreneurs will avoid any such calamity by restriction of investment whenever their expectations begin to fade. That is, Hobson traces the crash to savings that are invested, Keynes to savings that are *not*. On the other hand, Keynes would accept the necessity, so stressed by Hobson, of bringing about a greater equality of income, but only as a last resort, after the various measures which might stimulate and control investment have been tried and found inadequate.[7]

------

[7] See Keynes, *General Theory*, 324–325, where he states his position in relation to the underconsumption theories.

On Certain Controversies in Regard to Saving and Investment

We have noted that Keynes has so defined saving and investment that they appear always and by necessity to be equal. They are simply two faces of the same thing. While Keynes feels that these definitions are in accord with "common sense" meanings of the terms, he has by no means satisfied his fellow economists, many of whom feel that saving and investment do not necessarily coincide, especially in short periods, and that it is precisely their divergence that is most characteristic of the transitions which make up business cycles. Furthermore, there is a certain ambiguity in Keynes' handling of saving and investment that increases the suspicion that their definitional equality is not so useful as it seems at first sight.

To be precise, although saving and investment are equal by definition, it seems as if they have to be *made* equal by approximate changes in income. Increased investment causes income to expand and so "induces" people to do the "necessary extra saving." That is, saving *must* equal investment, for, if it does not, the action of the multiplier will make it. This proposition is not merely confusing; some even think it is foolish. Says Hawtrey:

> The idea that a tendency for saving and investment to become different has to be counteracted by an expansion or contraction of the total of incomes is an absurdity; such a tendency cannot strain the economic system; it can only strain Mr. Keynes' vocabulary.[8]

Probably the "strain" arises from the fact that the full effect of any investment *takes time*. During this time, a process of change goes on which, given the propensity to consume, adjusts saving to investment. If we regard this period of time as the unit of measurement, then we may say that, in all "times," saving and investment are equal, just as we say that prices and

---

[8] R. G. Hawtrey, *Capital and Employment,* Longmans, Green and Company, New York, 1937, 176.

cost of production are always equal in a "normal" period. But if we are thinking of the process of change and the passage of time, it is more natural to say that saving and investment, although unequal, have been brought to equality.

It would seem, therefore, that the concept of equality of saving and investment is more appropriate to picture the completed process of investment than the changing process itself. At the end of the process, investment and saving are equal. During the process, they can be regarded as equal only by interpretations that seem unnecessarily strained.

For this reason, critics of Keynes have offered alternative definitions of saving and investment which we will now examine.

Active and Passive Investment

Mr. Hawtrey suggests that "there is a sense in which saving and investment, suitably interpreted, while not identical, do tend to equality." The clue to the problem lies in the distinction between "active" and "passive" investment.[9]

Investment, in general, is the excess of output over consumption. It is unconsumed wealth. As the total of unconsumed wealth is obviously identical with the total of saving, there is an identity between saving and investment. Active investment includes only that part of unconsumed wealth which is *voluntarily* acquired, under the inducement to invest which operates when the yield of investment outweighs the rate of interest. There is no reason to suppose that it is equal to the total of unconsumed wealth which is saving.

If active investment is not equal to saving, note what happens. If it falls short of saving, some part of the increment of unconsumed wealth (all of which must be held by someone) will not be acquired voluntarily—that is, there must be an involuntary accumulation of unsold goods. This accumulation is "undesigned" or "passive" investment. It represents the differ-

---

[9] *Capital and Employment,* 176–180.

ence between total investment and saving. If active investment exceeds saving, then the excess is represented by "undesigned" or "passive" disinvestment (or, alternatively, by negative passive investment). That is to say, stocks of unsold goods undesignedly decline.

When active investment thus differs from saving, a cause of disequilibrium is at work which brings about various (cumulative) changes. An increase of passive investment causes a decrease of productive activity and probably a fall in prices; an increase of passive disinvestment, the reverse. This passive investment is the real cause of change, the real factor which increases or decreases income until active investment and saving once more are equal. As long as active investment and saving are equal, equilibrium endures.

Plans and Realizations

A second variation on Keynes' definitions, with some resemblances to that of Hawtrey, has been expounded by Bertil Ohlin, who represents what he calls the "Stockholm Theory of Savings and Investments." [10]

Ohlin's theory, which appears to be the accepted approach of Swedish economists, is based on the difference between anticipations or expectations and realizations; or, if you like, between plans and results. The behavior of today is based upon the expectations of the future. Entrepreneurs base their plans for investment on their profit expectations. Consumers base their plans for saving, and hence the level of consumption today, on the expected income of the future. These are planned savings and planned new investment, and the plans are actually carried out by the savers and investors. The savers determine their consumption, and the entrepreneurs their business expenditures, on these plans.

Now there is no reason to suppose that these planned savings

---

[10] B. Ohlin, "The Stockholm Theory of Savings and Investment," *Economic Journal,* March and June, 1937.

and investments are equal.   Indeed, every probability indicates
that they are not.   As Keynes himself has shown, it is impossible that the expectations of two different groups looking at the
future from two widely different angles would be the same.
But the point is, they must be equal if realizations are to be in
harmony with expectations.   If they are unequal, then a process
is set in motion which makes realized income differ from expected income, hence realized savings from planned savings,
and realized new investment from planned investment.   When
the process is over, realized savings and realized investment
are equal; for if they are not, the process goes on until
equality is reached and equilibrium attained.

Thus suppose that profit expectations rise and the volume
of investment expands with planned savings unchanged.
What is the result?   The community, in general, finds
that it has a larger income than it had expected.   Realized
income exceeds planned income.   That is to say, the community's income exceeds its expenditure by a larger amount
than planned.   Thus savings in realization exceed anticipations,
and they are equal to the volume of investment.

Obviously, as a result of these realizations, new plans are
made by the entrepreneurs and the savers.   If they happen to
coincide, so that planned investment equals planned savings,
then no further expansion can take place.   If they again differ,
and if again planned investment exceeds planned savings, then
total purchases and total income continue to grow, incomes
continue to increase, and so on, until coincidence of plans
brings about equilibrium.

Similar but opposite results come about when planned investment falls below planned savings.

In fine, planned savings and investment may and do differ;
realized savings and investment are equal by definition.   To
use Ohlin's phraseology, investment and savings *ex ante* may
differ; investment and savings *ex post* must be equal.

Keynes and Ohlin thus offer alternative ways of describing

the same process. In general, they are in agreement. Both agree that the expectations of the entrepreneur are the dominant factor of change. Both apparently agree that a process of income increase or decrease set in motion by changes of new investment is the means by which equality of savings and investment comes about. Both would agree that forced saving is not the appropriate term to apply to the increased saving that tends to accompany an increase of income. (The increase is unexpected and unplanned, it is true; but is hardly "forced." Perhaps "unintentional" is the right word to use.) But Ohlin's *ex ante* and *ex post* concepts seem more accurately to describe the actual process of change than Keynes' somewhat ambiguous terminology.

Robertson's Picture of the Process

The proposition that Keynes' method is better adapted to show a completed process than the process itself is defended by D. H. Robertson, who offers an alternative method of approach adapted to show the process and for this purpose retains the divergence of saving and investment which seemed to illustrate this so conveniently.[11]

Robertson points out that Keynes' identity or equality (whichever it is) of saving and investment is only true on the assumption that the income received during any period of time is equal to the income expended in the same period, or, in short, that output gives immediately disposable income. But this assumption in turn can be valid only in an economic system in which there are no lags of any kind or if "immediately" is defined in such wise as to include the whole period of time during which all the processes involved in acts of saving and investment are completed, and there are no lags because everything is over and done.

Lags are the very essence of cyclical behavior. The various

---

[11] D. H. Robertson; "Saving and Hoarding," *Economic Journal,* Sept., 1933.

processes do not expand and contract at the same time; particularly the changes in various prices, including prices of production factors, which are so characteristic of cycles, are never synchronous. This phenomenon is the source of the profit changes which as Keynes himself puts it, are "the mainspring of change." Hence economists who insist on the, importance of monetary changes, whether or not they regard them as the "cause" of cycles, cannot easily accept theories of change which leave out lag and the phenomenon of time.

To meet this objection, Robertson re-introduces time. He conceives of the process of expansion or contraction proceeding through a series of short slices of time, so short as to be "homogeneous"—that is, involving no important changes within them. These periods of time he calls "days," the principal characteristic of which is that income received during a given "day" is not available for disposal during that "day," but only on the following "day." This means that decisions in respect to the disposal of current income, which will determine whether it is to be used for expenditures or for addition to money balances, really pertain not to the income received on that "day," but to the income received on the previous "day." Saving, then, which in any definition seems to be the difference between income and consumption, is, in Robertson's scheme, the difference between yesterday's income and today's expenditure.

Now if income is not increasing or decreasing, this division of "days" has no particular significance, for the income of any day will equal that of the previous day, and income earned or received in any day is equal to disposable income. But if, for example, income is increasing, then income earned in any day is clearly greater than the disposable income of that day. This situation can come about only by an increase in the rate of investment, and this, in turn, cannot be financed from the income of yesterday, which, by hypothesis, must be insufficient both to purchase the consumers' goods and to supply the funds for the increased total of investment. That is to say, on

Robertson's definitions, investment has increased over saving and has done so from some inflationary source. This inflationary source may be either an increase of the total stock of money by banks or an increase in the velocity of circulation of money. As Robertson says, the aggregate income can be changed by "the power possessed by the public and the monetary authority to alter the rate of income flow, the former by putting money into and out of store, the latter by putting it into and out of existence." [12] There is, therefore, a rise in the price level, an increase in profits, and a general expansion of activity induced thereby; and this process goes on as long as the difference between investment and saving, so defined, continues. Doubtless, in due time, the increase of income will induce more saving; so much so that, presently, saving may exceed investment; but, in the meanwhile, day-by-day disequilibrium goes on.

We come back then to the proposition that the idea of disequilibrium of investment and saving is a convenient way of throwing light on the process of expansion (and contraction) which constitutes the business cycle. The criticism that may legitimately be raised against Keynes is that his definitions of the terms do not do a good job of illumination. The definitions as given in the *General Theory* are logical enough, but they seem to refer to a succession of static equilibria rather than to a process of change such as the business cycle. Probably what Keynes is interested in is *results* rather than *causes,* and, because of this, Robertson's definitions may be more fruitful in seeking out what are the impelling factors of change.

-----

[12] *Ibid.,* 411.

CHAPTER XVI

GENERAL CONCLUSIONS ON CYCLE THEORY

The Conflict of Theories

. The survey of business cycle theory to which the chapters of this section have been devoted reveals how complex are the forces which seem to make for cyclical change. Some of these are originating causes coming from the outside and making cycles seem a series of isolated but similar episodes. Others are the cumulative responses which any stimulus elicits from our business system and which, once started, seem to generate themselves in endless succession. Some forces are active, like invention, imposing new data on business; others are passive, but indispensable to expansion and contraction, such as an elastic currency. Some are physical, like weather changes; some psychological, such as the waves of optimism and pessimism that accompany boom and depression; some "institutional," such as the tendency of wages toward rigidity or the "stickiness" of some prices in the presence of a degree of monopoly.

Our survey of cycle theories further shows by what diverse routes one can develop a plausible explanation of the cyclical process. Concentration on some particular aspect of business behavior has made possible the production of one explanation after another, each reasonably convincing and consistent. As . Robertson humorously puts it, "in the deathless words of the Dodo, everybody has won and all must have prizes."

It must be admitted that this agreeable competition has

brought forth an embarrassingly plentiful supply of apparently contradictory explanations. For example, consider how many different theories have been advanced to explain the observed tendency to excessive fluctuations in the production of capital goods. This tendency has been attributed to: (1) an excessive tendency to save; (2) "forced" savings extracted from the people by an elastic currency; (3) the result of increased profits in a period of rising prices; (4) bursts of invention; (5) excessive additions to equipment during a period of gestation; (6) inflexible prices of producers' goods causing great variations in output in response to given changes in demand; and (7) the principle of acceleration.

It may be, of course, that these apparent contradictions really mean nothing more serious than differences in emphasis among the numerous factors which operate in our intricate economic mechanism. Were this the case, it should be possible to achieve a reasonable synthesis of these various approaches into a comprehensive and convincing explanation.

Haberler suggests that, although there is much dispute as to the determinants of the upper and lower turning points in the cycle, there is a considerable measure of agreement as to the nature of the cumulative process of expansion and contraction.[1] Let us examine this in detail.

Probably all would agree that expansion and contraction are cumulative processes. How this cumulative process gets started is a controversial issue, but once under way it seems established that it derives from the joint operation of the following causes: (1) the interrelation of all business enterprise via prices, markets, finance, ownership, and so forth; (2) the active or passive coöperation of a banking or monetary system capable of supplying an elastic currency; (3) the principle of acceleration; and (4) the profit inflation or deflation arising in an institutional

---

[1] G. von Haberler, "Some Reflections on the Present Situation of Business Cycle Theory," *Review of Economic Statistics*, February, 1936.

setting which causes certain costs, especially interest and wages, to lag behind prices of commodities. These various forces make for self-reinforcing expansion and contraction.

Turning points, however, offer more difficulty and occasion much more disagreement. In respect to the downturn, this much is agreed: that, although outside "accidental" causes, such as bad harvests, wars, and so on, may be important on particular occasions, expansion engenders within itself the forces that in any event will bring it to an end. Self-reinforcing forces are finally overcome by self-limiting forces. In this broad sense, the cause of depression is boom. But here agreement ceases. Some hold the monetary factor responsible, as bank credit reaches its inevitable limits. Others see the problem in maladjustments of production, either vertical or horizontal, that strain our system to breaking. Some believe we save too little and spend too much, so that investment outruns available capital. Others think we save too much and spend too little, so that investment outruns effective demand. Still others see the fading of entrepreneur's expectations as lagging costs, which made excess profits possible, now begin to close the gap and make them disappear.

The upturn after depressions is an even more formidable problem for the theorists, for, whereas the downturn is commonly attributed to self-limiting forces developed in expansion, even this measure of agreement is lacking in respect to the upturn. Some hold that such favorable forces as are generated at the end of a depression are not powerful enough to bring about recovery. To their minds, recovery is not a self-generating process. Instead, it must await the appearance of some "starter" or originating force capable of lifting the economic system out of stagnation.

The result is confusion both in theoretical explanations and in practical precepts. On the one side are those who hold that depression itself gradually generates the forces capable of overcoming deflation and bringing about recovery. The fall of interest rates, the slow but sure reduction of wages, the restoration of reasonable relations between various prices, the exhaustion of consumers' goods on hand, the need of equipment replacement—all these restore the expectation of profit and begin a revival of production first by the bold then by other entrepreneurs. The rest is cumulative expansion of the familiar kind.

On the other side are those who, while admitting that these developments are the necessary foundation for recovery, see no permanent revival therein. Production may recover to some degree, but only in a sort of rebound from the low level of depression; and there it will stay until a new impulse from without, not conditioned by the weak forces of the system itself, comes to make a real revival possible. Inventions, increased agricultural output, wars, new gold, and their like must appear to begin a new cycle.

These divergent views, moreover, impose different ideas of appropriate economic policy. Self-generation theorists, thinking in terms of "natural" recovery, tend to oppose governmental interference to end depression; or, if they consent to any measures, they are such as will merely reinforce what they believe is tending to come about in any case. Hence, even conservative opinion supports central banking policy to ease the money market and lower rates of interest. Those who have no such faith in self-generating recovery impatiently await the force from without that is to solve the riddle of revival. When this force is slow in coming (and its coming seems certain to be capricious and subject to no rules of forecast), they tend to demand government interference to hasten the end of depression, making public works, or inflation, or a similar governmental instrument, the substitute for the lagging starter. Thus, when the low level of agricultural fortunes that coincided with the great industrial depression of 1929–1932 removed one of the presumed traditional starters for a new cycle of prosperity, and when, further, no great new industry seemed to be in sight to give the impetus to revival that railroads, electric power, and automobiles had given in the past, then a great demand arose for government intervention that culminated in the recovery program of the New Deal. The acrimonious disputes this program has occasioned even in professional economic circles is proof enough that the causes that make for recovery are still pretty much an unsolved riddle.

The Difficulty of Statistical Verification

It might be thought that empirical investigation would throw light on the validity of any given cycle theory and enable one to determine which of many theories is valid. "Look and see" is good advice to follow in testing any hypothesis. But the difficulties involved in the task of verification are most formidable; formidable enough even for the explanation of a single cycle, much more so for a theory of cycles in general.

For example, take the crisis of 1929. What does the statistical evidence have to say about the cyclical behavior that led to this specific crash?

, It is argued, for example, that the preceding boom was a typical investment boom that collapsed, not because of inadequate consumption, but because of shortage of capital. If this be true, then producers' goods industries should show the first decline. What are the facts in regard to this important point?

H. G. Moulton states that no decline occurred in the important indexes of construction before October 1929 with the single exception of residential building.[2] Yet F. C. Mills puts 1928 as the peak for practically all construction, and 1927 as the peak for factory and commercial buildings, although the figures were nearly as high in 1929.[3] J. M. Clark, having in

---

[2] H. G. Moulton, *The Formation of Capital*, Washington, 1935, 56.
[3] F. C. Mills, *Economic Tendencies*, New York, 1932, 265–267.

mind durable goods, it is true, asserts that the decrease in consumption goods preceded that of other industries.[4] S. H. Slichter states that producers' goods led down in 1926 and probably in 1929, but regards the whole evidence as inconclusive.[5]

Moulton, again, wondering whether the cause of trouble might not lie in an excess of savings over investment (which he regards as likely to occur in a society where wealth is unequally distributed), made some estimates of the volume of savings and investment, respectively, previous to 1929. The result seemed to confirm his hypothesis. Sums available for investment ranged from eight or nine billions in 1923–1924 to as much as 15 or 16 billions in 1928–1929, while new corporate issues including mortgages remained stationary at about five billions a year.[6] Simon Kuznets, in a study for the National Bureau of Economic Research, puts the annual average of gross capital formation 1919–1932, as measured by the flow of producers' durable commodities to enterprises plus the volume of total construction, at over 18 million dollars. If we allow for differences in terms, this seems ample to absorb Moulton's apparently excessive savings.[7]

Underconsumptionists commonly find the source of trouble in wage payments not keeping pace with the value of output. Let us see what the facts are in this regard. Professor Douglas, supporting this hypothesis, quotes from the Census of Manufactures to show that both wages alone and wages and salaries together have been falling relative to value added in manufacture. Here are the tables: [8]

---

[4] J. M. Clark, *Strategic Factors in Business Cycles*, New York, 1934, 113.

[5] S. H. Slichter, "The Period 1919–1936 in the United States," *Review of Economic Statistics*, February, 1937.

[6] Moulton, *The Formation of Capital*, Chap. X.

[7] National Bureau of Economic Research, *Bulletin* 52, "Gross Capital Formation 1919–1933."

[8] P. H. Douglas, "Purchasing Power of the Masses and Business Depressions," in *Economic Essays in Honor of W. C. Mitchell*, New York, 1935, 123–124.

Year	Wages as a Percentage of Value Added by Manufacture	Wages and Salaries as a Percentage of Value Added by Manufacture
1919	42.2	
1921	44.7	
1923	42.6	53.4
1925	40.1	51.0
1927	39.3	51.0
1929	36.4	47.7

So far as it goes, this evidence seems to support his point.

But the purchasing power of the masses of the people does not come merely from manufacture. It arises from all enterprise, and it is quite possible that the apparent (relative) decline in manufacture is offset by (relative) increase in other fields. That this may be so is indicated by the percentage which wages and salaries are of the national income. This percentage shows *no such decline* as is found in data drawn from the limited area of manufacture.

The following table is from the estimates of the Brookings Institution:[9]

Year	Wages as a Percentage of Total Income Produced	Wages and Salaries as a Percentage of Total Income Produced
1922	41.2	63.3
1923	42	62.7
1924	41.5	63.6
1925	40.5	61.7
1926	41.8	63.8
1927	41.3	64.6
1928	40.0	63.5
1929	42.1	65.1

This more comprehensive picture gives no support to the supposition that either wages or wages plus salaries were not keeping pace with output as a whole.

Possibly the discrepancies which appear in the evidence in

---

[9] Leven, Moulton, and Warburton, *America's Capacity to Consume*, 158.

respect to 1929 arise from faulty statistical data and will disappear with more adequate knowledge; but even then the problem of verification will remain. It is not enough to establish causal factors in a particular cycle. What we want is to verify a theory for cycles in general. Cycle theory aims to transcend the individual cycle and the specific peculiarities which surround each instance. It must discover the common and universal element in all cycles. It is the typical, not the individual, cycle which it aims to explain; and its validity must be established by other means than the investigation of particular cases.

Correlations Not a Proof of Causation

The favorite means of verifying such general causation is to find whether there appears to be any statistical correlation between the supposed causal factors and the actual industrial fluctuations recorded over some considerable period of time. If a significant correlation is discovered, it will be assumed that a relation has been established, and some light thrown upon the process of causation; but establishing a relation throws no light upon the relation of cause and effect. For example, it is possible to discover a high degree of correlation between variations in the volume of bank credit and variations in industrial output. But whether this is because changes in bank credit cause changes in output or, on the contrary, because changes in output move bankers to equivalent changes in the issue of credit, the statistical relation in itself does not enable us to say.

Furthermore, the correlation established between two sets of changes may arise because both are joint effects of some common cause. For example, there is evidence of a correlation between the yield of crops and the variations in industrial activity; and it is commonly deduced therefrom that agricultural changes affect business and are a cause of cycles. But this possibility is not the only one. Both the yield of crops *and* the variations of industrial activity may arise from changes in weather conditions, which affect, at the same time, the production of crops *and* the vitality and efforts of businessmen.

Sometimes it is held that, if the correlation is fortified by an established lag or lead, so that one set of changes constantly leads another, the leader may be assumed to be the causal factor, since cause comes before effect; but even this is not necessarily true, for if there is any degree of anticipation, expected occurrences will bring about their effects in advance of their cause. Thus, although an expansion of bank credit may be found regularly to precede an expansion of industrial output, this fact may be due to the expectations of businessmen, who anticipating a rise in demand (the real cause of expansion), arrange their bank credits in preparation therefor.

Indeed, the insuperable difficulty of interpreting the significance of lags and leads can easily be illustrated. Suppose it were found that the output of producers' goods tends to decrease before the output of consumers' goods decreases, what might this be supposed to mean? (a) It might mean that direct causes were at work pressing on the producers of capital goods (say, a rising rate of interest) so that they were led to reduce their output, reducing incomes of their work people and so bringing about a reduction in demand for and output of consumers' goods. This interpretation seems to refute the underconsumptionist theory. But (b) it might mean that a coming fall in consumption was anticipated by businessmen, who reduced their output in advance. Or (c) it might mean merely the operation of the principle of acceleration whereby, although consumption was increasing absolutely, its rate of increase was declining, with consequent absolute fall in the demand for and output of producers' goods. Either (b) or (c) would be consistent, as (a) is not, with underconsumptionist theory.

We are forced to conclude that in the present state of our knowledge, neither logical consistency nor statistical verification will enable us to choose with confidence between the important, and to some extent contradictory, theories of the cycle now offered. Perhaps, therefore, we should follow the eminent example of Professor Wesley Mitchell who, with a humorous eye on the various explanations offered, limits his lucid account of the cycle to a mere description, unencumbered with theory, of how one phase gives way to another in an endless round of fluctuation. This description may be sufficient as a reasonable means of forecast and, by incorporating all the multitudinous factors that valid theoretical analysis has brought to light, may serve as well to show those strategic points at which control in the interests of stabilization might be exercised with reasonable chance of success.

Even those who would regard this attitude as inadequate and unnecessarily skeptical might be willing to accept it as a useful but tentative position until persistent research into the behavior of cycles and continued exposure of the possible explanations to rigid logical sifting finally establish, for the generality of reasonable men, an acceptable explanation of these baffling phenomena.

Suggested Readings on Part II

The following books give systematic accounts of the various theories:

G. von Haberler, *Prosperity and Depression,* Geneva, League of Nations, Revised Edition, 1940, Part I. The most comprehensive and up-to-date survey available.

A. H. Hansen, *Business Cycle Theory,* Boston, Ginn and Company, 1927. An excellent analysis of the state of cycle theory before the great depression.

A. L. Macfie, *Theories of the Trade Cycle,* London, Macmillan and Company, 1934. A very useful, brief analysis devoted largely to English theories.

W. C. Mitchell, *Business Cycles, The Problem and Its Setting,* New York, National Bureau of Economic Research, 1927, Chapter I. Admirable, succinct summaries of current theories. Interesting classification.

The following books cover a somewhat more restricted field:

H. S. Ellis, *German Monetary Theory, 1905-33*, Cambridge, Harvard University Press, 1934. The most available account of German theory on business cycles.

R. J. Saulnier, *Contemporary Monetary Theory*, New York, Columbia University Press, 1938. These are studies of Hawtrey, Robertson, Hayek, and Keynes, in whose theories monetary and business cycle problems are closely interwoven.

A. H. Hansen, *Full Recovery or Stagnation*, New York, W. W. Norton and Company, Inc., 1938. Part One of this series of studies is devoted to a critical study of Keynes, Harrod, Hayek, and other recent trends in cyclical literature.

The following books, although not devoted to a review of cyclical theory, are so eclectic in treatment and cover such wide ground as to be valuable introductions to theory.

A. C. Pigou, *Industrial Fluctuations*, London, Macmillan and Company, 1927, Part I, "Causation." One of the best analyses of the part played by various forces in making for the cycle, by a leader in English economic thought.

D. H. Robertson, *Banking Policy and the Price Level*, London, P. S. King & Son, 1932. Short and compact, this little book covers a great area of theory and has had no little influence.

For more detailed accounts of the theories examined in this part, the reader is referred to the works listed in the several chapters.

PART III

STABILIZATION

CHAPTER XVII

MONETARY MANAGEMENT: CONTROL THROUGH BANK POLICY[1]

A LL theories of the cycle recognize the importance of variations in the supply of money. In some theories, the elasticity of the money supply as evolved by banks is held to be
the active cause of industrial fluctuations. In all theories, it is
regarded as a necessary condition of industrial expansion, without which disequilibrating impulses would be ineffective. Even
where the entrepreneur is the hero, the banking system must
acquiesce.

It is obvious, therefore, that one of the approved ways of
attacking the problem of fluctuations is through banking
policy. There is no reason, it is argued, to suppose that the
volume of money is inherently unstable. It is unstable because the banks have allowed it to be so, and because they are
swayed by the ordinary motives of private business rather than
by the dictates of intelligent public policy. It would seem
possible, in the light of our analysis of cycle theory, for banking policy, if properly directed, to smooth out the variations of
business, put brakes against undue expansion and barriers

---

[1] The best book to consult on the subject of this and the next two chapters is
Keynes' *Treatise on Money,* New York, 1930, Book VII, where will be found a learned
and often amusing discussion of the problem of the management of money. The student will find an excellent and critical discussion in A. C. Pigou, *Industrial Fluctuations,* Book II, Chaps. 4–8. For a popular but competent account of the problem as
current as the United States, see P. H. Douglas, *Controlling Depressions,* Part II.
Chaps. V–X. See also A. D. Gayer, *Monetary Policy and Economic Stabilization,*
2nd Ed., New York, 1937.

against undue contractions, and so bring greater stability into the operations of the industrial system. It is the purpose of this chapter to examine what devices can be used to this end, and how effective they are likely to be in practice.

Banking Policy

The fundamental problem of bank policy in its relation to cycles is to control the volume of credit in such a way as to make for industrial stability. This control might and probably does involve some attempt to control the price level; but bank policy as such may not be primarily designed in terms of prices. Fundamentally, it will be directed to the maintenance of stability of industrial activity, or, perhaps more exactly, to adjust activity to the normal trend. In any case, it is predicated upon the ability of the banking authorities to control the aggregate volume of bank credit. As we shall see in the ensuing discussion, this control is not easy to get and may demand quite radical measures if it is to be attained.

The Problem of Control

If the only source of credit in the country were a single institution, such as the government or a single central bank, then the control of credit would be relatively easy and simple, for a single authority could increase and decrease the volume of available credit by administrative order. As we shall see, even this task is not so easy as it looks (since it takes two to make credit effective, the issuer and the user, and the user cannot be compelled to take credit even though the issuer is ready to issue); still there is no doubt the problem of control is greatly simplified when there is only one issuer and one decision, and greatly complicated when the issuers are many, as in the banking system of the United States. This situation is one of the reasons why there are arguments for causing the volume of credit to be a function of the Treasury, or for creating a single national bank, or for nationalizing all the banks. Under any of these arrangements, one decision, and one only, is involved.

Many banks make control difficult. Where these conditions do not exist, however, the problem is more difficult to solve. Thus, in the United States, the aggregate volume of credit is determined by the practices of many thousands of banks, each one making its own decisions; and the problem, therefore, is to bring about stability in the aggregate volume of credit when issued under these conditions. Clearly, this task is not easy. If bank policy were subject to the law of averages, so that if some banks deviated in one direction from the normal, other banks would tend to deviate in the opposite direction, stability could still be attained; but the experience in booms and depressions is just the opposite—namely, a general tendency on the part of all banks to expand and contract in concert—and for very good reasons. If, when business is expanding, less optimistic banks put brakes on the expansion of credit, they begin to lose business to their competitors and soon find themselves with increasing stores of unprofitable cash; for, as other banks expand and checks are drawn upon their increasing deposits, some of these are deposited in the restricting banks and entitle them to cash from other banks via the clearinghouse. It is very difficult for banks with increasing cash in a time of expansion to resist the general tendency to expand (not to mention the needs of their stockholders). Under these circumstances, it is much more likely that even cautious banks will join the procession of expansion (arguing that they simply keep in step) than that any will be bold enough to act for stabilization, or powerful enough to have much effect even if they do. In short, as is so commonly the case in our competitive system, no one finds it possible or profitable to do what all in the long run would gain from doing; and all follow procedures which result in general damage.

A central banking system facilitates control. A central banking system, however, such as is found in most industrialized countries, makes the problem of control less difficult. A central bank like the Bank of England, or a system of central banks like the Federal Reserve System in the United States, can bring appropriate influences to bear upon all banks, so as to enable or encourage them to do in common what no one bank could venture to do alone. Fundamentally, the power of central banks resides in their ability to modify the reserves of their members and, through them, the scale of loans to customers on which the active supply of money in business largely depends. It is important to bear in mind that the central banking authorities have no direct control over the total supply of money, but only such indirect control as is found in the techniques by which they can influence the activities of the banks in general.

These techniques consist largely in appropriate modifications of the rate of rediscount, together with the fortifying assistance of open-market dealings in securities by the central bank. These two techniques, which may be denominated "the discount policy," are the classical weapons of central banks in dealing with such fluctuations of the activity of business as are capable of being affected by the management of money. To them, as moving in the same direction, may be added a third— namely, direct changes, either by agreement or by legal regulation, in the reserve ratios required of banks in general.

These three techniques will now be examined in detail.

Rediscount Rate as a Means of Control

The rate of rediscount is the rate charged by central banks on specified kinds of bills or commercial paper discounted for the banks in general. In the United States, it is the rate charged by a Federal Reserve Bank to its members; a rate determined separately for each Federal Reserve Bank, subject to review by the Federal Reserve Board. As rediscounting adds to the reserve of the bank involved, it may be said that the rate of re-discount is the price paid to add to the bank's reserves.

If this rate is raised, then the volume of rediscounting by banks tends to be reduced. This outcome reduces the reserves of banks, or, more exactly, lowers the rate at which they have been increasing, and hence tends to reduce the amount of additional accommodation which they, in turn, can advance to their customers. It cannot affect the existing volume of loans, but it does tend to restrict further expansion and does make for some unwillingness to renew loans when due, at least for marginal borrowers.

This restrictive influence on the volume of bank loans (and deposits), which is, of course, a restrictive influence on the total volume of monetary purchasing power in the community, may be brought about without a rise in the market rate of interest, by a more cautious loan policy on the part of banks, who now scrutinize borrowers and their security more intensely than before. Or on the contrary (and this action might be regarded as more normal), they may raise the market rate of interest and so bring about the natural restriction of total advances that comes about by the rise in the price of loans. In either case, some advances will presumably be restricted, and progressively so, as the rate of rediscount presses still harder on the bank's reserve balances in the central banks.

A rise in the market rate of interest, if it occurs, may discourage borrowing in a cumulative fashion, for not only does it make some current ventures unprofitable which might otherwise have been profitable, but it tends to change the expectations of businessmen and put some brakes on optimistic antici-pations. A rise in the rate of interest increases the cost of holding both securities and commodities and puts a premium on present sale. The result is a tendency for both security and commodity prices to fall; and enterprises that have been count-ing on the continued rise of these prices will postpone otherwise attractive projects. Thus a rise in the rate of rediscount may set off a whole train of effects which are much larger than would appear to be justified from the original change—so much so that a very moderate change in the rate of rediscount, if properly timed, may be all that is needed for stabilization purposes. Indeed, it might be even argued that it is a very powerful weapon which has to be used with the utmost discretion and intelligence, if it is not to cause many more reactions than are desirable in the interests of stability.

Similar and opposite effects would be anticipated from lowering rediscount rates. This reduction tends to increase the borrowing of member banks at the Federal Reserve, increases, therefore, their reserves, makes them more eager to advance funds to customers, and induces them, in order to be able to do so, to make equivalent changes in their own rates of interest. This change makes ventures feasible that otherwise would not be. The rate of borrowing should increase; consequently the aggregate of bank credit outstanding should grow, the more so as (according to influences similar to those described above) it is expected that prices of both commodities and securities would cease to fall and even rise. The accompanying conviction that the trend of bank policy it toward easy money tends to cause businessmen to be more sanguine in their business ventures and reinforces the tendency to obtain an increasing aggregate of bank credit, already set in motion by the change in the interest rate.

Rediscount rates may not be effective. The theory of changes in rediscount rates rests on the assumption that the banks in general will be promptly moved thereby to make equivalent changes in their rates to the public. This tendency may be because of the additional cost of borrowing thus thrown upon them; or it may be because of the psychological influence which the change might well exercise. Banks may be accustomed to look upon changes in rediscount rates as an important sign of impending business changes. They may regard the action of the central banking authority, based as it is on a more intimate acquaintance with all the pertinent facts than ordinary banks can enjoy, as an important warning of impending storm; and they may be led thereby to make changes in their loan policy to which they would not be moved by the mere addi-tional cost of borrowing at the central bank.

This assumption may not necessarily hold true. For exam-ple, in the beginning of periods of expansion, the banks may have such large reserves that borrowing at the central bank is unnecessary. In this case, a rise in the rate of rediscount is nominal and may have no important effects. This outcome was certainly the situation in the United States during the years 1934 to 1937, when, largely due to the great importations of gold, the excess reserves of banks were so large that the quite different device of regulating reserves by administrative order had to be used to bring the situation under control.

Again, even where rediscounting is resorted to, market rates may not reflect, or reflect but slowly, changes in the rate of rediscount. This result may be due in part to the expansive power of bank credit. When several dollars of bank credit can be built up on a single dollar of reserves, increase in the cost of borrowing at reserve banks need not mean a proportional increase in the rate charged to the public. The situation may come about by local habits of banking which tend toward rela-tive stability of local rates. This tendency seems to be indi-cated in the experience of the various money markets in the United States. While open-market rates on commercial paper, where competition is keen, may reflect changes in rediscount rates, rates on customers' loans, especially in the smaller towns and in the South and West in general, appear to be relatively inflexible and insensitive. They change slowly and fluctuate much less than rediscount rates.[2]

For these reasons, monetary authorities must be prepared to supplement changes in rediscount rates by further action if dis-

---

[2] W. W. Riefler, *Money Rates and Money Markets in the United States*, New York, 1930, 68–76.

count policy is to be made effective.   This further action resides in the open-market operations of central banks.

Open-Market Operations as a Means of Control

Open-market operations include all kinds of dealings by central banks, but for our purposes they may be held to consist in the purchase and sale in the open market (that is, transactions not merely with banks) of such securities as central banks are allowed to deal in, usually securities issued by the government.

Open-market operations have substantial and immediate effects on the reserve balances of the banking system.   If the central bank buys (say) $1,000,000 of securities, paying for them by check, the check is deposited with a commercial bank, adding to some customer's account, and the bank deposits and adds the check to its reserve in the central bank.   The commercial bank, consequently, has new credit which it can lend direct to its customers or use to buy securities.   As these uses diffuse funds throughout the banking community, they make it possible to increase in multiplied fashion the general volume of credit outstanding; and if the original purchase of securities is widespread, so as to affect the generality of banks, the total credit made available will then become whatever multiple of the reserves rules for the system as a whole.   If this multiple is (say) 10, then the purchase of securities to the volume of $1,000,000 by the central banks will add to the available credit volume an amount of $10,000,000.

For similar reasons and by a similar mechanism in reverse, sale of securities to the volume of $1,000,000 would contract total available bank credit by $10,000,000.

These open-market operations may be (and probably are) more effective than mere changes in rates of rediscount for two reasons.   (1) They depend on the volition of the central bank, not on that of banks in general.   Here they contrast with rediscounting which arises from the voluntary action of banks, for banks cannot be prevented from rediscounting if they insist on doing it, and they cannot be compelled to rediscount if they do not want to. If their demand for central-bank accommodation is inelastic, there is nothing that can be done about it. The volume of their reserves and of the deposit currency based thereon may be uncontrollable. Open-market operations, in contrast, are at the discretion of central banks, who can buy and sell securities if they want to, as long as there is a security market and any sellers and buyers. (2) In the second place, the effect of open-market dealings on the reserves of banks is direct and immediate. Purchase of securities adds to the reserves of banks; sale of securities reduces their reserves. Thus, whereas changes in the rediscount rate only make it *advantageous* for banks to change their reserves, open-market operations actually change them. Furthermore, it might be said that, while rediscount-rate changes may not result in any action whatever by member banks, open-market dealings almost *compel* them to do something.

Making rediscount rates "effective." The actual and (presumably) unwished-for changes in reserves have a powerful tendency to make rediscount rates "effective." In expansion, either the banks are compelled to replenish their reserves by rediscounting and so come under the influence of a rising rediscount rate, or they have to reduce the volume of their accommodation to customers, which, of course, is the result the central bank set out to attain. In depression, on the contrary, either the banks utilize the funds from the sale of securities to pay off their indebtedness to the central bank, in which case the ease of their position and their freedom from interest would presumably make them more willing to lower rates to their customers, or they immediately utilize the funds to increase accommodation to their customers, which, again, is the result the central banks set out to attain.

One should note, however, that there is some difference in the immediate effectiveness of open-market operations arising from the working of the two alternatives open to the banks. If, when their reserves are depleted or increased by open-market operations, the banks proceed immediately, without rediscount or debt reduction at the central bank, to decrease or increase their loans to customers or their investments, then the effects desired are quick, although, even at the best, there is bound to be some time lag as the cumulative influences of open-market operations get into full swing. But if, on the contrary, the normal effect of open-market purchases is to cause member banks to reduce their debt at the central bank, and the normal effect of sales is to cause them to rediscount, then there is introduced an intermediate stage between open-market operations and their effects on the volume of bank credit, which substantially increases the time lag involved in the operations, and in some cases may actually counteract the intentions of the central bank.

Under the latter alternative, the central bank cannot directly vary the volume of its investments, for what it loses or gains in securities it gains or loses in advances to the banks. Consequently, open-market operations become simply an adjunct to discount policy (not an alternative or a substitute) and serve merely to reinforce it and make it more effective.

This difference in effectiveness of open-market operations *per se* is nicely illustrated by the working of the English and American banking systems, respectively.[3]

English banking practice.   The essential peculiarity of the English banking system is the fact that the great Joint Stock Banks never, and the rest of the money market rarely, allow themselves to be in debt to the Bank of England. Rediscounting by the Joint Stock Banks is not done, and the rest of the market makes use of the facilities of the Bank of England only in emergencies. This practice is partly a result of custom or convention, partly (perhaps fundamentally) because the Eng-

---

[3] See Keynes. *Treatise on Money,* Vol. II, Chap. 32.

lish method of maintenance of bank rate above market rate makes borrowing unprofitable. On the face of it, this practice would seem to make a policy of stabilization by changes in bank rate impracticable, since such changes would be purely nominal and have no direct effect on the balances carried by the banks at the Bank of England. One would suppose, therefore, that the only factor making for increase or decrease of these balances (and hence of the aggregate of loan-credit at banks) would be increase or decrease of gold as determined by movements out of or into circulation, or into or out of the country, the control of which by changes of bank rate would be too slow to be of value in stabilization. (Indeed, this outcome is the precise reason why the discount policy of the Bank of England was regarded as ineffective by such authorities as Hawtrey.)

It is true that the further custom of the banks of paying heed to the change in bank rate as a signal for increasing or decreasing the scale of their accommodation to customers made these changes more effective than they certainly could have been otherwise; but, for all that, the peculiar situation of the banks would seem to reduce the effectiveness of central bank policy.

But this conclusion neglects the factor of open-market dealings which, while not important before the war, began to be used in the postwar decade as a purposeful instrument of stabilization. With the introduction of these dealings on a substantial scale, the virtues of the banks' attitude toward borrowing at the Bank of England are revealed. A sale of securities by the Bank of England will certainly reduce the reserve resources of the banks, and, as they will not replenish these by borrowing or counteract the fall by reducing the ratio of their reserves to their liabilities, their only alternative is to reduce their investments, or the volume of their advances to customers, or both. In either case, the effect is restrictive. Contrary effects arise when securities are purchased by the Bank of England.

American banking practice. In the United States, the situation has been, and still is, substantially different, although, as we shall see, changes have been going on under the practices of the Federal Reserve Board that are tending to reduce the dissimilarity.

The essential features of interbank relations within the Federal Reserve System are two, both of them opposite to the practice of the English banks. The first is that banks are not averse to being in debt to the Federal Reserve Banks and that rediscounting is common. The second is that the rediscount rate is normally *below,* not above, the general market rate for accommodation to customers. These features, particularly the rediscounting, were apparently incorporated into the Federal Reserve Act in order to carry out the declared intention (see the preamble) to create an elastic currency that would expand and contract with the needs of trade.

The full effects of open-market operations in these circumstances are inevitably delayed. The first effect of purchases is to cause member banks to reduce their debts to the Federal Reserve Banks; the first effect of sales is to cause them to rediscount. It is only as a *secondary* consequence of these reactions that changes occur in the total bank credit (the banks from being out of debt tending to increase their credit to customers, contrariwise because of the cost of rediscounting tending to decrease it). Thus, in the United States, open-market operations have delayed effects: in expansion, only after the higher rediscount rates are passed on to the public; in contraction, only after loans are paid off to the Federal Reserve System.

To some observers in the postwar decade, this outcome seemed to prove that open-market operations had essentially no effect at all, save to change the composition of Federal Reserve assets as between advances and investments. The better view is that open-market operations under these conditions are not an independent agency, but an adjunct to discount policy and to make discount rates "effective." Indeed, Governor Strong of the Federal Reserve Bank of New York argued that open-market operations are largely useful to prepare the way for discount policy, holding that discount changes are apt to be, under American conditions, dramatic and alarming, and that they should be prepared for by previous selling (or buying) of securities.

Making open-market operations more effective. The feeling that the open-market operations were of only minor direct effectiveness, but that they could be made more effective, apparently led the central reserve authorities to approximate the condition of the English money market by a purposeful effort to discourage member banks from the practice of rediscounting, save for meeting the temporary and seasonal needs of their customers. Efforts were made to make banks realize that loans merely to enlarge the operations of the bank were not good policy. The rules of eligibility were interpreted to include not mere legal qualifications, but considerations both of the general state of trade and of the reasonable quota for any one bank. As far as possible, loans likely to be used for increasing the volume of loans on securities were definitely discouraged.

Whether or not such measures could create a custom of non-borrowing at Federal Reserve Banks is, of course, open to question. Member banks able to borrow at Federal Reserve Banks in 1929 were not only doing so, but were lending their funds to banks that already had borrowed as much from the Federal Reserve Banks as they dared to, or were permitted to. Indeed, skepticism in regard to this was so considerable as to lead to the provisions of the Bank Act of 1933, which allowed Federal Reserve Banks, in granting accommodation to member banks, to be guided by whether such accommodation was likely to be used for excessive carrying of securities, commodities, or real estate, or other purposes not consistent with the maintenance of sound credit conditions. Even this would not prevent widespread expansion due to the "legitimate needs" of trade, which, as Keynes [4] points out, may be just as inflationary as any other use.

However that may be, in so far as the effect of these various regulations and extra-legal pressures lead to an approximation of the nonborrowing attitude of English banks (especially if this were reinforced by a changed relation between rediscount rates and market rates), open-market operations would become more directly effective, and the present time lag of their influence would be reduced. In the meanwhile, the inherent characteristics of American banking will continue to present some difficulties to effective stabilization of bank credit through the operations of the central banks.

Even though central bank policy is reasonably effective, in the sense of imposing suitable changes in the lending policy of the generality of banks, the question remains as to how far these changes in their turn are capable of controlling the expansion and contraction of business which, one may suppose, is the ultimate end of policy. As we shall see, even when reinforced by open-market operations, discount policy faces some serious difficulties—to some extent in good times, but even more so in depressions, especially severe depressions.

The Effectiveness of Discount Policy in Expansion

(1) In a period of expansion, the demand for credit by business may be seriously inelastic. When the spirit of confidence is running high, the demand for bank accommodation is not easily checked by changes in interest rates. If interest is a relatively small fraction of the cost of operation, the inelasticity of demand for credit is increased. For some types of borrowers, merchants for example, interest cost may be relatively high. For manufactures and production in general, it is not likely to be so high. Doubtless, in due time, a continually rising rate of interest will have its effect, largely by the pressure it exerts

---

[4] Keynes, *Treatise on Money*, Vol. II, 243.

on the stock market, and hence on business expectations; but this may come so late in the phase of expansion that the evil is already done, the seeds of trouble are already sown, and the overextension of activity is already impossible to prevent.

(2) The very rise in the rate of interest may attract funds into the market and so assist in counteracting its own desired effects. This result is likely to happen where a stabilizing policy is used by a country on the international gold standard at a time when other countries are taking no action. The rise of the local rate of interest will prove a powerful attraction for liquid funds which, to the extent they are in gold, will increase the reserves of banks and make them to that degree independent of the action of their central banking authority. Thus the stringent money market conditions of 1928–1929 attracted large sums from abroad, despite the fact that the high rates were in themselves a warning of unsound conditions and had been accompanied by the gravest kind of caution from the Federal Reserve authorities.

(3) It is possible also that the restraining influences of open-market policy, intent upon reducing the expansion of bank credit, may, in times of optimism, be offset by changes in bank practice or in the velocity of circulation of money or credit. The velocity of circulation is not directly under the influence of banks. Bank policy may determine how much credit there is to be, but it is the businessman who decides how fast it will be used. It is true that rising rates of interest, designed to check the volume of bank credit, may discourage business expectations and weaken the enthusiasm that makes for increases in velocity; but this cannot always be relied on, especially in times of speculative furor, and, if velocity moves contrary to volume, bank policy will be by so much counteracted.

In the United States, some counteraction will arise from changing proportions of time and demand deposits, which, by law, require different ratios of reserves. Thus, with legal reserves averaging 10 per cent against demand deposits, but only

3 per cent against time deposits, a shift of funds from the former to the latter would seem to permit further expansion and make discount policy less effective. This result, for some reason, seems to have happened in the period 1922–1929. While demand deposits increased from 15.5 billions to 19 billions (a rise of 22 per cent), time deposits increased from 7.2 billions to 13.3 billions (a rise of 85 per cent). This relative increase in time deposits enlarged the possible ratio of expansion. ·

(4) The ability of the central bank to affect market conditions through open-market operations is, of course, strictly limited by its current supply of suitable securities, and in addition by its own preparedness to buy securities at a (probably) high price and incur the loss of selling them at a low one. If the central bank, even where it is privately owned like the Bank of England, is ready and willing to take losses on security dealings as its contribution to stability and as part of its normal responsibilities as a central bank, it still remains possible that its supply of securities will be inadequate for control—the more so as the securities in which it is permitted to deal may be mostly government securities, so that its control is determined at any moment by the size of the government-debt and the current policy of government in regard to surplus and deficit. As Keynes says, "The Reserve banks can only fire off against an incipient boom such ammunition as they have been able to pick up while resisting a slump." That this might in itself be inadequate is nicely shown by the situation of the Federal Reserve Banks during the recovery of 1935–1937, when the excess reserves of member banks reached some 3,300 millions with the total holdings of United States securities in the Federal Reserve Banks of 2,400 millions. Even the disposal of all these holdings would have left the excess reserves at 900 millions. Indeed, the sale of such extensive holdings would undoubtedly have been resisted by the government in the interests of the Treasury, for the result would have depressed government bonds at a time when its fiscal operations would have been injured thereby.

Hence, even the ammunition the banks have cannot always be fired off.

The problem of timing. (5) Finally, one must note the difficulty of proper timing in the application of bank policy. Brakes must be applied at the right time, and in the right quarters. Applied too soon, they may bring an expansion to an end with factors of production not fully employed. Applied too late, they may find a runaway expansion now out of control. Perhaps the latter outcome is the greater danger, for expansions are insidious in their approach. Their seeds are sown some time before the sprouting appears, and it is not easy to know when the sowing occurred. Nor is it easy to persuade the banking and business community to accept restrictions on bank loans when business is good and profits coming in. Bodies sensitive to public opinion, like the Federal Reserve Board, may well delay action until they are quite convinced that action is needed.

Much depends on the guides, statistical or otherwise, by which policy is determined. For many years, for example, the Bank of England was guided by the state of its reserve ratio—that is, the ratio of gold to deposits—raising or lowering its rate of discount as this ratio fell below or rose above some conventional level. But it seems that this index is bound to be defective. Gold movements and central reserve ratios are lagging indexes. They are the effects of expansion and contraction, and not the earliest at that. Hawtrey, it will be recalled,[5] regards the preoccupation of the Bank of England with this ratio as a prime cause of the trade cycle.

Pigou advances evidence to show that changes in the reserve ratio actually tend to precede changes in the wholesale price level, which may be taken to be a good current measure of the state of trade, and that it is only the discount rate (because of natural delay on the bank's part in acting on its changed posi-

---

[5] Chap. XI, p. 231.

tion) that lags behind the price level. Even with this qualification, it is clear that, if the early seeds of expansion are to be controlled, a more sensitive and barometric index should be used.
Pigou suggests that, if the signal for action were found in movement of security prices, or of volume of monthly new orders
in important industries, or of stocks of finished goods in dealers'
hands, or possibly in the percentage of workpeople out of employment, corrective discount changes could be brought into
play early enough to have an effective stabilizing influence.[6]

In the 1920's in the United States, the Federal Reserve Board
seems to have been dominated by the concept of a stable price
level, and to have felt that maintenance of the price level would
insure stability in the industrial world. Consequently, the rationale of discount policy throughout the decade was to guard
the price level from notable change. That this was a good
guide to policy was completely disproved by events, for the decade was one of rapid technological change and falling costs,
and a falling rather than a stable price level was called for.
Since the policy of the Board was to prevent this very fall and
to keep money easy to bring this about, the result was a great
inflation of profits and, in the end, one of the most remarkable
of American booms. Even as late as 1928, the Board was still
resisting corrective measures, and, when at last they were put
into force, the crisis and disaster were inevitable.[7]

The Effectiveness of Discount Policy in Depression

Whatever the difficulties in the way of effective discount policy in expansion, they seem to be even more serious in depression, especially severe depressions. Any depression involves
tedious and unavoidable readjustments of one sort and another
that take time. Serious depressions, in addition, deliver a blow

---

[6] A. C. Pigou, *Industrial Fluctuations*, Part II, Chap. 6.
[7] Cf. C. A. Phillips, T. F. McManus, and R. W. Nelson, *Banking and the Business Cycle*, New York, 1937, Chap. VIII.

to business confidence that apparently only considerable time can overcome.

Under these circumstances, the demand for accommodation at banks falls rapidly away and is, at the same time, extremely inelastic. Businessmen do not want to borrow even on the most favorable terms, and nothing that the banks can do can force them to borrow. In prosperity, when there is always a fringe of unsatisfied borrowers, bank rate can reduce the total of bank credit, and the total of effective purchasing power in use. In depression, the banks cannot increase the effective purchasing power in use; they can make it as attractive as they like, but only the public can decide to use it; and the evidence is that they will not. In times of depression, when sales are falling and idle capacity increasing all over the field, business enterprises cannot be coaxed readily to increase or even continue their borrowing. Current output continues to be unprofitable, and any demand for additional equipment or capacity is almost fantastic. Nobody is going to install productive equipment for a remote and uncertain need, not to mention the difficulty of knowing what kind of productive equipment will be needed.

Under these conditions, cuts in interest could hardly be great enough to overcome the anticipated losses which seem to face the business community. Even a negative rate of interest would be unattractive if borrowers anticipated loss on any use to which they could put their money. If the fall in prices is expected to continue, any conceivable reduction in interest rates would be counteracted. Prices falling 10 per cent per annum turn a money rate of —5 per cent a year into a real rate of +5 per cent.

Hence open-market purchases may turn out to be a very blunted weapon of attack. They may free banks from indebtedness to the Federal Reserve System and put them in possession of increasing volumes of cash, but they cannot bring about, merely by easing the money market, an effective increase in the flow of purchasing power in use. The banks will merely

add to their excess reserves without thereby stimulating industrial activity, for the only safe investments at such times are the
very government securities which the open-market policy of
the Federal Reserve System would deprive them of.

Easy money no sure cure for depression. This potential
difficulty is vividly illustrated by the experience of open-market
operations of the Federal Reserve Banks in 1932 and 1933.

During the year 1932, under the influence of President
Hoover, who, although conservatively inclined, favored open-
market purchases as the correct method of easing the money
market and making greater credit available to business (After
all, it was practiced by the Bank of England!), the Federal
Reserve Banks bought approximately one billion dollars' worth
of securities from the market. This purchase built up the
reserves of member banks to unprecedented heights; but the
loans to business did not increase. In point of fact, they steadily
declined. What is more, throughout the entire period of purchase, the velocity of circulation of deposits declined also, so
that not only did business not use the chance to increase its
borrowings from banks, but even what funds it had were
used at a slower place than before. As far as the banks were
concerned, their only benefit was to get out of debt to the
Federal Reserve Banks.

In 1933, under the Roosevelt administration, the Federal
Reserve Banks had a similar experience. Although net purchases of over half a billion of securities were made in the open
market by the Federal Reserve Banks, member bank loans increased only a few millions. The principal effect was to add
to the excess (and idle) reserves and free the banks almost
completely from dependence on the Federal Reserve System.
Doubtless all this was done in the hope that the excess reserves
of banks (which, after all, indicated lack of earning assets)
would induce them to adopt more liberal lending and investing
policies and so facilitate the recovery of business, but in point
of fact this desirable result did not occur.

Of course, it is quite possible that the banks did not go far enough. Mr. Keynes had already argued in his *Treatise* that, when severe slumps come, central banks should overcome their nervous fears of "causing the total volume of money to depart widely from its normal volume" and intensify open-market purchases to "saturation" or to whatever degree is necessary to bring down the long-time rate of interest to levels attractive to business.[8] In 1933, a group of economists of the University of Chicago called upon the Federal Reserve Banks to increase the flow of their funds into the market via purchases of securities, and to continue to do this until the low level of interest and the high price of securities would "take," and business would be pushed into expansion. Whether this expansion would have been the result or whether idle reserves would have risen thereby the higher cannot precisely be known, for, by February 1934, further open-market purchases of securities by the Federal Reserve Banks ceased (not to begin again until 1937), and the government settled back for its recovery program on devaluation, the NRA, and the public works.

However, that it would have continued to be difficult to stimulate expansion merely by easing the money market and making funds available for business is indicated by the extraordinary conditions of bank reserves in the period 1934–1937. During these years, the net gold inflow into the United States was at a rate of over a billion dollars per year. Up to early 1937, when the restrictive policies of the government through changing legal reserves reached their peak, over four billions (net) of gold had come to this country. This gold being transferred to the Treasury in exchange for checks on Federal Reserve Banks, as required by law, resulted in enlarging the reserves of member banks, and on easy money theories should have caused a proportionate (multiple) expansion of loans to

---

[8] Keynes, *Treatise on Money*, Volume II, 369–387.

business. This expansion did not occur. Perhaps a billion of the gold served to back the increased liabilities of banks; but over three billions more were added to the reserves back of existing liabilities, raising excess reserves to unprecedented heights. This outcome proves beyond all dispute that mere increase in reserves does not necessarily lead to proportionate expansion of bank credit in use.

The great difficulty, therefore, with the Keynes theory of pushing ease of the money market to the point of saturation seems to lie in the problem of forcing funds into circulation and possibly the danger, always imminent, that the increasing volume of potential credit thus piled up may eventually burst out in a sudden rush of inflation. These funds are a great pool of dammed-up purchasing power, held back partly by the reluctance of banks to lend, partly by the timidity of borrowers in periods of depression; but if the dam gives way, perhaps with a sudden return of confidence, or perhaps because fears of inflation start a runaway spending before high prices arrive, then a rush of inflation may set in which is not to be controlled easily. Therefore, efforts to end depression may make it less easy to keep the next recovery within reasonable bounds.

Conclusion

Looking back, now, over the discussion of credit control in booms and depressions, the general conclusion must be that manipulation of discount rates and open-market dealings by central banks should be reasonably effective, if applied quickly and continuously, in preventing booms from developing and, consequently, depressions from arising. But it is apparent that the ability to seize the right moment may be lacking or made ineffective by various neutralizing effects, and that, if powerful forces are at work, an extravagant expansion, despite all efforts at credit control, may develop. When this result happens, the possibility of averting a depression by credit operations is very slight, and it is highly probable that, once depression has set in, the best that can be done is to have the central banks keep the money market easy and liquid, and then fall back on other methods, such as expansion of public works, to make the spark for recovery.

CHAPTER XVIII

MONETARY MANAGEMENT: PROBLEMS OF THE MONEY SUPPLY

Direct Control of Reserve Ratios

Central bank policy, as described in the preceding chapter, is designed to influence the behavior of the banks in general by bringing about changes in the volume of their reserves; but no attempt is made to control the volume of deposits which the banks erect upon their reserves. This attitude, clearly, is a weakness in the armory of control, for, unless the banks deliberately maintain a fixed proportion between reserves and deposits, they can defeat the purposes of control by varying their reserve ratios. The credit creation possible with a reserve of one million dollars would be 10 millions with 10 per cent reserves, 12½ millions with 8 per cent reserves, and 8 millions with 12½ per cent reserves. Thus an unchanging volume of legal reserves would permit wide variations in total credit.

It is, therefore, arguable that reserve ratios themselves must be brought under control if monetary stabilization is to be reasonably complete. On this ground, the Macmillan Committee appointed by the British Government in 1929 to inquire into the effectiveness of banking, finance, and credit recommended that the banks accept the advice of the Bank of England as to the average figure at which they should keep their reserve balances and as to appropriate changes therein from time to time (such changes to be small on any one occasion);

and, furthermore, that the ratio, when agreed upon, should be rigidly adhered to, seeing that success of the measures of the Bank of England designed to control the aggregate of credit essentially depends on the rigidity of this ratio.[1]

In the United States, as is well known, bank reserves have been regulated by law for many years; but the regulation has been in the interests of solvency and the protection of the depositor, rather than for stabilization of economic activity. Minimum reserves, not actual reserves, have been controlled. Such variation as has been prescribed has been between city and country banks on the one hand, and between time and demand deposits on the other, and has had no relation whatever to the problem of monetary stabilization. It has, therefore, been proposed that the reserve basis be changed and be determined for all banks according to (a) the total volume of deposits and (b) the activity of these deposits as measured by an index of velocity of turnover. That is, the required reserve ratio would not be constant but would rise as the volume of deposits rose and/or the activity of deposits increased, and fall under the opposite conditions. Thus, as business expanded and contracted, the expansive power of credit would be decreased and increased.

Control of reserve ratios by the Banking Act of 1935. This kind of regulation was projected for the Banking Act of 1935. What actually was enacted was somewhat different. The projected provisions would have established a sliding scale of ratios by legal enactment; the actual provisions rejected this procedure and substituted control through the discretionary power of the Board of Governors of the Federal Reserve System. "In order to prevent injurious credit expansion or contraction," the Board of Governors may change the legal reserves of member banks against either time or demand deposits; but these changes may not require reserves lower

---

[1] Committee on Finance and Industry, London, 1931, Report, Paragraph 370 (6).

than those previously required nor more than twice as high. This provision clearly gives discretionary power over a substantial range of reserve ratios, and one, which in times less abnormal than those now ruling, may be of considerable importance.

The effectiveness of this kind of regulation remains for the future to reveal. Presumably it will depend on the wisdom of the Board of Governors, and even more on its ability to escape political domination and subservience to the fiscal interests of the Treasury. That the latter can be of overshadowing importance is indicated by the events of 1936–1937, when the first discretionary regulation was put into effect. At that time, under the fear of impending inflation, the Board, by two successive increases, one in August 1936, the other in May 1937, raised the reserves to the maximum figure of twice their former level.

The result, perhaps not unexpected, was a considerable sale of United States Government bonds by those banks whose cash did not enable them to meet, without some liquidation of assets, the higher reserve requirements. This result was not by any means universal throughout the system, for most banks' excess reserves were high enough to make the new reserve requirements no burden; and even after the change of May 1937, total excess reserves of member banks were approximately $900 millions. However, enough sale went on to depress the price of government bonds, already affected, incidentally, by previous fears of inflation.

The fall in government bonds, however, was anything but agreeable to the Treasury, not to mention banks in general whose holdings had greatly increased during the financial operations of the New Deal. Doubtless under government influence, the Federal Reserve Banks proceeded to buy considerable amounts of bonds for the first time since February 1934. Thus a strangely contradictory policy was displayed to an astonished country as the reserve authorities on the one hand

decreased the lending powers of banks by changing their
reserve requirements, and on the other hand increased them by
open-market purchases of securities. So difficult is the path of
the stabilizer!

Perhaps one lesson from this experience is that changes in
reserve ratios should never be very large at any one time, as
was recommended by the Macmillan Committee. But America
moves in large gestures, and the bold attempts to bring about
reflation through devaluation and other financial devices of
the New Deal seemed necessarily to lead to equally bold gestures in the opposite direction when the resulting excess of
idle reserves raised the spectre of imminent inflation. Perhaps, too, these are only the somewhat uncoördinated movements of the inexperienced performer, which, in time, will
give way to the graceful, effortless action of the fully trained
expert.

100 Per Cent Money

The proposal to control more directly the total supply of
money by fixing the reserve ratios of banks raises the questions:
Why would it not be more efficacious to remove completely
the elasticity of bank credit by fixing reserve ratios at 100 per
cent? What is the advantage of juggling with reserve ratios
in the probably vain attempt to stabilize bank credit, when
the simple act of raising ratios to 100 per cent would once and
for all limit changes of bank credit to changes in the volume
of reserves? If the deposit currency of banks were an inflexible function of reserves, then any operations successfully
controlling the reserves, would, *ipso facto,* control the volume
of bank credit. As long as currency is *not* an inflexible function of reserves, banks can defeat control by changing the ratio
of reserves to bank credit, and the aggregate of bank money
still escapes effective regulation by the central banking authorities.

For this reason, various reformers have advocated 100 per

cent reserves as a cornerstone of money management and a prerequisite to stability.[2] Let us now examine how this arrangement would work, using as an example the proposals advanced by Professor Irving Fisher, one of the leading advocates of such a plan.

The Fisher plan for 100 per cent reserves. Fisher proposes that the Federal Government, through some appropriate agency (say, a Currency Commission), buy sufficient assets of the commercial banks of the country to make their cash reserves against checking accounts 100 per cent. The assets would preferably be United States bonds so as to reduce the national debt, and the means of payment would be national currency issued by the government. He would also have the Commission buy enough assets of the Federal Reserve Banks to redeem all their outstanding liabilities in currency. This procedure would turn all the existing assets of the Federal Reserve Banks and a large fraction of the assets of other banks into cash; but as the cash would be needed for reserves, nothing thereby would be added to or subtracted from the existing total of the circulating medium.

For the banks, this cash, like other reserves, would be a credit on the books of the Commission, as present reserves are a credit on the books of Federal Reserve Banks, translatable in emergency into bank notes or similar appropriate "currency," but ordinarily transferred from bank to bank by simple entries on the books of the Commission.

With existing deposits thus secured 100 per cent, further demand deposits would then require 100 per cent reserve. Deposits would become what they were originally expected to be—namely, deposits in the literal sense. In respect to de-

---

[2] The arguments for 100 per cent reserves and various proposals for bringing them about will be found set forth in the following places: (a) Irving Fisher, *100% Money;* New York, 1935, (b) J. Lauchlin Currie, *Supply and Control of Money in the United States;* Cambridge, 1934, (c) H. C. Simons, *A Positive Program for Laissez-faire* (The Chicago Plan) Chicago, 1934. See also P. H. Douglas, *Controlling Depressions,* 184–188.

posits, banks would be storage warehouses for the spare funds of the community. Thus for an individual bank as well as for the aggregate of banks, deposits could rise only if cash rose, and in exact ratio thereto. As this situation would reduce the earnings of banks, no longer able to charge interest for loans of "fictitious" money, customers would doubtless have to pay some fee to banks for the privilege of deposits therein.

Savings deposits would be a different case. Savings would essentially be for investment, not storage, and the banks would be not warehouses, but rather brokers for investments. They would be middlemen bringing savers and investment opportunities together. As such, they would not keep on hand any more cash than they do at present—namely, just enough to meet the demands of customers who do not want to wait until their investments are cashed in by sale or maturity.

Loans under the 100 per cent plan. Moreover, banks could still make loans. They could loan their own money (capital and surplus). They could reloan the proceeds of loans paid back by customers. They could loan the sums placed in their hands for investment purposes by savings accounts customers. They could lend any new money advanced to them by the Currency Commission when it was necessary to do so in order to keep the total volume of currency in proportion with the growing needs of industry and trade.

But they could not under any circumstances lend the money placed with them in demand deposits; nor, *a fortiori*, could they lend this money, as they have done in the past, to several separate borrowers at one and the same time.

There is nothing in this arrangement, Professor Fisher argues, that will reduce the volume of available loans at banks. On the contrary, it ought eventually to increase them, yet with perfect safety. The existing loans will not be decreased because the required additional reserve will be had by selling or rediscounting, or borrowing on, the necessary amount of assets. When these assets fall due, the funds paid by the borrowers will revert to the Central Currency Commission, which is then in a position to supply with funds any bank that wishes to make a loan of similar amount.   Or if the assets had still been held by the original bank, they now have funds which make their reserves over 100 per cent and put them, with those excess reserves, in a position to lend up to the original volume of loans.   New loans will therefore come, whenever (and not until) investors are ready, through savings accounts, to save the necessary amounts.   But as the whole business structure ought to be safer without the unstable money of the partial reserve system, savings ought to be made with more confidence, and Professor Fisher thinks they will increase in the aggregate with advantage to the growth of wealth.

Naturally, variations of this procedure would suggest themselves to ingenious minds.   Thus the Currency or Monetary Commission, instead of buying up the bonds of the banking system, might lend the banks enough cash to raise their reserves to 100 per cent.   Or the banks might be allowed to count government bonds as reserve, with the right to cash them at will into currency issued by the Commission.   Again, as has been suggested in the so-called Chicago Plan, long-time loans might be made largely by separate institutions of the nature of investment trusts, whose securities the public would buy instead of depositing their "savings" in savings banks.

Creation of money not a proper function of banks. These are only details.   The essence of all such plans is to separate the function of creating money from that of retailing credit. The banks can continue to be the middlemen between lenders and borrowers, but the producers and controllers of the aggregate volume of monetary purchasing power of the community they can no longer be.

There are some who would accomplish this objective by nationalizing the banks.   The 100 per cent reserve does not go this far.   The banks continue to be, as they have been before, private institutions.   But it does effectively nationalize the function of currency creation. It is arguable that this is precisely what should be done, and what was expected to be done by the terms of the Federal Constitution. Article I, Section 8, of the Constitution specifically bestows upon Congress the issue and regulation of money. It is only by a historical accident that money has become so little gold, silver, and paper currency and so much the checkbook currency characteristic of our times. One may say that banks, unconsciously, without purpose, and without even knowing themselves what has been going on, have usurped an essential function of government. The underlying purposes of Federal Reserve policy and open-market operations have fundamentally been to get that function back. The advocates of 100 per cent reserves simply hold that this gets it back finally and without any uncertainty or ambiguity.

100 per cent reserves no panacea. Nobody claims, of course, that the 100 per cent reserve plan is a panacea. It does give to the government an apparently complete control over the available amount of monetary purchasing power, whether currency or bank credit. The volume of money as it stands at any moment would be a fixed and determinable quantity; and thereafter all changes will depend on the deliberate action of the currency authority, which presumably will so act as to keep this volume at levels which will make for stable and continuous growth of economic activity. Whether this action will abolish cyclical fluctuations and, particularly, whether it will prevent depressions are other matters.

A monetary authority can create money, but it cannot, as such, cause it to be used. The volume of money in use depends not merely on the volume supplied by the monetary authority; it is also a function of the velocity of circulation, and this is dependent on the will of people to use their funds. No authority can determine the intensity with which purchasing power is used. If people want to withhold funds from use, and put them in savings accounts and leave them there, they can. If the banks receiving these accounts do not lend them to bor-rowers either because of their lack of confidence in business ventures or because business is not in the mood to borrow, they cannot very well be compelled to do otherwise.

To meet this situation, therefore, the currency authority under 100 per cent reserves may be compelled themselves to put funds in circulation—say, by the purchase of appropriate securities from the community in general.   If this does not over-come the tendency to keep funds idle (and the experience of similar activity in the great depression indicates that this dan-ger may materialize), the government may have to go into action itself and get the funds into circulation by a system of public works or other government spending.

If booms and depressions were largely the result of credit expansion and contraction, this situation need not arise, for booms could be prevented by monetary control. Without booms to create tension, depressions would have no reason to occur, nor would hoarding or other forms of velocity reduction seem likely to take place.   But enough has been learned in-our survey of cycle theory to indicate how easy it may be for a rate of expansion to be begun that cannot be maintained, and how difficult it is to avoid the deflationary consequences when activity begins to slacken.

Wars, investment booms stimulated by invention, and ac-celeration of capital goods production begun by changes in consumers' demand may still bring about bursts of expansion, even with all our efforts to control the money supply. It will not be easy to prevent a community determined upon expansion from carrying it through.   Indeed, the banks may often have been merely passive instruments of expansion and contraction imposed by industrial leaders upon the economic world. It may turn out to be that even governments may not be able to resist the demand for expansion in times of great speculative or inventive or warlike urges; and the monetary authorities may be compelled to issue the volume of currency needed to satisfy the "boom" in industry.

The subsidence of activity which inevitably must follow such episodes will not readily be prevented by merely monetary measures. The lesson of the great depression may not be very clear, but it is clear on this point at least: that the volume of money available is quite different from the volume of money in active use; and that to prevent activity from falling below its normal levels, government spending and lending may have to be brought into play.

Will 100 per cent reserve reduce the cost of our money supply? It is argued in favor of the 100 per cent reserve that the profit from creating the supply of money which has been the perquisite of banks would be enjoyed by the public as a whole. The issue of money could be carried on at cost, only such charges being levied as are necessary to pay the unavoidable expenses of currency issue and management. Furthermore, the procedure by which, to get the 100 per cent reserve plan in operation, currency is issued in exchange for the banks' holdings of government bonds, would be on such a scale as practically to wipe out the government debt. Thus, by the exchange of noninterest-bearing currency for the bond issues of the government, the public saves the interest on the national debt.

This seductive argument may not be so good as it looks. If the creation of the money supply of banks is under competition, the charge for the service will approximate the cost. Only if (a) there had been a monopoly profit, or if (b) the government could perform the service at less cost, all things considered, would there be a real saving to the public by transferring the job to the government. Whether the latter condition would prevail only experience could tell. But it is easy to overestimate the saving. Under the fractional reserve system, checking accounts were frequently carried by the banks at their own expense, the procedure of drawing, paying, clearing, transfer, and exchange being carried on gratis. With 100 per cent reserves, this favor could not be done. If the cost were reimbursed by the government from taxes, as some suggest, it would be an obvious burden on the public. It is a cost on, the general depositor when charged up to him, as would probably be the case, by the banks. This charge is one deduction from the apparent gains to the public from the 100 per cent plan.

Furthermore, there is the problem of choosing, and taking care of the assets against which the monetary commission would issue notes. This job is not costless. The cost of managing the money system, the investigations, the current flow of statistical information; the cost of resisting political pressure; and the cost of "public relations" and propaganda are bound to add up to a considerable sum.

It has been pointed out by Angell [3] that the aggregate interest paid on government bonds to banks in the year 1935 was scarcely enough to pay the apparent service costs of the aggregate checking accounts. If this situation continued, and if, in addition, the cost of managing the money were taken into account, it does not appear that the public would gain much, net, by wiping out the public debt in exchange for the "right" (should it be called the "burden"?) of issuing money.

Administrative problems of changing to 100 per cent reserves. Perhaps one should add that the problem of reaching 100 per cent reserves is an administrative one of no mean order and one which may possibly not be solved without considerable economic disturbances. One might recall that the doubling of the reserve requirements in 1936–1937 was not accomplished without some agitation in banking circles, and not without a considerable fluctuation in the bond market. Indeed, the need on the part of the banks, especially the country banks, to acquire

---

[3] J. W. Angell, "The 100% Reserve Plan," *Quarterly Journal of Economics*, November, 1935.

cash put some strain on the price of bonds, had something to do with the serious fall in government bonds in early 1937, compelled the government to reverse its policy of anti-inflation, and caused the Federal Reserve Banks to buy considerable quantities of bonds for the first time since February 1934; and may have had consequences not unconnected with the stock market (and, therefore, with the business) recession that was precipitated in the second half of the year.

To change to 100 per cent reserves would be a much more formidable maneuver.

Angell reckons that one-half the total earning assets of banks would have to be taken over by the government (bank or commission, or whatever body it may be). Naturally, the government would prefer to have this half include its own bonds plus other assets necessary to make up the total. Naturally, also, it would prefer to have the best assets, and perhaps Congress would insist on this. In any case, it would have to pick and choose among the assets.

What would be the effect of this on the other half? That half would be protecting the savings deposits. If that half were less desirable, and the depositors knew or suspected as much, would there not be a rush to transfer from savings to demand accounts and would not this compel the government to take over a greater and greater amount of assets in progressive fashion? In any event, would the banks be moved to readjust their portfolios in order to take advantage from, or avoid evil consequences of, the situation? And what effects would this have on the banks themselves, on the investment market, on borrowers, and so forth?

One must be reminded of the fact that time deposits are frequently only delayed demand deposits. They represent temporarily idle funds of corporations placed where they can earn a little return. They are not investments. Would not such time deposits be quickly transferred to demand, or liquidated completedly, on any belief that the assets behind them were to be discriminated against, or even on any realization that the banks assumed them to be permanent investments?

So much for the 100 per cent reserve plan. There seems no doubt that it would reduce the hazards of deposits. It would probably increase the effectiveness of monetary control, although it might be argued that reasonable coöperation of the banks with the policies of the Federal Reserve System would be as effective in the long run. Whatever its effectiveness, it would leave some factors uncontrolled, particularly the velocity of circulation and the possibility of using forms of credit, such as book credit, not easily subject to banking restrictions. In any case, it would not be costless; it might not even be sufficiently less costly than the present arrangement to justify the hazards of its introduction.

The Proper Volume of Money

If the purpose of monetary management is achieved—that is to say, control over the volume of money—the first question that will have to be faced is: What is the proper volume of money? What, in other words, is to be the proper standard to which the volume of money should be made to conform?

The standards which have been suggested most commonly are the following:

(1) A constant volume of money.

(2) A constant volume of money per capita.

(3) A varying volume of money such as to maintain stability of some one of the possible price levels, wholesale prices, cost of living, general prices, and so on. This standard might be called "the constant purchasing-power standard."

All of these standards must start from some essentially arbitrary level. If the volume of money is to be kept constant, the start must be the volume of some given date or year. If the price level is to be stabilized, the start must be the price level of some given date or year. If it were possible to name any

,date or year which could be reasonably regarded as "normal,"
that date or year might be chosen. Thus the Roosevelt Administration in its early years was thinking in terms of stable
prices on the level of the year 1926, which was regarded as
normal. Not quite so sensibly, the Agricultural Adjustment
Administration was instructed to attempt to bring up agricultural prices to the relative level of the years 1910–1914, which
were, apparently, also regarded as normal.

But no price level and no volume of money are normal. Any
price level that is chosen, either directly or indirectly by choosing the volume of money, will be fairer to some than to others.
The price level of 1932, for example, would be more advantageous to creditors than that of 1939. If the price level of
1926 were chosen as the normal, all creditors whose money
was put out at interest in any year since 1929, including all
creditors of the Government itself in the years since 1933, would
be penalized. If the levels of the year 1939 were chosen, all
debtors whose debts had been contracted at a higher level
would be penalized.

To repeat, therefore, any standard must start from some
more or less arbitrary level. Granting that such a level is
chosen, what are the relative merits of these three standards?

1. A constant volume of money. The argument for a
constant volume of money is that changes in the price level
will no longer be propagated from the monetary side. Such
changes as occur will be from nonmonetary causes. Thus, as
the total volume of output in the typical industrial country is
normally on the increase, the price level, with a constant volume of money, must fall. This result is as it should be, for
the causes of the increase of output and the subsequent fall
in prices are nonmonetary in nature. They are improvements
in technology, growth of population, opening up of new resources, and so on. Monetary causes have been removed by
holding the monetary supply constant. Money, in short, is
"neutral."

That money should be "neutral" is the position of Hayek and a natural corollary of his theory of the cycle. The rhythmic expansion and contraction of the volume of bank credit, with its consequences in encouraging uneconomic changes in the structure of production that are impossible to maintain, are removed by fixing the supply of money; and no other causes are capable of generating cycles.

This standard, however, may need to be qualified in some particulars. A neutral money professes to remove monetary causes of fluctuation; but a constant money supply does not necessarily do this. There are two influences of a monetary nature which may even then affect price levels and may have to be removed for the sake of stability. These are: (1) changes in the velocity of circulation, which are as capable of initiating price changes as changes in volume of money; and (2) changes in the proportion of the total flow of goods effected by money (what Hayek calls "the coefficient of money transactions"), which clearly determines the demand for money, hence its value and the level of prices. Thus the merger of firms formerly independent releases money and is equivalent to an increase in money supply; just as, in the contrary case, a subdivision absorbs money and is equivalent to a decrease in money supply. For this reason, Hayek concedes that the volume of money should not be constant, but should change so as to cancel changes in velocity and changes in the coefficient of transactions, varying inversely with the former, directly with the latter. With this modification, the money supply would be truly "neutral."

It is possible that these modifications have no great importance. Snyder has shown that, over long periods, velocity of circulation has no noticeable trend; and it may well be, although there is no definite evidence of this, that the various changes in business relations that might affect the "coefficient of money transactions" are so numerous and so various as to cancel out fairly well. For short periods, it is highly improbable that the coefficient of money transactions would change much; but this cannot be said for velocity of circulation, which has had definitely marked cyclical fluctuations, rising in boom, falling in depression. For this reason, a "neutral" money (if there is such a thing) must take account of velocity changes.

2. A constant volume of money per capita. A constant volume of money suffers from one grave defect, which needs some examination. As noted above, a constant volume of money in the face of the gradual increase in aggregate output, which is the normal behavior of modern industry, must result in a falling price level. Now, where the increase of output is the result of technological advance, or of new discoveries, it is arguable that the falling price level will cause no trouble, for costs will be falling and aggregate profits may be maintained. Hence there will be no motive to decrease aggregate employment or to diminish the money earnings of the factors of production. Where the increase of output is the result of an increase of population, technical methods unchanged, then, unless production as a whole (agriculture and extractive industries included) were in a position of increasing returns, the fall in prices raises serious problems. There is no fall in costs of production; and unless money wages can be reduced, profits are bound to suffer. The result, therefore, is likely to be unemployment and depression.

An example of this difficulty can be found in the industrial situation in England following the return to the gold standard in 1925. The decreased volume of money which this return involved tended to lower the price level, especially of exported goods; but, as wages were relatively inflexible, profits were hit, and a chronic source of depression in many industries set in motion, which continued to operate until England went off the gold standard in 1931. This experience would seem to indicate that a fixed supply of money in the face of an increase of goods may offer the gloomy alternative of unemployment or serious industrial disputes over the level of wages.

For this reason, therefore, it would be best to have, not a constant supply of money, but rather a constant supply of money per capita. Under these circumstances, increase of output brought about by increase of population would be taken care of by an appropriate increase of money and would involve no change in the price level. But other increases of output (which can be summed up as increases in output per capita, and are due to "improvements") would not be accompanied by any increase of money and would involve a fall in the price level. Under this arrangement, if no change in population occurs, the aggregate money income of the community would be unchanged, irrespective of changes in aggregate output. The real income of the community would rise and fall in proportion to changes in the aggregate output.

It would be assumed, of course, that changes in velocity of circulation and in the coefficient of monetary transactions would be compensated for by appropriate changes in per capita money.

Is this standard a just one?   Even with all these precautions, there are objections to the constant-volume-of-money-per-capita standard. (a) Entrepreneurs introducing innovations and technological improvements would not enjoy any more than the normal level of profits. The fall in prices would remove all extra profits. Whether this result would leave a reasonable stimulus to undertake the risks of innovation is doubtful. To meet this, the alternatives are either some reduction of wages with attendant industrial conflict or a sufficient increase of money-per-capita to leave more than normal profits for the system as a whole. That is to say, it is arguable that some relative inflation is a necessary (and reasonable) price to pay for technological advance.

(b) A constant volume of money per capita means that, although real wages may rise, money wages cannot do so. If wage earners were educated to think in terms of real wages, this situation would not be objectionable. But, in fact, wage earners seem to reckon in terms of money wages. When these rise, people are getting on well; when they fail to rise, people are discontented, and they will resist reductions in money wages, even where real wages might thereby be raised. For this reason, it may make for less discontent and industrial conflict if a standard of money is adopted under which money wages as well as real wages may rise.

(c) A stationary per capita money income with a falling price level means that the gains of production from technology are shared throughout all society. All income receivers stand to gain, and gain proportionately, from the reduction of prices. Hence not only the wage earners, but the recipients of property incomes, incomes from rents, interest, and dividends share in the gains. There are some who argue that this is not socially desirable; that, on the contrary, a standard that will benefit earned, and penalize unearned, incomes is a more desirable one. A proper monetary policy will serve to redistribute the national income on a broader base. It should not attempt to be "neutral." One of the fundamental causes of our cyclical troubles resides in a faulty distribution of income; and here is a chance to correct it. (Underconsumptionists would be fond of this argument.)

These various reasons lead some to favor a fixed purchasing-power standard, which must now be examined in detail.

3. A constant-purchasing-power standard. Under this standard, the total monetary supply would be so regulated that the price level of some collection of goods would remain substantially constant. This standard involves the necessity of deciding which collection of goods shall be stabilized in price, and means that this kind of standard is more ambiguous than the fixed-volume-of-money-per-capita standard. Thus, to take two alternatives, the prices of goods at wholesale could be stabilized, using an index number similar to that of the Bureau of Labor Statistics; or, on the other hand, the prices of goods entering into common consumption, as reflected in wage earners' purchases, could be stabilized, using an index of cost of living. Which to use would depend largely on what was expected to be accomplished. If the aim were to eliminate the windfall profits and losses of entrepreneurs, the wholesale price level would appear to be the more appropriate. If the aim were to stabilize the consumption of the people as a whole, the cost-of-living index would seem more appropriate. Which aim is more desirable would have to be decided largely on one's theory of what causes cycles.

In any case, whatever the appropriate prices to be stabilized, this standard means that the aggregate volume of money must be increased with every increase of output. Thus whereas, in the fixed-money-per-capita standard, total money income can only increase when population increases, in this case total money income will always increase when aggregate output increases.

Now it is evident that, when aggregate output increases because of improvements in methods of production, so that costs are falling, the result of a stable price level will be to increase profits above normal, unless wages or other incomes are increased. This increase of profits above normal, what Keynes calls "profit inflation," is a prime factor in disequilibrium and must lead to the very boom which stabilization of prices was designed to prevent. Indeed, this outcome seems to have been our experience in the great American boom of the 1920's, when, although prices were remarkably stable, falling costs unaccompanied by equivalently rising wages brought about one of the greatest profit inflations in history.

It is, therefore, essential to the effectiveness of a fixed-purchasing-power standard that wages be raised to that level where wage earners may share adequately in the gains of production, and producers' profits be held at such levels as to prevent an expansion that cannot be maintained. Provided this level can be agreed on (and no merely monetary policy can determine it), then the result of the standard is essentially this. Ag-

gregate money wages and, with them, real wages would rise
with every increase of output; where the output was an increase
per capita, money wages per capita would also rise. Profits
would presumably be relatively stable. But the recipients of
fixed income, such as interest and rents, would be penalized.
Their real income would gradually fall; and the aggregate
would tend to represent a smaller fraction of the national income. They would not share, during the period of their
claims, in any increase of the national income, either monetary
or real.

Any monetary standard involves social policy. It is evident
from what has been said that the merits of the two principal
alternative standards, a fixed-money-per-capita standard or
a fixed-purchasing-power standard, must be judged in the
light of broad social policy rather than by purely monetary
considerations. Which standard will make fewer disputes between labor and capital? Which would better stimulate improvement and innovation while causing their advantages to
be widely diffused? Which better satisfies the requirements
of social justice, which, in the long run, may turn out to be
requirements of social efficiency? More particularly, which
works out the better in the long run, a system which shares
gains with everybody, or one which penalizes the *rentier* for
the benefit of earned incomes such as wages?

In short, monetary stability turns out to be no easy road to
industrial stability. There are problems involved here which
no monetary policy can solve. There will still remain the
acute problem of the division of the product between capital
and labor. Lying concealed in this is the extremely difficult
problem of adequate reward for the risky innovations which,
in the past, have seemed to be the source of our advance. For
the sake of avoiding the evils of alternating booms and slumps,
we may, as Keynes puts it, be condemning ourselves to a chronic
situation of semislump.

There still remains the question of price inequalities and

divergence. Even though the general level of prices is controlled, there may still be instability and inequality of individual prices owing to different degrees of monopoly and competition in different fields. If a standard is adopted which is designed to cause prices to fall with improvements in production, it is vitally important that the right prices fall. If concentration, of control happens to give power over price to the very concerns whose prices should fall, trouble is bound to emerge, for they would be certain to resist price reduction, and their increased volume of output could then be sold only by attracting an undue share of the limited money volume of the community. This situation must put a heavy strain on the price levels of all other producers, who, with no reduction of costs to help, would be in a sad condition. The general fall in the price level may be attained therefore by a fall not in areas where costs have gone down, but in areas where costs have stayed up. That this result would be disruptive of the productive and exchange mechanism of the community is hardly to be denied.

In other words, even though means are available to eliminate the disturbing effects of monetary influences, it is not implied that no other policy is needed. If prices are to fall, the right prices must do the falling. If frictions or monopolistic control, or any other institutional factor, prevents this from being attained, then society must proceed against these obstructive influences if it is to reap the complete advantages which monetary stabilization is expected to bring about.

CHAPTER XIX

MONETARY MANAGEMENT: INTERNATIONAL MONETARY RELATIONS

I T HAS been assumed, in the discussion to this point, that stabilization can be undertaken effectively by a single country without regard to international relations. But international relations definitely complicate the problem of control. Clearly, what is possible for a self-contained country with no international relations may not be possible for a country on an international gold standard, whose total stock of money is exposed to the continual inflow and outflow of gold occasioned by its economic relations.

An International Gold Standard Hampers National Stabilization

Suppose, now, a given community on the gold standard undertakes a stabilizing policy to prevent the expansion and contraction of credit associated with business cycles, and therewith the rise and fall of prices which are the heart of the monetary problem. If the general trend of world prices is upward, the stabilizing country tends to have a steady excess of exports. Gold will flow in and continue to do so as long as prices are kept artificially low. This continued flow of gold would make stabilization increasingly difficult even if all the gold were purchased by the central bank.

If the gold is paid for with cash, the result is to increase the balances of banks at the central bank, and therewith weaken the ability to control the market by changes in bank rate. If, on the other hand, the gold were paid for by sale of securities, then, although reserves of banks in the central bank are not changed, the open-market operations of the central bank are progressively weakened, as they "shoot all their ammunition away." Thus successful stabilization involves the costly exchange of cash or securities for useless and embarrassing gold which must either be sterilized at considerable cost or remain a constant and growing threat of sudden inflation.

If, on the other hand, the trend of world prices is downward, the stabilizing country will find its import balance increasing. Gold will flow out and continue to do so as long as there is any left to flow. If the central bank persists in its determination to keep prices up, the ultimate result must be the exhaustion of the gold supply and the abandonment of the gold standard.

Thus stabilization in a nonstabilizing world seems to land any one country in a serious dilemma, either forcing gold upon it which it does not want, or taking away gold which it would prefer not to give up; at the worst, exposing it to the risk of either serious inflation or the abandonment of the gold standard.

In short, central banks seem to suffer from the same limitations in respect to the world community that restrict national banks at home in relation to each other. Just as, in a multiple-bank system, no bank can increase or decrease its outstanding credit at a pace much different from that of its fellows, so central banks find their behavior regulated by the behavior of central banks in general. The gold standard, as Keynes puts it, essentially ensures "that no Central Bank shall inflate or deflate at a pace very different from that of its neighbours." "Each Bank is necessarily governed by the average policy of the Banks as a whole," and this situation "hampers each Central Bank in tackling its own national problems, interferes with pioneer improvements of policy the wisdom of which is ahead of average wisdom, and does nothing to secure either the

short-period or the long-period optimum if the average behavior is governed by blind forces such as the total quantity of
gold, or is haphazard and without any concerted or deliberate
policy behind it on the part of the Central Banks as a body." [1]

Some Individual Stabilization Is Possible

Doubtless some central banks are more exposed than others.
If the normal reserve ratio of the central bank is high, so that
loss or gain of gold can be readily absorbed in changes in the
volume of reserves, the national economy may be reasonably
protected from gold movements. Thus the United States in
the 1920's, or France before the First World War, would have
more freedom than England, where the Bank of England
normally operates on a low ratio of reserves. Low ratios are
economical but sometimes dangerous.

Again, if the country has a relatively small fraction of foreign
trade and investments, local stabilization will be so much less
restricted by the consequences of inflow or outflow of gold.
Similar results would follow from high tariffs or other impediments to foreign trade.

Furthermore, central banks, by appropriate changes in their
rates of interest, which cause the fringe of international financial business to be transferred, as it readily can be, from one
center to another, can clearly affect somewhat the flow of
reserve resources. Thus a loss of gold may be averted and a
gain shut off before the flow has had time to affect internal
stability. Of course, this process is limited to the central banks
of countries of major importance in international finance.

If a central bank, therefore, is ready to allow wide variations
in its reserve ratios, and if its national economy is not too
sensitive to foreign trade, it may enjoy considerable stabilizing
power over its internal price structure and industrial activity,
even though adhering faithfully to the gold standard. While

---

[1] J. M. Keynes, *Treatise on Money*, New York, Harcourt, Brace & Company, Inc.,
1930, Volume II, 286–287.

this holds out hope that at least minor fluctuations might be ironed out by the leading banking systems, enough has been said to throw strong doubts upon the ability of any country on the gold standard succeeding by individual action in adequately preventing or controlling the major booms and depressions.

International Agreement Desirable But Improbable

This conflict between the operation of the international gold standard and a deliberate policy of internal stabilization is not, however, unavoidable. It could be resolved by appropriate international agreements, and indeed this kind of approach was the hope of the 1920's, when restoration of peaceful economic international relations seemed still to be within reach.

That is to say, if the leading central banks could be persuaded to adopt broadly uniform policies of stabilization, the hindrances to effective action might be greatly reduced. For example, if reserves could be varied by law or convention within reasonably wide limits (Keynes suggests a maximum variation of 20 per cent above or below normal), expansion and contraction of total bank credit could be reasonably regulated, especially if all banks would adopt a uniform discount policy and adjust discount rates, fortified by appropriate open-market dealings, to a program designed to prevent undue differences in expansion and contraction between different regions. This policy would do for the financial world what the open-market committee of the Federal Reserve System was designed to do for the Federal Reserve districts—namely, prevent the controlling measures of one bank from being upset by the inappropriate action of others. These policies would be greatly facilitated if the central banks were attached to some permanent institution, the prime duty of which would be precisely the job of supernational monetary management. Indeed, such an institution is supplied at present (at least potentially) by the Bank of International Settlements.

But the circumstances of the world today effectively rule out these international measures. They were the hope of the 1920's, seeming as they did to point the way, by a logical development from the centralized banking systems of the several nations, to international coöperation for the benefit of all; but the world has chosen the other way. The conflict between internal stabilization and the international gold standard, itself the fundamental sign of international coöperation, has been resolved by abolition of the international gold standard. The world has pinned its hope of financial stability on national management of currency. There may be effective arguments for international monetary management (admirably set forth by Keynes in Book VII of his *Treatise on Money*); but they have a purely academic interest. A nationally minded world has ruled them out of practical importance. Hence our discussion will be limited to the problems which must be faced when the traditional gold standard is replaced, in the interests of stability, by a nationally managed currency, whether on a gold base, as that of the United States today, or a purely paper currency, as is advocated by some of the more radical reformers.

A Managed National Currency

A managed national currency must aim at some definite standard of prices. As we have seen, this standard need not necessarily be a stable or fixed price level. It might be desirable to have prices gradually fall; it is even arguable that they should be permitted gradually to rise. Whatever the choice, some standard is set up; and when such a standard is set up, the volume of money must be appropriate to maintaining it. Consequently, some mechanism must be set up to see that variations in the flow of gold, both over short and over long periods, do not disturb the standard. Except in the improbable event (which has never happened yet in the world as it is) of actual gold volume being precisely coincident with the theoretical volume required to maintain the standard of prices, disturbance will take place unless measures are taken to prevent it.

The problems which this kind of control involves can be visualized readily by examination of one of the best-known proposals for a managed currency—namely, the so-called "compensated dollar" advocated for many years, with variations of detail, by Professor Irving Fisher. The compensated dollar has been constantly in the background of administration policy ever since President Roosevelt announced to the World Economic Conference of 1933 that "the United States seeks the kind of dollar which a generation hence will have the same purchasing and debt-paying power as the dollar value we hope to attain in the near future."

A dollar of such stable purchasing power means a radical departure from the traditional gold standard. The familiar dollar of a fixed weight of gold but fluctuating purchasing power is abandoned, and in its place is set up a dollar of fixed (or controlled) purchasing power but of fluctuating weight in gold. Having determined some price level that might be regarded as normal, the monetary authorities would seek to maintain this by appropriate fluctuations in the legal gold content of the dollar. When wholesale prices were rising (owing to an increase in gold relative to commodities), the gold content of the dollar would be proportionately increased. In the opposite circumstances, with prices falling, the gold content of the dollar would be proportionately decreased. All these changes would be made upon such small variations in the price level (1 per cent in the Fisher plan) as promptly to compensate for these variations, tending therefore to correct them, and hence to avoid cumulative price increases and decreases. Of course, gold would cease to circulate as money. Indeed, all gold would be held by the Treasury or the central banks, its exchange for currency (at varying rates) being allowed only for foreign economic transactions.

To put it in another way, when prices rose, the currency

available for bank reserves would be automatically decreased, and, when prices fell, would be automatically increased. The decrease of reserves in the former case would set in motio 1 deflationary influences; the increase of reserves in the latter case would set in motion inflationary influences. The result of both is to maintain the price level stable within narrow limits, for increasingly powerful brakes would be applied if prices moved in either direction.

Clearly this regulation of prices could not be upset by the normal reactions from abroad, as would be the case in the unregulated gold standard. Thus, under the gold standard, if prices were prevented from rising, more and more gold would flow to the country, making the problem more and more acute. Under the Fisher standard this is avoided. The increased amount of gold in the dollar makes the dollar more expensive to buy with foreign currencies and completely and precisely cancels the relatively lower prices ruling in the country. Thus, although prices fall for internal buyers, they do not fall, but are unchanged, for foreign buyers, and no movement of gold need take place. Similarly, if, while prices in general are falling, national prices are maintained, no gold need leave the country. The lowered content of gold in the dollar makes the dollar less expensive in foreign currency and so cancels the relatively higher prices ruling in the country.

It would, therefore, seem theoretically feasible by the Fisher plan to regulate the total volume of gold reserves within the country and to prevent this regulation from being broken down by movements of gold, into or out of the country, induced by the levels of prices ruling at home.

Various complications, however, interfere with the success of this ingenious scheme.

Other Monetary Factors Must Be Controlled

(1) What the Fisher plan does is to maintain stability in the gold reserves of the country. It can only maintain sta-

bility in the total money supply of the country provided the bank deposits, which are the principal currency, are a fixed multiple of the reserves. But bank deposits are not necessarily a fixed multiple of reserves. They rise and fall relative to reserves in periods of boom and slump, respectively. It is just this variability in the ratio of deposits to reserves that central bank policy tries to control. Consequently, either central bank policy must still be relied upon to bring complete stability, or some other device must be invented to complete the mechanism of control. The uncertain results of central bank policy, as expressed in its discount rates and its open-market operations, and the necessity of relying on the uncertain supply of human wisdom embodied in boards have, characteristically, led Professor Fisher to become an ardent advocate of 100 per cent bank reserves. As we have seen in a preceding section, 100 per cent bank reserves tend to make the supply of money absolutely and finally equivalent to the supply of reserves, so that, if the reserves are controlled (and the Fisher plan assumes that they are), so also is the supply of money.

Even then, it must be admitted, variations in the velocity of circulation may still prevent complete control, unless the authorities are prepared to compensate for them also by appropriate inverse changes in the total supply of money.

Freedom from Foreign Influences Not Attainable

(2) While, theoretically, a stabilized dollar of the Fisher type will not be made more difficult by persistent inflow or outflow of gold, since exchange rates vary with internal prices, actually it may not work out so smoothly.

This difficulty arises from the varying relations between the change in the foreign exchange rates of the stabilized currency and its purchasing power at home as measured by the internal price level. Theoretically, changes in the external and the internal values of the monetary unit should be identical, so that the relation is a permanent one. Thus, if the gold content of the dollar is decreased, prices at home and the exchange value of foreign currencies rise equally. If the gold content is increased, prices at home and the exchange value of foreign currencies fall equally. While this theory is (approximately) true of commodities that enter into foreign trade and have an international price, it does not appear to be true (except for the long-run tendency) of the price level in general, including the price of securities. On the contrary, there is a marked difference in the flexibility of prices on the one hand and foreign exchange on the other, the former being much slower to move than the latter. Whereas the exchange rates reflect quickly and faithfully the changes in the gold content of the currency unit, internal prices, although moving in the same direction, move more slowly and much less.

The consequence is an unbalanced situation which has much the same results as would occur under a traditional gold standard when prices are being controlled. If the standard is devalued downward (that is, the currency depreciated), the great depreciation in external as compared with internal value penalizes imports, makes exports a bargain, and tends to attract gold into the country. If, on the contrary, the standard is revalued upwards (that is, the currency appreciated), then exports are penalized, imports are a bargain, and gold tends to leave the country, as long as the situation persists. Furthermore, if the circumstances of stabilization are such as to demand more than the small changes in the gold content of the currency unit postulated in the Fisher plan, then the flow of gold into or out of the country may be so considerable as to be not merely embarrassing but destructive of the very stability sought after.

Thus the external depreciation of the United States dollar following the devaluation of 1934 was so considerable compared to its internal depreciation as to cause a persistent flow of gold into the country; a flow that arose partly from payment for export balances, partly because of the relative undervaluation of stock exchange securities, and partly also because of the expectation of internal price rise, which, although delayed, would ultimately follow the depreciation of the dollar.

The contrary case is nicely exhibited in the experience of Great Britain following the return to the gold standard in 1925. The appreciation of the pound sterling which this occasioned, while substantial abroad, was seriously delayed at home, where, apparently owing to rigidity of wage rates and other costs, internal prices were not easily brought down. The result was to discourage exports, increase the volume of unemployment, and set up a chronic tendency to depression of trade and industry which stubbornly resisted treatment.

Further Complications of a Managed Currency

Thus the unequal consequences of stabilizing measures on internal and external prices seem to expose the Fisher standard to embarrassments similar to those afflicting efforts toward stabilization under the traditional gold standard. Countries operating without reference to the behavior of others find themselves exposed, on the one hand, to influxes of gold which may be burdensome and, if continued, dangerously provocative of inflation; and, on the other hand, to an outflow of gold which, if continued, might drive them off the gold standard.

Perhaps this difficulty merely means that, in periods of unusual instability, a simple managed currency on the Fisher plan, designed as it is for minor and quickly correctable fluctuations, must be supplemented by other devices. Indeed, in those countries where a managed currency now rules (as in England and, with some qualification arising from the fixed gold price established by law in 1934, in the United States), other devices are used. The device for this purpose is the equalization or stabilization fund, designed primarily to ensure that local stabilization will not be upset by inappropriate changes in foreign exchange rates. Thus if, in the United States, whether for reasons arising internally or externally, the dollar appreciates unduly over foreign currencies (encouraging imports, discouraging exports, and so forth), the Treasury may use its stabilization fund to buy foreign currencies, forcing their price upward until the desired level is reached. The opposite is done when the dollar depreciates unduly.

Thus the stable dollar involves more than the simple Fisher formula and forces on the government a considerable expansion of discretionary authority.

Stabilization is a game, however, that every country might like to play, and, the interests of each not being the same, the result may be a good deal of conflict for all and stability for none. Currency depreciation during the depths of the great depression came to be a weapon of international strategy. It seemed a seductively simple way of curing internal distress, for, by stimulating exports, it helped to get rid of unwieldy surpluses of goods, especially agricultural goods, and it seemed to promise a gradually increasing internal price level brought about by the contagion of higher export and import prices. Although it was all very well for any given country, this way does not work out so simply when all countries join in the game. Then currency depreciation ceases to be an effective weapon, for the depreciation of each is met by the similar depreciation of all, and, if this goes on on a competitive basis, international monetary relations become increasingly precarious. It was to meet this situation that France, England, and the United States entered into the tripartite currency agreements of 1936, the avowed purpose of which was the maintenance of stable exchange values between these three great democracies.

Thus we have a very curious and unexpected result of the attempt to free the monetary systems of the several countries from the dominance of an international gold standard. National stability, based on a managed currency, proved to be exposed, for all the efforts of the stabilizers, to international disturbance; and compelled bringing in by the back door, as it were, the international standard which had been pitched out the front. This result, as far as it went, was what the tripartite agreement amounted to.

External Stability Sacrificed for Internal Stability

(3) These considerations indicate that the advantages of stabilization, even though attained, are not attained without a price, and, under some circumstances, a heavy price. The price is instability of exchange rates. It is impossible for a single country acting alone to achieve stability of internal prices without sacrificing stability of external exchange rates. It can have one or other of these advantages, but it cannot have both. More exactly, it cannot have both except under exceptional behavior of the other countries of the world. If all important countries happened to be introducing a managed gold currency on the same principles, then both could be achieved; or if many countries happened to be off the gold standard and regulated their paper currencies according to no particular principles, so that exchanges in any case would be subject to uncertain fluctuations, then at least the adoption of a managed currency in one country might be achieved without adding anything to the instability of exchanges that were, in any case, unstable and unpredictable. This case would certainly have been true in the period immediately following the war. But a single country moving towards internal price control in a gold standard would meet neither of these conditions and would inevitably be compelled to face whatever disadvantages arose from instability of exchange rates.

These disadvantages may be serious. Specifically, they consist in the impediments that fluctuating exchange rates make both for international trade and for international investment.

Hindrances to Trade and Investments from Unstable Exchange Rates

In regard to trade, the fluctuations of the exchanges may change the value of foreign currency even in the relatively short

Interval between sale of the goods and receipt of payment. This fluctuation introduces a risk into commerce that adds to its cost, and, both because of the cost and because of direct discouragements arising from the risk, the volume of trade may be reduced. One must observe, however, that these risks can be reduced by the use of "forward exchange." By this device, banks dealing in exchange will, for a price, contract to buy or sell exchange on specific foreign countries at future dates at definite agreed-upon rates. This device does not remove the risk as such, but it does shift it to the shoulders of the banks. If they in turn can hedge their purchases of currency from exporters by corresponding sales of currency to importers, they not merely shift the risk, but eliminate it altogether. Whether or not this mechanism would work effectively in the event of wide fluctuations of exchange, such as would occur when powerful price movements had to be counteracted in the stabilizing country, is problematical; but at least the exchange difficulty in regard to trade has some possible corrective.

In investment, however, the difficulty is more profound. Here the contracts cover a much longer period than could possibly be covered by forward exchange. The risk of loss by exchange fluctuation is greatly increased and would have to be borne by either borrower or lender. If the stabilizing country were a creditor nation, it might shift the risk of loss to its debtors by providing that payments of interest and principal be made in its own currency. But this provision would not increase the enthusiasm of debtors in regard to borrowing and, in extreme cases, might lead to the defaults which marked so much foreign investment in the great depression, when unfavorable exchange rates added greatly to the burden of the debt. One would have to admit, therefore, that a nationally managed currency would necessarily involve some more or less considerable contraction in the volume of international investment. As international investment is a direct cause of the expansion of international trade, one would have to accept a relative contraction of international trade also. The degree of this handicap would depend on how important foreign trade and investment happened to be. For Great Britain, it would be a high price to pay not only because of the high importance of foreign trade and her great investment position, but because, through these things, Great Britain had gained and maintained a supreme position as an international financial center, which might not continue if exchange stability were gone.

In fact, any country that aspires to get or keep a large share of international banking business will have to sacrifice some domestic stability to do so, and will have to ask just how high a price in internal instability it is prepared to pay. For the United States, with its large holdings of gold and its relatively autonomous position in regard to both trade and finance, the difficulties may be less important. If the current wave of economic nationalism persists, and the popular distrust of international lending arising from the sad experience of the last 15 years also continues, then the disadvantages of exchange instability might look small in the face of the advantages of the stability, if it can be gained, of internal prices.[2]

Why Keep Gold at All?

(4) The Fisher plan of a stabilized dollar is essentially a compromise system. It is divorced from the conventional international gold standard, yet it is not divorced from gold as such. This compromise, like any compromise, is distasteful to

---

[2] J. M. Keynes suggests (*Treatise on Money,* Vol. II, 308–309, 334–336) that the supposed advantages to England from stabilized exchange rates were based on ignorance of the degree to which ease of foreign investment could disrupt the internal economic machine. This ease of investment made foreign lending extremely sensitive to outside influences and often caused it to outrun the foreign balance available for investment. When this occurred, the reaction necessary to bring about the necessary increase in foreign balance, either by increasing exports or by reducing imports, was so severe as to put a heavy strain on the economic machine; the more so as the flexibility of prices and particularly of costs necessary to bring this about was ceasing to be characteristic of the modern economic system, which, indeed, was beginning to show quite the opposite—namely, a hardening of these particular elements. Thus an increase of foreign lending may not cause the assumed increase of exports necessary to make it effective, the result being a tendency to a loss of gold, high bank rates,

logical persons, who raise the question: Why not be divorced from gold completely? What is the merit of a scheme which maintains a costly and useless reserve, when a much simpler solution, and one which would lend itself to management more readily (that is to say, a paper standard), is at hand?

The Fisher plan is clearly costly. The Treasury must stand ready to acquire increasing stock of gold bullion, which must be stored, and often to sell these stocks at a lower price in currency than it paid for them. Moreover, as for internal purposes at least gold ceases to circulate, the upshot of the plan is the continuous revaluation in currency of a permanent (and permanently large) stock of hoarded gold. The hoarded gold in itself serves no useful purpose. It is not seen by the public; it never gets into circulation. If it were not there, the public might never know the difference. Yet it has to be stored away at considerable cost, particularly if it might be endangered by possible attacks in war and has to be moved to some *cache* well away from the frontiers. This way of maintaining a stable currency seems very crude and irrational and seems an unnecessary concession to what may be nothing but an easily uprooted prejudice of the public for a gold basis. Clearly, it is a relic of a time when commodity monies were the rule, and it may well have no place in a world where the essential money of every country is a representative one.

Furthermore, this costly and useless gold base is being continually affected by variations in the inflow and outflow of

---

deflationary influences in general, and the imminent danger of a depression, just as an increase in foreign borrowing unaccompanied by a reasonably immediate increase of imports leads directly to boom.

In short, *laisser faire* and extreme mobility in one element of the economic system, accompanied by relative rigidity and control in other parts, such as wages, tariffs, or interest rates, may work far less effectively than would be true if all the elements were mobile, as is assumed by the defenders of the gold standard. As Keynes puts its, "to introduce a mobile element, highly sensitive to outside influences, as a connected part of a machine of which the other parts are much more rigid, may invite breakages."

These considerations may make it necessary to reassess the relative advantages of external and internal stability, and may weigh the decision more in favor of the latter than would have seemed likely at first glance.

gold, arising from relative deviations of exchange values and internal purchasing power.

Why Not a Paper Currency?

These considerations raise the question of whether a sensible kind of managed currency is not a paper one. A paper standard will not be exposed to any greater disturbances from outside than the Fisher standard turns out to be on examination; and, on the other hand, it does not submit the country to the quite unnecessary expense involved in what may be nothing more than a fetish—that is, the gold base.

Public opinion, however, is hardly prepared for such a radical step as this; and one may presume that a managed gold standard is quite as far as any country is likely to go at the present time. Furthermore, paper standards have a dishonorable history behind them that cannot be lived down easily. The great merit of the Fisher plan is the mechanical rules under which it operates. The paper standard, by substituting human judgment for an automatically functioning standard, exposes the monetary system and hence the whole business structure to the consequences of unavoidable mistakes, political considerations, and sheer folly. Economic wisdom is not easy to find, nor does it always reside in authoritative bodies such as would be in control of the monetary volume; and many feel that the shortcomings of a mechanical system, whatever they are (particularly if they are reduced to a minimum by the flexible standard of the Fisher plan), are easier borne than the risk of folly, mistakes, and pressure involved in more human control. Political pressure is bound to arise from time to time from powerful economic groups interested in specific and limited gains, and there will be times also when the whole business world may be opposed to the wise financial course. The first kind would arise, for example, if, when the general price level were stationary, the prices of some considerable group (say farm products) were falling. Who can doubt that strong pressure would be exerted to raise the prices of farm products even though it had the effect of unstabilizing the price level in general? The second would come in every period of prosperity. While, should depressions come, little objection might be made against a policy of raising prices, a great vocal opposition might start against measures designed to prevent the rise from going beyond reasonable levels.

Because of these considerations, a managed gold standard seems more likely to be adopted than any paper one. The public likes to have its prejudices catered to, and, even though the supply of gold is rigidly excluded from circulation and not even allowed in banks, it seems more consistent with stability to have it there than finally to give up the last vestiges of what may be an obsolete system. It may be well, as Keynes suggests, to give "formal homage and the courtesy title" to gold, even though this involves (it is all it can involve) a certain annual expenditure on purchasing the current output of the mines.

Conclusions on Monetary Control

We have now completed our survey of the problem of controlling the available supply of the monetary means of payment. We have seen that, for any one country, the problem is essentially two-fold: (1) controlling the gold or other lawful reserves of the banking and currency system, and (2) controlling the volume of credit and currency based upon a given volume of reserves. If the volume of credit and currency based upon a given volume of reserves were a fixed ratio of the latter, then the problem would come down to the control of the volume of reserves. As, in practice, what we have is not a fixed but a variable percentage, the problem remains twofold. It has been shown that the first part of the problem is not easily solved with a metallic standard like gold, for the gold standard is exposed to influx of money metal from mines and from abroad and to undesirable and unstabilizing variations in this influx. But even the gold standard can be made to supply controllable

reserves through the Fisher plan, provided a country is willing
to pay whatever price is involved in unstable exchanges. Stability of exchanges, along with stability of total internal monetary purchasing power, can be had only by international agreements. This kind of agreement might, through central banks,
bring about reasonable stability of the world's total gold reserves; but the more complete theoretical stability of international paper standards, controlled in the interest of world-wide
stability, can be ruled out as beyond the realm of practical
politics.

If some reasonable stability of gold reserves exists, whether by
national or international action, there remains the problem of
stabilizing the total monetary purchasing power made available
through the banking system. Clearly, as long as the generality
of banks are private institutions, and so long as they are allowed
the measure of freedom of action that all private institutions
must have if they are to serve the public with efficiency, this
stabilization can be only approximate. Aggregate money can,
however, be made a reasonably stable multiple of the volume
of reserves by proper discount policy (aided by open-market
dealings) and, where the reserves themselves are subject to
fluctuation as in the unmodified gold standard, by proper adjustments, through law or otherwise, in the reserve ratios of
the banks.

It has been further noted, however, that the total volume of
purchasing power in the form of both currency and bank credit,
but particularly bank credit, although its available volume can
be approximately controlled, cannot be forced into use unless
the business system is interested in using it. This limitation,
we have seen, means greater powers of control over the periods
of expansion than over the periods of contraction; for, whereas
there can be limits placed to the credit offered in times of stress,
there can be no limits placed on the volume of credit unused in
periods of slump. Indeed, even the control of credit in times
of stress may be made more difficult by increases in the rate of

velocity of turnover of money (currency and bank credit) at the will and initiative of the users. Hence, the paradoxical situation may arrive wherein the credit authorities may be compelled in good times, not merely to slacken the rate of increase of credit, but positively to reduce the volume available, in order to counteract undesirable increases in velocity. Even this, however, would not be impossible. What is impossible, apparently, is to force money into use, in times of depression, merely by the operation of the banking system.

The problem, however, may not be so severe as it looks if one takes into account the fact that depressions do not usually arrive except as a consequence of booms. If the banks can control booms, they may not have to worry about their problem of controlling depressions. But it still remains true that if depressions come, whether as a result of an unpreventable boom or because of other causes, then even the control of the volume of available money must be supplemented by measures designed to get this money into active use. The only measure clearly adapted to this purpose is for the government itself to put funds into circulation via some kind of "public works."

CHAPTER XX

PUBLIC WORKS AS A STABILIZER: [1]
ADMINISTRATION AND FINANCE

WE have examined in preceding chapters the devices by which the monetary authorities may remove or counteract certain causes such as price changes, or credit expansion and contraction, which tend to promote undesirable fluctuations in business activity. These devices might be regarded as methods for inducing business to stabilize its expenditures, which, being the greatest source of the income of society, make regularization of first importance for a stable economic system. But we have seen also that the monetary measures at the disposal of the authorities cannot be completely successful. Even in booms their efficacy is limited, and in depressions they may be quite unable to stop the process of deflation. Even the cheapest money may not be a stimulant to business, and the flow of purchasing power which business can set in motion, particularly in its expenditures for plant and machinery, may, despite all efforts, be undesirably reduced.

In these circumstances, the government may have to resort

---

[1] The best economic analysis of public works is J. M. Clark's *Economics of Planning Public Works*, a study made for the National Planning Board, Washington, 1935. A. D. Gayer, *Public Works in Prosperity and Depression*, New York, 1935, is comprehensive. Two excellent short essays are "The Economics of Public Works," by S. H. Slichter in *American Economic Review Supplement*, March 1934, and G. Bielschowsky, "Business Fluctuations and Public Works," *Quarterly Journal of Economics*, February 1930. The multiplying effects of public expenditures are discussed by R. F. Kahn in his much quoted paper "The Relation of Home Investment to Unemployment," *Economic Journal*, June 1931.

to other means of control.   Of these, the best known lies in the purposeful manipulation of those expenditures of governmental bodies which are known as public works.

Public works are defined by Clark [2] as "durable goods, primarily fixed structures, produced by the government." They commonly include all public buildings, roads, airports, canals, sewage systems, projects for conservation and development of natural resources such as water power and forests, flood and erosion control, river and harbor development, and similar projects. What they include, of course, depends on the scope of activity normally carried on by governmental bodies as well as on the state of public opinion in respect to the extension of this activity into relatively new fields.   Thus, in countries where public utilities are commonly operated by the government, railroads and telegraph and telephone facilities are included in public works, whereas they are private works in the United States.   In depressions, deep ones particularly, there is a tendency to widen the scope of public works in order to increase to its maximum the work-giving area.   Thus, in the United States, public works under the Roosevelt administration were extended to include slum clearance and the construction of low-cost housing on a large scale.   Such an extension of public works is obviously a matter of public policy and social conscience, dependent at any time on the degree to which, in an emergency, public opinion is prepared to see government invade territory normally occupied by private enterprise.

How Public Works May Serve as a Stabilizer

The stabilizing possibilities of public works lie in the fact that the government in its various units normally exercises a large demand in the field of durable goods, and that this demand, to a very considerable degree, can be arranged in such a manner as to modify the instability of private expenditures.

---

[2] J. M. Clark, *Economics of Planning Public Works,* 1935, 2.

Not being subject to the profit-making commercial considerations that surround private business, government may postpone or advance its demands within wide limits; and this power enables it to stagger its operations in the field of durable goods against those of private enterprise. This possibility is particularly important because it is in the field of durable goods, such as are involved in public works, that the greatest fluctuations of output and employment occur and that the greatest social benefit can come from stabilization.

If government followed the habits of private consumers, including business consumption, it would enlarge its purchases when business is good and reduce them when business is bad. In so doing, it would tend to increase the expansion of industrial activity in boom and increase its decline in depression. Moreover, this practice is more or less what it is actuated to follow under its ordinary impulses, for, when times are good, not only do taxes flow in more freely and revenues rise, but the demand for government works of all kinds—on roads, bridges, canals, docks, post offices, and so on—rises also. On the contrary, in depression, revenues gradually shrink, ordinary demand for public works falls away, and economy becomes the watchword for all governmental units. In short, government tends to be inflationary in times when inflation is already under way, and deflationary when deflation is already dangerous.

It would seem, therefore, that, if government would revise its practices and deliberately arrange its expenditures to counteract rather than exaggerate the fluctuations of business spending, increasing its activity when business is dull and decreasing when business is active, the aggregate of business activity in general should certainly be more stable than it now is.

Activity as a whole might, therefore, be made to avoid periods of feverish and unhealthy activity. If depression comes, a means is at hand for utilizing the human and material resources of the community which otherwise will be idle and useless. The use of these resources is then almost costless to the community, and their output is nearly a free gift to society, for the resources are already there. They cost nothing to produce, and even their use costs but little. They have to be supported even in idleness—not only men, who cannot be allowed to starve, but also machinery, which must be kept from deterioration. In idleness, the expenditures on their support bring no material result to society. At work, society has works of public usefulness in return for its expenditures.

The effectiveness of this stabilizing agent depends on its importance in the economic system as a whole, and this in turn depends on the volume of public works as compared with comparable private expenditures and on the fraction of this volume which can be brought under effective control.

The total volume of public works in the United States under normal conditions is considerably smaller than the volume of the investment expenditures of private business. If one compares the estimated totals of public and private construction, for example, one finds that, in the 11 years from 1923 to 1933, public construction averages about 30 per cent of total construction, although this proportion has tended to rise, especially since 1929. In 1929, public construction was estimated at 3,555 millions as compared with a total of 12,279 millions.[3] But in depressions, the proportion tends to rise, and in the Great Depression rose greatly, partly because of the shrinkage of private investment and partly because of the great extension of the scope of public works under the urge to find employment for the many out of work.

If we grant the probability that such an extension of the scope of public works will be favored by public opinion in depressions, it would seem that the total expenditures involved are of such a size as to enable government to exercise significant stabilizing power, provided it can bring these expenditures under control.

---

[3] A. D. Gayer, *Public Works in Prosperity and Depression*, 1935, 23.

Can the Volume of Public Works Be Controlled?

In the United States, the degree of this control is affected primarily by two considerations:

1. The first is the proportion of federal as compared with state and local expenditures. The total expenditure for public works is normally heavily weighted by state and local activities. In normal times, state and local expenditures average 10 times as much as federal expenditures.

Thus, for example, expenditures in millions are as follows:

	1928	1929	1930
Federal construction	268	307	339
Nonfederal construction	3,363	3,248	3,293

These proportions considerably affect the power of control over public expenditures as a whole, for only federal expenditures are reasonably flexible and readily controlled. They are under one authority, not several. Experience shows the utmost difficulty of increasing in step and in some coördinated plan the public expenditures of the vast number of local jurisdictions. Federal authority, too, enjoys continued credit even in depressions, where state and local authorities, particularly local, find credit sadly reduced, if not completely gone, as depression proceeds.

2. The second consideration is the extent to which expenditures, whether federal or nonfederal, can be shifted without raising problems greater than those to be solved.

Even though government is not moved by profit-making motives, it may, for other reasons, be prevented from manipulating expenditures to the degree demanded by a policy of stabilization. Army and navy expenditures cannot be dictated by these considerations. A government cannot foresee its future need for armament or afford to store up what may become obsolete types; and when need arises, it cannot delay. When war comes, stability of industry must become a secondary consideration. Education suffers from similar limitations; schools will be required as need arises, not merely because of depressions. While there might be greater flexibility in the building of, say, post offices, political motives may require at least some building for votes at times when votes are needed, and votes are as much needed in prosperity as in depression. On the other hand, public convenience would be but little affected, in the case of many services, were these varied within a year or so to meet the conditions of stability. Here the cost of changing the time of public works is relatively small. Probably this applies to roads, canals, and harbors. Certainly it applies to long range public works such as power development, or forestation, or the development of recreational facilities such as parks, game preserves, and so on.

How much of the public works expenditures can safely be left to manipulation no one can say. Much depends on the state of public opinion and on the composition of the public works program as a whole. It would probably be safe to estimate that not more than one-half the normal program of public works can be shifted from one period of the cycle to another.

Planning Public Works

Unlike monetary control, the use of public works involves an elaborate planning machinery. Monetary control, whether by changes in the price of gold or operations of a central bank, or both, is essentially a simple mechanism. It requires extensive statistical and economic data and analysis thereof, but beyond this the administrative mechanism is simple. In fact, most of the statistical knowledge would be gathered, in any case, as a necessary incident of the ordinary operations of central banking, irrespective of business cycle control. The administrative mechanism is of the simplest type—at the most, the organization of an effective board for the conduct of open-market operations.

But a program of public works is a much more formidable affair. There must be an engineering commission with appropriate plans and specifications. There must be all the administrative facilities for expanding and accelerating a program of construction when need comes. There must be some mechanism for taking care of financial reserves.

Doubtless any public works involve a proper arrangement of finance, engineering, and contracting. But, clearly, the success of a controlling program, adjusted to other than the original purposes, depends on its being able to fit into the traditional procedure for public improvements and the administrative habits of many hundreds of governmental units throughout the country. Public officials, especially in local units, are concerned with the routine of the job and with the placating of the electorate, not with stabilizing theories. They think in terms of meeting local demands when they arise or are insistent. They are concerned with the possibility of selling local bond issues, which are not particularly adaptable to cyclical regularization.

Furthermore, considerations of caution against reckless expenditure have created an administrative machinery for public works that is extremely complicated. For example, take the practice of local governments in Ohio.[4] A project is initiated by popular petition. Plans and specifications are then prepared and presented to the proper legislative body. Assessment boundaries are fixed, and assessment maps are prepared. Assessment notices are then served, and a month is allowed to property holders to protest. Often appeal is made to courts, and two or three years' delay intervenes.

Whatever the jurisdiction, public works necessitate determining the legality of loans, preparing plans and specifications, acquiring the property, raising the funds from the public, bidding and selection of contractors, and all the routine of legislative action.

These delays are formidable for all local projects. How

---

[4] L. Wolman, *Planning and Control of Public Works*, New York, 1930, 165.

formidable can be seen from the experience of PWA delays in the early years of the New Deal.[5]

Federal projects do not suffer from such a complication of delay, and the increasing proportion of federal projects will, of course, reduce the average delay for public works as a whole. Even local delay could be avoided were some kind of long-time planning set up which would enable plans and specifications to be ready when need arose. Planning would be most likely to be available for works of broad popular use, forestation, parks, conservation, roads, and so forth, rather than for those for which local demand is a prerequisite, such as schools, sewers, and public buildings. We always want conservation projects. Local projects are not so easy to foresee.

The efficacy of public works for stabilization can probably be increased in those areas where a long-time regional plan has been worked out under the efforts of engineers and public administrators eager to avoid the disbenefits of haphazard development. Regional planning, where it is in force, reduces delay in utilization of projects. A set of carefully considered projects, already investigated, is an enormous advantage in depression, where delay is costly. The PWA laboriously, but of necessity, passed on many projects, often worthless, with much loss of time. Regional planning speeds this up. Areas where regional planning was in operation, as in Cincinnati, made a much better record than others in submitting sound projects for approval.

Furthermore, regional planning helps to maintain continuous interest in public works projects, and thereby overcome the ease with which depressions are forgotten when prosperity returns. People may become accustomed to long-term thinking, and so avoid the futility of spasmodic efforts when what is wanted is to keep the problem alive at all times.

---

[5] See P. H. Douglas, *Controlling Depressions*, New York, 1935, 127–128.

It is true that regional planning tends to work on fairly uniform schedules with relatively stable year-to-year expenditures,
and that this might conflict with the demands of cyclical stabilization. But the disruptive effects of depression in long-time
plans are so considerable that it might not be difficult to persuade the regional planners to modify their timing (and, possibly, their financial policies) with a view to reducing cyclical
swings. Business stability might make long-time plans more
likely to work out. Since costs are high in prosperity and low
in depression, the projects as a whole might be substantially
cheaper.

The Timing of Public Works

The theory of public works as a stabilizer indicates that the
postponable portion be held as a reserve, to be put into action
upon the arrival of depression. The approved arrangement
for this is the adoption of a medium long-time schedule of
public works, with an annual average budget, and a provision
that a certain percentage of this work shall be earmarked for
reserve. Then, upon the signal of some designated authority
or upon the fall of some designated index below normal, these
deferred works would be set in motion. Thus, if an index is
used, a reserve would accumulate in all years of "normal" or
above, and, if it should happen that depressions were proportional to previous booms, the fund of works thus set aside would
be reasonably adequate for the coming need.

Thus, in England, the Poor Law Report of 1909 (the original
source of many stabilizing plans of this order) recommended
that 3 to 4 per cent of the annual total of all public works
be set aside for development whenever the unemployment index, as shown by the Labor Exchanges, rose above normal. In
the United States, the Jones Bill before Congress, following the
depression of 1921, authorized a reserve of $150 millions to be
spent on public works whenever the volume of all construction
contracts in any three months' period fell by 10 per cent below

the average of the same three months in the preceding three years.

A procedure of this sort is not free from serious difficulties.

It is not easy for legislative bodies to live up to such schemes, even though they may be persuaded to adopt them. Public persons like to point to their achievements during their terms of office, and do not care to forego the prestige this carries to prevent some future danger.

More important, the amount of public works which can be reserved is not unlimited, and even on the most generous calculations may not be adequate to deal with any except minor depressions. Most advocates of public works seem to agree that 50 per cent of the normal program is the most that can be deferred. Indeed, this amount would be very large compared with the modest figures suggested in the English plans. It means increasing public works from 50 per cent of normal in good years to 150 per cent of normal in bad years—that is, trebling the minimum rate at which public works are normally carried on. A shift of this sort applied to the public works of the United States, as estimated by Clark,[6] would expand employment directly and indirectly during bad years by as much as two and three-fourths millions of workers. Yet even then it would not be nearly adequate for the job. Employment in the Great Depression shrank by not less than 25 per cent and involved probably 12 millions of workers (not counting part-time unemployment). In other words, a program of public works, involving the probably unattainable fraction of 50 per cent postponement in good times, could neutralize only one third or one fourth of the shrinkage of employment and national income involved in a major depression.

These considerations indicate the strong probability that the system of reserves, while logical, must be supplemented by other means. Irrespective of reserves of public works earmarked for

---

[6] J. M. Clark, *Economics of Planning Public Works*, 1935, 62.

depression, it may be necessary, unless the depression is a minor one, to expand these operations in volume and in scope much beyond the limits set up in formal reserve measures. Hence, the appropriate public works policy would be to arrange necessary expansion in depression, leaving the burden of amortization charges in the coming period of recovery to put effective and automatic limits on capital expenditures in those years.

When should additional public works be started? The stabilizing efficacy of public works depends not only upon the volume available but also upon their being used at the proper time. Improper timing may cause even an adequate program to do more harm than good. Proper timing will greatly enhance the effectiveness of what otherwise might seem very modest efforts. But opinion as to the best time to launch public works is by no means unanimous.

Some believe that public works should be begun as soon as recession is definitely established. The argument is that a relatively small amount of expenditure thrown in promptly at a strategic time will check a depression before its cumulative deflationary effects get momentum. It is these cumulative effects which make depressions serious, and, if they could be averted, business might recover its equilibrium before great damage was done. The reserve of public works contemplated in the English schemes mentioned above, with their relatively small volume initiated at the movement of an index, implies this attitude toward timing.

There are several objections to this view: the difficulty of spotting a genuine recession until after it is well under way; the inevitable delay in launching public works under the best of circumstances; the possibility that only a prolonged expenditure by the public, and not merely a prompt but small outburst of spending, is needed to restore activity to predepression levels, for, if cyclical depressions are the result of overexpansion of productive equipment by private industry, a severe shrinkage of private expenditures for capital purposes may be unavoidable.

Others insist that expansion of public works should be timed to take place when depression has reached the bottom, when industry is in a trough, and when the stimulus of public spending may be the one thing needed to speed recovery. This view is based on a particular theory of depression. The point is that the recession and its cumulative effects are the inevitable consequences of the previous boom. They are the necessary readjustments imposed on industry by the distorted price and cost structure built up in prosperity. As long as these adjustments are not made, recovery cannot come. They can be postponed, it is true, but they cannot be avoided. Until they are made, business will stagnate or move in a quite artificial activity.

Now public works, if improperly timed, may prevent these adjustments from being made. Introduced too early, they keep up prices of materials and wages when they are on the way down and when they should continue downward if business is to be once more on a profitable basis. The proper time to begin public works is when the readjustments have been worked out as far as they will go—that is to say, at the end of the cumulative decline called "depression." Then public works may become a stimulus to an exhausted patient and be of positive help in lifting it once more into recovery.

Proper timing an unsettled problem. There seems no adequate reason to prefer this view to the other. Doubtless, readjustments have to take place, but sheer deflation seems not to be needed and might be prevented by earlier use of public works. Readjustments are never completed, nor is there adequate evidence to indicate how much readjustment should have gone on before public works are started. Possibly, when prices cease to fall or fluctuate within a narrow area for some time, one may assume practical readjustments to be over. But even then wages and other costs may still be going down.

Moreover, the end of a depression is partly a psychological matter. Adjustments are over when the business community thinks they are over. If businessmen think wages will continue to fall, they postpone expansion still longer, and their expectations are affected by the public works policy of government. If this policy is averse to early starting of projects, lest wages be pegged too high, it will be a factor in making business postpone commitments until wages fall. If, on the contrary, it is likely to start works early, business may become resigned to existing wage levels and be willing to expand more quickly.

Cautious waiting for the precise time for placing public works may, indeed, so delay the onset of these projects that depression may be over and recovery on the way by the time the peak of activity in public works has arrived. One must remember the exasperating but unavoidable delays incident to all public projects: the legal and engineering investigations needed to avoid waste and graft; the elaborate scrutiny of plans required when local projects are submitted to the federal government; and the fact that public works, even when plans are ready, have the slow development characteristic of all capital projects. All these are time-consuming processes and may well overrun the depression into recovery itself. If this delay occurs, it may not be easy to avoid making it more costly for business ventures to proceed and more difficult to restore normal activity when public works are withdrawn. The case for public works is definitely weakened if they cannot be carried on in depression without overlapping into periods of revival and boom.

For these reasons, it is not wise to assume that interrupting or shortening the rigors of depression is impracticable.

In practice, however, only experience will locate the best time for launching public works and determine the best speed at which, once launched, they should be carried on. Until these facts are determined, and their determination requires economic indexes not yet available, other considerations will doubtless be paramount. These considerations are of such a nature—public pressure, the demand to get something done, unrest among farmers or workers—that public policy is more likely to move in the direction of early, rather than delayed, decision in putting projects into action.

Placing Public Works

Public works not only need to be properly timed but also need to be properly placed. Clearly, if public works are to be most effective, they should be expanded most in areas where unemployment is greatest. Thereby they will relieve the most distress and be least likely to interfere with any possible private expansion. But this placing is not easy to accomplish. The volume of unemployment is heavily concentrated in the industrial areas. In eleven industrial states in the north central and northeastern areas of the United States will be found a very large fraction of the unemployed. To concentrate public works in these areas in volume comparable to the unemployment is both economically and politically difficult—economically, because the marginal utility of projects in these areas may fall quite low; politically, because the people of other states expect some tangible compensation in their own areas for the present and future burden of taxation which they will surely be called upon to bear.

The problem could be solved if labor were much more mobile —able to change not only place but occupation at call. But the great distances involved, the unwillingness to sacrifice home ties, and the uncertainty of changing circumstances make territorial change not easy. Although occupational change is not difficult for unskilled, it is not always feasible to make construction workers out of other specialized labor. Unemployment among textile workers, for instance, cannot be solved easily except by the simplest kind of alternative occupations.

When the difficulties involved in this transfer become so considerable as to interfere with the adequate success of a public works program (which may happen in any major depression, as it undoubtedly did in the depression of the 1930's), the authorities are moved either to adopt projects calling for such unspe-

cialized ability that all labor may readily take part, or else to
create work for specialized and trained workers in the field of
their normal employment. Both of these alternatives may
involve some trouble for the authorities. The first will extend
the scope of public works into projects of diminishing usefulness, from such work as roads, bridges, and public buildings,
into the creation or beautification of parks, forestation or clearing work, and other projects of remote future utility. The
second will tend to encroach on the field of private enterprise,
as, for example, in the theatrical, musical, and other "white
collar" projects of the WPA. Opposition will certainly arise
against both of these developments: against the first as a waste
of public money; against the second also as a waste of public
money ("boondoggling" is the word applied thereto), but more
because of its competition with private business. For these reasons, immobility of labor has far-reaching effects, reducing the
efficacy of public works no matter how they are arranged to
solve the problem.

Fiscal Problem of Public Works

The fiscal problem of public works is that of financing the
expansion of government outlays during depressions. This
problem can be handled in either one of two ways: (1) by
collecting reserves from taxation during good times, to be spent
on public works in bad; or (2) by borrowing the necessary
funds for public works in depression and paying off the loans
from taxation during prosperity.

On the face of it, these two methods are essentially the same,
since both mean raising funds in good times by taxation in order
to have funds in bad times for public outlays. It would seem
to be a question of administrative detail whether the taxation
should precede or follow the expenditures involved.

But the question is more complicated than this. The two
methods involve substantial differences in practical results,
which have now to be examined.

1. **Reserves.** The use of reserves seems to be a businesslike method of handling the problem. Taxes are relatively easy to raise in good times; surpluses are likely to emerge, and it seems wise to raise funds in these circumstances. Moreover, the funds, once collected, seem to remove any uncertainty as to the amount available, such as is likely to attend reliance on borrowing. While it may be possible to postpone public works in a physical sense, so that what is not done now is available for the future, the financial arrangements involved may not be postponed so easily. Merely to refrain from borrowing in prosperity does not necessarily create a reserve of borrowing available in depression. Depressions have a way of affecting borrowing power adversely. They bring about decided differences in security, and there is no guarantee that capacity to borrow will remain intact. Security may fall in depressions, for governments as well as for other money-raising bodies. Ability to borrow in depression cannot be relied on merely because a reserve of borrowing was left from prosperity.

Hence there is, at least in theory, something very attractive about a reserve of actual funds. There they are, and there is no question about them; and, when emergency arises, they can be used immediately.

Reserves not so good as they look. There are, however, serious difficulties in the use of reserves, which may make them much less suitable to the problem in hand than it would seem at first glance.

(1) In the first place, reserve funds are easily raided for increased expenditures by public officials seeking popular approval. Although this danger may possibly be avoided in federal administration, it is one that is never far removed in state finance.

(2) Secondly, the problem of investment of the funds and their realization when needed is a serious one. This problem is more specifically dealt with in considering unemployment insurance and other devices for equalizing and stabilizing con-

sumer income.[7] Here it is enough to point out that it is a
formidable problem to find suitable investments for taking care
of the funds without expanding industry still further, and even
more to liquidate these investments without demoralizing the
investment market at a time when its ability to absorb securities is reduced to a very low ebb.

(3) These two difficulties, however, are obviously administrative and should lend themselves to final solution. The third,
which is more serious, is that the amount of reserves which
could be reasonably laid aside, public and business opinion being
taken into account, may be far short of the necessities of anything save a minor depression.

If no special taxes are levied for the purpose of reserves in good
times (unemployment insurance levies are of this sort, but they
lead to special funds that are not usable for public works), then
the best method would be to set aside all tax yields that rise
above, say, a five-year average to be used in years when yields
fall below the average. What would be the result of this in
practice? Clark points out that, had such a formula been used
for federal revenues from 1925 to 1934, the result would have
been the accumulation of 246 millions during the years 1925-
1930, and the withdrawal of 198 millions for expenditures in
the years 1931-1934.[8] These are not sums that would do much
toward meeting the problems of a major depression.

It is possible, therefore, that the exigencies of a public works
program, in any save minor depressions (and minor depressions
might even be left to take care of themselves) are such as to
make reliance on reserves bring disappointing results, and to
make depression borrowing the more effective policy.

2. Depression borrowing. The creation of a deficit in depression to be written off in recovery involves problems of both
borrowing and repayment. These problems will now be examined.

[7] See Chap. XXII.
[8] Clark, *Economics of Planning Public Works*, 116.

In order to be effective, a policy of depression borrowing may have to overcome certain obstacles which arise, partly from traditional attitudes towards government deficits and partly from the credit difficulties which are apt to surround state and local bodies even though the federal government may be free thereof.

The problem of balancing the budget.

(a) First, there is the tradition of a balanced budget, which creates hostility to the more than seasonal deficits which a stabilization policy is bound to bring about.

A balanced budget is an important protection against the constant and insidious danger of a progressive increase in the public debt. It forces governmental bodies to live within their income, and adopts a policy of pay-as-you-go. Doubtless, budgets should be balanced. What is in dispute is the proper period over which budgets should be balanced. The traditional period is, of course, the calendar year. It is within this period that the public expects revenues should equal expenditures. But there seems no compelling reason why pay-as-you-go must be interpreted to fit into the fixed framework of the calendar year. There is no overwhelming merit except usage in 12 months as compared with 6, or 18, or 24. The calendar year is a conventional period, doubtless adopted because it fitted the traditional processes of agriculture when agriculture (and other seasonal vocations) dominated activities. But other periods are quite as rational and probably better suited to industrial conditions. Business itself, in its own financial practices, by no means follows the budget balancing it commonly demands of government. Corporations lay aside reserves for bad times, and throughout depression continue to pay not only dividends but salaries and wages in excess of current revenues. Indeed, they regarded their doing this in the depression of the 1930's as a particular claim on public commendation. Essentially, what they are approaching is a period for budget balancing coincident with the business cycle. Just as the seasonal fluctuations of business and of revenues average out in the calendar year, and justify thereby deficits in one part, surplus in another, of this period, so cyclical fluctuations average out, and equally justify deficits in one phase if they are counterbalanced by surpluses in another. A cycle seems to be just as rational a period for budget balancing as the more commonly recognized year. Let us adopt pay-as-you-go by all means, but during a cycle of business, not a year of seasons.

Indeed, it may be said that, in actual practice, governmental bodies. *never* live up to their pay-as-you-go intentions in any but the most normal periods. Any emergency will wreck the policy and make some compromise necessary. Furthermore, public opinion tacitly accepts the compromise. Thus tax-anticipation warrants, the running up of bills, transfer from one fund to another, and other short-time expedients of state and local finance, although designed to be cleared up currently within conventional budget periods, never get cleared up in this way, but in emergencies fall into continuous renewals and thus become, without formal recognition, a kind of cyclical deficit financing acceptable to public opinion. Possibly a more appropriate attitude would see the problem straight and approve regular funded loans.

It is true that the great virtue of yearly budgets is the certainty of the period, for the use of longer periods than the fiscal year introduces an unpleasing vagueness as to the length of time within which balance is to be attained. Cycles, as has been pointed out elsewhere, are not periods. They do not have regular time intervals, and we must regard this aspect as a serious disadvantage. Nobody can foresee how long a depression is going to be, save that the depressions in which borrowing is most needed are usually not only severe but long. This uncertainty is a serious matter for the balancing of a budget, for all deficits are, in theory, to be cleared away in revival. But long depressions may not be followed by revivals great enough to balance budgets out. Indeed, there is some evidence that prosperities following major depressions are shorter than average.[9] Revival in such times starts from very low levels, and even considerable recovery may not mean a great enrichment of the nation; and when one adds to this the further difficulty that repayments of large deficits may be a distinct drag on recovery, there seems to be good reason for the fear lest cycle budget balancing may turn out to be, in the long run, an insidious process of a gradually increasing debt.

The usual compromise and its disadvantages. The public willingness to accept compromise, however, may indicate that its attitude toward yearly budget balancing is a matter of convention rather than conviction, and could be broken down in favor of cyclical balancing were good reasons for the change to be advanced. If so, then a new convention would be adopted, and it would be regarded as correct for government to run on deficits during depression, surpluses during prosperity, provided that, over the cycle as a whole, the excess of good times pays off the deficits of bad. Unfortunately, public opinion is likely to lag behind the necessities of the situation and, for a time at least, to force upon government certain illogical compromises such as marked the depression of the 1930's.

One of these compromises was the double budget set up by the Roosevelt administration: the first or ordinary budget, which was to be "balanced," and the second or extraordinary budget, the expenditures of which were to be met by borrowing. The balanced budget maintained intact the "correct" attitude toward the fiscal year; the unbalanced budget was "abnormal."

This concession to public opinion, however, is bound to lead to absurdities whenever the limitations of tax receipts force the abandonment of relatively important services which happen to fall in the "regular" activities of government, while relatively unimportant services which can be included in the extraordinary budget are being expanded. The most glaring example of this

---

[9] See E. C. Bratt, *Business Cycles and Forecasting*, 2nd Ed., 1940, 402.

is the experience of the school systems in the great depression. School budgets are of the group which is supposed to be balanced in the calendar year. If receipts fall off, then salaries must be reduced, or, at the worst, schools closed early, or entirely. This calamity may happen when, through deficit financing, the government is building roads and sewers, or making parks, or cleaning streets—admirable things in their way, but no substitute for the fundamental services of education. It would seem wiser to forego the public works, which, after all, if not built now can be built later, and use the borrowed funds to maintain services such as education or health, which, once foregone, can never really be made up. Yet this policy cannot be followed under orthodox canons of fiscal practice which make it possible to borrow for permanent works but not for current services.

So obvious is the objection to the kind of compromise we are apt to get in depression that services cut off from ordinary departmental budgets had, during depression, to be put back through the agencies of the WPA. Especially was this true of education. School teachers released from regular services were re-employed by government agencies in adult education projects, or other educational activities of the WPA. In some instances, artists have been employed painting murals on the walls of schools, where inability to raise school funds had already reduced the schedules of classes. While, doubtless, adults need education, and schools may be brighter for murals, it would seem that these are no exchange for the ordinary services of teaching the children of the community. Yet this arrangement is what we get under the compromises which lagging public opinion forces upon fiscal practice. Perhaps, in other depressions, public opinion may have been educated out of these arbitrary distinctions between budgets which may and budgets which may not be balanced. Until they are, it may be necessary to hold with Clark [10] for "actual evasion of the principle of

[10] *Economics of Planning Public Works*, 107.

the divided budget," by using public works or relief funds to maintain regular services which have been reduced or omitted under the urge to balance the "regular" budget. The thing to do is to spend money where it will do most good, without worrying about artificial fiscal categories in respect to deficits.

Limitations on government credit in depression.

(b) A second difficulty in the way of borrowing in depression is found in the credit standing of governmental units. Even though public opinion, especially business opinion, has been educated to government debt-creation in depression, this is no guarantee, in itself, that debts can be easily or quickly expanded. There are various limits on the debt capacity, particularly of state and local bodies, that put up formidable barriers to such expansion.

Federal credit would seem, from the experience of the recent severe depression, to be free from serious direct limitations. But state and local credit are other matters. The fiscal difficulties of states and cities in depressions are notorious. This situation arises from several causes. Part of the difficulty comes from taxes that too readily reflect the cycle of business and fall away too much when business goes into major depressions. State tax systems are apt to be built up on too narrow a basis, and prove, for this reason, too sensitive to business fluctuations. This characteristic seems true of net income taxes, unless they are based, not on a single year's income, but on the average of several years so as to include a complete business cycle. Even property taxes, still the foundation of many state revenue systems, and long regarded as maintaining stable revenues in periods of less than normal business, have proved to be unreliable as revenue producers in a severe depression. Moreover, this sensitiveness to depression is reflected not merely in a reduction of estimated yields, but perhaps even more startlingly in a great increase in the volume of tax delinquency, which is reported by Clark to amount to an average of 20 per cent for a group of 17 states. Nor can this delinquency be effectively checked. There is great difficulty either in enforcing penalties or in realizing on property taken over for taxes. Indeed, this delinquency is a thinly disguised (and unscientific) method of tax reduction. Furthermore, in depression, tax receipts are extremely elastic, so that raising the tax rate or even extending the tax base may turn out to be only a means of increasing delinquency, and not an important and effective device for enlarging fiscal receipts.

This tax difficulty in itself weakens the credit status of government units. But apart from this, borrowing is still further impeded. Many fiscal units enter a depression in poor financial condition. Unless a regular program of long-time financing has been set up to replace the more or less opportunistic arrangements of state and local bodies, credit may have already been endangered by unwise or excessive borrowing in good times, when political ambition finds easy expression in expanded local activities. Thus several states and one of our largest cities entered the depression in 1929 on the verge of bankruptcy.

Even states or local bodies with reasonable credit standing may be stopped from borrowing by statutory limits on debt expansion. In some instances, these limits have the additional inflexibility of being written into the Constitution. Originally designed for preventing wild-cat construction schemes by local public bodies, these limitations doubtless had (and still have) their justification, but they certainly were never set up with any realization of the necessities of fiscal policy during booms and depressions, and they put severe restrictions on the success of stabilization programs—so much so that the State of Washington, for example, had to invoke the insurrection clause of its Constitution in order to enable it to borrow funds for relief works. This way of doing things seems unnecessarily hard.

State and local credit need fortifying. The result of this situation is that, while federal borrowing can be readily expanded, it is not easy either to expand the very important body of local public expenditure or (what is more important, perhaps) to work out a reasonably coördinated system of public works by federal, state, and local bodies. This result is particularly unfortunate since state and local expenditure has been (and can continue to be) greater in the aggregate than federal, as well as more adaptable to particular local situations. The figures of federal and nonfederal public construction in the depression of 1929–1933 show this situation clearly enough.

	1928	1933
Federal	268 millions	553 millions
Nonfederal	3,363 millions	747 millions

If excessive reliance on federal debt creation is to be avoided, it will be necessary to fortify the credit of state and local governments. This task could be accomplished by various means. (1) Debt limits should be made more flexible either by constitutional change or by modification of existing laws. (2) More intelligent avoidance of debt creation in prosperity might be achieved. To this end it might be advisable to discourage the issue of tax-exempt securities which too easily facilitate expansion. (3) Try to get more stable tax systems. Great reliance on the general property tax is probably a source of instability. Single taxes, like single crops, may have to give way to a more diversified structure. (4) Give federal aid by grants and loans to assist state and local projects in depression. This aid reduces the cost of borrowing and is equivalent to raising the credit rating of the local units. It enables the federal government, in return for such aid, to enforce general standards throughout all jurisdictions and to bring about the all-important coördination of federal and nonfederal projects.

Repayment

The theory of public works as a stabilizer assumes that loans contracted in depression will be repaid in the following period of recovery and prosperity. Only thus will the public credit be maintained and the margin of credit capacity for the next depression be restored. This assumption does not imply that the aggregate of public loans should, on the average, remain constant, but only that the long-time rate of expansion of loans be not arbitrarily increased by unpaid deficits accumulating from depression periods. The aggregate of public loans will clearly increase, both with the general wealth of the country and with any underlying tendency to increase public economic functions relatively to private. Stabilization finance will merely cause the aggregate of loans to fluctuate about this rising trend as the community goes through expansions and contractions of general economic activity.

The source of repayment is, of course, in a general sense taxation. But it may be convenient to distinguish two sources of revenue from which depression expenditures can be recovered. (1) The first are specific revenues from so-called self-liquidating projects. This category includes not only prices, as for the use of museums or baths or stadia, and so on, but also special assessments, as for sewers, and specific taxes such as gasoline taxes, and other levies (license fees, and so forth) that are used to pay for public roads, and all interest and amortization payments, such as for home and farm mortgages. (2) The second is general revenues from any kind of taxes to repay all other advances and expenditures. These may require special taxes or special increases of rates or rate bases, or they may come without such special changes from the increased earning power and revenue-producing power of the community in good times. Such revenues are not thought of as arising from self-liquidating projects, but the term "self-liquidating" is not precise, and only convention gives it its present rather narrow meaning. Further experience with cyclical fiscal policy, and particularly more insight into the possible gains from investment in human resources as compared with physical resources like roads and sewers, may substantially broaden the concept of self-liquidation. In any case, if public expenditures actually stimulate revival, as is claimed, they are all self-liquidating in the broad sense of the term.

To fulfill the requirements of cyclical policy, depression loans should have short periods of amortization—say five years on the average. But this arrangement is not always possible, partly because of the burden on industry during the period of recovery and partly because in some of the projects often advanced as a particularly desirable medium for public works, such as low-cost housing, short periods of amortization cannot very well be utilized. On the assumption that major depressions do not come too frequently, and further that the deficit expenditures of government are really conducive to recovery (a problem in itself to be examined in the following chapter), it would seem possible to clear off the burden of excess debt during periods of prosperity. Thus the prosperity of the 1920's so greatly increased the revenues of the federal government that even the high levels of its outlays (a legacy of war and postwar depression) did not prevent a substantial surplus from arising and being used to retire the public debt. Had it resolutely set itself to do so, and imposed appropriate taxation to this end (especially taxes on large incomes), it could have increased greatly the speed and volume of repayment.

How to Prevent Repayment Starting a Boom

Some hold that large-scale repayment of government loans, if based on broad tax levies, may lay the foundation of an excessive investment boom. The collection of taxes from a wide base, and their use to repay the banks, institutions, and wealthy individuals who constitute the chief creditors of government, tend to shift resources from the spending to the saving classes. If the government has been successful in stimulating recovery, the further stimulus of debt repayment may create the conditions of an unhealthy capital expansion. From this viewpoint, the boom and crash of 1929 were in part caused by the Republican policy of heavy repayment of war loans at the same time

as high surtaxes were reduced.   The same argument was used
to justify the taxation of undistributed corporate surplus in the
Revenue Act of 1936, it being held that such tax would enlarge
the field of spending and check undesirable saving and investment.

To guard against this outcome, government should take care
that the amortization funds are raised by taxes that rest on saving rather than consumer expenditure.   Taxes on consumption,
such as sales taxes, should be avoided, as should any extension
of income taxes into the lower brackets.   Instead, taxes should
be levied on large incomes, on inheritances, and on corporate
surplus.   With these fiscal policies, untoward results need not
be feared.

This reasoning, however, is purely conjectural.   It assumes
that oversaving is the cause of crises.   It assumes that we know
who belong to the spending and saving classes, respectively, and
how they behave in the various phases of the cycle.   But oversaving may not be the cause of crises.   It may even be over-
spending.   We know little enough about the varying behavior
of those who save and those who spend.

This uncertainty makes it unwise to rely on fiscal policy as a
certain means of heading off undesirable expansion.   If there
is danger in this quarter, it would be more advisable to use
weapons supplied from the armory of the Federal Reserve
System.

If the repayment of loans has too expansive effects, the Federal Reserve Banks could counteract them by appropriate sale
of securities.   Or even better, the government could invest its
repayment funds directly in the bonds held by the Federal Reserve System. If the volume of these holdings is large
enough (as it may *not* be in major depressions), expansive
effects could be reasonably neutralized.

In the ideal situation, the government would borrow exclusively from the idle funds of the Federal Reserve Banks in depression and repay the loans in prosperity.   Such repayments,

involving as they do merely an addition to the funds of the Federal Reserve Banks and not to those of private investors, need not, on the face of it, add any more to the formation of an investment boom than the Federal Reserve is willing to permit. In fact, under these circumstances, fiscal policy would seem to be fulfilling its ideal function—namely, adding to expenditures in depression, and reducing them (net) in expansion; in other words, making for stabilization of aggregate purchasing power in use.

But this ideal situation is not likely to be achieved except in minor fluctuations. In a major depression such as that of 1929–1933, the volume even of federal government deficit expenditures is so large that bonds are sold not only to Federal Reserve Banks, but heavily to the generality of banks and to private investors and institutions. The aggregate of government securities owned by the Federal Reserve Banks reached a maximum of some 2,400 millions in February 1934 and stayed there for over three years. The member banks carried four times as much. Repayment under these circumstances puts funds in the possession of banks that are not necessarily interested in, or capable of, restraining investment use. Once more, the problem reverts back to the effectiveness of the control residing in Federal Reserve Banks over the expansive activities of the money and investment market, a subject which is treated at length in the chapters on monetary policy.

CHAPTER XXI

PUBLIC WORKS AS A STABILIZER: ECONOMIC PROBLEMS

WE have examined in the previous chapter some of the administrative and technical problems of public works. Now we have to consider the economic aspects involved. More particularly, we must ask these questions: If the administrative difficulties are solved, if a sufficient fund of projects can be made available for attacking depression, and if the proper financial procedure has been set up, will the exploitation of these works actually tend to bring a depression to an end and serve to restore prosperity? Is the employment brought about by public works a real addition to employment? Is the purchasing power made available by public expenditures a net addition to purchasing power? Has the government succeeded in transferring employment and purchasing power from good to bad times and, by this degree, stabilized the total of employment and purchasing power over the period involved? In short, is the apparent economic effect the real economic effect, or are there hidden consequences which must be considered? These questions we shall now examine in detail.

The effectiveness of public works is best measured by the net increase in employment they bring about. This increase may be the direct result of the expenditures set in motion by the government, expenditures which, as we shall see, are not indicated accurately by the immediate outlays involved. Or the increase of employment may be the indirect result of the rise of prices which is started by increasing the aggregate volume of purchasing power in actual use. Unless supply, especially of consumption goods, is perfectly elastic, purchasing power will outrun output, and an increase in the price will take place, whereby the margin of prices over (relatively) fixed unit costs will increase and so stimulate a general expansion of business.

Direct and Indirect Effects of Public Works

The total employment which may be brought about by public works expenditures may be considerably larger than appears on the surface. Such expenditures have cumulative consequences which tend to make the increase in total employment a multiple of the original employment upon the projects themselves. This increase in employment is commonly classified into *primary employment* and *secondary employment*.[1] Primary employment is the immediate outcome of the public works projects. Some of it is employment of workers on the project itself, which may be called "direct primary employment." Some is the employment in producing and delivering materials of all kinds for the work in question, and the performance of all associated services, which is "indirect primary employment." *Secondary employment* is the employment resulting from the expenditures of all those who receive their income from the outlays involved in both direct and indirect primary employment. To meet the increased expenditures from these incomes, which include not only wages, but interest, rents, and profits, production and employment are generally increased, particularly in consumers' goods industries. The incomes thus generated are spent, and so give rise to further activity and employment, and so on. This increase of employment in consumers' goods industries extends indefinitely as expenditure goes on from group to group, but it is convenient to group it all as secondary employment, which then covers all the further

---

[1] See p. 307, where investment increases are similarly classified in the discussion of the "multiplier."

series of increases resulting from the original primary employment involved in the public works proper.

The numerical relations between these various series of employments are of fundamental importance, for they determine the practical effectiveness of a public works program not only in adding to total employment but in adding to employment where it is most needed.

As to the relation of direct and indirect primary employment, Clark hazards the guess that, under ordinary working conditions, the two are about equal, but that, under conditions of acute depression, the urge to minimize the use of machinery may reduce the ratio of indirect to direct employment to three fourths or two thirds. In practice, the percentage seems to vary with the quality of work done. Investigations carried on by the PWA on work done from June 1933 to June 1936 indicate much higher ratios of indirect employment. Measured by man-hours of employment, work created in industries supplying building materials averaged two and one-half times that done in the building trades constructing the projects.[2] If an average expenditure of $3,000 per year per man (Clark's estimate) is assumed, this outlay would mean approximately $850 for direct employment and $2,150 for materials of construction. Nearer to Clark's ratios are the WPA projects begun in 1935, on which it was expected to spend $100 per month per person, of which $50 was to be in wages and $50 in materials. At the other extreme are the relief projects of the leaf-raking variety on which, in the year ending April 1934, the expenditure averaged $630 per man-year. The way in which this work was done and the low total of expenditures indicate that most of this must have been paid in wages, and that the fraction of indirect primary employment must have been uncommonly low.

---

[2] *New York Times*, Dec. 7, 1936, 3.

Relief Work Versus Public Works in Creating Employment

° These varying ratios of direct and indirect employment must occasion some variation in the effects of public works upon further industrial activity. Where there is practically no indirect primary employment at all, as in straight relief work, the entire stimulus must arise from the secondary consequences of expenditures by relief workers, consequences which in the first instance would be felt exclusively by a few consumption industries catering to the elementary needs of workpeople. In elaborate construction projects, on the other hand, where indirect primary employment substantially outweighs direct employment, an important stimulus is given to all kinds of industries supplying materials, thus widening the range of employment instead of concentrating it on relief workers and, at the same time, diverting considerable fractions of the outlay via profits and interest into other than wage-earning hands. Quite apart from secondary employment, this result creates a significantly different set of conditions. For one thing, the additional workers employed are likely to be more skilled, and it is possible also that fewer of them will be drawn from the totally unemployed. That is, some of the effects are to increase the hours of employment of already employed workers. Again, the diversion of some of the outlays to nonworkers may mean different secondary consequences, for such receipts are more likely to be spent in different ways, or saved in different proportions, from the receipts of wage earners. The fact that some of the receipts is profits may have the effect of causing employers to desire to invest, and draw upon idle funds, thus adding further expenditures to those arising from the original outlays. A dollar in wages, of course, enters into the circulation and has a series of (probably diminishing) effects, as does also a dollar in profits; but a dollar in profits may, in addition, draw out (say) an additional dollar from idle resources, to have its own circulation and further effects; and these may be very important indeed.

In a depression, especially a major one, a controversy is likely to develop between those who favor relief works and those who favor public works of the usual sort. The first group is thinking of the number of persons to be relieved and argues that a given sum of money will relieve the largest possible number if paid out mostly in wages. It further is likely to argue that the secondary effects are the same, no matter who gets the money. The second group thinks rather of the stimulus to industry and favors larger expenditures on materials as helping precisely the industries in which unemployment is the greatest and which are in most need of stimulus. One result of this conflict is the usual compromise, such as is found in WPA projects, where wages are a larger fraction of total expenditure than in PWA, but not so large as in relief works. Such a compromise is an unstable solution continually attacked on the one side by those who want to relieve more people with the available sums, and on the other by those who deplore the feebleness of many of the projects and argue for more valuable work, not only as supplying the community with something for its money but as giving the greatest possible stimulus to private industry.

Secondary Employment

The volume of secondary employment, which, it will be remembered, covers the whole series of employments brought into being by the use of incomes by primary recipients of all kinds, is very much a matter of conjecture. We have no statistical evidence available, and the estimates made by such writers as Keynes must be regarded as most tentative.

Were the incomes received for primary employment all expended without delay, and again re-expended by the second rank of recipients, and so on in endless series, then the original outlays moving on from circle to circle would, unless reduced by leakage or stopped by friction, in due time bring about the full employment of all the employable resources of the country. If the original outlays were themselves repeated, as they would be, every month, this constant stream of expenditures, turning over at some recognizable rate per annum, would in relatively short time bring full employment.

This possibility of a flow of income moving into circulation at unchanging rates was apparently the theoretical basis for the claims of the Townsend Plan, which, by putting out $200 per month for, say, 10 million persons, hoped to be able to bring industry not only to the levels of 1929, but to the very much higher levels of which optimistic engineers believed industry to be capable, if worked with the best technical methods.

The Multiplier Once More

Analysis, however, indicates that this is not what happens. Various "leakages" prevent the effectiveness of expenditures in each period from maintaining its full or 100 per cent level, so that only a fraction of the original outlays are spent in such ways as increase the activities of the community. Of that fraction, only a fraction is spent in the third cycle, and so on. If the fraction remained the same through these successive cycles of use (although there is no reason to suppose it would), then the result is a series of rapidly diminishing expenditures, the aggregate of which (at infinity) would be a definite quantity. Thus, if the fraction spent in industrially stimulating ways were one half in each successive use, then the total secondary expenditure from an original $1 would be an additional sum of $1, the greater part of which original sum would be derived from the first few cycles of expenditure.

For example, let us suppose that the original outlay was $1, and that the primary recipients spend 50 per cent, as do all other recipients in succession. The additional spendings then are as shown on the next page.

$$(1)\ 50\% \text{ of } \$1.00 = \$.50$$
$$(2)\ 50\% \text{ of } .50 = .25$$
$$(3)\ 50\% \text{ of } .25 = .1250$$
$$(4)\ 50\% \text{ of } .1250 = .0625$$
$$(5)\ 50\% \text{ of } .0625 = .0312$$

$$\overline{\qquad\qquad}$$
$$\$.9687$$

Thus, in five stages the additional sum aggregates $.9687 and the total expenditure attributable to $1 of original outlay is nearly $2.

The ratio of total expenditure (and presumably total employment) to primary expenditure (or employment) is, in the phraseology made celebrated by Keynes, the "multiplier," the use of which in his theories has been set forth in Chapter XV. It will be noted that the size of the multiplier depends on the fraction spent, or, to put it in another way, the multiplier is the reciprocal of the fraction not effectively entering into use as purchasing power.

We must, therefore, examine what determines the fraction which is not spent, or, if spent, not spent in such ways as to add to the total activity and employment of the community. It is this fraction that limits the total benefits which may be expected from any given outlay on public works in depression. We may conveniently sum up all the ways which determine this fraction under the general term *leakages*.

Leakages

Leakages occur in a great variety of ways. Some income is hoarded or, if "saved," not immediately invested. Some is spent in the stock market and merely affects the prices of securities. Some is used to pay off debts to banks or to those who in turn pay off debts to banks, and, because of inadequate demand for loans, remains idle for shorter or longer periods of time. Some income is spent abroad (this would be a heavy source of leakage in England, not very important in the United States), and, while this may occasion equivalent spending from abroad in due time, the lag causes leakage.

Leakage occurs also if expenditures cause price increases, for these reduce the purchasing power of all fixed or relatively fixed incomes and so cancel out some of the increase of expenditures. Some of the actual demand for goods that remains after this leakage is deducted does not itself constitute net additions, for it may merely replace sums that would have been spent for relief or charity in regard to formerly unemployed workers now employed. This result, however, does not happen if public expenditures for works are made from loans, where previous charitable payments or relief payments or dole have been made from taxes or by voluntary private contributions. In this case, the burden of charity and dole being removed from private expense enables private spending for other things now to go on; and to this will be added the further expenditures made possible by public works. But where doles are met from loans and are now replaced by public employment also from loans, clearly the net addition made by the latter is much smaller than the gross outlay would indicate. Of course, any public works financed from taxes would be subject to this kind of leakage.

We might sum up by saying that leakages occur either by limiting the amount of money which becomes genuine additional income to the community or by limiting the effective spending of this additional income. In his pamphlet, "The Means to Prosperity,"[3] Mr. Keynes suggests that ordinarily not less than 60 per cent of the total outlays of government are "new income" (that is, allowing for replacement of one income by another) and that, of this "new income," perhaps 75 per cent is spent in ways that stimulate industry. In deep depression, when "doles" are a heavy drain on resources, "new income" may be as high as 70 per cent of outlay and 70 to 75 per cent thereof be spent. Hence, at least 50 per cent of the

---

[3] New York, 1933.

original outlay is used for effective purchasing, and on this basis the multiplier would be 2.

Clark arrives at about the same figure.[4] He estimates 75 per cent of public expenditures is new money, and that about one third of this new money may be lost in leakages. This result makes a net addition of 50 per cent to effective purchasing power, and again the multiplier is 2.

The Changing Multiplier

It is probable that the multiplier falls as expenditure is increased. It is true that some of the leakages which hold the multiplier down may actually be reduced. For instance, as incomes increase, the need to pay off debts or back taxes or to restore reserves, and other deflationary actions, is not so imperative. But this effect may be outweighed by other important influences. For one thing, it becomes more and more difficult to maintain the inflationary effects of public expenditures, as it becomes harder to ensure that they are obtained from unused funds and do not encroach on and are not a mere substitute for private expenditures. The more effective public works have been in encouraging recovery, the more certain this limit is to arise. Furthermore, as revival proceeds, the rise in prices and profits puts further limits to the multiplier—the price rise by canceling the effects of outlays, the rise in profits by directing increasing percentages of received income into the hands of the saving classes. This result seems to diminish the efficiency of the remedy as time goes on, but in truth it merely indicates that the remedy is successful.

This success, which fundamentally takes the form of a revival of industry, is reflected back to the government in a reduction in the burden of its public works expenditures, for two reasons. First, relief expenditures of the government or,

---

[4] *Economics of Planning Public Works,* 89.

where such systems are in use, unemployment insurance expenditures by government are reduced as employment increases. This saving reduces the cost of government by amounts which, for England, Keynes estimates as high as one third of public works outlays. Second, there is an increase in the yield of taxes as the income of the community rises under the impact of public expenditures. These added to the first may, if they are as successful as the multiplier indicates, reduce the net cost of public works by as much as 50 per cent.

Neutralizing Effects

We must now examine critically the assumptions on which the cumulative possibilities of public works expenditures are based. We shall see that there are many hindrances to the full effectiveness of these expenditures, and that cumulative expansion may be substantially counteracted by unfavorable conditions, some of which may be almost unavoidable incidents of the public works policy itself.

The essential meaning of public works is the creation of additional purchasing power and the use thereof to build up employment and production at a time when private expenditures are shrunken. By public works, government maintains, or attempts to maintain, a stable level of income to the end that there may be also maintained a stable level of employment. It fills in the gap of purchasing power opened by the deflationary processes of the depression. It is a policy, in short, designed to counteract deflation.

For this reason, it may be said that any aspect of public works that is deflationary is harmful, and that any policy related to public works that is deflationary is unintelligent. Unfortunately, it is not always possible to avoid various deflationary by-products, as it were, of public works; and it is not even easy, public attitudes and congressional psychology being what they are, to rule out deflationary policies, despite the fact that these would seem to be reasonably subject to intelligent control.

The following sections will show the nature and extent of these deflationary offsets.

Fiscal policy demands loans, not taxes.

(1) The first, and perhaps the most obvious, of these offsets is the result of an inappropriate fiscal policy for financing the expansion of public expenditures. Clearly any form of fiscal arrangement that reduces or tends to reduce private incomes and outlays prorata with the increase of public outlays is to that extent deflationary, tending to neutralize the effects desired, and therefore inappropriate to the end in view. Taxes in general, therefore, are inappropriate as means of revenue for public works. Usually they constitute a transfer rather than a net increase of purchasing power. What is gained by the recipients of government outlays is lost by the payer of taxes. As it may be assumed, as a general rule, that taxes are paid from current income rather than from savings or hoardings, the result is to neutralize public outlays.

Of course, not all taxes operate in this way. Some taxes might well tap currently unused resources, and, if taxes must be relied on for at least some of the revenues for public works, clearly taxes that tap unused resources rather than taxes that do not should be employed. The most desirable taxes, therefore, would seem to be inheritance taxes and surtaxes on large incomes, since in times of depressions the sources of these taxes are reasonably likely to be idle funds which in good times might be invested in business. Even these, however, might encroach on expenditures; or if not, they might cause heavy sales of securities, which as such have deflationary effects. At the other extreme, sales taxes, which come directly from current expenditures and bear most heavily on the great mass of incomes, must be regarded, from this standpoint, as the least desirable tax. They may have to be used, particularly by local and state units desperate over loss of regular revenues and unable to float loans, but they would be a particularly inappro-

priate form of tax to be levied by the federal government either
to replace regular revenues or, more especially, to raise funds
for public works. The persistent drives in Congress for such
taxation during the depression of the 1930's merely show how
deep-seated is convention in fiscal policy and how hard it is
to meet new situations rationally.

The most effective method of raising funds for public works,
if deflationary consequences are to be avoided, is by loans.
Loans, as compared with taxes, have smaller deflationary effects. Under the most favorable circumstances, indeed, they
may have no deflationary effects whatever, and involve no can-
cellation or neutralization of the public works outlays. But
for this to occur, loans must tap resources that would otherwise lie idle. Loans made direct from the public do not necessarily do this, as the funds subscribed thereto might otherwise
have been invested in the securities of private business. Even
in this quarter, the general prostration of business activities and
the almost complete disappearance of new issues from the market indicate that uninvested resources are there, if they can be
reached.

Where public loans are sold to banks, whose earning assets
in such times are greatly reduced and whose loans to business
are at a minimum and not easy to increase, it is fairly certain
that idle funds are being tapped. Most certain of all would
be for the government to borrow from the Federal Reserve
System. There is little doubt, certainly in the early stages of
borrowing, that the great resources of the Federal Reserve
Banks can be drawn on at such times without encroaching in
any important degree on their lending power to the banks in
general and, through them, to private business. Indeed, if the
bonds of the government are made eligible for loans by individuals at banks and by banks at the Federal Reserve Banks,
then it would seem that all government borrowing, whether
from individuals, banks, or Federal Reserve Banks, would be
inflationary.

Doubtless even the reserves of the Federal Reserve System are limited, and the amount of loans they can support has definite limits also. That is to say, as the increase of government borrowing proceeds, deposits in the Federal Reserve Banks gradually increase. These deposits accrue first to the credit of the government, but as these are drawn on by check to finance public works outlays, and as these checks are deposited in banks in general and sent by them to be credited to their accounts in the Federal Reserve Banks, the increasing deposits emerge as deposits to the credit of banks in general. Against this growing volume of deposits, the reserves of Federal Reserve Banks, unless they are fortified, as they fortunately were in the 1930's, by an increase of gold from abroad, or by devaluation of the currency unit, or from the product of home mines, gradually become a smaller and smaller percentage until, as they approach conventional or legal limits, a restriction on loans, coupled with a rising rate of rediscount, is certain to emerge.

When this situation is reached, further borrowing by government creates no net increase in purchasing power but only a transfer of potentially active resources from private business to government. But it is to be hoped that, before this situation arrives, business will have been encouraged to expand, and the depression, together with the need for public works, will have given way before the forces of recovery.

Great expansion of public loans makes a peculiar situation for banks, which find a greater and greater proportion of their investments taking the form of government securities. Banks have absorbed the major proportion of all new federal issues floated since 1931. Indeed, the advantages of government issues are so great that no other investments have much chance.

But this kind of investment tends to reduce, theoretically, the liquidity of banks. To have less and less self-liquidating business paper and more and more bond holdings makes for an apparently less desirable banking situation—apparently, because there are those who hold that the differences in liquidity are purely fanciful. However this may be, if bankers regard the situation as less liquid, it *is* less liquid as far as their behavior is concerned. Particularly it may lead them to stress liquidity in other assets—to be cold to commercial loans and prefer in their stead abnormal amounts of cash. This hoarding by banks may be deflationary and thus counteract to that extent inflationary effects from budgetary deficits.

Misplaced governmental economy.

(2) The second deflationary aspect arises from the irrational demand, which appears during depression, that government should reduce its expenses in all its regular services. Economy in the regular budget and reduction of the cost, and often of the amount, of the established services of government are demanded not only because of shrinking revenues from taxation, but as a concession to that section of the community which regards such economy as the best contribution government can make towards encouraging the revival of private business. It is conceivable that such economies are the right way to proceed in meeting a depression. But they obviously detract from the success of a policy of public works, once this has been decided upon as the correct policy to follow. It is absurd to increase expenditures and employment in one direction while reducing expenditures and employment in another. As government, is practically the only body able to maintain consumption and incomes in depression, and as public works are specifically designed to see that just that is done, it would seem to be worse than folly to listen to economy pleas, at least until recovery is once more under way.

We have already seen what compromises have to be adopted in the various departments of public expenditure in order to satisfy a public opinion which at one and the same time demands public works for recovery and reduction in current regular expenses for the sake of balancing the budget. Some compromise, however, can scarcely be avoided. Thus, if wages and prices are falling, as happens in a depression, fiscal policy may reduce government salaries and wages proportionately, so that only real, not nominal, expenditures are maintained. Or again, economies may be introduced into governmental departments by eliminating less essential services and by consolidation and rationalization. This economy is loudly demanded by public, especially business, opinion, and in the long run is good. But it is deflationary as far as it goes, and poorly timed.

If the reduction of such current expenditures released funds for business uses, no harm would result. Indeed, it is a common statement of business that it stands ready to go ahead if government balances the budget. Unfortunately, this advance is not likely to happen, particularly in the early stages of depression. As long as depression is proceeding, there is not much chance of business expansion and great likelihood that business will take the gain from reduced taxes to increase cash reserves, improve liquidity, and generally fortify their economic position. For this reason, reduction in government expenditures on current services, together with whatever reduction of taxes this may involve, merely leads to an increase of idle resources and a deeper depression.

We may conclude that the reduction of governmental expenditures in depression is a deflationary influence and neutralizes to a proportionate degree the effectiveness of a public works program.

Public works may be depressant to private business.

(3) A third neutralizing effect arises from any reduction of investment by business as a result of the public expenditures. This reduction may be caused either by the competitive effects of public works projects or from the psychological effects of loss of confidence or other fear of government encroachment. It is always assumed that public works must be and can be

of such a nature as not to compete with private enterprise; otherwise, the net stimulus to business must be reduced. On the face of it, the noncompetitive character of public works seems to be assured by their limitation to fields in which private enterprise does not ordinarily enter. Public buildings, roads, canals, docks, parkways, and so on are not financed by private investment. But the boundary between public and private projects is not a rigid one, and in depressions, particularly if they are severe, public enterprise is apt to be pushed into controversial areas. The development of the TVA, with its production and transmission of power, is an example. Its activities competed not only with the business of private utilities in the region, but even with the local coal industry, which claimed that its sales were affected by the spread of cheap power and light. Similarly, housing projects carried on as part of a public works program definitely encroach on a field occupied by private business. True it may be that the low-cost housing field in which government operates is one that has never been, nor is likely to be in the near future, exploited by private agencies, but the limits of private enterprise can never be foretold, and competition at the margin is theoretically unavoidable.

Even if the government limits its enterprise to its orthodox fields, it cannot avoid being to some degree a competitor of private business. Every project undertaken constitutes a demand for labor, for materials, and for capital. The sum of projects together is a powerful influence in the market for these means of production. Wages, prices of materials, and interest rates, all important costs of industry, are higher than they otherwise would be. Even though the depression is accompanied by apparent surpluses both of men and of capital, market rates may be tightened. Public works are often undertaken, indeed, in a spirit of wage maintenance. If there is common acceptance of underconsumption theories, public officials can be persuaded easily that reduction of wages is reduction of the consumer purchasing power which supports industry. Furthermore, the entry of the government into the capital market, try though it may to tap idle resources, does not make it easier for other borrowers. Even though interest rates are not affected, government issues make a tough competitor for private issues, for which there is small chance of sale as long as the superior credit of the government is being actively used. Government securities take a larger and larger place in the investments of banks. They offer advantages in safety and liquidity no other security can offer. In the face of this, banks may be cold to commercial borrowers, preferring to hold, apart from government issues, abnormal amounts of cash.

These dangers may be particularly ominous in the field of construction, where public works cause such heavy concentration of demand.

Construction costs seem to have an abnormal power of resisting deflation in depression. Prices of building materials are "sticky" prices, and wages in the building trades are notoriously inflexible. Labor unions in construction seem to prefer an extraordinarily high percentage of unemployment in depression to any substantial concession in wages. Indexes of construction costs exhibit this tendency clearly. The Standard Statistics Company, in February, 1934, showed building materials at 87 per cent and total building costs at 89 per cent of their 1926 levels.[5] The effect of government expenditures is to reinforce this tendency. It stiffens costs in an industry with a chronic tendency to stiffness, and at a time when deflation of costs may be a prerequisite to any early large-scale revival of private demand for the real capital, buildings, machinery, and so on, which the construction industry produces.

The discouraging effects on private investment by this stiffening of costs may be intensified by the general weakening of confidence and the widespread distrust produced by the unaccus-

---

[5] Quoted in Douglas, *Controlling Depressions*, 132, n.

tomed extension both of public expenditures and of the area occupied by public enterprise. Uncertainty concerning the wisdom and the outcome of government expenditures may cause business to postpone commitments. In the fear lest business collapse when the artificial support of government is withdrawn, improvements and extensions which might be carried on may be withheld. There may arise a dread of runaway inflation engendered by excessive budgetary deficits, for inflation makes any business venture a gamble. The fear thereof is a damper on conservative enterprise.

One cannot safely assume, therefore, that public expenditures are, as their advocates hold, stimulating to private enterprise. They may, indeed, be quite the reverse. If they actually retard private business activity, the efficacy of public works may be substantially reduced, for so great are private compared with public expenditures that even a small reduction in the volume of private enterprise may neutralize a relatively large part of public works.

The gold standard as a limit to public works.

(4) Finally, there are neutralizing influences arising from foreign trade, more particularly for countries that try to maintain the gold standard.

Countries on a gold standard are limited in regard to the possibilities of inflationary expenditures such as public works are expected to cause, for, to the degree that these expenditures are successful, they are likely to bring about, as a normal incident of the increase in aggregate purchasing power, some rise in prices. This rise in prices cannot go far, if the gold standard is maintained, without causing a continuous outflow of gold. As prices rise at home and fall abroad (at least relatively, and, if depression is general, even absolutely), the purchase of imports, foreign securities, and services abroad is encouraged, while, contrariwise, purchase of exports, home securities, and home services by foreign buyers is discouraged. These changes

increase the passive balance of accounts and lead to an outflow of gold. This outflow presumably goes on, more
or less continuously, and to a certain extent proportionately
with the increase of purchasing power supplied via public
works outlays.

This situation is deflationary, and deflationary in a serious
degree, for gold is the foundation of bank reserves. Its loss
is increased many times in the shrinkage of potential bank
credit. Every dollar of gold leaving the country may reduce
bank credit, or potential bank credit, by 10 dollars. Not only
that, but the weakening of bank reserves tends to raise rates
of interest and so discourage the use of funds at a time when
funds are not greatly in demand; makes for selling of securities
and stock market deflation; and in time increases the tendency
to hoarding, causing runs on banks, and all the dangerous accompaniments of a weakening of public confidence.

If the supply of goods were sufficiently elastic, so that output
could be increased as purchasing power is expanded, this rise
in the general price level need not occur. Or if the major
nations happened to inaugurate or could agree to inaugurate
simultaneous programs of public works, even an increase in
the price level would have no untoward consequences. But
neither of these occurrences can be counted on in depression.
Output lags are likely to be unavoidable. Periods of economic
stress usually find nations too absorbed in local problems and
too determined to find solution in local remedies to be interested in international coöperation. One may expect, therefore,
that public works expansion on a large scale will not be easy
to accomplish in countries that adhere to an international gold
standard.

The extent of this difficulty depends on the relative importance of a country's foreign trade. For a country like the
United States, it might not be formidable; in England, it might
well cause a choice between expansion of public works and
maintenance of the gold standard. Indeed, even in the United

States a severe depression might bring about this very dilemma, and there are those who see a very good example thereof in the circumstances of the years 1931 to 1933. Thus Mr. Hoover, convinced of the importance of maintaining the gold standard (especially after England had abandoned it and the United States seemed likely to be the inheritor of its dominance in the world money market), was averse to public works and gave but grudging consent thereto even under the compulsion of urgent demand. Eager to avoid inflationary consequences, he advocated, instead, retrenchment and economy in all government expenditures. Mr. Roosevelt, himself determined to expand greatly the volume of public works, was apparently hopeful of staying on the gold standard. But the realities of the situation were soon borne in upon him. He had to choose between public works and the gold standard, and, preferring the public works, he took the country off gold.[6]

This dramatic outcome, however, may have resulted from the peculiar circumstances of the great depression. It may not be necessary, under proper safeguards, to make this heroic choice. These safeguards should be found in the powers available to the monetary authorities for controlling the volume of bank credit in use and stabilizing within narrow limits the general level of prices. In other words, public works policy must be supplemented by monetary policy if it is to avoid the neutralizing consequences of outflow of gold under the gold standard.

What Is the Net Efficiency of Public Works?

We have seen in the early sections of this chapter that the effectiveness of public works as a stimulus cannot be measured merely by the volume of primary expenditures. Our survey of the neutralizing possibilities to which public works are exposed now discloses that the total expenditures, both primary

---

[6] See Gayer, *Public Works in Prosperity and Depression*, Chap. 1.

and secondary, do not tell the whole story. It is certain that these total expenditures are never 100 per cent efficient. Some deduction, large or small, must be made to allow for deflation. It is true that this deduction cannot readily be estimated. It is true also that some of the deflationary influences can be avoided by proper policy. But some counteracting deflation there is bound to be, especially that undertermined but possibly formidable amount that springs from the hesitancies of the business community.

It is unfortunate that the calculations by which the efficiency of public works might be measured cannot at the present be anything but intelligent guesswork. The expansive possibilities associated with the multiplier are quite conjectural. No reliable investigations are available for establishing the volume of secondary employment. We know little as to the extent of leakages and how they change as expenditure proceeds. There is nothing whatever on which to estimate the deflationary effects which an unprecedented public works program might set in motion.

It might seem that the practical experiment in public works provided by the Roosevelt administration in the years from 1933 to 1940 would throw light upon the effectiveness of these stabilizing policies. If it does, the light is a very uncertain one. Indeed, the experiment turns out on examination to be a battleground of conflicting claims, ranging from those who find therein the source of all the recovery the country has enjoyed to those who, on the contrary, see in it nothing but a drag on the natural recuperative powers of private industry.

The defenders can point to the undeniable facts of recovery. The national income, which had fallen as low as 40 billions in 1932, rose to 60 billions in 1937 and 70 billions in 1939. The fluctuating but generally upward trend of business from 1934 to the summer of 1937 was one of the longest periods of expansion we have known. This expansion coincided with the increase of deficit spending by the federal government. When the deficit was increasing, business recovered; when it was cut down as in 1936–1937, business fell away.

Against this position the opponents have equally persuasive arguments. The national income increased, it is true, but the increase was substantially less than in other industrial countries of the world. There may have been recovery up to 1937, but it was continually punctuated with relapse, and, even at the top, business indexes had failed to reach the line of normal. Nineteen hundred thirty-seven was a peak but a submerged peak, not even up to the level which the normal growth of the country would justify. Furthermore, the recovery was artificial in its nature. Dependent on government aid, it fell away as soon as the aid was withdrawn. The boom of 1935–1936 and the relapse of 1937, far from proving the effectiveness of government expenditures, merely indicated how artificial the whole situation had become.

Conclusion

These confusing testimonies mean that practical verification of the effectiveness of public works cannot yet be had. They do not mean, however, that our analysis of the economics of public works is of merely theoretical interest. It does lay bare the favorable and unfavorable influences at work. It indicates the direction which intelligent planning must take in order to obtain the greatest net effectiveness from public works. Specifically, it indicates that if the government guards against illogical economy when public works are in progress, raises its funds from loans rather than taxes, and uses the resources of monetary control to prevent drains of gold abroad, the deflationary influence of all factors save one can be greatly reduced. The one that cannot so easily be reduced—that is to say, the hesitant attitude of business in the face of expanding public expenditures—may perhaps gradually disappear as business becomes accustomed to stabilization measures and regards them as rational devices from which all will draw benefit. That this is not impossible is seen from the contemporary experience of Sweden, where public works as a stabilizer are accepted as readily in business circles as are the open-market operations of Federal Reserve Banks in those of the United States. Until this attitude arrives, the adverse effects of business hesitancy can be reduced to a minimum by keeping public works to the orthodox fields which now enjoy acceptance and by avoiding the tendency to utilize them under the influence of purchasing-power theories merely as a means for putting more money into circulation.

This conclusion clearly means that public works will be most effective when they are used as *one* of the armory of weapons available for attacking a depression, not as a panacea for spending our way into prosperity.

CHAPTER XXII

STABILIZING THE VOLUME OF CONSUMPTION

ONE way of looking at the business cycle is to regard it as a varying flow of purchasing power or a varying stream of monetary income. This monetary income stream, which is constituted by the aggregate of the incomes of individuals in the economic system, rises in boom and falls in depression. Its size is, in a very large part, determined by the activities of the producers of goods and services on the one hand, and by the activities of government on the other, these two agencies acting as the principal distributors of income to those who supply the agents and services of production. But the size of the income stream may be affected also by the autonomous decisions of consumers, who, apart from the variations of income imposed on them by the producers (including governments), may themselves vary the income stream within limits by hoarding in slumps and "dishoarding" in booms. In the unregulated business cycle of the classical type, all three sources of income increased and decreased in step. When private business was good, government business was good, because taxes were easy to collect, and the consumer felt the urge to spend and moved what income he had at a greater speed. In reverse, business fell; government, its reserves shrinking, reduced its activities; and the consumer, fearful of his shrinking income, shrunk its activity still more by hoarding what he had the nerve to hoard

Can Consumers' Income Be Stabilized?

The question now is: In what way might this income, visualized as a stream of purchasing power, be stabilized? The degree to which this can be done by direct operation on the essential sources of income—namely, producers' expenditures and the activities of government—has been examined already. In the chapters on monetary management, the problem of inducing variations in business expenditure was attacked; and in the chapters on public works, the problem of making government expenditures contribute to stability was examined. But if the measures outlined therein fail to remedy the situation, would it not be possible to attack the problem directly (and immediately) by measures stabilizing the flow of income to consumers? After all, as we have seen, monetary management may not be completely successful, and public works may be unavoidably slow in taking effect; but if funds could be paid to consumers as soon as depression begins, would not expenditure on consumption goods be immediately restored, and through their influence the demand for production likewise be maintained?

On the face of it, if, as soon as depression emerges, new money could somehow be put in the hands of consumers to be spent as they chose, there need be no falling off in the demand for consumption goods. Prices would not fall, and the falling profits of industries making consumption goods (which commonly remove the incentive for capital development) would be averted. If, as recovery is brought about, the normal level of activity is restored, making the additional money paid to consumers redundant and a source of potential inflation, then consumers' incomes could be assessed in some way and the funds so raised removed from circulation, so that consumers' expenditures would be checked and the rise of prices and profits that make for booms prevented.

Let us examine now more closely various expedients that

might, more or less completely, make for this desired stabilization.

I. Business Reserves

Common business prudence leads most businesses to carry reserves for various purposes. To the extent that these reserves happen to fit into the cyclical pattern, in the sense that they are laid aside in good times to be expended in bad, to that degree they do seem to make for stabilization, for they tend to make some of the expenditures more stable than they otherwise would be. Not all reserves are of this nature. Insurance reserves, for example, have to do with other types of emergencies. Depreciation reserves, too, probably the largest single type, may be laid aside in growing volume in expansion, but their use in depression is uncertain. Indeed, the replacements for which they are designed may actually be postponed and the funds, instead of being put into the stream of circulation, may be added to hoards and so be deflationary. Other reserves, on the other hand, are specifically designed to furnish purchasing power in depression—for example, dividend equalization reserves which help to maintain dividends to stockholders when current earnings begin to slump. If the business carried unemployment reserves, these, too, would tend to maintain consumer expenditures. One might add that, in deep depressions, all reserves of corporations, irrespective of their original purpose, may become a source of expenditure, as the necessities of the business cause depreciation reserves, insurance reserves, or even reserves for sinking funds to be taken from their destined use (which for the moment is not emerging) and thrown into the consumer spendable fund. It is the existence of these funds (whether called "reserve" or "surplus") and the possibility of their being a mainstay of consumer purchasing power in depression which led many critics of the administration to deplore the 1936 taxes on undistributed corporate surplus. They felt that, if this important source of income stabilization were dissipated, depressions would be deeper than ever.

Business reserves not effective for stabilization. There are two formidable limitations, however, to the effectiveness of business reserves, which make them probably of minor importance.

(1) In the first place, they are not sufficiently universal to cover more than a fraction of the volume of purchasing power necessary for stabilization. Many concerns do not attempt dividend equalization; very few of their own volition have even tried to set up unemployment reserves, the particular kind of reserves most likely to be effective and most adapted to the task of stabilization. The fact that, although some reserves have clearly been in use, business cycles have gone on, certainly with no sign of diminishing intensity, is proof enough that private business reserves are not adequate to the task, even though it be conceded that, as far as they exist, such reserves *should* make fluctuations less than they otherwise would be.

(2) But this consideration leads us to the second limitation, which is precisely that the way in which private business reserves are handled in practice tends to perpetuate the very fluctuations they might seem designed to alleviate. Naturally, the source of any effective corporate reserves to be used on the emergence of a depression must be accumulations held over from prosperity; otherwise, corporations could hardly add to their disbursements when depression arrived. What is more, on the face of it, not only would such accumulations be feasible, but the very fact that they are accumulated would seem to modify the extent of the boom. Unfortunately, this outcome is not quite what happens. Reserves are not merely held back from payment. They are commonly invested in the corporation. They thus add to capital formation and tend thereby to exaggerate rather than diminish expansive tendencies. The effect, therefore, is to make a device which is supposed to prevent depression turn into an influence which makes depressions more likely to arrive, and more severe if they do.

This possibility is the principal justification for taxes on undistributed corporate surpluses. While no one would deny that corporations that enter depressions denuded of surplus are not able to contribute anything to the increase of consumer purchasing power at the time, it is equally true that piling up surpluses in the way in which they have ordinarily been handled —that is, investment in capital expansion—may be an added incentive to boom.

But taxes on corporate surplus are not an appropriate way to approach the problem of income stabilization. All they do is to cause additional disbursements to stockholders. If these are made in prosperity, they *may* (if excessive saving is the cause of boom) prevent undue expansion; but they make no direct contribution to the problem of adding to consumer purchasing power whenever, for any reason, depressions actually emerge.

What is really necessary, if purchasing power is to be stabilized, is: (a) that adequate funds be forthcoming on the emergence of a depression, either from reserves or from some other source; and (b) that, if reserves are the source (and it may be that reserves are the only effective source), they be collected and maintained in such a form as not to aggravate the conditions making for boom.

II. Unemployment Insurance

Legal provision for unemployment insurance, if properly handled, seems best adapted, as far as it goes, to meet the problem of maintaining consumer income. It can, apparently, eliminate the two great difficulties of ordinary corporation reserves—that is to say, (1) by being compulsory over the general field of industry, it will not suffer from the limited volume of voluntary corporation reserves; (2) if properly invested and disbursed, there is no reason why the fund should defeat itself, as do corporation reserves, by accentuating the instability it is designed to remove.

The ordinary and primary purpose of unemployment insurance is to furnish a means of support for unemployed workers in a form which is free from the uncertainties and humiliations of "doles" or charity in any form of "relief." But it has, or may have, the further consequences of stabilizing industry by stabilizing the volume of consumers' income. Whatever the details of insurance in law and practice (and these details are numerous and complicated), its essence is the collection of funds from employed workers and/or their employers during active employment to create reserves from which, as long as they last, payment can be made to the unemployed. As far as cyclical fluctuations are concerned, this scheme amounts to collecting reserves in good times in order to distribute them in bad times, a process which, in the face of it, is an active force for stabilization. It reduces expansion during good times by the collection of reserves from all wage incomes, and in bad times it puts purchasing power to use through the maintained consumption of unemployed workers. In addition, it serves, to some degree, to prevent the further source of deflation that, in depression, is always added to shrinkage in the volume of disbursements to consumers—that is to say, the reduction in the velocity of monetary circulation as the masses of the people, dreading unemployment, lay aside funds for the emergency. Without unemployment insurance, this hoarding may be a potent cause of cumulative deflation. With unemployment insurance, fear psychology should be at least to some degree removed, and the tendency to hoarding, with its concomitant of idle funds finding no outlet in new investment, should be stopped or substantially reduced.

It is further claimed that the existence of the insurance burden has a more direct influence making for stabilization. Employers, being anxious to avoid the cost of insurance, seek to stabilize their production and, by reducing unemployment to a minimum, reduce the burden on their reserves. Most laws, indeed, are deliberately drawn so as to bring about this result. In the recent state laws, reserves, instead of being pooled, are commonly kept separate for each employer (except a small emergency reserve for the support of all) and so arranged that those who succeed in regularizing their work not only keep their reserves intact but, as soon as reserves reach a certain level, are freed from the burden of further contributions.

It may, therefore, be claimed for insurance reserves that, in one way or another, they are bound to exercise a stabilizing influence. If employers are moved to measures of stabilization, the problem is to that degree solved. If they are not, then the variation in the aggregate of consumers' demand, brought about by the alternate collection and disbursement of the funds, will bring about stabilization in any case.

Let us now examine the merit of these claims.

Unemployment Insurance as a Stabilizer

(1) Experience shows that not much stabilization can be expected from the voluntary efforts of employers. The incentive to stabilization is not strong, and, even if it were, the power to stabilize is lacking.

The incentive to regularization arising from the cost of reserves is, after all, relatively small. Only in those industries where the wage bill is large relative to the total costs would the direct burden of unemployment reserves be sufficiently important to encourage the employer to tackle the extremely complex task of stabilization. Thus, in 1929, wages for manufacturing industries as a whole in the United States constituted but 16.5 per cent of the total value of products. This fact would mean that the ordinary insurance burden of 3 per cent of wages would amount to less than ½ of 1 per cent of the total value of products. In the petroleum industry, where wages are some 6.3 per cent of the value of products, the importance of the 3 per cent assessment is almost negligible. Even in railroad repair shops, which, with a wage cost of 50 per cent of the value of products, stands highest in the list, the 3 per cent reserves would be only 1½ per cent of the value of products.

When one adds to this that, quite apart from the influence of unemployment insurance, every intelligent employer must know that stabilizing output would reduce his overhead costs and enable him to get workers at lower hourly wages, and that the gains from these sources would be much more substantial than the gains from avoiding insurance payments, one can readily see that, if these advantages have not led to stabilization, it is hardly probable that the desire to escape insurance payments would.

But there is an even more formidable difficulty. The major reason why we will not get stabilization from unemployment insurance (and the reason why we have not got it from employers in the past despite the powerful advantages that it would give) is that such stabilization by individual concerns is practically impossible to achieve. Most of the stabilization effected by individual concerns in the past has been in reducing seasonal fluctuations. Making for stock, diversifying output, transferring workmen from department to department, budgeting production, and so on, are possible, within limits, for the short-time fluctuations of the season. But even here there are limits, and when it is a question of the relatively long-time fluctuations of the business cycle, when all business is booming or all depressed, the simple devices appropriate to seasons are not of much use. What is needed is not the isolated action of individual concerns, nor even of individual industries, but rather the combined action of the whole industrial process. Even the monopolies and monopolistic groups that control the affairs of an industry do not have power to achieve the stability wanted. They talk stability and achieve a sort of stability; but the stability they get is price, not production, stability. Indeed, stabilizing prices without concern for the general state of demand increases instability of output, making it greater in good times and less in bad times than a flexible price would have produced.

In short, cyclical unemployment is a problem not of the firm, nor even of the industry, but of the economic system as a whole, variations of which only centralized action can correct. This centralized action can be achieved in practice only by government.

Can insurance reserves stabilize consumer income?

(2) Now let us examine the effectiveness of the greater stability of consumers' income which unemployment insurance is designed to bring about, for in this, rather than in pressure on individual producers, lies the hope of stabilization.

The shifting of consumers' income, which is implicit in unemployment insurance, superficially seems easy; but, as a matter of fact, it involves considerable difficulties arising largely from the possible consequences of the collection and disbursement of unemployment reserves.

Let it be assumed that such reserves consist exclusively of deductions from workers' wages paid by employers into a government-controlled fund. This process, as such, reduces *pro tanto* the consuming power of wage earners and, tied as it is to the total of wage payments, should serve as an increasingly powerful brake upon expansion. If, however, the collected reserves are offered for investment so that their earnings may reduce the burdens of the tax, the effect is to lower the rate of interest, or retard its rise, and encourage business thereby to proceed with more expansion, add more to capacity and output, than it would otherwise have done. If the fund is invested in government bonds, as commonly required by law, it would raise both their prices and the prices of all bonds, and thus give obvious encouragement to the expansion of capital issues. In so far as the conditions of boom are caused by failure of interest rates to rise relatively to profits, this outcome of the use of insurance fund is in direct opposition to the needs of stabilizing policy.

To put it in another way, if conditions of boom are caused

by a rate of saving (and investment) that is excessive and cannot be maintained, then insurance reserves, by transfer of resources from consumption to the market for savings, would seem rather to reinforce conditions of boom than to counteract them.

Furthermore, the arrival of depression and the consequent demand for the reserves call for the liquidation of the bonds in which the reserves are invested. As this occurs when the bond market is weak and considerable liquidation of other holdings is in process, a powerful deflationary influence would be set in motion. If the bonds were sold directly or indirectly to those who might otherwise have spent their money on consumption, no addition to purchasing power in the aggregate is made, and the total of consumer purchases cannot rise. Furthermore the sales of bonds depress their price and raise interest rates—a process which is just the opposite of that demanded by a stabilizing policy.

It is, therefore, possible that unemployment insurance reserves, if uncautiously handled, and under certain conditions, would actually serve to increase booms and depressions instead of reducing them.

How should reserves be invested? How can this unfortunate outcome be avoided? If the reserve funds were invested in government bonds, it would be possible to prevent undesirable effects in business through open-market operations of the Federal Reserve Banks. If easy interest rates unduly encourage industrial expansion, open-market operations through the sale of the appropriate volume of securities would serve to neutralize the effects of the fund. Similarly, in depression, sales of bonds from the fund could be kept from deflationary effects by the appropriate purchase of bonds by the Federal Reserve System. This method- means that consumer income stability *cannot* be expected to work out solely via the operation of insurance reserves, but must be fortified by the powerful stabilizing machinery of central banking; another illustration of a probably general situation—namely, that stability can be achieved only by the appropriate and intelligent use of *all* the weapons in the economy armory.

It seems, however, to be a somewhat cumbersome method to cause one government agency to buy bonds in the market, and another to counteract this (as far as is needed) by selling. A simpler mechanism, avoiding the cost and uncertainty of buying and selling through the intermediacy of the capital market, would be to have the insurance funds (or at least part of them) deposited directly in the Federal Reserve Banks. This outcome is what happens anyway (to the extent that the banks sell bonds to neutralize the purchases of the reserve fund), and it would seem more expeditious to do it directly.

What would happen then is this: As the collections exceed disbursements (good times), the fund would pile up in the hands of the Federal Reserve Banks, diminishing equivalently the aggregate reserves of member banks of the system. This reduction in reserves would serve to put the Federal Reserve Banks more and more in command of the investment situation. If net collections rose too high, so as drastically to limit the reserves and lending power of banks, the reserve banks could relieve the situation by appropriate investments, either by purchases of bonds in the bond market or by loans or discounts to member banks (with accompanying fall in the rate of interest). If, on the contrary, the reduction of reserves seemed to be desirable and in the interests of checking untoward expansion, then the funds could be held intact and withheld from investment by the reserve authorities. All this process would tend to reinforce the efforts every central bank makes to control booms, for, whereas in some booms easy money conditions (often arising from previous depressions, and certainly so, if government has done much to relieve them) make banking control difficult, the continual and compulsory flow of funds into the insurance reserve and thence into the reserve banks would keep the banks in much closer touch with the money market and enable them to check credit expansion more quickly and more effectively than they otherwise could do.

The use of reserves in depression. With the onset of depression, when disbursements from the insurance fund must exceed, and in time greatly exceed, the collections, payments from the fund (via checks on the Federal Reserve Banks) add to member banks' reserves, ease their financial situation, enable them to pay off loans at the reserve banks if they need to, and, in general, maintain that ease of money conditions and lowness of interest rates that are necessary to cope with depression conditions. There would be no large sale of bonds, to be counteracted by equivalent purchases by the Federal Reserve System (a roundabout way of withdrawing funds from reserve banks); indeed, investment conditions as such could hardly be affected unfavorably. The result would be to transfer funds to unemployed persons, not from the balances of other individuals who might otherwise have spent or invested the money, but from the unutilized resources of the central banking system, the use of which is not likely to have anything but inflationary and buoyant effects. The expenditures of unemployed persons put new purchasing-power to work that would otherwise have been idle, and is a support to all business activity. The fact that the funds come from such a respectable and businesslike source as insurance would tend to prevent the offsetting effects of deterioration of confidence in the government such as would arise when, because of lack of insurance reserves, resort must be had to "doles" or other forms of "relief" expenditures.

Thus operated, insurance funds would turn out to be funds in reality. To a very considerable degree, they would be cash reserves held for emergencies as though by an individual. As such, and to the extent of their volume, they would involve some cost. Cash funds earn no interest; therefore, such procedures probably would add to the cost of insurance, and for this reason the amount of assessments upon the workers (or whoever pays them) must be larger. As the amount of such assessments, it is agreed, reaches the apparent limits of endurance at rather low levels, this might be a very important consideration. This difficulty, however, would not be so great as one would think. It would not be necessary to maintain in cash, and thus "sterilize," the entire reserve of the fund. Indeed, to do so would be extremely deflationary. Under a fractional reserve system of banking, such as rules in the United States, any reduction of member bank reserves (such as is involved in every payment to Federal Reserve Banks) reduces bank credit by perhaps 10 times as much (depending on the ratio of deposits to reserves). Hence, in order to prevent expansion of loans in time of boom, only a fraction of insurance reserves would need to be sterilized, and the cost of sterilizing this fraction would be the real additional cost of the procedure. Assuming that 3 per cent interest is the expected earnings of the fund, and that one tenth of the fund must be "sterilized" on the average, the cost to the scheme of sterilization would be only three tenths of 1 per cent.[1]

This cost is not large. Any scheme must incur costs; and any successful scheme would be worth a good deal. Even if the loss of interest amounted to 1 per cent of the fund, success in stabilization would amply repay this loss.

The above analysis seems to indicate that unemployment insurance is adapted, in theory, to the task of stabilization, and that proper policy in the use of the funds will, within limits imposed by their size, actually make stabilization effective. If embodied in a law of wide scope, as is the assumption, the fund is large enough to be reasonably effective; and, if handled through the agency of or under the direction of the central banking system, there seems no reason why its beneficent effects should be seriously neutralized by its being inflationary or deflationary when it should be the reverse.

---

[1] Cf. P. H. Douglas, *Controlling Depressions*, 258–259.

Limitations of unemployment insurance. There are, however, other possible difficulties in unemployment reserves that prevent them from performing an adequate job of stabilization.

(1) Those who hold to the underconsumption theory of business cycles would regard the basis of collection as quite the wrong one. The ordinary plan for collection of reserves is deductions from wages paid into a fund. (These may or may not be accompanied by further payments from the employer or the state.) But there are many who hold that what is wanted in prosperity is increases, not decreases, of wages; that the flow of purchasing power tends in any case to be too much diverted from wages to nonwage incomes such as profits; that insurance does nothing to cure this, and may make it worse; and that the proper source of insurance funds for unemployment is taxes on high incomes, excess profits, and other large receipts. By taxing such incomes society gets at the essential source of excessive expansion—namely excessive investment by persons of great wealth; and thereby not only collects a fund for such depressions as occur, but may even prevent depressions from occurring.

(2) A second difficulty is found in the probably unexpected and certainly undesired tendency of unemployment insurance to increase the inflexibility of wages in depression. In another chapter, wage inflexibility is discussed in some detail.[2] Here it is enough to point out that wage earners have always stubbornly resisted wage reductions in depression and that the consequent wage rigidity, by maintaining costs in the face of falling prices, is a cause of greater reduction in industrial activity and employment than would otherwise occur. As insurance reserves, by giving workers something to fall back on in depression, tend to bolster their determination to resist wage

---

[2] See pp. 481–484.

reduction, they have the consequence of adding to some degree to the extent of depression. How important this consequence is cannot be estimated. At most it is only an addition to forces which would be operating in any case. As insurance payments are usually limited to 50 per cent of current wages, they may not, in fact, prove a very attractive alternative even to somewhat lower than normal wages.

For this reason, the most that can be safely said is that unemployment insurance gives the worker and his labor unions somewhat better bargaining power in a time of distress.

(3) A third difficulty is more serious. It is that no workable and practically acceptable scheme of insurance can be expected to cover anything save relatively short periods of unemployment. Douglas has estimated that an assessment of 3 per cent of average total earnings, in occupations commonly covered by insurance, would permit benefits of 50 per cent of wages with maximum of $15 a week for 16 weeks per year after a three-weeks' waiting period, provided unemployment over a major cycle were 10 per cent.[3] While this scale of benefits would provide purchasing power adequate to cushion a minor slump, it would hardly be adequate for major depressions, in which output and employment, particularly in the capital goods industries, fall far more than 10 per cent, and for periods considerably longer than 16 weeks. In such times, insurance reserves built on normal levels of contributions will quite certainly prove inadequate. More and more people as time goes on will exhaust their total benefit claims, and those added to the groups commonly excluded from the insurance system, such as agricultural workers and domestic servants, may make a formidable total. To maintain the purchasing power of these people involves either extended benefits, such as were devised in England in the 1920's, or other supplementary payments not available through normal insurance channels.

---

[3] Douglas, *Controlling Depressions*, 259–260.

These supplementary payments would be best made through a broad system of relief, financed largely by national funds. Those unable to work would receive relief in money or in goods. Those able to work would be engaged in projects of general value, approximating public works, but perhaps now more familiarly described under the New Deal title of "relief works."

Thus unemployment insurance *must be coördinated with other measures of stabilization* to be of greatest benefit. Unemployment reserves cannot be properly invested and disbursed without the assistance of the central banking authorities. They cannot effectively prop the purchasing power of workers in depression without the potent aid of a broad policy of governmental expenditures, ranging from public works down through various work projects, more or less important, to outright relief.

III. Stabilizing Consumers' Income in General

Insurance against unemployment is clearly a form of consumption stabilization. But it is not the only form, nor does it cover the whole ground. True, it covers a lot of ground, and it tends to stabilize, as far as it goes, the income of a class that definitely needs the security it gives. But it does not stabilize consumers' income as such; it stabilizes that part which comes to a certain fraction of the wage-earning class, during a particular and limited period of time. It is worth considering whether it would not be possible by similar devices to stabilize consumers' income as a whole.

Unemployment insurance suffers from the limitation that it is insurance. It is designed to be insurance, not a stabilization mechanism. Its primary purpose is to insure, as far as can be done safely by insurance methods, against the specific risk of unemployment. If it contributes to stabilization of consumers' income, it does this incidentally, and not as its principal purpose. Hence it covers only a limited field. More specifically, it covers unemployed persons only for a limited period, say 26 weeks, or whatever time is justified by the state of their respective contributions when employed. Moreover, it does not touch unemployed persons not in wage-earning groups, nor does it restore or stabilize in any way (except indirectly) the income of those who receive profits or interest, and so on. If, therefore, income stabilization is the aim, and if income stabilization as such can be made effective, then the stabilization (as far as possible) of *all* incomes would seem to be the correct policy.

A partial, but relatively unscientific, approach to this problem is found in such programs as Social Credit and the Townsend Plan, both of which owe their popularity with low-income groups to their insistence on the importance of maintaining consumption as a means of avoiding or curing depression.

Social Credit. Of these, the Social Credit plan [4] is the more comprehensive and, as far as it goes, more defensible. Social Credit is based on two fundamental propositions: (1) that the processes of technology and science (which are essentially a social heritage belonging to all of us and to which many persons and groups, alive and dead, have contributed) make it possible, were they effectively used, to bring a high and continuous level of income for all; and (2) that our accounting and monetary systems so limit the supply of consumer purchasing power as to make it impossible to market the reasonably possible supply of producible goods and services; and that hence we run into depressions every time we try to make use of our industrial equipment and methods in the way engineering and scientific considerations would dictate. The cure for this evil, therefore, is for the community to supply its citizens as consumers with the purchasing power which, on the one hand, is due to them as a social dividend on their heritage of technology and science, and, on the other, is necessary if the product of

---

[4] See also the theories of Major C. H. Douglas, pp. 262–268.

industry is to be adequately salable. This purchasing power the Social Credit plan would supply by appropriate advances to consumers, via the Treasury, or via banks, or in whatever way seems most effective. These advances would be large enough to supply the demand for all the goods that industry is, at any given time, capable, technologically and physically, of producing; and, furthermore, they would be increased with every further increase, through invention and discovery, of the technological powers of industry. It appears to be the belief of the Social Credit advocates that, by this means, industry would reach and hold full employment of its resources, and that depressions would be made to disappear. They hold that this mechanism would bring output to a level never reached even in the greatest boom, and hold it at this level without serious interruption.

The Townsend Plan. Somewhat similar claims are made for the Townsend Plan. This plan, as it originally was stated, would provide an income of $200 a month to every person in the United States over 60 years of age, who was a citizen of the United States, and who agreed both to drop whatever employment he or she had and also to spend the "pension" within the month. Apart from the atmosphere of social justice to the older members of society in which the plan is immersed, and apart also from certain personal moral angles which seem characteristic of all such schemes, the essential beliefs on which the plan is based are these: (1) that the reason for the abnormally low level of production in depression, and the chronically and unnecessarily low level of production even in booms (considering our technical abilities), lies in the lack of consumer purchasing power; and (2) that the increase of purchasing power in the hands of consumers, when coupled with some device to prevent mere hoarding, will stimulate industry; and, if the increase of this purchasing power is carefully measured to fit the need, it should bring industry to the highest level justified by our technological and scientific knowledge.

The mechanism by which these payments are to be financed is by a general tax on transactions, the yield from which seems to Townsendites to be sufficient to meet the demands. Obviously, quite apart from the possible consequences of the payments in stimulating industry, this method of raising funds is inappropriate. Taxation, as a general rule, merely transfers purchasing power. It does not add to the aggregate in use. It is conceivable that taxes might be paid from idle resources, but this outcome is unlikely, particularly in the case of a transactions tax. It is possible, too, that the forced circulation of pension money might increase the velocity of circulation of money provided the funds flowed from a slow-velocity to a fast-velocity area of use. But this result is improbable and uncertain; and it may be repeated, therefore, that a transactions tax is a particularly inappropriate method of financing attempted additions to consumer purchasing power. Indeed, this characteristic is the most obvious and certain defect of Townsend or similar plans.

But the fundamental defect of both Social Credit and the Townsend Plan lies in their inability to serve as a means of stabilization. Based as they both are on the assumption that what is needed is continuous expansion of purchasing power, they are not adapted to cyclical variations. Instead of expanding in depression and contracting (relatively) in boom, their means of payment continuously expand. Hence, except in the most favorable possible assumptions, they must make for inflation and be wrecked on the normal consequences thereof.

Despite their defects, however, Social Credit, the Townsend Plan, and similar schemes raise the question of whether, with proper methods of finance and with appropriate timing, consumer credits might not be an effective device for stabilizing industry and employment; or, to put it in other words, whether the relatively narrow field of unemployment reserves might not be enlarged to cover the whole area of consumer purchasing power.

A bold proposal for consumers' credits. An interesting analysis of this problem has been given by J. E. Meade in his recent book, *Consumers' Credits and Unemployment* (1938). The essence of Meade's proposals is to pay out credits to consumers in general on the advent of depression; and to recover these by appropriate taxation upon the restoration of good times, with the purpose of restricting at the very start the deflationary processes of depression and restoring prosperity at the earliest moment. In detail, there is involved: (1) the problem of getting payment into the hands of the right persons, and (2) the problem of providing an effective means of retiring the credits when the need for them is over.

Who should receive consumers' credits?

(a) As the persons most in need are the unemployed, a simple means would be to make payments to all persons out of work because of depression. This method would be different from unemployment insurance, although in a broad way it might affect the same group of persons. Unemployment insurance is paid to all persons insured, on account of any kind of unemployment and for limited periods of time. Consumer credits on the other hand would be paid only for unemployment due to depression, for only this kind of unemployment can be said to be due to a deficiency of consumer demand. Seasonal unemployment, on the one hand, and technological unemployment, on the other, which are not due to a deficiency of consumer demand in this sense, cannot be cured by consumers' credits. They are an appropriate occasion for unemployment insurance, but the insurance will have no stabilizing effects.

On the other hand, consumers' credits to all persons unemployed because of depression would reach farther than unemployment insurance, since it would be unaffected by previous contribution or by length of unemployment period.

In short, consumers' credits to all unemployed because of

depression would be both more and less embracing than un-employment insurance as such—less, because meeting only one kind of unemployment; more, because of covering greater numbers of persons.

Even then the coverage would not be precisely what is wanted. Workers still employed but with diminished incomes would get no aid, nor would other persons whose incomes are reduced by depressions (unless they happened to be unemployed), such as the recipients of rents, dividends, profits, and so forth.

(b) A second method which would meet those objections would be to distribute benefit to all persons losing income by the depression. There is no simple method of arranging this, but, on the assumption that the injury is widespread, a roughly proportional benefit could be paid by reducing all taxes and financing an equivalent volume of government expenditures by borrowing. This method would restore, to whatever degree was considered feasible, the purchasing power of all tax-payers, without at the same time canceling out the benefits by reduction in government expenditure. (This method is suggested by the official of the Bank of England, mentioned in Roger's *Capitalism in Crisis,* who said that England needed a deficit so badly that he was prepared to recommend the remission of all taxes.)

As a means of enlarging expenditure, however, remission of taxes is cumbersome and slow. Taxes are paid at intervals, often only once a year, occasioning undesirable delays in the expansion of purchasing power. Furthermore, governments being what they are, it might be dangerous to put in their hands such a device as remission of taxes. Popularity might too easily be won by tax reduction at inappropriate times.

(c) A simple device would be to pay consumers' credits to everybody at such times as an index of depression unemployment (that is, unemployment due to depression and not to seasons or technological change or other cause) showed positive figures. This arrangement would approach the devices advocated by the Social Credit theorists such as C. H. Douglas, but under such statistical control as would prevent them from being made at inappropriate times. Douglas would give Social Credits at all times, boom as well as depression, until industry was at its technological maximum; whereas, for the purposes of stabilization, such credits should be used only when unemployment was due to inadequacy of demand. Otherwise, it would only result in inflation.

But consumers' credits for everybody will result in payments being made to people who do not need them. This outcome violates our notion of social justice. It may not even be effective in stimulating the demand for goods, since it is persons in this class who are said not to spend their incomes promptly. Hence Meade proposes that payments be made only to those members of the community, whether workers or not, whose income falls below a certain level. This provision would give payments to those in need as long as need existed, and it would place money in the hands of persons who are most likely to spend and least likely to resort to the hoarding which depression psychology often encourages.

Retiring the credits when the need is over. Effective use of consumers' credits demands the withdrawal of outstanding credits in the advent of recovery; otherwise, inflation will occur, with its undesirable results. When, therefore, the index of depression unemployment falls to zero (that is to say, when all remaining unemployment must be attributed to seasonal or structural causes, not curable by increased credits to consumers), then credits should be withdrawn, and industry should be allowed to carry on with its (normal) volume of purchasing power.

How, therefore, should this be brought about? A tax of some sort must clearly be levied to bring about this retirement, but on what persons, or what groups, should this tax be levied? Should it be levied on the persons who received the credits, as,

for example, by a general tax on social security payments?
Should it be levied on the higher incomes of society as a means
of maintaining a more equal distribution of wealth? Should
it be levied on everybody in general via a sales tax?

As to these alternatives, Meade makes the following observation: A tax on social security payments may not be equitable.
If paid by workers themselves, then others who have gained
by the stimulating effects of the credits will have made no contribution to the recovery. All classes gain. If paid by employers, a form of discrimination is set up which clearly penalizes industries that are stable and have continued to pay out
relatively unchanging incomes through the depression.

These considerations suggest the levy of such a widely based
tax as would be paid to some degree by every recipient of income. For this purpose, a sales tax is often held up as a model.
But sales taxes have unequal incidence not only on rich and
poor, but also in respect to industries which have different rates
of turnover of output, or in which goods pass through different
numbers of hands.

For these reasons, Meade suggests a tax on the beneficiaries
of the credits (those in receipt of or contributing to social insurance), half paid by the workers, half by employers (who, by
shifting their share, spread it widely, and presumably with
some approach to equity, over the whole body of consumers).

There is something seductively attractive about this kind of
stabilization that entitles it to serious consideration. It is simple, it is direct, and it works with the least possible delay.
Unlike monetary management, which, in the last analysis, is
a scheme to *induce* businessmen to regularize their expenditures,
it is not likely to suffer from the embarrassment of offering
funds to people who do not want them. Nor is it likely to be
bothered with the delays and conflicts too often found in public
works. For, after all, the real purpose of public works is quite
often not the utility of the projects, many of which are hastily
set up and often of little lasting value (like public buildings in

an economically declining locality), but quite frankly the purchasing power which is, as it were, incidentally put into the hands of otherwise idle people. Advocates of consumers' credits claim that this can be accomplished more quickly and more effectively by their proposals.

CHAPTER XXIII

WAGE POLICY

The Problem of "Rigidity"

It has always been claimed for an economic system based
on free enterprise that it and it alone is capable of spontaneous
adjustment to the constantly changing data of economic life.
Shifts from one industry to another, expansion here and contraction there, readjustments of output to changes of demand
and to changes in methods of production and the relative
availability of the productive factors must be brought about
continuously, rapidly, and spontaneously if balance is to be
maintained and production continue uninterrupted.

It is a commonplace of economic reasoning that a system of
free enterprise where no values or prices are subject to control,
but all are free and quick to react to changing conditions, is
best adapted to this necessity of constant adjustment.

But evidence is piling up that this flexibility on which adjustment depends is being reduced, and that some of the values
and prices are tending to become more rigid as time goes on.
This rigidity has always been present in the important element
of contract interest rates. These are fixed charges, which, although to some degree flexible by negotiation and by the more
painful process of bankruptcy, have been accepted as a relatively rigid element in the structure of costs. But other values
are moving toward inflexibility. We hear much these days
of inflexible prices, and we are told that many of our industrial prices are "administered" so as to vary within narrower

limits than they otherwise would and less than the needs of flexibility seem to demand. Particularly have wages tended to become less flexible. That they have long since been to some extent less flexible than prices is, of course, well known. They rise and fall less than prices and are less quick to move either up or down. This relative rigidity is most marked in depression, and it may well be that developments are increasing the strength and scope of this tendency.

Whatever the relative importance of this tendency to rigidity in contrast to the flexible elements in the economic structure (and it is well to be reminded that this cannot be measured with our present knowledge), to the degree that it exists it will interfere with the self-adjusting process which is supposed to be the great virtue of free enterprise. Rigidity of prices and wages could be particularly dangerous in depression, when readjustments are inevitable, and, when delayed, serve only to prolong the period of stagnation.

What are the causes of this rigidity? What consequences does it have upon cyclical fluctuations of business? What policy should be followed to restore greater flexibility if such flexibility is desired?

The Causes of Rigidity of Wages

Wage rigidity works both ways. It makes wages rise less than proportionately to prices in good times, fall less in bad times. But it is particularly strong in bad times, when various reasons conspire to create stubborn resistance to wage reduction. What are the reasons for this?

(1) The first is the general preoccupation of workers with the standard of living. Workers are not businessmen engaged in making money; they are primarily human beings making a living. They have never been willing to regard their labor as a commodity subject to the mechanical operation of supply and demand. Fair wages, they argue, are not market-controlled wages but rather wages that will ensure a just standard of liv-

ing. Hence workers strive for wages that gradually rise, rather than wages which rise and fall with the vagaries of industrial fluctuations. They are willing to have them go up, but not go down. This attitude, which has become almost traditional, tends to make wages a matter of status rather than contract. Furthermore, it is increasingly defended as appropriate social philosophy in a democracy wherein the general welfare of the people demands stabilization of wage income. While perhaps the more appropriate way of achieving this would be to stabilize the whole national income, in the meanwhile this philosophy finds expression in the demand that wages become a fixed charge on industry, like interest.

(2) A second cause of rigidity is the common conviction among workers that the demand for labor, particularly in depression, is inelastic. If this conviction is true, any given drop in wage rates will produce a less than proportionate increase in the demand for labor and a smaller aggregate volume of wage payments. Resistance, therefore, to wage reductions is, from labor's point of view, a good policy. It is, of course, possible that wage earners are wrong, and that the demand for labor even in depressions is elastic. This elasticity would certainly be more probable if wage cuts were general, for then each industry would gain not only by reduction of direct wages but also by the probably more important reduction of indirect wages which is found in the cost of their materials. But ill-founded or not, there the belief is, like the possibly equally ill-founded belief of industry in the inelastic depression demand for their commodities. As long as it is there, it makes for rigidity.

(3) Thirdly, resistance to reduction of wages is stimulated by the fear that wages are easy to get down but hard to get up. Once wages are reduced, only prolonged pressure can get them up—pressure which at the best makes for friction and at the worst leads to costly strikes. This fear is the counterpart of that fear of "spoiling the market" which, as is pointed out

later,[1] plays such an important part in causing industry to oppose price reductions.

(4) A fourth cause is the existence of unemployment insurance, work relief, or any other alternative to money wages that society has to offer. The "short-time normal" to which wages might be expected to fall in depression will clearly depend on the alternatives open to workers. If the alternative is starvation, wages may fall very low; if the alternative is insurance payments or work relief, and so on, wage levels will be supported to that degree. The emergence of these alternative payments during the last two or three decades has led some observers to attribute to them the apparently increasing inflexibility of money wage rates during this period. It has been a common argument that the prolonged stagnation of English industry since the First World War and the inability to reduce the volume of unemployment can be traced largely to this source.

(5) Finally, rigidity of wage rates in depression has been supported both in theory and in practice by the spread of purchasing-power theories of wages. The growing tendency to emphasize that wages are not merely a cost, but also the main constituent of effective demand for commodities, has given added strength to resistance to wage cuts. It has become the accepted theory of organized labor and has gained ground even in academic economic circles, especially under the influence of Keynes, who has ingeniously rationalized the instinctive opposition of labor to wage reduction.

These reasons indicate what powerful influences make for rigidity of wages and give a measure of the difficulties which any policy of greater wage flexibility must be prepared to face. With this in mind, we will now examine the effectiveness of various wage policies designed to make for more stable production.

---

[1] See p. 502.

Wage Policy in Cycles

The problem of wage policy is complicated by the fact that wages are both an element of cost and a means of effective demand for goods. Rigidity of wages regarded as an element of cost is a force increasing the amplitude of cyclical fluctuations. By lagging behind prices both on the rise and on the fall, they will, to the extent of their importance, open up abnormal areas of profit and loss. On the upswing, they encourage undue expansion; on the downswing, they force undue contraction. As long as profits are the driving force of enterprise, so long will the rise and fall of profit caused by lagging costs make for alternating periods of expansion and contraction. Therefore, proper policy will increase the flexibility of costs. This flexibility is one of the aims, indeed, of banking and monetary control which, by raising and lowering interest rates more promptly, tends to remove such profit inflation as arises from lagging interest. Similarly, raising wages earlier in expansion would put brakes on the enthusiasm of the entrepreneur. If depression comes, a more ready reduction of wages would adjust costs to prices, restore the profitability of enterprise, and encourage the maintenance of normal levels of activity.

But wages are not only an element of cost. They are, as underconsumptionists hasten to point out, the most important source of purchasing power. As such, their variations are bound to modify the profit expectations of entrepreneurs, not through the effect of wage rates as cost, but through the influence of aggregate wages on effective demand and hence on the sales 'expectations of the producer. As the latter influences may be favorable when the former are unfavorable, or vice versa, wage policies viewed from one angle may demand different, if not completely opposite, measures from those seen from the other angle.

Thus, if the cause of crisis is held to be a level of output which has outrun the purchasing power of the masses of the people, proper policy in expansion demands steady increases in wages. Only in this way will a continuous foundation be laid on which expansion can be maintained. Where improvements in technology have been made, it is particularly imperative that wages rise proportionately. Otherwise, even with stable prices, abnormal profits will emerge, an investment boom will be propagated, and a crisis will impend.

But it is not in order to put brakes upon the producer by raising his costs that wage rise is necessary. What is needed is a steady increase in consumer purchasing power. Raising cost serves merely to bring expansion to an early end, which, considering that even in boom times equipment is never fully used, seems to condemn us all to a much lower level of real income than our technological advantages should enable us to enjoy. But raising purchasing power encourages activity to go on. Instead of giving us the unhealthy kind of boom which inevitably ends in crisis, it gives us steadily rising prosperity, limited only by the state of the industrial arts.

Thus, although both those who think of costs and those who think of purchasing power can advocate rising wages in expansion, the former aim to keep this expansion in bounds, the latter to remove the bounds. The former put up barriers to prevent rates of expansion they regard as impossible to maintain. The latter remove barriers that hold back an expansion which can continue as long as science and technology flourish.

Disagreements as to wage policy in depression. But if, although for different reasons, these two groups advocate superficially similar wage measures in expansion, all agreement disappears when depression comes. While considerations of cost demand more speedy reduction of wages in depression, considerations of purchasing power can do so only under very specific conditions which may, in fact, not be present.

Those who think of wages as cost imply that the demand for labor as a whole has an elasticity greater than unity. Were this so, reduction of wages would involve no conflict between our two points of view, for not only would cost per unit of output be reduced, but aggregate wages and, therefore, aggregate purchasing power of the workers would increase.

But the assumption involved is by no means justified. Various accompaniments of reduced wages in depression may falsify it completely.

(1) In the first place, the reduction of wages may be followed by a reduction in prices. Were this to happen, the gains to employers would be canceled out and the forces of deflation continue. Even at the best, the total active purchasing power would not increase, and since some of the gains from falling prices go to bondholders and others of the *rentier* class, whose tendency to save rather than to spend may immobilize at least a part of their gains, there is a strong probability that aggregate purchasing power in use would fall. This result is not an encouragement to maintenance of output.

(2) In the second place, initial reductions in wages tend to encourage the expectation of further reductions, causing entrepreneurs to postpone commitments until wage levels should have reached their minimum. There emerges, for short periods of time, a "perverse elasticity" for labor, whereby reductions in wages decrease rather than increase the demand for labor and rapidly reduce the aggregate of wage payments. If there could be a single reduction of wages that could be considered final, this outcome might be avoided. Such a reduction could hardly be accomplished save by the dictatorial orders of the government, not available in systems of free enterprise.

(3) If, despite the temptation to do so, prices are not reduced with the reduction of wages or reduced with a time lag so that there accrues an additional profit to entrepreneurs, even then there may be no expansion. The entrepreneur, surrounded as he is by the uncertainties any depression produces, may prefer not to invest these profits but to pay off bank loans or put his business in a more liquid condition. Should

he decide to do this, the total effective demand for commodities is most likely to be reduced, since resources are transferred from wage earners, who would presumably have spent them, to entrepreneurs, who under these assumptions would not. When this result happens, the profits themselves turn out to be illusory.

(4) It is possible, indeed, that reduction in the wage and price level will correspondingly reduce the demand for money, create a margin of unused credit, and so bring down the rate of interest, and that this will give the needed encouragement to expand. But a lower rate of interest, as we have seen, may not be an effective stimulus; and even if it were, it could be more easily brought about by the deliberate operations of the banking system than by the reduction of wages with all its attendant uncertainties and difficulties. Wage reductions are strongly resisted by workers, and their resistance not only adds to entrepreneurs' costs, but may be accompanied by so much popular discontent as to weaken general confidence, thereby upsetting any influences that might be favorable.

Keynes comes to the aid of wage maintenance. These arguments against reducing wages in depression have been strengthened lately by the powerful support of J. M. Keynes, whose *General Theory of Employment, Interest and Money* may be said to be devoted largely to the proposition that "the volume of employment is uniquely correlated with the volume of effective demand measured in wage-units." Mr. Keynes puts his argument for wage maintenance as follows: [2]

Reduction in money wages can only be favorable to entrepreneurs provided the total volume of effective demand is maintained. With reduced wages in general, this result can happen only either (a) if the additional income thus accruing to others is consumed (that is, if the community's marginal propensity to consume is unity), or (b) if not consumed, it is invested by entrepreneurs, which in turn can happen only

[2] Keynes, *General Theory*, Chap. 19, "Changes in Money Wages."

provided their expectations are improved (that is, that the schedule of the marginal efficiency of capital is raised relatively to the rate of interest).

These conditions do not make a very promising picture. If prices are reduced, additional income largely accrues to the *rentier* class, whose standard of living is relatively inflexible. If prices are not reduced, additional income accrues to entrepreneurs, who are more likely to save than consume. On either count, consumption seems likely to suffer. This outcome puts the burden on investment, which will expand only if expectations are made relatively favorable. As the considerations already advanced indicate that the marginal efficiency of capital is not likely to rise, about all that is left is the possible fall in the rate of interest, which, as already pointed out, is likely to be more effectively brought about by the banking authorities. If the entrepreneur foresees all these results, he will not be tempted to increase his output. If he does not foresee them but acts on optimistic expectation engendered by reduced wage costs, then he is almost certain to be disappointed with the outcome and to be led to reduce his employment to its former level.

° **Can these policies be reconciled?** We have, then, two quite different wage policies to choose from, as a means of reducing depression. On the face of it, one or the other of these policies must be wrong. If it is good economics to lower wages in depression, it cannot be right to maintain them. Yet it may be that there are elements of truth in each and that different circumstances may justify different policies. There are cycles, perhaps minor ones, in which readjustment comes quickly, and revival emerges as a result of low interest rates and the consequent stimulus to investment. In these cycles, the demand for capital is elastic, and it seems possible that reductions in wages would add to the stimulus.

But there are other cycles in which depressions seem prolonged and serious. Deflation continues unduly, even after reasonable readjustments are made. Confidence has disappeared, and the demand for capital has become completely inelastic. The symptom of this is the total inability of a prolonged period of low interest rates to rouse enterprise out of stagnation. In a cycle of this sort, wage reduction serves merely to reduce the volume of active consumption and can have no other result than to prolong the depression.[3] In fact, elasticity of the aggregate demand for labor may be so low that very severe reductions in wages may be necessary to bring about adequate re-employment of labor. Doubtless in any depression, no matter how severe, there is *some* level of wage rates which would restore full employment, but, if this level is so low as to violate the moral standards of the community, it must be ruled out as impracticable. That such a situation might occur is indicated by the similar experience of interest rates which, in depression, may approach zero without encouraging a revival in the demand for capital.

Raising Wages for Recovery

Looking on wages as purchasing power, then, causes one to favor a wage policy of raising wages in prosperity and maintaining them in depression. If, however, wages have not been maintained in depression, then an extension of the policy indicates that wages should be raised to bring about recovery. A depression can end only if somebody begins spending money. Entrepreneurs will not produce without a market; and markets cannot be there as long as wage disbursements are unduly low. Therefore, the right thing to do is to raise wages in industry in general. The increased purchasing power this generates constitutes the market that is needed for recovery and for encouraging entrepreneurs to expand production and employment. This view of things finds great popular support. It is the favorite panacea for restoring good times. It

---

[3] E. Lederer, "Industrial Fluctuations and Wage Policy," *International Labor Review*, Jan., 1939.

is accepted readily by politicians and enthusiastically by labor leaders. It has played an outstanding part in the economic policies of the New Deal, which has been enormously influenced by underconsumption points of view. It found concrete expression in the wage policies of the National Industrial Recovery Act (NRA), in the Wages and Hours Act establishing minimum wages and maximum hours, and in the aid given by the New Deal to the revival and expansion of labor unions. It is the background of the popular demand, to which the A. F. of L. has given its official blessing, for a 30-hour week in industry in general. This proposal, although ostensibly a means of creating more jobs, is really a means of increasing the total disbursements to labor, as is shown by the provision that hourly wages should be sufficiently increased to maintain the prevailing weekly earnings for labor.

The idea of bringing about recovery by raising wages, considering that this must be at the expense of entrepreneurs, seems like lifting oneself by one's own bootstraps. Certainly it would not be easy to find support for this except in relatively unorthodox circles. Nonetheless, because of its great popular appeal and the devotion it has found in some governmental circles, it deserves detailed examination. For this purpose, let us take the wage policy of the NRA.

The wage policy of NRA. Everybody agrees, of course, that no individual employer can be expected to raise wages in the hope that he will recoup his outlay via the increased purchasing power of wage earners. There is no reason to suppose that any more than a negligible fraction of his outlay will come back to him in purchases, and even what comes will be delayed. But it is arguable that, if employers in general raise wages, they will, as a body, receive back in sales what they pay out in additions to wages; and that if they could be induced to act together, a wage-raising policy ought to be feasible. With this in mind, the government, through the somewhat authoritative persuasion of NRA, aimed to bring about

an increase in aggregate wage payments by agreements with
employers to raise the general level of wage rates and lower
hours of labor. As the effect of the latter was to encourage
an increase in numbers employed, aggregate payrolls were
substantially increased. This method was expected to protect
individual employers from the hazard of isolated action and
supply the increased volume of purchasing power needed as a
basis for general expansion. Most important of all, the increase in outputs that this would occasion, in plants running
to only a fraction of capacity, would substantially reduce
unit overhead costs and so enable employers to meet the additional wage costs imposed by NRA without reduction in profit
and without increase in price—particularly without increase in
price, for otherwise real purchasing power could not be effectively increased.

Now, even assuming that the increased volume of wage
payments would be promptly spent or otherwise put to active
use by the recipients, return of wages in purchases is bound
to be delayed. Some of the funds would be used to pay bills or
other debts; some of them would go through banks and be delayed in reissue. To producers of consumers' goods, wage
outlays would come back very fast. To producers of capital
goods, in proportion to their remoteness from the consumer,
they may come very slowly. For the producing community
as a whole, there would be an unavoidable lag between outlays
and receipts; and the question of how the increased costs
should be financed in this difficult interval would arise.

NRA wage policy of doubtful value. It is evident that
whatever financial means are used they must be such as to
add to the total purchasing power in active use. They must
come from "new money" obtained through bank credit, or
they must be otherwise idle funds. If they come from other
active uses, so constituting a mere transfer of active funds from
one use to another, they will not add to aggregate spending
and will make no contribution to recovery. If, for example,

entrepreneurs meet additional wage bills by reducing expenditures on replacement or inventories, cutting down on repairs and additions, letting inventories run down, and so forth, purchasing power is reduced in one place to be increased in another. At the opposite extreme, if employers have idle reserves at banks or can borrow at banks, and make use of these funds to meet wage payments, a real net addition is made to purchasing power. If wage increases are met at the expense of dividends, or, provided arrangements can be made, by reducing interest on outstanding debt, the *active* purchasing power would be increased, if it can be assumed that this process shifts resources from slow spenders to rapid spenders, or from those who tend to save to those who are sure to spend.

The prospects of successfully financing increased wage payments from these means do not look very promising. Payments from other current expenditures are of no net value. Payments at the expense of whatever dividend money is available in depression would be small in the aggregate and of doubtful efficacy in any case, as payments from interest and other contract incomes would be also. This situation leaves cash reserves and bank loans as the main resources. As to these, the general attitude of businessmen in depression does not seem favorable either to releasing cash reserves (which they cling to with great tenacity at such times) or to incurring the risk of borrowing at banks for the certain outlays and the very uncertain gains increased wage costs must involve. Hence, business is apt to finance their expense either by reducing nonwage expenditures or by the normal business procedure of raising prices. Neither of these expedients can possibly be effective in raising the general level of purchasing power. Either of them, if practiced, will produce disappointing results to entrepreneurs and confirm their natural hostility to "unorthodox" measures.[4]

---

[4] For a detailed study of these points, see *The National Recovery Administration*, a study by the staff of the Brookings Institution, 1935, 757–772.

For these reasons, most economists would hesitate to recommend a policy of raising wage rates at the end of depression in the hope that it would bring about recovery through increase of purchasing power.

Can Wages Be Made More Flexible?

The upshot of this analysis seems briefly to be this. More rapid wage increases as production increases in expansion are definitely desirable. Drastic wage reduction in depression may be ruled out, as may also rigid wage maintenance. Moderate wage reductions, made once for all, with certainty of no further fall, would perhaps be the compromise most likely to find favor enough to be adopted and involve the least economic risks. Wage increases as a means of promoting recovery are undesirable. This outcome sums up to a program of promoting some flexibility in both the rising and falling phases of the cycle. What, then, are the best methods in practice for bringing this about? Can employers, on the one hand, or wage earners, on the other, make any important contribution in this matter? Or must we fall back on the regulatory power of the government to bring about the desired flexibility?

Formulas for flexibility.

(1) Professor Pigou, speaking from English experience, suggests that employers would be more ready to promote wage flexibility if they could be assured that it works both ways. It would probably be found that employers in general would more readily concede higher wages in good times if they could be sure they would be not unreasonably maintained in bad times. In fact, the same might be said from the other side. Wage earners would be more ready to concede reductions in bad times if they could be reasonably sure they would be restored in good times.[5]

---

[5] A. C. Pigou, *Industrial Fluctuations*, Part II, Chap. IX.

Barriers to flexibility that are the result of the mutual suspicion of capital and labor should not be insuperable. Like
other conflicts between these great groups, they ought to yield
to the skillful procedures of experienced collective bargaining.
One possible means of solving this problem would be a sliding
scale of wages whereby, without protracted argument, they
would be adjusted by formula to variations in industrial activity or to variations in some index of prices. Thus wages
could be increased and decreased from some agreed upon normal level, in proportion to the variations of a price level indicating changes in the demand for labor. Or they might be
tied to variations in the cost of living, which, themselves, are
indicative of changes in the purchasing power of labor income

It would seem from experience, however, that no such formula is adequate to the task certain to be imposed upon it.
The "normal" level of wages to which the actually varying
wages are tied cannot be readily determined. There is no
unique "normal" which can be discovered by scientific procedure. It has to be arbitrarily determined, and it is not easy
to find a base satisfactory to both parties. Even when determined, new methods of production will make it obsolete, and
agreements on the proper readjustment are not easy to reach.
A situation may readily arise in which a given upward revi-
sion of wage rates will be regarded by employers as the temporary increase of a period of prosperity, but by workers as the
readjustment to a new and permanently higher normal, justified
by new methods of production. In such a case, workers will
stand out for wage maintenance in depression, on the ground
that otherwise they would be deprived of their reasonable
share in the gains of technological advance. This situation
is particularly likely to emerge where wages are tied to indexes of the cost of living, the effect of which is to maintain
relatively constant real wages throughout the cycle. Constant
real wages, in the face of increasing productivity in industry,
would bar workers from the fruits of progress and condemn

them to a gradually decreasing share in the national income.

Doubtless, constant real wages would serve the needs of flexibility better than the relatively rigid money wages of common experience; which actually mean real wages that fall in prosperity and rise in depression. But they still fall short of the demands of stability. What appears to be necessary is such a changing level of real wages as would maintain labor's share in the total national income. Otherwise it would be difficult to prevent the excessive profits that make for untenable expansion, or, alternatively, to ensure that distribution of purchasing power which is needed to make for uninterrupted advance.[6]

While, therefore, industrialists, moved by the hope of escaping the formidable machinery of collective bargaining, frequently look with favor (at least in advance) on sliding scales or profit sharing, and other wage adjustments of the formula type, the limitations from which these schemes suffer do not make them appropriate means, at least over short periods, for maintaining labor's share in the national income.

Collective bargaining as a means of flexibility.

(2) From the workers' standpoint, the most obvious method of achieving this result would be a strong body of organized labor, and the most immediate need to encourage the spread of unions and strengthen their effectiveness wherever they exist. From the point of view of flexibility, workers might be more willing to make concessions when bad times come if they could be reasonably sure of getting wages effectively back again in good times—even more, if they could feel convinced that wage earners had shared adequately in prosperity and that depressions, when they did come, did not spring from failure of wages to keep pace with the level of output. Would not a strong labor movement be the best guarantee that this desir-

---

[6] P. H. Douglas, *Controlling Depressions*, 210–214.

able outcome would be achieved? Could they not so raise wages in prosperity that they would be willing to accept the wage adjustments employers feel ought to be made in depression?

But labor unions rarely show any willingness to make flexibility work both ways. Strong unions are as resistant to wage reductions in depression as are weak unions. Even the strong unions of Great Britain have not noticeably budged from this common attitude.

It may well be that this is but the reflection of the various causes making for rigidity that have been set out above. Labor unions are the quintessence of the general viewpoint of wage earners. What wage earners think, they think. They systematize the relatively unconscious and spontaneous attitudes of their class. But there is another reason for their position. Labor unions, with all their power, suffer from serious limitations. There are definite bounds to what they can accomplish by economic pressure in a world based on private enterprise and the profit motive. It may not be easy to wring from entrepreneurs, even in prosperity, what wage earners regard as equitable wages. Two reasons particularly are worth noting.

(a) The general wage level at any time tends to be determined by the marginal productivity of labor. If wages are below this level, effective pressure may bring them up, but beyond this level they cannot go without causing unemployment. Small highly organized groups, if they keep their ranks closed, may force wages up substantially, partly at the expense of the public in prices, partly by squeezing employers, and partly at the expense of other less organized workers. But the wider the area covered by unions, the farther they reach down into the ranks of semiskilled and unskilled workers, the greater the difficulty of this monopolistic policy, and the smaller the range over which wages can be raised without throwing workers on the margin out of work. Furthermore, wages being dictated by marginal levels, unions have no adequate means whereby workers may share in the gains of that considerable body of producers in any industry who produce under various differential advantages, advantages of position, or management or sheer monopoly. Were wages to share in any such differential, they would be rapidly cut down by the inrush of workers from less favored places. Under such circumstances, wages in the aggregate may find it difficult to keep pace with the value of output.

(b) Even granting the level of wages at any given time to be adequate for stability, the progress of technology and improvements in management tend to increase the national income faster than the share of labor. Most improvements being labor saving in nature, they tend to reduce the marginal productivity of labor relatively to that of capital and managerial ability and to make it difficult for even the most powerful unions to encroach on the additional earnings of the other factors of production. Under these circumstances, the demand that workers, for the sake of stability, maintain their share in the national income may be futile. In the event that they were able to do so, they would reduce the profits from innovations to ordinary levels and remove most of the stimulus that makes for progress.

It may well be, therefore, that these limitations which are imposed on the effectiveness of unions in raising wages have caused them to adopt the purchasing-power theories which would raise wages in booms and maintain them in depressions, rather than the alternative policy which would make wages flexible both ways.

Flexibility by legislation.

(3) These difficulties in the way of advancing wages have tended to some extent to shift the interest of wage-earning groups from the economic to the political field, where the powerful machinery of legislation can be drawn in to supplement and extend the work of labor unions. The wider the

scope of labor unions, the farther they extend into the great masses of wage earners, the more likely this alternative aim will be relied upon. It is characteristic that the leaders of the C.I.O., not those of the A.F. of L., look with favor upon the extension of legal enactment to the field of wages and prices and even the control of production. But it does not seem that adequate flexibility of wages is likely to be obtained by legal enactment. In societies based on private enterprise, laws to this end have but little scope. Specifically, they are commonly limited to minimum wage legislation, the purpose of which is to raise to some socially acceptable minimum the wages of the lowest-paid workers. This wage provision may or may not be accompanied by some maximum limits on working hours. As the wage levels established have to be low enough not to penalize unduly the less effective employers, lest unemployment should increase, they are more advantageous in putting a floor to wages in depression than they are in adequately raising wages in prosperity. The number of those whose wages in prosperity would fall below the minimum figures established in the recent Wages and Hours Act cannot be large. Under no circumstances would they be able to tap the possible sources of high wages such as are to be found in monopolistic positions or in industries of advancing technology.

It would be theoretically possible, by appropriate taxation rather than wage legislation, to get at business income which seems to evade the pressure of unions. Excess-profits taxes on corporate earnings would gather in the earnings of differential advantages and monopoly, as well as the additional earnings from technological and managerial improvement. Unlike wage increases, these are not limited by production at the margin. They are discriminatory and can leave marginal production without any additional burdens. If these taxes are then distributed to labor in some appropriate way, as, for example, in social services which otherwise would have

to be paid from other taxes, or even by granting a consumer dividend to all people as advocated by the exponents
of Social Credit, then, indeed, it might be possible to maintain
in prosperity the worker's share in the national income.

But taxation of this sort may well penalize industry and
reduce, rather than expand, the national output. In so far
as it rests entirely on differential advantages from monopoly,
or from favored location, or from possession of particular
managerial talent, it may not be followed by any ill effects.
The income is a quasi-rent, not part of the supply price, and
may be taxed with impunity. But taxes on the earnings of
technological innovations and managerial improvements stand
in a different case. The effect thereof is to reduce the profits
of progress to the ordinary levels and to remove the stimulus
that, in the past at any rate, has made for progress. Doubtless some level of tax on excess profits might be found that
would not reduce noticeably the forces of innovation; but no
level of tax that reaches the ideal of maintaining labor's share
in the national income could fail to be burdensome. Thus
society is in a dilemma. If we gain stability, we may lose
progress. We can have stability, or we can have progress; but
we cannot have both.

It may be, therefore, that, in the world as it is, flexibility of
wages cannot be had. The forces which are needed to bring
wages up in prosperity are not likely to be adequate. And
as long as this is so, labor unions backed by public opinion,
or public opinion alone if labor unions are absent, will demand
the maintenance of wages in depression. We may fairly conclude that wage policy based on considerations of costs will
tend to give way before wage policy based on considerations
of purchasing power. As far as it goes, this outcome means
essentially the adoption of the Hobsonian point of view that
the fundamental cure for cyclical fluctuation is a more even
distribution of income. It means, too, that whatever stabilization we are going to get must come from other sources than
wage policy.

CHAPTER XXIV

PRICE POLICY

Price Inflexibility

Wages are not the only relatively inflexible element in the economic structure. Prices, too, can be inflexible. They can be inflexible in good times when lowered costs due to innovation may fail to be passed on to the public. They can be particularly inflexible in bad times when business in general, but particularly monopoly, prefers to reduce output rather than to make the concessions in price necessary to maintain existing scales of consumption.

The tendency to hold up prices in depression has long been pointed out by economists and may be taken to be a normal policy for all business in a position to carry it on. On the face of it, this policy implies some limitation on competition, for otherwise prices would tend to fall in depression to the short-period normal determined by marginal variable costs, with no allowance for overhead. As it is, wherever tacit understandings make it possible, wherever imperfect competition dictates it to the producer, and particularly in the event of monopoly proper, prices tend to be maintained at levels higher than the short-period normal, and reduction in output is greater than it otherwise would be.

What are the reasons for this attitude? [1]

---

[1] See A. Marshall, *Principles of Economics,* Book V, Chap. V; A. C. Pigou, *Industrial Fluctuations,* Part I, Chap. XVIII; J. M. Clark, *Economics of Overhead Costs,* Chap. XXI, Sec. 3.

Spoiling the market.

(1) In the first place, we have the fear of "spoiling the market." Prices cut to variable costs do not cover the total costs of production; once down, they may not easily come up, with bankruptcy menacing in the background. The ethics of the trade will heap moral condemnation on too much cutting. There is a fear, too, lest the market be spoiled for future sales in better times. Buyers stock up when prices are low, and the normal recovery of demand is delayed by consumption from stock. The consumer may become habituated to lower prices and regard higher prices, if restored, as unfair. If goods have been intensively advertised and become associated in the buyers' mind with a definite price, there is an added motive to maintain prices lest the advertising appear to be mere ballyhoo designed to make products seem worth more than they really are.

Fear of inelastic demand.

(2) A second cause of price maintenance is the common belief in business that demand in depression is inelastic and that to lower prices is merely in varying degrees to reduce the aggregate receipts. Businessmen are commonly skeptical of any favorable reactions to price reductions. They tend to regard depressions as storms which have to blow themselves out, and about all that can be done is to take in sail until the gale is over. This attitude is particularly prevalent in industries producing capital goods and the instruments of production. Here is a derived demand which, under the influence of the principle of acceleration, tends to fall to a low and apparently inelastic level. Business demand, it is felt, depends on the state of confidence, not on the price level. As long as confidence is low, low prices, like low interest rates, are ineffective to stimulate revival.

This attitude is stronger, wherever there is any degree of monopoly. In pure competition, the demand for any firm's output is infinitely elastic. Any small cut gets business away from rivals. But monopoly has its particular market, and elasticity of demand, even in good times, is not perfect. Cuts in price cannot then be as effective, and the temptation to avoid them is particularly strong. The apparent scope of imperfect competition indicates that the area of relatively inelastic demand may be greater than competitive equilibrium theory has assumed.

It may be added that the fear of demand inelasticity may, in part, derive from the experience of piece-meal reductions in prices. As in the similar case of wages, such practices set up expectations of further reduction, cause consumers to withhold purchases in anticipation thereof, and create a situation of "perverse elasticity" greatly annoying to business. This outcome, of course, might be avoided by drastic once-for-all reductions, provided the buyers did not take them to be a bluff.

The influence of the accountant.

(3) These causes are reinforced by the influence of accounting concepts which lead business to oppose any prices which do not cover "costs." The aim of any business is to sell at such prices as will cover costs and leave a margin of profits. It regards prices properly related to costs as fair prices. It does not like to sell below costs, and regards prices below cost as unfair and the mark of the "chiseler." Furthermore, these costs which prices should cover include not only the variable costs such as wages, materials, and so on, but also the overhead costs which go on irrespective of the volume of output. The accountant discovers what these costs amount to, and these, spread out over the output, are taken to be a measure of the price which must be charged. If prices cover these costs, well and good; if they do not, the business is losing, and proprietors must reduce output or incur the odium of "selling below cost."

Now in depression with falling demand and reduced output, what happens to "costs"? Some costs, of course, such as materials and wages under the pressure of unemployment, fall. But overhead costs, including depreciation charges as long as plant values are not promptly written down, do not fall, or fall but little. From the accountant's standpoint, those relatively fixed charges spread over a smaller volume of output, raise unit costs, and, as such, balance (possibly over-balance) any fall in variable costs. The greater the overhead, the greater is this possibility. Under these circumstances, producers, thinking in terms of covering "costs," resist price productions. In large-scale industry, with expensive capital installations, this resistance is particularly strong and, in the field of producers' goods, it may conspire with the fear of inelastic demand to make the utmost price rigidity.

Accounting concepts may conflict with good sense. Logically, these accounting obsessions might even demand price increases, and sometimes they appear actually to do this. This attitude is irrational, leading as it does to raising prices in periods of falling demand. Carried to its logical conclusion, it would cause prices to rise and rise, each rise producing smaller consumption, and each reduction of output raising units costs, until finally no business whatever would be done, and costs per unit would be infinitely high. That this result may be the direction of policy is indicated by the following conversation between Feller, TNEC council, and Weir, of the National Steel Company, in hearings before the TNEC on price policies of the steel industry. Weir had made the statement that it was the "patriotic duty" of every steel producer to make a profit and that in depression profit margins could be maintained only by raising prices.

Mr. Feller: As the demand for steel declines, and the cost of production goes up, prices should increase?
Mr. Weir: Absolutely.
Mr. Feller: Then as the demand goes down, prices should go up to meet it?
Mr. Weir: Absolutely.[2]

---

[2] Quoted in *New Republic*, March 11, 1940, 338.

Again, in the operation of the codes under NRA, the opportunity to raise prices was seized on so quickly as to arouse the complaint of the Consumer's Advisory Board. To quote the report of the board to General Johnson in March 1934:

Many of the provisions (against selling below cost) include such elements of cost as charges for excessive and obsolete equipment, selling expenses and even returns on investment. Such provisions raise the question of whether or not recovery can be secured while basing minimum prices upon charges for the use of plant and equipment, etc., which would only be appropriate to a larger volume of sales and a far larger volume of consumers' purchasing power than now exists, and in some cases than has ever existed.[3]

If it could be assumed that price competition were the rule, these impediments to price reduction would have to be ruled out. Presumably this situation exists in agriculture where prices in depression must approach the short-period normal. In manufacture, on the other hand, various degrees of imperfect competition make it possible to follow the dictates of restriction, and all the influences mentioned will play their part in keeping up prices. Where there is actual monopoly, either by the form of organization or through various kinds of agreements, the tendency to restrict under these circumstances would be particularly powerful.

The Extent of Price Inflexibility

Pigou, reflecting English experience, does not attribute great importance to price rigidity. He gives it a weight of one sixteenth as a factor determining the amplitude of fluctuation, one half as much as wage rigidity. Indeed, he considers that some steadiness of price may be of great convenience to buyers, and that resistance to excessive price cuts may stave off the highly disturbing consequences of bankruptcy. But, in the United States, economic opinion has tended to give much

---

[3] *New York Times*, March 5, 1934, 2.

greater weight to price rigidity and to suspect that its influence has been gradually increasing. The apparently expanding scope of large-scale production, the concentration of corporate power revealed in studies such as Berle and Means' *The Modern Corporation and Private Property,* and the reasoning of economic theory on the restrictive possibilities of imperfect competition have concentrated attention on the increasing possibilities of price rigidity. An important section of economic opinion claims price rigidity to be an important, even dominant, factor in the prolonged depression of the 1930's, when the appropriate readjustments in some prices seemed uncommonly long in coming.

The scope of "administered" prices. Evidence in this regard has been set forth in the well-known studies of Gardiner C. Means.[4]

In order to ascertain degrees of flexibility, Means examined the monthly changes in price of the various commodities entering into the Bureau of Labor Statistics wholesale price index. Some 750 items were checked over the years 1926 to 1933, a period including 94 months and 94 possible price changes.

Classifying the items into 10 groups by frequency of change, Means got the following result:

Group	No. of Items	Frequency of Change
I	14	0
II	77	1-4
III	76	5-8
IV	82	9-13
V	96	14-21
VI	88	22-35
VII	86	36-60
VIII	85	61-87
IX	83	88-93
X	63	94

---

[4] G. C. Means, "Price Inflexibility and the Requirements of a Stabilizing Monetary Policy," *Journal of the American Statistical Association,* Vol. 30, 1935, 401–403. See also National Resources Committee, *The Structure of the American Economy,* Part I, 1939, 129–149.

Thus at one end of the scale are 14 items showing no change at all over this whole period and 91 with less than 5 changes; while, at the other end, 63 changed every month and 146 changed 88 times or more. The prices at one end of the group are "administered"; the items at the other end are subject to the uncontrolled vagaries of the market.

Furthermore, in depression, frequency of price change and magnitude of price change tend to go together. Over the period 1929 to 1932, items which changed most frequently showed also the larger drop in price. The most flexible prices tended to drop, on the average, 50 per cent; those that changed least often fell, on the average, only 10 per cent.

The result of these varying degrees of change is to create great discrepancies in production as depression emerges. Where prices are held rigid, production is greatly curtailed. Where prices are flexible, production is relatively little affected. The following table is offered by Means in proof:

PRICES AND PRODUCTION—1929 TO SPRING OF 1933

Industry	Per Cent Drop in Prices	Per Cent Drop in Production
Agricultural Implements	6	80
Motor Vehicles	16	80
Cement	18	65
Iron and Steel	20	83
Auto Tires	33	70
Textile Products	45	30
Food Products	49	14
Leather	50	20
Petroleum	56	20
Agricultural Commodities	63	6

Similar conclusions are reached in the more extensive study made under Means' direction for the National Resources Committee.[5] Examination of price changes in the depression of 1929–1932 showed that depression sensitivity was, on the whole,

---

[5] *The Structure of the American Economy*, 132–137.

associated with raw materials, agricultural products, market-dominated prices, nondurable goods, and standard commodities; and insensitivity was associated with fabricated products, manufactured goods, administration-dominated prices, durable goods, and differentiated products. It was held, further, that the dominant factor in making for depression insensitivity is "the administrative control over price which results from the relatively small number of concerns dominating particular markets."

Such great discrepancies in prices and production seem to Means to constitute a serious impediment to balanced economic functioning, the more serious as they appear to be the result of the growth of economic concentration, which has gradually been increasing in pace. We are approaching an economy half free, half controlled. This situation would be dangerous in any age, but in a period subject to rapid technological change, like our own, anything which interferes, as this growing inflexibility must do, with the effective process of continuous adjustment will hinder progress and, in depression, may bring about prolonged stagnation.

Means' conclusions challenged. It cannot be said, however, that these conclusions are accepted without challenge.

Means himself has pointed out that price statistics give no clue to improvement in quality, and that price quotations are often nominal and not representative of actual prices reached by negotiation. But other more formidable criticisms have been made.

(1) It has been shown that flexible and inflexible prices are the mark of all depressions. Rufus Tucker has produced evidence from four great depressions showing not only the persistence of this phenomenon but apparently no essential increase in the spread between the two levels of prices.[6] It is

---

[6] R. S. Tucker, "Reasons for Price Rigidity," *American Economic Review*, March 1938. Also "The Essential Historical Facts about 'Sensitive' and 'Administered' Prices." *Annalist*, Feb. 4, 1938.

commonly conceded that price rigidity is by no means a phenomenon of recent origin.

(2) The persistence of inflexibility over such periods raises the suspicion that concentration of economic power, which is of relatively recent origin, is not the sole important factor in price maintenance. Other conditions than control keep prices up; other conditions than lack of control bring them down. Tucker suggests that, where labor costs are important and have not fallen, prices may be maintained even under competition. Again, that persistence of demand keeps prices up in areas of production where control seems insignificant.

(3) While economic reasoning indicates that maintenance of price in depression tends as such to reduce the volume of consumption and hence of output, statistical inquiry into the experience of 1929–1933 does not seem to confirm this relation so strikingly as Means seems to claim. Further investigation into the behavior of prices and production in this period shows most diverse relations. Where prices have been continuously maintained, the reduction of output for different commodities has a wide variation. Where prices have been reduced, output changes accompanying them range through varying degrees of both increase and decrease.[7] These facts justify the conclusion that many other factors in addition to prices must be taken into account to explain the observed variation of output.

This controversy indicates that our knowledge of the significance of flexible and inflexible prices is too limited to be sure that inflexibility is increasing, or that it is caused by concentration of economic power, or that it was a substantial factor in the great reduction of output in the depression of 1929–1933. We must be content with the undeniable fact that some prices in depression are relatively inflexible, and that, all other

---

[7] J. Bachman, "Price Inflexibility and Changes in Production," *American Economic Review*, Sept. 1939.

things being equal, they tend to increase the amplitude of fluctuations in output, particularly where they occur in industries producing capital goods.

Price Flexibility Desirable

A purposeful policy of price flexibility seems, therefore, to be one of the important weapons of stabilization.

(1) It would help to prevent profit inflation in periods of rapid technological progress and thereby reduce the danger of an investment boom such as that of the 1920's.

(2) It would reduce the amplitude and duration of depressions and, by lessening the disparity between controlled and uncontrolled prices, avert the sectional antagonisms and internal economic strains displayed in the 1930's.

(3) It is an indispensable adjunct to any monetary policy directed to maintaining a managed price level. Supposing the aim of money management is, via a fixed volume of money per capita, to allow the price level to fall with improvements in technology; it is quite as important that all prices fall as that prices on the average be lower. Were some prices maintained in the face of falling costs, then other prices must be reduced unduly. Thus industries possessing an element of monopoly power could put an intolerable burden of price adjustments on the more competitive fields. To avoid this situation, flexibility of all individual prices must be achieved.

We must now inquire what measures to achieve price flexibility are available.

Flexible Prices by Exhortation

It is conceivable that customary attitudes of business could be broken down and that businessmen could be persuaded to take larger and longer views. This position means that they must forego the advantages of monopolistic action in good times, and in bad times overcome their fears of spoiling the market and give up their ingrained belief in inelastic demand. This result might well be accomplished. The earnest writers inspired by H. G. Moulton of the Brookings Institution have urged businessmen to see the larger wisdom of continuous price reduction as technology proceeds on its triumphant course. Let them adopt a "dynamic" concept of price based on the encouragement of potential demand, rather than their present "mechanical" concept that is a mere adding up of costs. Then it would be found that production is no longer held up by lack of effective demand, but will expand within limits determined only by the state of our industrial arts. Perhaps they can be brought to realize that only thus can they restore vitality to private capitalism and avert the onward march of the controlled economy that otherwise is surely bound to come upon us.[8]

Whether this method would meet the problem of depression is another matter. Where goods are specialized and prolonged efforts made to build up particular markets, heavy barriers are raised against "spoiling" them by price reductions. Perhaps, in less specialized fields, fear of inelasticity of demand might be overcome, but the testimony of businessmen in the great depression is not favorable. If reduction of prices could occur promptly and, once made, not be repeated, the producers' fears of delayed demand might be overcome, but this would need a community of action such as would hardly be expected from a multitude of business units. For this reason, more might be expected if business were organized into trade associations, which might be able to bring unity of action over much wider fields. A business might be much more willing to risk prompt price reductions if it knew that other businesses from whom it buys commodities were going to do likewise.

Trade Associations as an Instrument for Flexible Prices

At first thought, trade associations seem to be an unpromising instrument, because they have been suspected of using

---

[8] See E. G. Nourse and H. B. Drury, *Corporate Price Policies and Economic Progress*, Chap. XI.

their powers, when they could, for maintaining rather than reducing prices. Hence, they normally live a suspected life in the looming shadow of the antitrust laws.

But trade associations have a genuine interest in stability. The economic disruptions of depression are as disastrous to business as to other victims. The popular hostility to private capitalism which the miseries of recurrent unemployment generate is a menace that justifies every effort made to avoid it.

Consequently, trade associations, along with their other more specific functions, have been offering remedies for industrial fluctuations. Their most thoughtful exponents argue that they can regularize and stabilize production and employment, coördinate production and consumption, and attain balance in the economic system. Fundamentally, they accept the businessman's explanation of booms as due to "overproduction," overproduction as due to the unregulated output of competitive industry, where each unit, working under the spur of rivalry and in the dark as to the doings of its rival, expands unduly, to the inordinate expansion in aggregate outputs. They would remedy this situation by coördination and planning. Production would be kept within bounds, and, with the disappearance of booms, depressions would be avoided. Or, if they should emerge, coördination of production could still achieve stability. None need shrink his output, since the output of each would constitute the demand for all.

Stability of production is an admirable end. All wish that trade associations could reach it. Unfortunately, these are interested not only in stability of production but also in stability of price; and while one or the other of these can be obtained, only the most unusual circumstances could enable them to obtain both. If demand did not change, there is no reason why a trade association should not achieve stability of both production and price. Having determined on a price that would sell the output proper to its capacity as a whole, the trade asso-

ciation would proceed to produce that output and hold that
price indefinitely. But if demand changes, and demand, under actual conditions, is sure to change, then the group can
have production stability or price stability, but it cannot have
both. If output is stabilized, prices are sure to vary. If demand falls, as in depression, price reduction cannot be avoided.
On the other hand, if prices are stabilized, output cannot remain constant. If demand falls, price maintenance must reduce consumption.

Doubtless, if contraction and expansion of demand could be
accurately foreseen, and if deviations from average levels were
not of long duration, both production and prices might be
stabilized by production for stock when demand fell and sales
therefrom when demand rose. But this device, while successful for the short and predictable variations of seasonal demand,
is usually neither physically feasible nor financially possible
for periods as long as the cycle.

Trade associations may use wrong policies. What trade
associations have to offer the public, therefore, is not price
stability *and* production stability, but price stability *or* production stability, and the evidence seems to indicate that, in the
face of these two alternatives, trade association lean toward price stability. The codes of fair competititon set up
under the NRA give the most comprehensive picture of what
trade associations would like to do if they could be freed, as
they were, from the dangers of prosecution under the antitrust
laws. Many of them contain provisions which, although
doubtless explicable by obsessions about unfair competition that
afflict these associations, seriously interfere with price flexibility.
Some three fourths of the codes had provisions against selling
below "cost," which frequently includes the cost of idle overhead. One half of the codes required their members to file
prices with the code authority and give notice of change.
Such provisions discourage price reductions. Indirect price

concessions of all kinds were discouraged, and indirectly price maintenance was protected by limitations on machine and plant hours, by restrictions on addition to capacity, and even by production quotas.

The result was a general tendency to raise prices at a time when depression was barely giving way to recovery, and, thereby, not only to retard recovery but to cancel to some degree whatever stimulus might have come from the AAA payments to farmers and the NRA payments to wage earners.

The truth of the matter is that trade associations express the quintessence of the general economic philosophy of businessmen, and it is idle to expect that, left to their own devices, they will do other than fortify and extend existing business practices. They will, therefore, continue to insist on keeping prices above cost, on the determination of which they will continue to be dominated by accounting conceptions. It will be easy to convince them that demand is inelastic, especially in depression; and they will continue to fear any concession that seems likely to "spoil the market." From such sources, price flexibility may be hard to obtain.

Regulated trade associations. Those, however, who think of business cycles as a normal consequence of an unplanned economy, where keen competition is naively expected to bring about good results, are not prepared to give up trade associations as a means to stability. The coördination of production which they might give should not be sacrificed merely because of an apparently incorrigible tendency toward price inflexibility. By appropriate governmental regulation it should be possible to get the advantages without the attendant evils. Let the principle of codes be retained. The codes were all right, but they did not go far enough. Through dominant representation in the code authorities, or by some public commission with appropriate power, government should regulate prices in the interests of stability and the widest use of capacity. If the associations will listen to persuasion, well and good.

But if not, appropriate prices should be imposed by administrative decree.

But the difficulties inherent in price regulation are enormous. Even in relatively stable industries such as railroads and public utilities, the problem of the right price is not easy to solve. In dynamic industries exposed to variability of demand on the one hand and continual changes in methods of production on the other, price control by public body meets almost insuperable difficulties. It might be possible to bring prices down gradually where technical progress justified, but the machinery of public control is not likely to be sensitive enough to make for quick adjustments, and the short-period changes demanded for cyclical stabilization might not be easy to bring about. Experience with the regulated prices of public utilities is not an encouraging one. Regulated producers are too apt to devote resources to influencing the controllers that should have been more usefully employed in improving their business. Further extension of this economic waste is not a pleasing prospect—so little pleasing, indeed, that any reasonably effective alternative for reaching our goal is to be preferred.

Why Not Restore Competition?

The question, therefore, might be asked: Why not go down to the core of the problem by restoring competition in our industries? If flexible prices are desired, competition offers the most effective means of getting them, far more so than the clumsy method of bureaucratic control. In a competitive society, prices are flexible, and readjustments are prompt and continuous. The hindrances which block and clog the adjusting mechanisms arise from monopoly, and the elimination of monopoly will effectively remove the power to "administer" prices. Instead of encouraging trade associations, what we need to do is precisely the opposite. Let them be limited to such coöperative activities as raise no suspicion of price or output control. Prosecute combines in restraint of trade. Let

the overgrown concentrations of corporate power be broken
up into a sufficient number of units to ensure effective competition.

But antitrust laws in the United States have been singularly
ineffective. Prosecutions, even when successful, have not prevented the divided units from reuniting in less vulnerable
forms, particularly in the mergers which are more difficult to
construe as combinations in restraint of trade. So persistent
has been this tendency as to indicate that competition in many
industries, especially those with great overhead costs, may be
as economically inappropriate as in such "natural" monopolies
as railroads and public utilities. If this be so, then, although
it may be possible to enforce competition in industries where
the number of producing units is still fairly large, the restoration of competition in those where a few large-scale units
dominate might be so expensive and involve the loss of such
considerable productive advantages as to be quite impracticable.

Is Competition Feasible?

Whether, in fact, this situation exists in industry today is,
however, an open question. Competent students are by no
means agreed on the matter, nor is the available evidence adequate to justify a confident stand. There seem to be two ir-
reconcilable factions. One group, inspired by the writings of
the late Justice Brandeis, denies that our existing large concentrations in industry are based upon effective producing and
marketing economies. Size, indeed, is a handicap. Monopoly
tends to stagnation and inefficiency. Economies of large-scale
operation could not and did not bring about many of our
large concerns. The motives that brought them into existence
were not engineering or economic; the motives were financial
and promotional. The profits derived from stock issue and
manipulation, not from effective operation, were the dominant
factor. They hold their own by the sheer threat of size. In
a fair field, they could not be maintained.

Now there is some impressive evidence in support of this view. There is the actual history of the promotion and financial operation of our great corporations. There is Dewing's well-known examination of 35 outstanding consolidations of the 1898–1902 period, showing that the earnings of the companies after consolidation were lower than before: lower in the first year, lower in the tenth year, and lower on the average for the whole 10-year period after the consolidation.[9] There is the evidence of various statistical studies of recent years disclosing that the largest concerns are not those that make the largest profits. There is the evidence, too, of the sprawling and uncoördinated structures of some great holding companies in the field of railroads and public utilities.

But this evidence is not convincing to those who find the clue to size in the productive and marketing advantages of large-scale units, and who desire to escape the destructive warfare to which competition on this scale of operation tends to degenerate. This group, while admitting that promotional motives and sheer megalomaniac ambition may carry the size of corporate units beyond the point of optimum efficiency, denies that what evidence is forthcoming upholds the advantage of reducing the average unit to a size capable of ensuring effective competition. Some of the largest units might be broken down, but technological considerations make the most efficient size in many industries a fairly large one—large enough, indeed, to limit sharply the probable number of concerns. Beyond this, further parcellization would begin to be costly, and price flexibility would be achieved at the expense of the general standard of living. From this standpoint, therefore, a new dilemma emerges. If we want the economies of size, we must submit to a concentration of output which, even if it avoids "monopoly," cannot avoid "monopolistic competition," with some control over price, some degree of "price

---

[9] A. S. Dewing, *Financial Policy of Corporations*, 3rd Ed., New York, 1934, 747–751.

jurisdiction," and, with that, some degree of price inflexibility. If, on the other hand, we want flexibility of price, we must submit to such an increase in the number of operating units as may sacrifice the advantages of size and lose economies of operation that society can hardly afford to give up.

One may fairly conclude that price flexibility, on examination, will prove to be as illusive and, in our large-scale industry, as difficult to achieve as its counterpart in the labor field— namely, wage flexibility. Whether we should exhort business to behave itself, whether we should encourage trade associations in the hope that government chaperonage might make them useful without qualification, or whether we should move to the regulative extreme of price fixing by administrative body or to the *laissez faire* extreme of restoring active competition— none of these alternatives seems to offer any certainty of success. About all one can say with reasonable assurance is that the last alternative offers the least chances of all. It seems likely that we will have to accept a relatively noncompetitive industrial order as a fact. Whether we can get flexible prices out of such a setup is the problem.

CHAPTER XXV

CONCLUDING REMARKS ON STABILIZATION

NOW that we have completed our survey of stabilizing measures, we should be able to decide better whether, on the whole, stabilization of the cyclical process is worth while attempting.

The Social Gains from Stabilization

That stabilization is desirable is indicated by both common sense and economic analysis. It is conceivable, as Professor Pigou points out,[1] that an economic activity which runs in alternate sprints and stoppages would best satisfy the needs of society. If the aversion to work or the desire for goods underwent periodic changes of several years' duration, so that men left to themselves would arrange their lives as alternating periods of active work and relative idleness, then the cyclical process would contribute to economic welfare, and its stabilization reduce it. But common sense, as well as the behavior of workers in good and bad times, confutes this view, and we may assume that stabilization would increase, not diminish, economic welfare.

Stabilization substitutes regular income and work for irregular income and work. If the principle of diminishing utility holds good, then this substitution is an economic gain. "A real income varying from $(A + a)$ to $(A - a)$ yields less

---

[1] A. C. Pigou, *Industrial Fluctuations*, Part II, Chap. 1, where the net value of stabilization is acutely analyzed.

satisfaction than one constant at *A,* the arithmetic average of
these two magnitudes."[2]   Unless a person is of a speculative
turn of mind, he will pay more for a regular income than for
an irregular income of the same aggregate.   That most people
are like this seems to be indicated by the high value of fixed-
income securities.   For the masses of the people whose incomes
are small, regularity is particularly important.   Their consumption has no great leeway; reductions in income encroach
on important items in the standard of living.   As the poorest-
paid workers are most liable to unemployment because of economic fluctuations, the loss of welfare by instability is unduly
large.

As for work, it is not possible to deny that irregularity is
an evil.   Instead of reasonably constant effort, our cyclical
fluctuations demand exhausting pace and overtime in expansion, unemployment and short time in contraction.   This variability is an evil in itself.   The uncertainty which it involves,
the constant fear of discharge which hangs over all workers
like a nightmare, makes the evil greater.   Add to this the loss
of skill and the destruction of morale, which depression brings
ever more seriously as months go on, and one has piled up a
formidable total of disutility.

To this must be added the consequences of irregularity in
making for restrictions on production.   This outcome is due
partly to industrial disputes over the terms of work, notoriously sharpened by irregular employment, and partly to restriction of output to make the jobs last longer.   In depression,
it arises from the refusal to cut wages and its consequence
in increasing the total volume of idle men and idle capacity.

As to resources, cyclical fluctuation reduces their effective
placement and use.   Prosperity encourages speculation, ex-
travagance, and waste, with all the misdirection and loss of
capital these involve.   The variation of aggregate output

---

[2] Pigou, *op cit.,* 218, n. 1.

from high to low compels excessive expansion of capacity for peak loads, adding thereby to the extent of each expansion and increasing the total volume of idle resources when depression comes.

These considerations mean that, even if the reduction of output and income in depression were counteracted by the equal and opposite expansion of output and income in prosperity, stabilization would still be desirable. If the effect of cycles is to reduce the average level of production below what might be expected from a stabilizing policy, the argument for stabilization is even stronger. That the latter is a possibility is indicated by the investigations of W. C. Mitchell and W. I. King on the experience of the period 1890–1919. By comparing the actual yearly production in mining, manufacturing, and transportation with a hypothetical level based on the output of certain "active but unhurried years," they found that, in 10 years of the 30, production exceeded this reasonable level; in 20 years of the 30, it fell below it. If we subtract the gains from the losses, there remains "a net loss of nearly 3 percent of the output of a whole generation of effort." [3]

The Social Costs of Stabilization

While these considerations all indicate that stabilization will have good results, it does not follow that stabilization is desirable. It will be desirable only if its gains are greater than its costs, and that the costs may be formidable has been foreshadowed throughout the preceding chapters of this section.

It is evident from our review of the various methods of stabilization and the specific problems they raise that it will not be an easy task to bring the business cycle under control. Business cycles, under their statistically smoothed front, conceal an amazing complexity of relations, which the most acute analysis has not yet succeeded in explaining. Control, in such

---

[3] *Business Cycles and Unemployment.* A report made to the President's Conference on Unemployment, 1923, Chap. III, 34–37.

a situation, finds itself continually meeting unexpected difficulties, starting off a train of unforeseen consequences. It is the economic system as a whole which we are trying to bring into stability, and it is no wonder that the task turns out to be formidable.

As we have seen, each method of attack has its own particular problems. Monetary control seems the simplest of all the procedures. It involves no interference with business management; it is not a "regimentive" type of device. It does not "put the government into business" or make the government a competitor of business. It attacks the system through one of its strategic channels, the bottleneck of money and credit through which all business transactions tend to pass. Yet we have seen that its essential aim of controlling the quantity of money may not be successful short of methods which deprive banks of one of their historic functions, such as "100% money." At the best, monetary control seems helpless as a means of recovery from depression, since, although money can be made available in almost any quantity, business cannot be made to take it.

A remedy for this situation of heaps of funds but no takers is public works, which go one step further and, by appropriate deficit financing by the government, get the idle resources into circulation. But while public works can seemingly avert the mere stagnancy of resources, we have seen that they do not necessarily thereby remove the causes which impede recovery. There are many neutralizing factors which prevent full efficiency of public expenditures; and while the strength of these cannot be exactly measured, they appear to be strong enough at times, not only to retard revival but to cause renewed slump when public works are temporarily reduced in volume. Experience with public works shows how difficult it is, in a system based on private enterprise, to promote a public good without the danger of incurring a private loss.

Again, effective stabilization of consumer expenditures turns out to be a more complicated problem than it would appear on the surface. It seems easy to set up a scheme of unemployment reserves on the ordinary model of all insurance plans of setting aside funds in one time for use in another. But doing this on a national scale raises questions of quite different magnitude, in respect to the investment and liquidation of funds, the effects of saving, and so on; questions that may be solved only by unexpected as well as unacceptable extensions of governmental authority.

Similarly, while flexibility of prices and wages is an important aid to business stability, the means of getting it may strike hard at some of the vital citadels of private enterprise. More particularly, the search for means of reducing the rigidity of some industrial prices may run from unsuccessful antitrust measures, through "codes of fair competition," to the regulation of the price policy of trade associations. When this situation comes about, the serious possibility that price regulation may be no more successful in this field than it has been in the field of public utilities brings a demand for public ownership of "monopolies" so close as to be just round the corner.[4]

These problems, however, are but instances of the inevitable conflict between public control and private interest which all regulatory measures stir up. They are frictions which indicate part of the "cost" of stabilization. But there are other costs which may be even more important—costs which come from the sacrifice of various incidental benefits which cyclical fluctuations may confer. Cyclical fluctuations are not an unmixed evil, as the following examples show.

Some Fluctuation May Be Beneficial

(1) Robertson[5] points out that some industrial fluctuations are "appropriate," as being the natural reactions to "real" changes that are not in themselves undesirable. Thus changes

---

[4] Cf. P. H. Douglas, *Controlling Depressions*, 247–250.

[5] D. H. Robertson, *Banking Policy and the Price Level*, Chaps. II, III, and IV.

in real cost such as by invention, or changes in derived demand via the principle of acceleration, or changes in the supply offered from agriculture, all occasion "justifiable" changes, often of rhythmic nature, in the aggregate of industrial output. These changes are still "justifiable" in a wage system with a relatively rich employing and a relatively poor wage-earning class, even though they are larger than would have occurred in a system of self-employed workers.

But superimposed upon appropriate responses are inappropriate responses which carry reaction to various impulses to undesirable and unjustifiable lengths. Thus the imperfect divisibility of units of production causes undue investment. Heavy overhead costs may dictate an otherwise inappropriate rate of output. Often, means of production have to be kept working to prevent damage, and so forth. Always the competitive illusion of businessmen and their tendencies to psychological waves of sentiment cause them to make exaggerated responses to any given stimulus.

Now, clearly, the needs of policy demand that only inappropriate fluctuations be suppressed. A policy which, in the urge for stabilization, hinders appropriate fluctuations is doing society not good but harm. As long as the changes which stimulate response are desirable, appropriate responses are also desirable. But the precise degree of control which this requires could be expected only from men whose knowledge of appropriate responses was as discriminating as their use of control mechanism was wise. This virtue not being available short of Utopia, we run the danger of some immeasurable loss of value which is the hidden cost of any enthusiastic urge to stabilization.

(2) If cyclical fluctuations are caused by waves of innovation, as has been argued by Professor Schumpeter, or, put in another way, if the process of innovation expresses itself as a boom and a depression, then stabilization may interfere with the effective introduction of technological change and hinder

the reasonable progress of society. In this theory, boom is the expansion caused by innovation; depression is the inevitable adjustment of values and costs which must follow. All progress is painful. Reduction of costs by innovation is rough on less gifted producers who must be eliminated or reorganized on a more economical basis. If innovations were gradual and continuous, adjustment could be also, and the violent oscillation of boom and slump might be avoided. But innovations come in spurts, and, as long as this is so, excess and adjustment cannot be avoided.

In these circumstances, we can have stabilization or we can have innovation, but we cannot have both. It is the fundamental conflict of the present stage of capitalism, the conflict between progress and security. Business cycles are the price we pay for progress. Possibly we pay too much, but we need more wisdom than we now have to know how much this excess is, or what precise degree of control would eliminate the excess while leaving the necessary alone.

(3) The French economist, François Simiand, has approached the question of progress from another, rather diverting, angle.[6] As he sees it, the alternating phases of expansion and contraction are due to changes in the supply of money (gold or credit); and both phases are necessary for progress. The upward phase, with its rise of prices, causes activity and income to increase up to limits set by diminishing productivity, and so on. When these limits are reached, and depression sets in, we do everything we can to hold the standards reached in expansion. Wage earners try to keep up wages; employers try to meet their costs by invention and improvements. So, while we desperately try to prevent slipping, we prepare our way for another effort with improved methods, and so we go on higher and higher.

Both phases then are necessary for progress. If prices always

---

[6] R. Marjolin, "François Simiand's Theory of Economic Progress," *Review of Economic Studies,* June 1938.

fell, we would have no outbursts of high standards to pin our hopes to. If prices always rose, we would get slack and never improve our methods. Rising prices increase our activity under the spur of profits. Falling prices increase our invention under the spur of losses. So we progress under the beneficent influences of a variable money supply which gives us the boon of cyclical fluctuation.

Stabilization would change all that and, for the sake of a probably illusive security, deprive us of progress.

Investment Must Not Be Discouraged

The dangers inherent in stabilization would be particularly threatening if, as some economists see the world, the investment opportunities which made the nineteenth century such a "magnificent episode" are facing a decline.

The enormous growth of capital formation which characterized the nineteenth century may have been conditioned by certain definite sources of investment opportunity, particularly the growth of population, the opening up of new territory and the discovery of new resources, and the spread of technical innovations. There is no way of estimating with any exactness the relative importance of these, but Professor Hansen has hazarded the guess that the growth of population and the opening up of new territory were together responsible for (say) one-half the total volume of new capital formation.[7] But this important outlet for savings is shrinking. Population growth has slowed up and will reach stability in a few decades at the most. The world has been charted, occupied, and developed; and while further development in areas of low standards of living is not ruled out, the easy expansion of the nineteenth century is over. The restrictions on international investment imposed by a totalitarian world make this more certain. Should all these apparently certain developments materialize,

---

[7] A. H. Hansen, "Economic Progress and Declining Population Growth," *American Economic Review*, March 1939.

the outlets for new investment which once were manifold will largely narrow down to those made possible by the progress of technology. If the enormous growth of savings characteristic of our thrifty societies continues, this shrinkage of investment outlets will, in the absence of some forceful measures, lead to a state of chronic stagnation and underemployment of resources.

In this situation, what is wanted is not so much stabilization as energizing the economic system to much higher levels of activity. Somehow we must find a means of outlet for the potential capital which the habits of society pile up in such volume.

As Keynes puts it:

The right remedy for the trade cycle is not to be found in abolishing booms and thus keeping us permanently in a semi-slump; but in abolishing slumps and thus keeping us permanently in a quasi-boom.[8]

This remedy might be found as Mr. Keynes has suggested, in drastic lowering of the rate of interest, so that investments that lie below the existing level of profitability might be carried on. How this is to be done effectively is not clear. In any case, it would involve, as Keynes puts it, the euthanasia of the *rentier*.

Or, again, the government might set out to discourage saving, by such taxes on the sources of savings, or by such limitation of income, as would transfer resources from habitual savers to habitual consumers. This avenue of escape does not seem a happy one, involving, as it does, a serious risk to the accumulation of the real means of future income.

Or, as was done in the New Deal, the government might substitute public for private investment as long as the flow of savings tends to outrun the opportunities offered in the latter

---

[8] J. M. Keynes, *General Theory of Employment, Interest, and Money*, New York, Harcourt, Brace & Company, Inc., 1936, 322.

field. This method seems to be a last resort which, pushed progressively, may dangerously cramp the efficiency and reduce the buoyancy of private investment.

But the most effective means of averting stagnation would be to encourage by every device the progress of technology. New methods, new resources, and new industries are what is wanted to give outlets to the savings of society. It was the railroads, the electrical industry, and the automobile which, in the past, helped to get society out of depressions and made possible the long rise in the standard of living. The new processes and industries of the future are the best guarantee that these standards will continue to improve. Hence programs of stabilization designed primarily in the interests of security rather than progress may be particularly risky at this time. In the process of removing undesirable fluctuations of industry, it may not be easy to avoid encroaching on the sources of innovation; always there is the risk that fear of overinvestment may lead to restrictions on expansion in a society in which underinvestment is the real evil.

Suggested Readings on Part III

E. C. Bratt, *Business Cycles and Forecasting,* Chicago, Richard D. Irwin, Inc., 1940. Chapters XV to XVII have a compact analysis of all possible methods of stabilization.

P. H. Douglas, *Controlling Depressions,* New York, W. W. Norton & Co., Inc., 1935. Popular and readable, but scholarly.

A. H. Hansen, *Full Recovery or Stagnation,* New York, W. W. Norton & Co., Inc., 1938. Parts II and IV are devoted to analyses of various current proposals for recovery and cyclical control.

A. C. Pigou, *Industrial Fluctuations,* London, Macmillan and Co., Ltd., 1927. Part II, "Remedies." Professor Pigou of Cambridge exposes various stabilization schemes to his keen and lucid economic analysis.

S. L. Slichter, *Towards Stability,* New York, Henry Holt and Company, 1934. A systematic and incisive analysis of possible measures of control. One of the best short books on the subject.

Columbia University Commission, *Economic Reconstruction,* New York, Columbia University Press, 1934. A series of essays by various hands on the problem of a more stable economic society.

The following books, which occupy a more special field, have already been noted in the particular chapters concerned, but they are here again recommended as of particular value and interest.

J. M. Clark, *Economics of Planning Public Works,* Washington, United States Government Printing Office, 1935. This analysis of the problem of public works, prepared for the National Planning Board, is shrewd, readable, and comprehensive. The best survey of the subject available.

A. D. Gayer, *Monetary Policy and Economic Stabilization,* New York, The Macmillan Company, 1937. A comprehensive study in its particular field.

J. M. Keynes, *A Treatise on Money,* New York, Harcourt, Brace and Company, 1930, Book VII, "The Management of Money." Most recent literature on money management is heavily indebted to this section of Keynes. Like all his work, it is stimulating, provocative, and amusing.

INDEX

INDEX

R

CPSIA information can be obtained
at www.ICGtesting.com
Printed in the USA
BVOW06*1937030417
480185BV00006B/17/P